Prima Games
A Division of Random House, Inc.

3000 Lava Ridge Court
Roseville, CA 95661
1-800-733-3000
www.primagames.com

Credits
Created By: **Kaizen Media Group**
President: **Howard Grossman**
Author: **Casey Loe**
Designer: **Tim Davis**
Gameplay asstance: **Bryan Lane**

Acknowledgements
Special Thanks to **Chuck McFadden** for all his expertise and assistance (not to mention his wit and wisdom) **Rachel Bryant** for helping put this project together. And the rest of the super helpful LucasArts team **Robert Blackadder, Jim Rice, Chris Susen,** and **Alison Gaiser.**
Very Special Thanks to all the folks at Prima especially **Christy Curtis**!

This guide covers all console versions of Gladius.

ISBN: 0-7615-4232-9
Library of Congress Catalog Card
Number: 2003108349
Printed in the United States of America

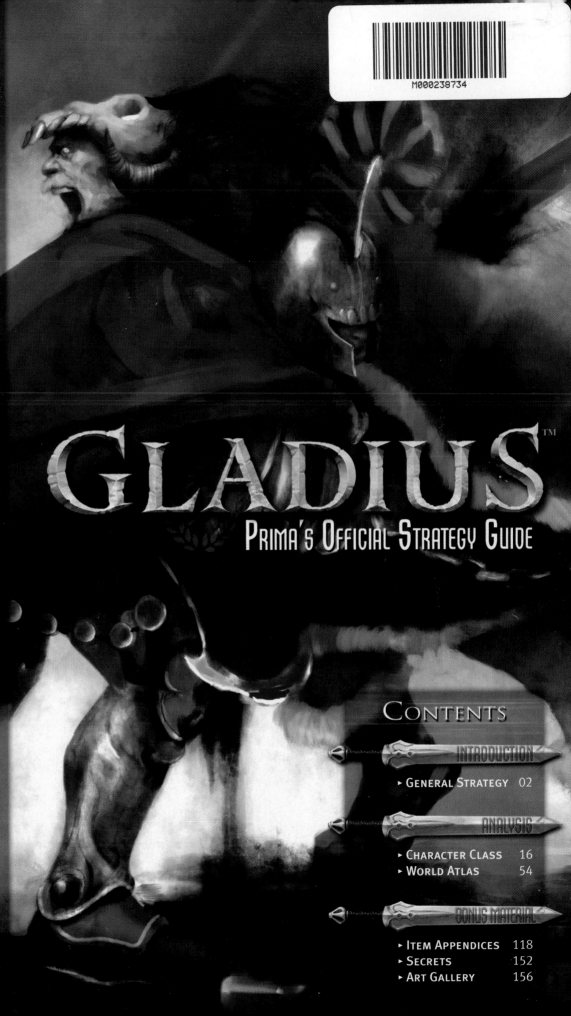

GLADIUS™

Prima's Official Strategy Guide

GLADIUS
STRATEGY

CONQUERING GLADIUS

> **AUTHOR'S NOTE:** Gladius is a very involved game, and we don't want to waste your time recapping the manual. The intent of this section is not to teach you how to play the game, but to advise you how to win. Please read this section after you've completed Usus's tutorials, and read your League Handbook.

PLAYING THE GAME

CHOOSING YOUR HERO

Gladius offers a selection of two characters: Ursula the Barbarian and Valens the Imperial Warrior. Your choice is largely a matter of personal preference, because the two unite midway through the game, and all leagues and quests (but not all event scenes) will eventually be available to both players.

| URSULA | VALENS |

Ursula begins the game in Nordagh, which she must conquer before moving on to Imperia. You'll have an easier time getting started with her, because Nordagh's leagues have easier entrance requirements, and the local schools use many light-type classes. This will leave them at a disadvantage when battling medium-type Ursula and Urlan. However, Nordagh doesn't have the wide variety of recruitable classes that Imperia offers, so your school will be slightly weaker when you begin Chapter 2. If you play as Ursula, use your mystical powers every chance you get (no matter what Urlan says), as they're the key to her developing powerful skills later on.

Valens begins the game in Imperia, and moves on to Nordagh after clearing his home region. Valens is the "advanced" character, because Imperial schools have a much wider variety of units. You'll need to use all the tricks in the "Seizing the Advantage" section to carve out a victory. Many of the leagues have entrance requirements you won't be able to meet the first time around. This leaves you with limited league options as you try to qualify for the tournament. However, Imperia has a wide variety of powerful units to recruit, including heavy units, which are practically non-existent in Nordagh.

CHOOSING YOUR BATTLES

Gladius offers a stunning variety of leagues, and while you're certainly welcome to try them all, wise players will want to choose their battles carefully early in the game. **The early tiers have a level cap (5 for Amateur and 10 for Semi-pro),** and when your characters hit their maximum level, any further experience they earn is wasted. Because your enemies get harder as you get stronger, doing unnecessary battles won't get you ahead of the game.

The amount of experience you'd earn doing just the leagues you need to obtain tournament qualifications will put you most of the way toward your level cap. If you'd like to max out your characters eventually, **it's best to leave most of the optional leagues, until you can return as a Pro-tier school, and your level cap has been lifted.** At that point, your large school roster will make it much easier to meet the entrance requirements. Of course, exceptions should be made when optional leagues offer unusually good prizes, like powerful accessories or recruitable gladiators.

♦ LEVEL UP ♦
URLAN

5 → 6

Urlan cannot level up until Orin's School progresses to Amateur tier by winning the regional championship.

MAXIMIZING YOUR EARNINGS

Equipping a school full of gladiators can be incredibly expensive, and that's in addition to the costs of recruiting the gladiators themselves. Money is important in Gladius, so keep a careful eye on your dinar total. Here are a few tips on how to maximize your earnings:

I   Keep an eye on the prizes

Some battles within a league have far better prizes than others. Sometimes this reflects a higher level of difficulty, but other times it's seemingly random. Even if you don't intend to complete a league, it's often a good idea to play these aberrantly lucrative battles.

II   Keep an eye on the fees

There's no rule that says every battle has to be profitable. In fact, there are times when the prize won't cover the entry fee! Avoid these like the plague, and keep an eye out for bargain leagues early in the game.

III   Master leagues when possible

In Gladius, a league is "Conquered" when you earn the necessary amount of Battle Points. If you clear every single battle, it's considered "Mastered." Some leagues offer bonus cash prizes for mastering a league, and it's often more than the purse for conquering it. If you're close, go for it.

IV   Sell recruits' gear before you expel them

There will be times when you need to free up a slot, or an early recruit simply isn't cutting the mustard anymore. Make sure that you strip 'em and sell all their gear before you kick 'em to the curb. Sometimes you can even turn a profit by recruiting a cheap gladiator, selling his gear, and immediately expelling him.

RECRUITING CHARACTERS

There are a few story characters who will join your school whether you want them to or not, but the vast majority of your gladiators will be ones you choose to recruit from local arenas. Here are a few tips to make sure you get the most for your money:

I   Don't recruit temporary gladiators

Unless you desperately need a gladiator of some exotic class to enter a league, recruiting temporary gladiators is always a waste of money. You can't control temporary recruits, so they often fare poorly in battle, charging off to get killed when the right play is to wait and let your foes come to you.

II   When you see two recruits of the same class and level, one will always be better, and it won't always be the more expensive one

You can compare their stats, but that won't tell you how much of the difference is because of the gladiator and how much is because of the gear. Stats also won't tell you what skills higher-level gladiators have purchased. When deciding between two gladiators of the same class, save your game, recruit both, and check them out. You'll find that some have better abilities, and others have expensive equipment you might want to steal before expelling them

III   Early in the game, you should usually choose lower-level gladiators

The tight level cap gives you a good incentive to rotate your team, so they'll have plenty of opportunities to fight and level up. You can then guide their development, ensuring they don't waste all their job points buying weak or redundant skills.

Additionally, it's a good idea to recruit as many gladiators as you can as soon as you get to your first arena (where you go through the training battles). Because experience points are given to all members of your school, the earlier you recruit characters into your group, the more experience points they'll get as you play through the training battles.

IV   Don't be afraid to expel your gladiators

This is especially true of Ursula's game, which will be entering Imperia with a roster full of sub-par characters if she recruited widely in Nordagh. New gladiators might make old ones redundant, and there are more gladiator classes to try than there are slots in your school. Just make sure you steal their gear before you give them the boot.

EQUIPPING YOUR TROOPS

If you buy every marginally improved piece of gear for every one of your gladiators at every town, you'll bankrupt your school quickly. Try to win your equipment if possible, and only buy gear that is significantly improved. A few tips:

I   Shop stock changes from day to day

Check back at old shops from time to time. Shop affinity specialties never change, however.

II   Don't change your affinity specialty for a good weapon

You can never afford to waste job points by buying different types of Affinity Attacks for one character, so you might want to skip the weapon upgrade or look for it elsewhere. Of course, this only applies to the gladiators you've made "affinity specialists." Keep the rest affinity neutral, so they can capitalize on whatever the best gear is, and leave them on the bench for battles in which affinity matters.

III   Watch your secondary stats

A marginal increase in Defense isn't worth the money when it comes coupled with a significant decrease in Initiative. The same is true of Power and Accuracy. In general, Initiative and Accuracy (Accuracy is less of a concern if you can master swing meters.) penalties rise as weapons get better, but certain types of gear have greater penalties.

GENERAL STRATEGY • CHARACTER CLASSES • WORLD ATLAS • MATERIAL

IV Keep an extra couple of shields on hand

When you equip a shield of which you have multiple copies, you can set it to automatically re-equip (at the end of the battle) when the shield is destroyed. Because shields get shattered all the time, this is worth the extra cost of picking up a few spares. Headgear can break as well, but because it happens much less often, buying spare helmets isn't necessary.

V When you're desperate for cash, replay Treasure Hunt battles

Types section, but it's worth noting that the items you earn can be attained more than once. The prizes are mostly gear, but it can almost always be sold at a profit.

In addition to the Leagues and

SIDE QUESTS & RANDOM ENCOUNTERS

Tournaments available in each town, there are also encounters on the world map. **If a recruited character dies in one of these fights, he is dead for good. If the main character dies, the game is over.** So always, always, always save the game before you leave a town.

Random Encounters can be escaped with the Back button, but if you've saved the game recently, give them a shot. Fallen opponents often drop treasure chests you can open during the fight and gladiators gain more experience from random encounters than from normal league battles. Most side quests involve battles on the World Map. **All the side quests come from shopkeepers, if you talk to them at the right time.** Typical side quests involve you going to a designated spot on the World Map, getting in a fight, and then going back to collect a prize from the shopkeeper. The same if-you-die-you're-dead rules apply, and side quest fights tend to be harder than random battles, so always save before the fights. You'll find more detailed coverage of side quests in the Atlas section of this book.

GLADIATOR TYPE: LIGHT

Light gladiators have high Initiative and Accuracy scores, and often get movement skills like Running Attack. Poor defense and damage scores balance their speed. Make sure to spend a few early skill points on defensive skills like Evasion, or your light fighters might not last more than a round or two.

Light fighters specialize in dealing with heavy gladiators. They don't get significant damage bonuses, but the heavy gladiators have little chance of dodging their quick attacks, and their evasive nature makes it virtually impossible for the heavy gladiators to land a hit in return. Some also have access to the Incapacitate Heavy skill that can effectively take a heavy gladiator out of the fight.

DERVISH

BANDIT

BERSERKER

GENERAL STRATEGY · CHARACTER CLASSES · WORLD ATLAS · BONUS MATERIAL

GLADIATOR TYPE: MEDIUM

Medium gladiators are well rounded and versatile. Their power can't match that of heavy gladiators, but they often make up for the difference with their superior Initiative and variety of techniques. Both Ursula and Valens are medium type, as are their companions Urlan and Ludo, so no player will be lacking in this area.

Unlike heavy types, medium gladiators have a good chance of hitting light types, and do major damage when they do. But they have serious trouble against heavy gladiators. They take extra damage from the heavies' powerful attacks, and can barely scratch their tough armor in return. **Even a perfect series of critical hits may not tilt the odds in a medium-on-heavy match-up.**

BARBARIAN

LEGIONNAIRE

MURMILLO

SEIZING THE ADVANTAGE

You'll rarely be facing even odds in Gladius, since your opponent sometimes gets more guys on the field, they may be a higher level than yours. But **there are a few ways in which the game favors *your* team,** and if you exploit these advantages, you can turn the odds around completely.

THE SCOUTING ADVANTAGE

Your single strongest advantage comes from your ability to peek into the enemy's roster before you choose your participating characters. If their roster is full of medium-type characters, you go heavy. If it's full of light-types, you go medium. The advantages can go beyond mere type matching: If they're playing lots of support characters, you can bring in your Murmillo and Undead Summoner (two classes that have strong defense against projectiles). If they're playing lots of Channelers, you can play characters with no affinity, so they have nothing to steal.

If their roster is simply too strong, you can back out of the battle and re-enter it. Some battles have entirely random schools as opponents, so a tricky Samnite army could suddenly become an easy pack of Satyrs. But even when the school is fixed, most schools have a mix of classes, and you can pick the one that plays best to your strengths. **There is also a small random element to the difficulty of your opponents:** Their total levels might drop by one or two if you keep trying, or their levels might merely be distributed differently, but more to your advantage. You might find it easier to face one level 6 Bandit and two level 4 Wolves, that two level 5 Wolves and a level 4 Bandit, because Bandits are easier to type-match against.

THE PATIENCE ADVANTAGE

Unless the computer AI has characters capable of long-range attacks, its troops will always immediately rush yours. This is to your advantage, because when the two sides start far apart, playing defense is by far the stronger strategy.

I   Use your free turn wisely

While the computer spends its first turn on movement, you can spend it using skills like Empower Self, Motivate and Crowd Pleaser. This raises your stats and puts you ahead in the crowd favor meter.

II   Form a strong defense

Group your characters so the strongest are in the way of the attackers, and support characters are in position to get a hit when opponents arrive. If you have innate defensive skills, like Garrison or Inspiration, you can cluster your team to take advantage of them. Many ranged characters can set ambushes with the Cover Area skill, while some heavy fighters can ready blows with skills like Back Off.

III   Take them one at a time

In large arenas, your opponents' characters will arrive at different times, with the fast, high-initiative light characters usually arriving first, and the heavy gladiators showing up last. Sometimes the turn or two of difference is all you need to gang up and kill the early arrivals before the stragglers arrive. Resist the temptation to meet the slower opponents halfway, and instead, concentrate on killing whoever gets there first.

THE PLACEMENT ADVANTAGE

In some arenas, playing defense isn't an option. And in some situations, there are even better options. This is because you get to place your gladiators after the computer has placed its units, which lets you set the terms of the fight. In battles where your characters start intermingled with the enemy, the following offensive strategies can be brutally effective:

I   The Type Matching ploy

When both players have the same number of characters, and you have a wide range of starting placements, simply place each character so it will be able to immediately engage an opponent of a weaker type in combat. Even if the opponents' units are slightly higher levels, their light Bandits will have no chance versus your medium Barbarians; their heavy Samnites will be impotent against your light Dervishes, and their medium Legionnaires will be crushed by your heavy Centurions.

II   Divide and Conquer

The opponent seems to choose its placements at random, and in large arenas, that can lead to his characters being far away from each other. You can start all or most of your units around a single unit who is at one of the corners, and quickly kill it. The other enemies will gradually charge into your secured area one at a time, and have to face your entire force.

Heavy gladiators are slow and cumbersome. They get fewer turns than their light and medium colleagues and often have to spend them lumbering over to the action. But when they get there, they often dominate the fight by dishing out obscene amounts of damage and laughing off blows from weaker fighters. Opportunities to recruit them don't come around as often as they do for light and medium types, so don't let them pass you by.

Heavy gladiators cut through medium gladiators like a Bladed War Axe through tissue paper, while easily absorbing the damage they do in return. Light gladiators give them fits, however, and their percentage chances of scoring a hit often plummet to the single-digit range. Well-timed critical hits can solve that problem, however, so this match-up isn't quite as bad as the tutorials suggest. Just make sure the light types that know Backstabber don't get a chance to slip behind you and plant an ax in your back.

CENTURION

OGRE

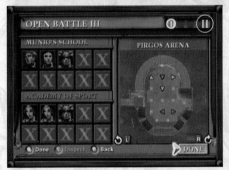

III The Surgical Strike

Backstabber is a powerful skill, and in battles where you can position your characters anywhere, it's easy to set key foes up for a shiv between the ribs. Simply put a backstabber (like a Bandit or Secutor) and one other gladiator on opposite sides of the strongest foe, or a key unit you want to eliminate early, like a Channeler. Have the backstabber pass its turn until your other character's initiative, and have that character engage the target in battle. The backstabber's turn will come around immediately (since you recover from passing very quickly), and he'll be in place for his strongest melee attack, with a double damage backstab bonus. Most crowds disapprove of such treachery, but since it's the beginning of the battle, you'll have no good will to lose.

IV Hold the High Ground

There's no rule saying you can't place your characters directly onto crates and other objects with height bonuses. You can even place them directly atop the hill in certain King of the Hill battles! Crates and such don't appear on the placement maps, so you'll have to start the fight, figure out where you want to be (by counting squares from some landmark), and remember for next time.

THE REFLEX ADVANTAGE

If you can master the swing meters in Gladius, you'll have an advantage against the computer opponents because **anytime you hit the critical (red) zone on the swing meter, your character will deliver an unblockable hit to the enemy.**

That means that if your reflexes are sharp and you choose the right attacks, your heavy gladiator will have no problem taking out an opponent's light gladiator, no matter how evasive your target is.

If you play with the Swing Meters turned off, your gameplay strategies need to change accordingly. Pay special attention to the little bull's-eye mark that appears by an opponent's stats when you target them. It shows the odds that you'll hit with your selected attack. If it's less than 50 percent, switch to an attack that provides a higher chance of hitting the target. Because it's generally easier to play Gladius with the Swing Meters on, the strategies provided in this guide assume that you haven't turned the option off.

SPECIAL BATTLES

Wiping out your enemies is the most common battle objective, but it's far from the only one. There are a number of special battles that you'll see time and time again, and we'll cover the best tips for those fights in this section. Less common special battles, like the ones in Cro Beska's "Condemned Hope" league, will be covered in the Atlas.

POINTS BATTLES

The goal in these battles is to do as much damage as you can. Score is all that matters, because all combatants have infinite health. Obviously critical hits and such are good here, but they're not the best tactic. The judges don't care who you're doing that damage to. So **attacks that damage your own teammates, like the Gungnir/Peltast skill Exploding Javelin or Valens's Wide Swing, are invaluable**. The Undead Summoner is another MVP, because his Darkness From Life skill damages himself, then almost immediately gives him another turn (and a bunch of affinity) in which to damage others.

KING OF THE HILL

In King of the Hill, you have to hold a spot on top of a hill, earning a point for each turn your team is on top. The last minute is always worth double points. This makes come-from-behind victories possible. In general, the best strategy is to take the hill from the get-go, by placing your character as close to the top as possible. **The ideal hill-holder has a bunch of Innate skills to help him dodge, and a skill like Defend to make him virtually unkillable.** While he holds the hill, your other characters should use the fact that your opponents are engaged with the hill-holder to backstab his attackers.

If you can't get to the hill first, you'll have to kill its current occupant to retake it. Unless you use a character that can move people off the hill. Characters such as the Undead Summoner (with the Splintering Bones skill) or the Archer (with the Jolt Arrow skill) can allow you to move the King off the Hill with one simple attack.

Orders for Undead Melee
Retreat

GLADIATOR TYPE: SUPPORT

There are two types of support gladiators: Javelin-throwers, like the Nordagh Gungnirs and their Imperial twins, Peltasts; and bow-wielding Archers and Amazons. All are neutral in the light-medium-heavy game, but are very weak to direct attack. Support characters are only good when they're shooting their foes from a few squares away.

Virtually all support character skills are ranged attacks that require a clear "line-of-sight" to hit, even Combo Attacks and Affinity Attacks. To play these characters correctly, it is imperative that you understand what that means. **Line-of-sight means that you can draw a line from the center of the shooter's square to the center of the target's square without intersecting any part of any character or obstacle's square.** You can shoot diagonally through two obstructions (figure B) but not when any part of an ally's square is in the way (figure A). There is only one exception: **A support character can fire over a beast character, because they're low to the ground.**

Bow users can move, and then shoot, so it's easy for them to maneuver into a clear line of sight. But spear throwers cannot move and throw in the same turn, so positioning them (and your other characters so as not to block them) is vital.

(Continued on following page.)

Figure A

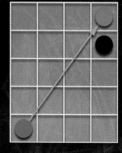

Figure B

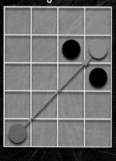

GENERAL STRATEGY • CHARACTER CLASSES • WORLD ATLAS • B/JUS MATERIAL

GLADIATOR TYPE: SUPPORT (Continued)

When an enemy can engage a Gungnir or Peltast in combat, it often blocks all of their line-of-sight options, effectively shutting them out of the battle. For that reason, melee skills, like Bear Form and Powered Throw, are very valuable. *Note: Use the line of sight button on your controller to help plan your projectile attacks.*

AMAZON

ARCHER

GUNGNIR

DOMINANCE BATTLES

Dominance battles are like King of the Hill, but with multiple hills (usually three). **The general strategy is to take and hold two hot spots, concede the third, and wait for the clock to run out.** Strategies vary arena by arena, but in general, you should divide into two teams, consisting of one hot-spot holder and one defender. While your opponents attack the hot-spot holder, the defender can backstab and kill them. Opposition is light in these battles, because your foolish opponent will often focus more on defending his one hill than retaking the two you took. Don't make the same mistake. If you're behind, throw every one but a single hot-spot holder at their most lightly defended hot spot.

VANDAL BATTLES

The point of Vandal Battles is to destroy more barrels (or whatever) than your opponents. These fights tend to have random barrel placement, so if there are a lot on your side, you'll have the advantage. If there aren't, you can back out and try again, but that shouldn't be necessary if you're sneaky about it.

Only the killing blow matters, so stealing barrel kills from your opponents is as easy as it is cruel. Use a few Support characters, and while half your team destroys nearby barrels, have them keep an eye on your opponents and target their barrels when they're heavily damaged.

RIVAL NATIONS

Playing defense is the key to these battles, where the goal is to destroy the opposing team's statue. The computer AI uses the same strategy every time: Send most of the team to attack your statue, while leaving one to defend. Get in position to block the routes to your statue, and take the attackers as they come, one-at-a-time. When they're all dead except the lone defender, move in, kill him, and attack the statue. Gungnirs and Peltasts are great in these fights, because if an attacker breaks through your defensive line, they can plug 'em while they whack at the statue. (The statues are quite strong, so a few hits won't matter.) The game also ends if you kill all opponents, it's not always necessary to take out the statue.

TREASURE HUNTS

Treasure Hunts are rarely called that. Their name changes from league to league. But they're easy to spot if you check the descriptions. … If they mention "non-critical chests," you're in luck.

Treasure Hunts are simply normal battles in which a few chests have been placed in a corner of the arena. If you think you can handle the fight with one less guy, you can send a light character to spend a few turns looting the chests. If not, you can eliminate all of your foes but the weakest one, and keep him alive while you collect the loot.

The treasure chests contain mostly common weapons and small amounts of gold. The weapons are never anything rare, but even common weapons are expensive, and **you can sometimes clear 10,000 dinars by selling a particularly good pile of loot.** If the assortment is lacking, you can replay the fights and get the loot again. (The exact chest contents change randomly from battle to battle.)

SERIES BATTLES

There are two different kinds of Series battles. In a standard Series, you simply have to clear all the battles in order, without losing any. In all other respects they're normal: You choose and place your characters at the beginning of each one.

Endurance Series (also known as Survival Series) are much tougher. In these, **the characters you choose at the beginning must battle through several waves of foes, and they don't regain hit points between waves**, except for characters with shape changing skills, that can regain health by doing so. Always use your best characters and make sure you have a variety of types. You do have a few small advantages though. **Affinity points *do* carry over**, so you'll want to use your affinity specialists, build up a lot of points, and unload powerful affinity attacks on enemies in later waves. **Skill points don't carry over** (you get a full batch at the beginning of each wave), so use your strongest combos and attacks on even weak enemies. When there's no healing, every point of damage you can prevent counts.

SKILLS

BUYING THE RIGHT SKILLS

Your Gladiators are only as good as their skills. This is one of the reasons it's better to recruit gladiators at low levels and raise them yourself. High-level gladiators raised by the computer just dump their skill points into whatever's cheapest, wasting them on redundant and ineffective skills. Here are a few guidelines so you don't make the same mistakes:

I   Save up for the good stuff

Don't let those job points burn a hole in your pocket! Unused job points carry over from level to level, so it's easy to save up for good skills like Riposte and Cover Area.

II   Avoid redundant skills

How many hit-the-square-in-front-of-you attacks do you need? Every early skill you buy should add a new capability to your gladiator; the ability to counter, to attack from a distance, to hit a row of enemies, to buff up when you have nothing else to do, etc. Versatility is the key.

III   Don't buy every skill in a series

Buying all four Long Throw skills is a waste, because each one increases your range only by a single square. And do you really need a choice of Combo Attacks? Buy Combo Attack 2 or 3 and then move on. There are better ways to spend job points than incremental improvements.

Bears fill the shoes of heavy gladiators, with devastating attacks and buckets of hit points. Wolves and Plainscats behave more like light gladiators, with high mobility and good Initiative. Scorpions and Scarabs are strange utility characters, not particularly strong in stats but with lots of versatile techniques. Beasts can vary widely, and must be judged as individuals. Still, all beasts do have a few strengths in common:

• **Beasts are cheap to maintain.** Beasts can equip nothing but accessories, so they lower your school's equipment budget.

• **Beasts do not obstruct support characters.** Don't overlook this detail! Heavy beasts and support characters make an amazing team. A Bear can thrash an opponent in melee while a Gungnir covers his back and fires spears over his head.

Earth Affinity Attack 3

PLAINSCAT

SCARAB

IV   Don't split your Affinities

Since you have to buy every Affinity attack in a series, it is a huge waste of job points to ever buy skills in more than one Affinity. Pick one and stick to it.

V   Not everyone needs Affinites

You might want to get Affinity Attack 1 for every fighter, since it's a decent can't-miss attack, but don't go beyond that for most of your school. It's best to pick only a handful of gladiators to be your Affinity specialists, and buy later Affinity Attacks only for them. Use these Affinity specialists whenever you're doing an Endurance Series, going up against the undead, or a league requires it.

SKILLS TYPES

I   Move Skills

Move Skills let you move a set distance and then attack. All characters get Strike, or its equivalent, for free. **Skills that let you move further to attack, like Running Attack, are very valuable for low-mobility characters.** However, anything beyond the first long-distance move skill is usually redundant.

II   Attack Skills

Attack Skills are generally more powerful than move skills, but you cannot move before using them. The best attack skills add to your capabilities, by letting you hit multiple enemies, or attack long range. **Attacks that are simply more powerful are usually a waste, since Combo Attacks usually do the same thing better.**

III   Combo Attacks

Combo Attacks let you unleash a series of normal attacks — the first at normal power, the rest at about half power. **Unless you have fantastic reflexes, don't go for the critical on the first hit, because a blue-zone miss will end the combo.** Combo Attacks cost a few skill points to use, but can do a great deal of damage, and **each hit fills your Affinity Power bar as much as a standard attack.**

Note that each hit of a combo counts as an attack for the purpose of triggering Innate Skills. For example, a three-hit combo that misses twice could trigger two Riposte counter attacks. Or, a successful five-hit combo will increase fivefold the chance that nearby allies will get a free hit off of Coordinated Attack.

IV   Special Skills

Special Skills are generally not attacks. They can do anything from boosting your stats to teleporting you across the field. **It's always good for each character to have a useful special skill he can use when he is playing defense and waiting for enemies to arrive.** Special skills that apply positive or negative effects to opponents usually require you to succeed at the added effect meter, so if you have poor reflexes, you should skip those.

V Affinity Attacks

VI Innate Skills

Affinity Attacks require Affinity Power to use. Arcane characters will find a wide variety of attack options in this slot, but all other characters simply have Affinity Attack 1 through 4 in the affinities that are available in their class. **Affinity Attack 1 and 2 do not do much damage, but they never miss.** This makes them useful when you're facing evasive characters. Affinity Attack 3 also applies a negative status effect to its target, usually incapacitating them temporarily, which is useful when you're outnumbered. Affinity Attack 4 summons an Affinity Beast that will damage every enemy in the arena, but unless you have a weapon that is very high in Affinity Power, it will usually come too late in the fight to matter.

Innate Skills are always on, and usually cost nothing to use. **In general, anything that lets you counter attacks or evade attacks is worth buying.** Innate skills like Indomitable can be useful in battles with Berserkers or Plainscats and also make Heavy units immune to incapacitate. Some classes have very powerful innate skills, like the Centurion's Garrison and Coordinated Attack, and these will be covered in more detail in the character section.

SKILL COMBOS

I On Guard + Riposte

Any skill that lets you counter attacks works great with skills like Evasion, Defend, Fortified Defense and On Guard. Simply

GLADIATOR TYPE: ARCANE

The rarest of gladiators, arcane types use Affinity Power for nearly everything, even Combo Attacks. Each arcane type has a special way of earning Affinity points: Summoners pull it from the gods, Channelers steal it from other gladiators, Undead Summoners convert their own hit points, and Mongrel Shamans get double points for melee attacks. They can spend these points on a wide range of magic attacks, like Ice Storm and Fire Cloud. Summoners and Undead Summoners can use it to summon Affinity Beasts and undead creatures.

Arcane types are not the best in combat, but they should never need to use melee attacks (except for Mongrel Shamans). **Arcane gladiators can use their Combo Attacks and Affinity Attacks from a distance.** Because of this, they often fill the same role as support characters. Mongrel Shamans and Channelers are fairly easy to recruit, but you'll need to conquer difficult challenges to get your hands on a Summoner or Undead Summoner.

MONGREL SHAMAN

SUMMONER

wade into the middle of the battle, so everyone attacks you, then Defend every turn. While enemies attack you, your allies can hit them from behind, while your counter attacks whittle away at their health. This combo is insane when done with the Bear's Raging Bear skill.

II   Suprise Attack + Backstabber

Normally, you can only backstab opponents who are engaged with an ally. But with Surprise Attack, they won't turn to face you, even if they're all alone. This Secutor special lets you backstab anyone, any time.

III   Combo Attack 4 + Affinity Attack

An obvious combo, but a good one. Whenever you're forced to fight one-on-one (it will happen a lot), this is the best strategy. Use up your skill-points-hitting

foes with powerful Combo Attacks, which will rapidly fill up your Affinity Power bar. Then unleash Affinity Attack 1 or 2 twice to do unblockable damage and refill your skill points. Affinity Attacks have quick recovery times, so your foes often won't be able to get an attack in edgewise.

IV   Reaper + Teleport

You'll need an Undead Summoner and two expensive skills to pull this one off, but it's worth it. Reaper kills its target after a few turns, unless the caster dies first. The computer is smart enough to turn its attention to killing the caster, but Teleport will keep you beyond its grasp. This is great when you're fighting a single enemy who is many levels above you.

GENERAL STRATEGY   CHARACTER CLASSES   WORLD ATLAS   BONUS MATERIAL

TYPE: MEDIUM

URSULA

One of the unique things about Ursula is that she gains a number of her techniques through storyline events. Using Empower Self three times in Fjord of the Fallen, Mordare's Den, and/or Stadium Dreas will give Ursula the **Summon Shield** skill, which replaces destroyed shields on the battlefield. After using **Empower Self** three times in any combination of those arenas, simply go into the school menu and check Ursula's statistics. Usus will congratulate you on earning your new power. If you chose her as your main character, she'll learn other valkyrie techniques, like **Heavenly Blast**, **Healing Light** and **Icarus Wings**, later in the game.

With most of her unique techniques coming for free (they're marked with an *), Ursula is left with lots of skill points to spend. That makes her a natural affinity specialist; spend your points on **Combo Attacks** and **Affinity Attacks**, and use weapons that have a high affinity value. Ursula is not a great fighter overall, and can rarely do the damage her brother does. But she is better on defense, which is important in certain storyline and wilderness battles, where her death would mean the end of the game if she's your main character. Focusing on Affinity Attacks will keep her relevant, and using defensive ability like **Empower Self** regularly will keep her alive. **Spell Blast** is the best of her exclusive skills, since it can damage all enemies in a wide area, and as a magical skill is particularly potent versus the Undead.

Character Class Statistics

HP	●●●●●
Defense	●●●●●
Power	●●●●●
Accuracy	●●●●●●●
Initiative	●●●●●
Movement	●●●●

Weapons
Medium Sword, Medium Hammer, Medium Axe, All Legionnaire, All Ursula

Shields
Medium Shield, Legionnaire Shield, Ursula Shield

Armor
Barbarian Armor, Ursula Armor

Helmets
Ursula and Barbarian

Accessory
Runestone, Feathers (as Valkyrie)

Affinities

Fire	Water	Earth	Air	Dark	Light

→ Skill		◆	Description
Strike	0	-	Standard move to attack.
High Kick	4	3	Heavy damage kick attack.

＼ Skill		◆	Description
Energy Blast	18	3	Spell blast of energy.
Overhead Cleave	40	4	Heavy overhead attack; may break opponent's helmet.
Spell Blast	*	4	A powerful blast of light energy that damages all opponents within range.

✖ Skill		◆	Description
Combo Attack 1	6	2	Two hit attack, moderate speed.
Combo Attack 2	12	3	Three hit attack, moderate speed.
Combo Attack 3	22	4	Four hit attack, moderate speed.
Combo Attack 4	34	5	Five hit attack, moderate speed.

✿ Skill		◆	Description
Empower Self	0	2	A divine gift of increased combat abilities.
On Guard	10	0	Increase defense next turn.
Blinding Flash	22	2	Blind all opponents within range.
Summon Shield	*	0	Replaces destroyed shield with magical shield of Light.
Light Beam	*	0	Healing beam; damages those aligned with the Dark Affinity.
Icarus Wings	*	0	Teleport a short distance on the battlefield.

✦ Skill		◆	Description
Affinity Attack 1	4	40	Attack enhanced by the power of an affinity god.
Affinity Attack 2	10	60	Mighty attack enhanced by the power of an affinity god. *Affinity Attack 1 Required.*
Affinity Attack 3	20	80	Mightiest attack enhanced by the power of an affinity god, has added effect. *Affinity Attack 2 Required.*
Affinity Attack 4	36	100	Summon a servant of an affinity god to attack all opponents. *Affinity Attack 3 Required.*
Heavenly Blast	*	80	A heavenly blast of light hits an opponent (Light Affinity only).

⚐ Skill		◆	Description
Dodge	0	-	Standard defensive maneuver.
Shield Block	0	-	Standard defensive maneuver with shield.
Sibling Rivalry	2	-	Ursula is powered up when Urlan is on battlefield.
Awareness	20	-	No bonus given to enemies when attacked from behind.
Off Balance	38	-	Lowers opponent's defense if opponent misses attack.
Healing Light	*	-	When health is low, a light from the heavens heals Ursula.
Light Guard	*	-	Magic damage is reduced by the Light Affinity.

VALENS

TYPE: MEDIUM

Weapons
Medium Sword, Medium Hammer, Medium Axe, All Legionnaire, All Valens

Shields
Medium Shield, Legionnaire Shield, Valens Shield

Armor
Medium Armor, Legionnaire Armor, Valens Armor

Helmets
All Valens, All Legionnaire, Military Helmet

Accessory
Medal

Character Class Statistics

HP	●●●●●●●●●
Defense	●●●●●●●●
Power	●●●●●●
Accuracy	●●●●●
Initiative	●●
Movement	●●●●●

Valens has more hit points than Ursula, and higher Defense, but lacks some of her grace and agility. Both heroes are pretty middle-of-the-road as far as stats go, but differ widely in the skill department. Valens lacks Ursula's versatility, but makes up for it with sheer power. While Ursula has several skills she can gain by using her magic abilities, Valens has only two: **Munio's Spirit** and **People's Champion**. Both are good skills, and are awarded automatically as you play.

The most interesting Valens skills are plain old attacks. **Wide Swing** hits the opponent directly in front of Valens for heavy damage, and anyone to that character's left or right (potentially including your allies) for lighter damage. It's a surprisingly powerful and versatile attack for only 10 job points. **Bungle Enemy** isn't particularly special, but it's useful, powerful, and cheap. **Smack Back** is a fantastic skill that damages everyone near Valens and knocks them back a square, forcing them to waste their next turn on less effective move attacks.

Valens has a solid assortment of innate defensive skills. They're hard to get excited about, but if you start taking them late in the game (after getting the three attacks mentioned above) you'll eventually have a hero who is immune to all conditions and backstabs, and has three ways to block or evade attacks.

Affinities

Fire	Water	Earth	Air	Dark	Light
●	●	●	●		

➜ Skill	🗡	◆	Description
Strike	0	-	Standard move to attack.

↘ Skill	🗡	◆	Description
Stagger Foe	4	2	Effect: Reduce opponent's movement rate.
Wide Swing	10	3	Sweeping attack that damages multiple opponents in front of character.
Bungle Enemy	18	2	Effect: Reduce opponent's accuracy.
Shield Hit	24	1	Strong attack using shield.
Smack Back	30	4	Spinning attack that knocks back any unit around Valens.
Target Head	34	3	Effect: Reduce opponent's initiative.
Overhead Cleave	40	4	Heavy overhead attack; may break opponent's helmet.

✖ Skill	🗡	◆	Description
Combo Attack 1	6	2	Two hit attack, moderate speed.
Combo Attack 2	12	3	Three hit attack, moderate speed.
Combo Attack 3	22	4	Four hit attack, moderate speed.
Combo Attack 4	34	5	Five hit attack, moderate speed.

✚ Skill	🗡	◆	Description
Empower Self	0	2	A divine gift of increased combat abilities.
On Guard	6	0	Increase defense next turn.

◗ Skill	🗡	◆	Description
Affinity Attack 1	4	40	Attack enhanced by the power of an affinity god.
Affinity Attack 2	10	60	Mighty attack enhanced by the power of an affinity god. *Affinity Attack 1 Required.*
Affinity Attack 3	20	80	Mightiest attack enhanced by the power of an affinity god, has added effect. *Affinity Attack 2 Required.*
Affinity Attack 4	36	100	Summon a servant of an affinity god to attack all opponents. *Affinity Attack 3 Required.*

🏃 Skill	🗡	◆	Description
Dodge	0	-	Standard defensive maneuver.
Shield Block	0	-	Standard defensive maneuver with shield.
Evasion	12	-	More effective defensive maneuver.
Indomitable Will	18	-	Immune to root, petrify, blindness and freeze.
Awareness	22	-	No bonus given to enemies when attacked from behind.
Discipline	32	-	Immune to stun, confusion, charm and fear.
Off Balance	38	-	Lowers opponent's defense if opponent misses attack.
Munio's Spirit	*	-	Receive large defense bonus when Hit Points are low.
People's Champion	*	-	Crowd meter increases faster.

TYPE: MEDIUM

URLAN

Urlan is probably the most physically powerful medium gladiator in the game, and is a great asset for Ursula early in her quest. He has a lot in common with other Barbarians, but differs in a few crucial ways, mostly for the better.

Without the Running Attack skill that other Barbarians enjoy, Urlan is one of the least mobile middle types. But its replacement, **Break Defense**, is a very powerful late game Move attack that does heavy damage and cannot be blocked. **Lunge** is a little strange, as it can only hit enemies who are exactly two squares away. You won't have valid targets too often, but it's nice to have in your belt, just in case. Urlan can't get the other Barbarians' Innate Totem skills, but his replacements are solid. **Older Brother** is very nice, and **Riposte** is great on a heavy hitter like Urlan.

I'm far less thrilled about Urlan's various shape-shifting skills. Wolves aren't great (unless you have lots of other wolves), and Urlan is already a bear on offense, so there's little point wasting job points on **Bear Form**. That leaves **Cat Form** (an Urlan exclusive), which is a fun skill that can be useful in large arenas when Urlan's lack of mobility makes him fall behind. Still, don't start dabbling in such chicanery until Urlan has purchased Riposte, Break Defense, and a few good Combo Attacks and Affinity Attacks.

Character Class Statistics

Counterattack
Riposte

HP	●●●●●
Defense	●●●●
Power	●●●●●
Accuracy	●●●
Initiative	●●●●
Movement	●●●●

Weapons
Two Handed Sword, Two Handed Axe, Two Handed Hammer, All Barbarian, All Urlan

Shields
None

Armor
Barbarian Armor, Urlan Armor

Helmets
All Urlan, All Barbarian, Hat Helmet, Helm Helmet

Accessory
Runestone

Affinities

Fire Water Earth Air Dark Light

➜ Skill			Description
Strike	0	-	Standard move to attack.
Break Defense	34	4	Several fierce attacks that prevent defense.

↘ Skill			Description
Lunge	24	1	Heavy damage attack, effectively only at short range.
Crippling Blow	30	3	Brutal attack that may stun and knock down opponent.
Overhead Cleave	40	4	Heavy overhead attack; may break opponent's helmet.

✕ Skill			Description
Combo Attack 1	4	2	Two hit attack, slow speed.
Combo Attack 2	8	3	Three hit attack, slow speed.
Combo Attack 3	16	4	Four hit attack, slow speed.
Combo Attack 4	26	5	Five hit attack, slow speed.

✚ Skill			Description
Wolf Form 1	4	0	Shapeshift into a wolf of lesser ability.
Cat Form 1	6	0	Shapeshift into a cat of lesser ability.
Bear Form 1	10	0	Shapeshift into a bear of lesser ability.
Wolf Form 2	12	0	Shapeshift into a wolf. *Wolf Form 1 required.*
Cat Form 2	18	0	Shapeshift into a cat. *Cat Form 1 required.*
Bear Form 2	20	0	Shapeshift into a bear. *Bear Form 1 required.*
Wolf Form 3	32	0	Shapeshift into a wolf of greater ability. *Wolf Form 2 required.*
Cat Form 3	36	0	Shapeshift into a cat of greater ability. *Cat Form 2 required.*
Bear Form 3	38	0	Shapeshift into a powerful bear. *Bear Form 2 required.*

● Skill			Description
Affinity Attack 1	4	40	Attack enhanced by the power of an affinity god.
Affinity Attack 2	10	60	Mighty attack enhanced by the power of an affinity god. *Affinity Attack 1 Required.*
Affinity Attack 3	20	80	Mightiest attack enhanced by the power of an affinity god, has added effect. *Affinity Attack 2 Required.*
Affinity Attack 4	36	100	Summon a servant of an affinity god to attack all opponents. *Affinity Attack 3 Required.*

⚑ Skill			Description
Older Brother	0	-	Urlan is more resistant to damage when Ursula is on the field.
Parry	0	-	Standard defensive maneuver.
Inspiration	12	-	Give defensive bonus to adjacent Nordagh allies.
Riposte	22	-	Immediate counter attack when an incoming opponent attack misses.

CHARACTER CLASSES · GENERAL STRATEGY
WORLD ATLAS
BONUS MATERIAL

LUDO

TYPE: MEDIUM

Weapons
Medium Axe, Medium Hammer, Medium Sword, All Legionnaire, All Ludo

Shields
Medium Shield, Legionnaire Shield, Ludo Shield

Armor
Medium Armor, Legionnaire Armor, Ludo Armor

Helmets
All Ludo, All Legionnaire, Military Helmet

Accessory
Medal

Character Class Statistics

HP	●●●● —
Defense	●●●●● —
Power	●●●●● —
Accuracy	●●●●● —
Initiative	●●● —
Movement	●●● —

Ludo is Valens's right-hand man early in his quest, acting as a solid second middle-weight fighter. He differs only slightly from the typical Imperial Legionnaire, but those differences are in his favor, and are reason enough to keep him in active duty and leave the other Legionnaires to sip tea in the recruiting office.

The differences in his attack capabilities are minor: Ludo has **Upper Hand** instead of Precision Attack, and **Upward Slash** instead of Overhead Cleave. Precision Attack will be missed, but Upward Slash is probably the better of the two late-game power attacks, since it costs only 3 skill points to use. **Ripost** is also an important skill.

The more significant differences are in the Innate Skill department. Ludo dumps the extremely situational Orders and Practiced Maneuver skills in favor of **Toughness**, a great skill that effectively raises his defense well beyond that of other Legionnaires, and **Peoples Champion**, a crowd-pleasing skill that should pay dividends for the whole party.

Affinities

Fire	Water	Earth	Air	Dark	Light
●	●	●	●		

➜ Skill			Description
Strike	0	0	Standard move to attack.
Upper Hand	10	2	Successful attack knocks opponent down.

↘ Skill			Description
Target Leg	4	2	Medium damage, may reduce opponent's movement rate.
Bungle Enemy	18	2	Effect: Reduce opponent's accuracy.
Destroy Shield	24	1	Successful attack may destroy opponent's shield.
Target Head	34	1	Effect: Reduce opponent's initiative.
Upward Slash	40	3	Heavy damage attack.

✕ Skill			Description
Combo Attack 1	6	2	Two hit attack, moderate speed.
Combo Attack 2	12	3	Three hit attack, moderate speed.
Combo Attack 3	22	4	Four hit attack, moderate speed.
Combo Attack 4	34	5	Five hit attack, moderate speed.

✳ Skill			Description
On Guard	6	0	Increase defense next turn.
High Guard	30	2	Increase defense next turn.

◗ Skill			Description
Affinity Attack 1	4	40	Attack enhanced by the power of an affinity god.
Affinity Attack 2	10	60	Mighty attack enhanced by the power of an affinity god. *Affinity Attack 1 Required.*
Affinity Attack 3	20	80	Mightiest attack enhanced by the power of an affinity god, has added effect. *Affinity Attack 2 Required.*
Affinity Attack 4	36	100	Summon a servant of an affinity god to attack all opponents. *Affinity Attack 3 Required.*

⚲ Skill			Description
Dodge	0	-	Standard defensive maneuver.
Shield Block	0	-	Standard defensive maneuver with shield.
Toughness	6	-	Resist a portion of all incoming damage.
Evasion	8	-	More effective defensive maneuver.
Indomitable Will	18	-	Immune to root, petrify, blindness and freeze.
Awareness	20	-	No bonus given to enemies when attacked from behind.
People's Champion	22	-	Crowd meter increases faster.
Riposte	22	-	Immediate counter attack when an opponent's attack misses.
Discipline	32	-	Immune to stun, confusion, charm and fear.
Off Balance	38	-	Lowers opponent's defense if opponent misses attack.

TYPE: SUPPORT

EIJI

E iji may claim to be an Archer, but she sure has a lot more in common with Amazons. Particularly in the fact that she seems to share their issues with men... Many of her special skills are only effective on male opponents. Those skills, and her many Eiji-exclusive skills, are based around causing negative status conditions. They're nice when they work, but it's better to have the reliable damage that comes from a real Archer's bow.

Punch is a nice move attack, dishing out a bit of damage and offering a quick recovery time. Eiji differs from her fellow Support characters with a lot of strange arrow tricks: **Acid Arrow** poisons its target and slowly melts their shield (far too slowly for my taste). **Flash Arrow** is a solid area effect that can stun a cluster of opponents, while **Nerve Arrow** only stuns one, but more reliably. **Razor Arrow** is a strong offensive attack with a potentially deadly added condition.

Most of Eiji's skills cost too many skill points to be used frequently, so you'll end up alternating them with weak Move-Bow Shots. **Volley** is a nice exception to that rule, costing only 2 skill points for a very powerful effect. **Cover Area** is also a skill that shouldn't be underestimated. If used wisely, it can hit multiple enemies mulitple times during *other character's* turns. **Note:** Starting skills are listed for Eiji at level 10.

Character Class Statistics

HP	●● ●●●●●────
Defense	●●● ●●●──────
Power	●●● ●●●──────
Accuracy	●●● ●●●●●────
Initiative	●●● ●●●●─────
Movement	●●● ●●●──────

Weapons
Plain Bow, All Archer, All Eiji

Shields
None

Armor
None

Helmets
All Eiji, All Archer, Hat Helmet, Helm Helmet

Accessory
Belt

Affinities

| Fire | Water | Earth | Air | Dark | Light |

→ Skill	🗡	◆	Description
Move - Bow Shot	-	0	Standard move to attack.
Punch	-	1	Quick, low power attack.

↘ Skill	🗡	◆	Description
Long Shot 1	-	2	Standard range attack.
Low Kick	-	4	Kick attack that can only be used against male opponents.
Sparks	-	2	Electric shock attack that causes damage and stuns a male opponent.
Acid Arrow	-	2	Medium range poison attack that damages shield if blocked.
Flash Arrow	-	4	Range attack that can stun anyone in the effect area.
Long Shot 2	20	3	Long range attack.
Nerve Arrow	22	3	Range attack that stuns opponent.
Volley	30	2	Multiple arrow range attack with area effect.
Razor Arrow	32	3	Range attack that causes bleeding damage.
Long Shot 3	36	5	Extremely long range attack.

✕ Skill	🗡	◆	Description
Combo Attack 1	4	2	Two hit attack, slow speed.
Combo Attack 2	8	3	Three hit attack, slow speed.
Combo Attack 3	16	4	Four hit attack, slow speed.
Combo Attack 4	26	5	Five hit attack, slow speed.

✦ Skill	🗡	◆	Description
Cover Area	-	0	Automatically attack all opponents entering designated area.
Distract	-	2	Lower initiative of male opponent.
Wink	-	0	Set a trap for male opponents to miss their attack.
Blind	34	2	Male opponent blinded by beauty.
Charm	38	4	Charm male opponent.

🌑 Skill	🗡	◆	Description
Affinity Attack 1	4	40	Attack enhanced by the power of an affinity god.
Affinity Attack 2	10	60	Mighty attack enhanced by the power of an affinity god. *Affinity Attack 1 Required.*
Affinity Attack 3	20	80	Mightiest attack enhanced by the power of an affinity god, has added effect. *Affinity Attack 2 Required.*
Affinity Attack 4	36	100	Summon a servant of an affinity god to attack all opponents. *Affinity Attack 3 Required.*

🏃 Skill	🗡	◆	Description
Dodge	0	-	Standard defensive maneuver.
Evasion	40	-	More effective defensive maneuver.

GWAZI

TYPE: LIGHT

Weapons
Light Axe, Light Sword, Light Spear,
All Secutor, All Gwazi

Shields
Light Shield, Secutor Shield,
Gwazi Shield

Armor
Light Armor, Secutor Armor, Gwazi Armor

Helmets
All Gwazi, All Secutor, Gladiatorial
Helmet

Accessory
Ring

Character Class Statistics

HP	
Defense	
Power	
Accuracy	
Initiative	
Movement	

Gwazi is the last storyline character you get in the game, but it's hard to get excited about a modified Secutor who has horrible Accuracy (the worst in the game, in fact) and can't learn Backstabber. On the plus side, he is the game's quickest character, but you'll need to be an ace at the combo bar or rely heavily on Back Attacks to get any damage in.

Back Attack and **Infallible Aim** are crucial skills when your Accuracy sucks, and while both are reliable, neither do much damage. **Weapon Throw** is a nice trick, capable of hitting medium range foes (if you get lucky) that are within a straight or diagonal line from Gwazi.

Like his Secutor cousins, Gwazi gets a lot of mileage out of **Berate** and **Taunt**. Cough up the 30 job points for **Evasion** to make sure he can survive front line combat, and you'll have the crowd's undying devotion. Of course, that trick works just as well with Secutors, who also have Backstabber and reasonably good Accuracy. Gwazi's weaknesses can certainly be worked around when you have to use him, but I'd leave him on the bench when you don't. **Note:** Starting skills are listed for Gwazi at level 10.

Affinities

Fire	Water	Earth	Air	Dark	Light

➡ Skill	🗡	◆	Description
Strike	-	0	Standard move to attack.
Running Attack	-	2	Run across battlefield to attack (reduced damage and accuracy).
Back Attack	-	0	Target does not turn to face this attack.
Shield Bypass	32	0	Opponent cannot use shield to block attacks.

🗡 Skill	🗡	◆	Description
Trip	-	1	Successful attack knocks down opponent.
Destroy Shield	-	1	Successful attack may destroy opponent's shield.
Infallible Aim	-	0	Opponent cannot evade attack; attack may be blocked.
Weapon Throw	-	2	Throw weapon for ranged attack.
Target Head	34	1	Effect: Reduce opponent's initiative.
Slicing Attack	40	5	Heavy damage attack that may cause bleeding damage.

✖ Skill	🗡	◆	Description
Combo Attack 1	4	2	Two hit attack, fast speed.
Combo Attack 2	8	3	Three hit attack, fast speed.
Combo Attack 3	16	4	Four hit attack, fast speed.
Combo Attack 4	26	5	Five hit attack, fast speed.

✤ Skill	🗡	◆	Description
Sand Toss	-	1	Successful toss may blind opponent.
On Guard	-	0	Increase defense next turn.

⚪ Skill	🗡	◆	Description
Affinity Attack 1	4	40	Attack enhanced by the power of an affinity god.
Affinity Attack 2	10	60	Mighty attack enhanced by the power of an affinity god. *Affinity Attack 1 Required.*
Affinity Attack 3	20	80	Mightiest attack enhanced by the power of an affinity god, has added effect. *Affinity Attack 2 Required.*
Affinity Attack 4	36	100	Summon a servant of an affinity god to attack all opponents. *Affinity Attack 3 Required.*

👤 Skill	🗡	◆	Description
Evade	-	-	Standard defensive maneuver.
Shield Block	-	-	Standard defensive maneuver with shield.
Berate	-	-	Taunt opponent; crowd reacts positively.
Taunt	22	-	Taunt opponent; crowd goes wild!
Evasion	30	-	More effective defensive maneuver.

TYPE: SUPPORT

AMAZON

Amazons use bows, but differ from Archers in several important ways. They're more accurate, they can attack opponents in adjacent squares, they have several short range attacks, and they've traded most of the Archers' versatile arrow attacks for Special skills (such as **Charm**) that beguile and distract primarily male opponents.

The kick attacks, however, are quite disappointing; they're expensive but do only slightly more damage than a point blank bow shot. Skip them and focus on the Amazon's exclusive arrow attacks: **Venom Arrow**, which has a much wider "crit" range on the status effect meter, **Sparks**, which has a nice added effect for its cost, and **Volley**, a limited version of the Archer's Deluge.

There are times when temporarily incapacitating an opponent is more effective than picking away at their life total, but all of the Amazon's Special skills have a very limited range (most are only two squares in any direction), which negates most of the advantage of her bow. Additionally they don't work on females or beasts (even if that isn't specified in the skill description), so you'll often find yourself without a valid target.

Character Class Statistics

HP	
Defense	
Power	
Accuracy	
Initiative	
Movement	

Weapons
Plain Bow, All Amazon

Shields
None

Armor
All Amazon

Helmets
All Amazon, Diadem Helmet

Accessory
Bracelet

Affinities

Fire	Water	Earth	Air	Dark	Light

→ Skill			Description
Move - Bow Shot	0	0	Standard move to attack.
Strike	0	1	Quick, low power attack.

↘ Skill			Description
Poison Arrow	8	1	Successful attack may poison opponent.
Low Kick	10	4	Kick attack that can only be used against male opponents.
Sparks	18	3	Electric shock attack that causes damage and stuns a male opponent.
Venom Arrow	20	4	Successful attack may poison opponent.
Volley	30	2	Multiple arrow range attack with area effect.
Flip Kick	36	2	Strong kick attack.

✕ Skill			Description
Combo Attack 1	4	2	Two hit attack, slow speed.
Combo Attack 2	8	3	Three hit attack, slow speed.
Combo Attack 3	16	4	Four hit attack, slow speed.
Combo Attack 4	26	5	Five hit attack, slow speed.

✚ Skill			Description
Distract	0	2	Lower initiative of male opponent.
Enamor	6	2	Root male opponent.
Flirt	12	3	Male opponent stunned by beauty.
Cold Shoulder	22	0	Freeze opponent.
Cover Area	24	0	Automatically attack all opponents entering designated area.
Wink	28	0	Set a trap so when male opponents miss their attack.
Beguile	32	2	Confuse target opponent.
Blind	34	2	Male opponent blinded by beauty.
Charm	38	4	Charm male opponent.

◐ Skill			Description
Affinity Attack 1	4	40	Attack enhanced by the power of an affinity god.
Affinity Attack 2	10	60	Mighty attack enhanced by the power of an affinity god. *Affinity Attack 1 Required.*
Affinity Attack 3	20	80	Mightiest attack enhanced by the power of an affinity god, has added effect. *Affinity Attack 2 Required.*
Affinity Attack 4	36	100	Summon a servant of an affinity god to attack all opponents. *Affinity Attack 3 Required.*

⚘ Skill			Description
Dodge	0	-	Standard defensive maneuver.
Evasion	40	-	More effective defensive maneuver.

ARCHER

TYPE: SUPPORT

Weapons
Plain Bow, Archer Bow

Shields
None

Armor
None

Helmets
All Archer, Hat Helmet, Helm Helmet

Accessory
Belt

Character Class Statistics

HP
Defense
Power
Accuracy
Initiative
Movement

Affinities

Fire	Water	Earth	Air	Dark	Light

→ Skill			Description
Move- Bow Shot	0	0	Standard move to attack.

↘ Skill			Description
Rapid Shot	2	0	Close range attack with fast recovery time.
Exploding Arrow	4	4	Exploding range attack; causes area damage.
Standing Bow Shot	4	3	Longest range attack.
Long Shot 1	6	2	Standard range attack.
Jolt Arrow	12	3	Successful attack knocks opponent back.
Bulls Eye	18	2	Close attack that bypasses opponent's defenses.
Long Shot 2	20	3	Long range attack.
Poison Arrow	22	4	Ranged attack that may poison opponent.
Indirect Fire	30	3	Ranged attack that travels over obstructions.
Point Blank	32	4	Heavy damage attack for nearby opponents.
Spray	34	3	Medium range attack with multiple arrows damaging opponents within range.
Long Shot 3	36	4	Extremely long range attack.
Long Shot 4	38	5	Longest range attack.
Deluge	40	4	Long range attack with multiple arrows damaging opponents within range.

✕ Skill			Description
Combo Attack 1	6	2	Two hit attack, slow speed.
Combo Attack 2	12	3	Three hit attack, slow speed.
Combo Attack 3	22	4	Four hit attack, slow speed.
Combo Attack 4	34	5	Five hit attack, slow speed.

✚ Skill			Description
Whislting Arrow	10	0	Pump up the crowd.
Cover Area	24	0	Automatically attack all opponents entering designated area.

● Skill			Description
Affinity Attack 1	4	40	Attack enhanced by the power of an affinity god.
Affinity Attack 2	10	60	Mighty attack enhanced by the power of an affinity god. Affinity Attack 1 Required.
Affinity Attack 3	40	80	Mightiest attack enhanced by the power of an affinity god, has added effect. Affinity Attack 2 Required.
Affinity Attack 4	36	100	Summon a servant of an affinity god to attack all opponents. Affinity Attack 3 Required.

⚑ Skill			Description
Dodge	0	-	Standard defensive maneuver.

Archers are probably the best Support characters in the game. They're not quite as accurate as Amazons or as powerful as Gungnirs, but they have a stunning array of ranged attacks and unlike spear throwers, will rarely be without a target. That's because bow users can do two things javelin users can't: Move to a square where they have a clear shot and attack in the same turn, and shoot enemies at point blank range.

Archers have a number of excellent skills to choose from. **Rapid Shot** doesn't do much damage, but it's free to use and has very quick recovery time, so it's a great way to get in a few hits while rapidly charging your skill point bar. You can then use those skill points on skills like the area effect **Exploding Arrow** and highly accurate **Standing Bow Shot**, which are too cheap to pass up. They should keep your Archer busy in combat while you save up for the all-powerful **Deluge**, which has such a wide range of effect it can often hit every enemy on the battlefield! Many of the single-target attacks, like **Jolt Arrow** and the powerful, short range **Point Blank** are also excellent, but nothing tops Deluge.

TYPE: LIGHT

BANDIT

Bandits are quick, unerringly accurate, and deadly from behind. Heavy gladiators may be rare in Nordagh, but Iain the Bandit should still be your first recruit when playing as Ursula. In addition to pestering the heavies, Bandits are great at taking out low-defense light and support classes like Berserkers and Gungnirs. When you equip your Bandit, don't automatically go for the weapon with the highest stats; **Spear Attack** is so versatile and powerful that even a mediocre Light Spear is often the best choice.

Backstabber should be your first skill selection. Highly mobile Bandits shouldn't have much trouble slipping behind their foes, and **Backstabber** turns their weak jabs into powerful attacks. **Running Attack** and **Sprinting Attack** are fantastic, but should be used carefully; if you send your Bandit too far ahead, he'll be killed before the rest of your troop can catch up. Use them primarily to get behind opponents who are already engaged, or to shut down vulnerable Arcane and Support characters. **Incapacitate Heavy** is fairly redundant, but late in the game **Strong Incapacitate** will give you a good option for dealing with otherwise unbeatable medium-type foes.

Since Bandits can easily avoid Heavy unit attacks, don't forget the **Riposte** skill. For every attack your Bandit dodges, he/she will counter-attack. The Bandit won't hit for a lot of damage, but because they dodge so much, it's good to have this skill.

Character Class Statistics

HP	
Defense	
Power	
Accuracy	
Initiative	
Movement	

Attack
Running Attack

Weapons
Light Axe, Light Sword, Light Spear, All Secutor, All Bandit

Shields
Light Shield, Secutor Shield, Bandit Shield

Armor
Light Armor, Secutor Armor, Bandit Armor

Helmets
All Bandit, All Secutor, Hat Helmet, Gladiatorial

Accessory
Armband

Affinities

Fire	Water	Earth	Air	Dark	Light

➡ Skill		◆	Description
Strike	0	0	Standard move to attack.
Running Attack	6	2	Run across battlefield to attack (reduced damage and accuracy).
Pierce Defence	24	2	Quick attack that evades opponent's shield.
Sprinting Attack	32	2	Run a greater distance across the battlefield to attack.

⚔ Skill		◆	Description
Spear Attack	0	0	Attack from the diagonal using the spear's extended reach.
Trip	18	1	Successful attack knocks down opponent.
Vigor Theft	34	1	Successful attack reduces opponent initiative.
Slicing Attack	40	3	Heavy damage attack that may cause bleeding damage.

✖ Skill		◆	Description
Combo Attack 1	6	2	Two hit attack, fast speed.
Combo Attack 2	12	3	Three hit attack, fast speed.
Combo Attack 3	22	4	Four hit attack, fast speed.
Combo Attack 4	34	5	Five hit attack, fast speed.

❄ Skill		◆	Description
Incapacitate Heavy	0	4	Successful attack will Petrify a heavy opponent for a short time.
On Guard	12	0	Increase defense next turn.
Strong Incapacitate	36	4	Successful attack may stun opponent.

◗ Skill		◆	Description
Affinity Attack 1	4	40	Attack enhanced by the power of an affinity god.
Affinity Attack 2	10	60	Mighty attack enhanced by the power of an affinity god. *Affinity Attack 1 required.*
Affinity Attack 3	20	80	Mightiest attack enhanced by the power of an affinity god, has added effect. *Affinity Attack 2 required.*
Affinity Attack 4	36	100	Summon a servant of an affinity god to attack all opponents. *Affinity Attack 3 required.*

🧍 Skill			Description
Dodge	0	-	Standard defensive maneuver.
Shield Block	0	-	Standard defensive maneuver with shield.
Group Courage	8	-	Increase movement and initiative when near other Bandits.
Back Stabber	10	-	Damage doubled when attacking from behind.
Evasion	20	-	More effective defensive maneuver.
Riposte	22	-	Immediate counter attack when an opponent's attack misses.
Heightened Evasion	30	-	Most effective defensive maneuver.
Awareness	38	-	No bonus given to enemies when attacked from behind.

BARBARIAN

TYPE: MEDIUM

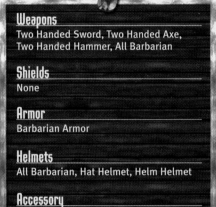

Weapons
Two Handed Sword, Two Handed Axe,
Two Handed Hammer, All Barbarian

Shields
None

Armor
Barbarian Armor

Helmets
All Barbarian, Hat Helmet, Helm Helmet

Accessory
Runestone

Character Class Statistics

HP	●●●●●● ───
Defense	●●●● ─────
Power	●●●●●● ───
Accuracy	●●●● ─────
Initiative	●●●●●●● ──
Movement	●●●●● ────

Barbarians are among the strongest medium gladiators, sporting excellent strength, a bucket of Hit Points, and no glaring weaknesses. But since both Ursula and Valens are Medium-class characters, and Urlan is basically an enhanced Barbarian himself, why would you ever want to recruit another? Ursula players may be tempted to recruit a few to add some beef to the party, but they should save those slots for the more diverse medium gladiators that await in Imperia.

One of the interesting things about Barbarians is the low cost of **Overhead Cleave**; they can get this powerful attack for only 24 job points, as opposed to the 40 most classes have to pay. **Wolf Form** and **Bear Form** are redundant on a class that's already good in melee, so spend the rest of your early job points on **Running Attack** and the Innate **Totem of the Bear** and **Totem of the Falcon** skills, which will give a hearty boost to their already strong offensive stats. **Destroy Shield** is also incredibly powerful and deserves mention. It can deal up to three to four times the damage of **Break Defense**, and for one skill point, can be used repeatedly.

Affinities

🜂	🜄	🜃	🜁		
Fire	Water	Earth	Air	Dark	Light

→ Skill			Description
Strike	0	-	Standard move to attack.
Running Attack	10	2	Run across battlefield to attack (reduced damage).

⬩ Skill			Description
Target Leg	4	2	Medium damage, may reduce opponent's movement rate.
Overhead Cleave	24	5	Heavy overhead attack; may break opponent's helmet.
Crippling Blow	32	3	Brutal attack that may stun and knock down opponent.
Break Defense	34	4	Several fierce attacks that prevent defense.
Destroy Shield	40	1	Successful attack may destroy opponent's shield.

✖ Skill			Description
Combo Attack 1	4	2	Two hit attack, slow speed.
Combo Attack 2	8	3	Three hit attack, slow speed.
Combo Attack 3	16	4	Four hit attack, slow speed.
Combo Attack 4	26	5	Five hit attack, slow speed.

❋ Skill			Description
Wolf Form 1	2	0	Shapeshift into a wolf of lesser ability.
Defend	6	0	Give up turn to reduce damage until next turn.
Bear Form	8	0	Shapeshift into a bear of lesser ability.
Wolf Form 2	12	1	Shapeshift into a wolf. *Wolf Form 1 required.*
Bear Form 2	20	1	Shapeshift into a bear. *Bear Form 1 required.*
Wolf Form 3	22	4	Shapeshift into a wolf of greater ability. *Wolf Form 2 required.*
Bear Form 3	30	4	Shapeshift into a powerful bear. *Bear Form 2 required.*

◗ Skill			Description
Affinity Attack 1	4	40	Attack enhanced by the power of an affinity god.
Affinity Attack 2	10	60	Mighty attack enhanced by the power of an affinity god. *Affinity Attack 1 required.*
Affinity Attack 3	20	80	Mightiest attack enhanced by the power of an affinity god, has added effect. *Affinity Attack 2 required.*
Affinity Attack 4	36	100	Summon a servant of an affinity god to attack all opponents. *Affinity Attack 3 required.*

🧍 Skill			Description
Parry	0	-	Standard defensive maneuver.
Totem of the Bear	18	-	Increase attack damage.
Totem of the Falcon	38	-	Increase accuracy.

TYPE: BEAST

BEAR

Good defense, solid defensive skills, and a nearly bottomless supply of Hit Points make Bears the hardiest class in the game. Their power is lower than the heavyweight characters they resemble, but a number of very powerful attacks easily make up the difference. Bears are perhaps the best of the beasts, and should be one of your first recruits.

Bears lack a versatile array of abilities, but they have a handful of truly eye-popping skills. **Raging Bear** is unbelievable—it grants you a counter attack whenever you're hit. You haven't lived till you've seen an opponent pull off a five hit combo, take off no more than a third of your Bear's HP Bar, and then get killed during his own turn by the Bear's five counter attacks. **Powered Pull Down** is a pricy but deadly attack that is guaranteed to hit, and **Smack Back** can be very useful when you're surrounded or want to push an opponent into another ally's range.

Winter's Fat is cheap, and should be the first skill you pick up. Pick up **Charge** if you're fighting in large arenas, and then start saving up for the big stuff. Basic attacks like **Swipe** and **Slash** are nice, but it's **Raging Bear** that will win you games.

Character Class Statistics

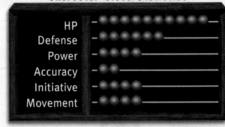

HP	●●●●●●●●●
Defense	●●●●●
Power	●●●●
Accuracy	●●
Initiative	●●●●
Movement	●●●●

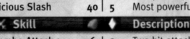

Weapons
None

Shields
None

Armor
None

Helmets
None

Accessory
Collar

Affinities

Fire　Water　Earth　Air　Dark　Light

➡ Skill	🗡	♦	Description
Snap	0	0	Standard move to attack.
Charge	14	1	Weak running attack with high accuracy.

↘ Skill	🗡	♦	Description
Bite	0	1	High power attack with low accuracy.
Swipe	10	2	Medium damage, may reduce opponent's movement rate.
Slash	18	3	More powerful attack.
Powered Swipe	24	4	Medium damage attack that may stun opponent.
Powered Pull Down	32	5	Prolonged stomping attack.
Raking Attack	36	2	Heavy damage claw attack that causes bleeding damage.
Smack Back	38	3	Push opponent backward and cause damage; move into the previously occupied square.
Vicious Slash	40	5	Most powerful move to attack.

✖ Skill	🗡	♦	Description
Combo Attack 1	6	2	Two hit attack, slow speed.
Combo Attack 2	12	3	Three hit attack, slow speed.
Combo Attack 3	22	4	Four hit attack, slow speed.
Combo Attack 4	34	5	Five hit attack, slow speed.

✳ Skill	🗡	♦	Description
Knock Back	2	1	Push opponent backward; move into the previously occupied square.
On Guard	12	0	Increase defense next turn.
Hibernation	22	2	Give up turn to regain Hit Points.

⬤ Skill	🗡	♦	Description
Affinity Attack 1	4	40	Attack enhanced by the power of an affinity god.
Affinity Attack 2	10	60	Mighty attack enhanced by the power of an affinity god. *Affinity Attack 1 required.*
Affinity Attack 3	20	80	Mightiest attack enhanced by the power of an affinity god, has added effect. *Affinity Attack 2 required.*
Affinity Attack 4	36	100	Summon a servant of an affinity god to attack all opponents. *Affinity Attack 3 required.*

🚶 Skill	🗡	♦	Description
Beast Dodge	0	-	Standard defensive maneuver.
Winters Fat	6	-	Reduce damage received.
Raging Bear	30	-	Counter attack after successful opponent hit.

BERSERKER

TYPE: LIGHT

Weapons
Light Axe, Light Sword, All Berserker

Shields
None

Armor
None

Helmets
None

Accessory
Runestone

Character Class Statistics

HP	
Defense	
Power	
Accuracy	
Initiative	
Movement	

Affinities

Fire	Water	Earth	Air	Dark	Light

Berserkers are the most versatile of the light gladiators. If you need a bit of ranged damage, they can hang back and use **Axe Throw**. If you need a heavy hitter, they can enter a berserker rage (with any of the Rage skills) and start dishing out damage that puts other light characters to shame. If you need to turn the tide of a tight battle, you can unleash a **Howl**, **Roar**, or **Metal Face** and make your foes lose a turn or two.

Unfortunately, while Berserkers can fill many roles in your troop, they aren't particularly good at any of them. **Axe Throw** doesn't do much damage, the loss of control over a berserk character can be problematic, and foes usually shake off negative effects very quickly. While the damage that can be dealt by an **Adrenaline** and **Rage**-boosted Berserker is nothing to scoff at, Berserkers can't wear armor and have very few Hit Points, so they rarely survive long in the front lines. Bandits, Mongrels and Dervishes are usually a better choice for your light gladiator slots. If you do recruit one, make sure to equip it with the common runestone Ingwaz, which will help reduce damage inflicted on them.

➡ Skill			Description
Strike	0	0	Standard move to attack.

⬊ Skill			Description
Target Leg	4	2	Medium damage, may reduce opponent's movement rate.
Axe Throw	10	3	Throw weapon for ranged attack.
Mad Rage	24	0	Successful attack strikes opponent three times.
Overhead Cleave	30	4	Heavy overhead attack; may break opponent's helmet.
Gouging Fury	34	3	A heavy attack capable of knocking an opponent back.
Destroy Shield	40	1	Successful attack may destroy opponent's shield.

✕ Skill			Description
Combo Attack 1	6	2	Two hit attack, fast speed.
Combo Attack 2	12	3	Three hit attack, fast speed.
Combo Attack 3	22	4	Four hit attack, fast speed.
Combo Attack 4	34	5	Four hit attack, fast speed.

✤ Skill			Description
Yowl	0	2	Successful attack may root nearby opponents.
Rage	6	2	Enter mild berserk status.
Howl	8	3	Successful attack may confuse nearby opponents.
Roar	12	4	Successful attack may panic nearby opponents.
On Guard	18	0	Increase defense next turn.
Rage 2	20	3	Enter berserk status.
Metal Face	32	5	Successful attack may petrify nearby opponents.
Rage 3	36	5	Enter intense berserk status.

⬤ Skill			Description
Affinity Attack 1	4	40	Attack enhanced by the power of an affinity god.
Affinity Attack 2	10	60	Mighty attack enhanced by the power of an affinity god. *Affinity Attack 1 required.*
Affinity Attack 3	20	80	Mightiest attack enhanced by the power of an affinity god, has added effect. *Affinity Attack 2 required.*
Affinity Attack 4	36	100	Summon a servant of an affinity god to attack all opponents. *Affinity Attack 3 required.*

⚑ Skill			Description
Dodge	0	-	Standard defensive maneuver.
Adrenaline	6	-	Receive large damage bonus when Hit Points are low.
Indomitable Will	19	-	Immune to root, petrify, blindness and freeze.
Riposte	22	-	Immediate counter attack when an opponent's attack misses.

TYPE: HEAVY

CENTURION

Centurions are team players all the way. They lack the wide variety of powerful attacks available to most heavy gladiators, like Samnites, but more than make up for it with a variety of effects that "buff" your entire team. They're no slouches in the statistics department either--Centurions are tanks on defense and brutal on offense.

Innate skills Coordinated Attack and Garrison should be your first two buys; **Garrison** toughens everyone around the Centurion while **Coordinated Attack** gives anyone in range a 50/50 chance of a free shot when the Centurion scores a hit. **Roam** is always good on a heavy gladiator, and essential for Centurions, who can't help the team if they fall too far behind. Finally, **Rally** is a rare healing skill that also raises your team's initiative, and since **Motivate** "stacks", you can use the skill multiple times to exponentially increase the damage your gladiators can do.

Due to their team-oriented nature, Centurions are best in fights with four or more gladiators, especially if they can all start in the same place. A good tip is to always recruit two; no foe will survive long when surrounded by a pair of **Coordinated Attack**-ing Centurions and a few other solid fighters.

Character Class Statistics

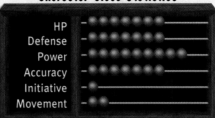

HP	
Defense	
Power	
Accuracy	
Initiative	
Movement	

Attack
ear Attack   186

Weapons
Heavy Sword, Heavy Hammer,
Heavy Spear, All Centurion

Shields
Heavy Shield, Centurion Shield

Armor
Heavy Armor, Centurion Armor

Helmets
All Centurion, Military Helmet

Accessory
Medal

Affinities

Fire	Water	Earth	Air	Dark	Light
◐	◐	◐	◐		

➡ Skill			Description
Strike	0	0	Standard move to attack.
Roam	10	2	Increased range move to attack.

↘ Skill			Description
Spear Attack	0	1	Attack from the diagonal using the spear's extended reach.
Target Leg	0	2	Medium damage, may reduce opponent's movement rate.
Bungle Enemy	18	2	Effect: Reduce opponent's accuracy.
Target Head	34	1	Effect: Reduce opponent's initiative.
Overhead Cleave	40	4	Heavy overhead attack; may break opponent's helmet.

✕ Skill			Description
Combo Attack 1	4	2	Two hit attack, slow speed.
Combo Attack 2	8	3	Three hit attack, slow speed.
Combo Attack 3	16	4	Four hit attack, slow speed.
Combo Attack 4	34	5	Five hit attack, slow speed.

✚ Skill			Description
Motivate	0	2	Increase attack damage of all allies.
Defend	6	0	Give up turn to reduce damage until next turn.
Reprimand	8	3	Remove charm, stun, or confusion effects from ally.
Impel	22	1	Increase movement speed of ally.
Spur	24	1	Temporarily increase accuracy of allies.
Rally	33	2	Recover Hit Points and increase initiative of allies within range.
Immediate Response	38	2	Give ally greater initiative.

● Skill			Description
Affinity Attack 1	4	40	Attack enhanced by the power of an affinity god.
Affinity Attack 2	10	60	Mighty attack enhanced by the power of an affinity god. *Affinity Attack 1 required.*
Affinity Attack 3	20	80	Mightiest attack enhanced by the power of an affinity god, has added effect. *Affinity Attack 2 required.*
Affinity Attack 4	36	100	Summon a servant of an affinity god to attack all opponents. *Affinity Attack 3 required.*

👤 Skill			Description
Parry	0	-	Standard defensive maneuver.
Shield Block	0	-	Standard defensive maneuver with shield.
Coordinated Attack	8	-	Successful attack that can grant an additional attack to allies within range.
Garrison	12	-	Give defensive bonus to adjacent allies.
Indomitable Will	18	-	Immune to root, petrify, blindness and freeze.
Shield Excellence	20	-	More effective defensive maneuver with shield.

CHANNELER TYPE: ARCANE

Weapons
Plain Staff, All Channeler

Shields
None

Armor
Arcane Armor, All Channeler

Helmets
All Channeler, Diadem Helmet, Arcane Helmet

Accessory
Charm

Character Class Statistics

HP
Defense
Power
Accuracy
Initiative
Movement

Affinities

Fire Water Earth Air Dark Light

Skill			Description
Strike	0	0	Standard move to attack.

Skill			Description
Steal Affinity	0	3	Steal Affinity Power from opponent.
Tornado	0	0	Teleport all within range to random location.
Invigorate	10	40	Recover some Hit Points for one ally.
Wind Stepper	12	10	Slightly increase all allies' movement rate.
Enliven	16	60	Recover Hit Points for one ally.
Teleport	18	0	Teleport a short distance on the battlefield.
Drain Affinity	22	10	Steal affinity power from opponent.
Wind Runner	24	30	Increase all allies' movement rate.
Ameliorate	36	80	Recover many Hit Points for one ally.
Stiff Wind	36	20	An attack that decreases opponent's movement rate.
Boost Affinity	38	10	Boost ally affinity power.

Skill			Description
Fire Bomb	0	20	Range attack damages and knocks back all opponents in explosion radius.
Affinity Attack 1	4	40	Attack enhanced by the power of an affinity god.
Fire Cloud	6	10	Attack that causes fire damage.
Combo Attack 1	8	20	Two hit attack, slow speed.
Sleet	8	10	Freeze opponent for a short time causing frost damage.
Affinity Attack 2	10	60	Mighty attack enhanced by the power of an affinity god. *Affinity Attack 1 required.*
Fire Tempest	14	50	Most powerful attack that causes massive fire damage.
Combo Attack 2	16	40	Three hit attack, slow speed.
Affinity Attack 3	20	80	Mightiest attack enhanced by the power of an affinity god, has added effect. *Affinity Attack 2 required.*
Combo Attack 3	28	60	Four hit attack, slow speed.
Ice Storm	28	20	Freeze opponent causing frost damage.
Affinity Attack 4	36	100	Summon a servant of an affinity god to attack all opponents. *Affinity Attack 3 required.*
Fire Storm	36	30	Powerful attack that causes intense fire damage.
Combo Attack 4	42	80	Five hit attack, slow speed.
Ice Tempest	46	40	Freeze opponent causing massive frost damage.

Skill			Description
Evade	0	-	Standard defensive maneuver.

Channelers are the primary spellcasters of the games. Skill Points matter little with this class, since all but a few of their skills use Affinity Power instead. All of these attacks are ranged, including Combo and Affinity Attacks, so as long as they have a steady source of Affinity, they can fall back and act as support characters.

Fortunately, Channelers are the only casters with a ranged affinity source: **Steal Affinity**. This offensive and defensive skill is useless on turn 1, when no one has any Affinity to steal, but after a few turns of positioning your Channeler and perhaps a few ineffectual Affinity-boosting Strikes, it will become a near bottomless source of Affinity. Best of all, you recover from **Steal Affinity** so quickly that you can usually do it twice in a row (if you're full up on skill points) and unleash an attack before the next character's turn.

Teleport is one of the Channeler's most effective abilities. It costs 0 skill points and has a very long range.

Most of the Channelers' special Affinity Attacks are underwhelming. **Fire Bomb** is a weak (but cheap) area effect that is useful at times, but your best bets are attacks that can temporarily disable key opponents, like **Ice Storm** and most types of **Affinity Attack 3**. Healing skills like **Enliven** are nice to have, but the effects are modest, and do require a success on the status swing meter.

TYPE: HEAVY

CYCLOPS

For a heavy type gladiator, Cyclopes are surprisingly versatile. They can dish out a savage melee beating, blast foes from afar with their **Eye Beam**, and cheaply incapacitate opponents from a distance. They share the heavy type curse of poor Accuracy (I'm sure the lack of depth perception doesn't help), so if you plan to run one in your school, do whatever you can to get your hands on the Blindman's Eye Accessory.

Punch is a great skill with high Accuracy, longer range than **Strike**, and faster recovery time. **Eye Beam** and **Heavy Handed** are no-brainers, but some tricky decisions await after that. **Overhead Smash** is worth the job points, but most of the Attacks should be skipped in favor of Special abilities like **Devastating Glare**. If you can hit the sweet spot at the status meter, this will cause debilitating fear in one character within medium range. Any skill that can incapacitate a character from several squares away is worth using, especially when it only costs two skill points. **Penetrating Stare** is also worth learning; it lacks the long range, but is a lifesaver when you're surrounded.

Character Class Statistics

HP	●●●●●●●●●
Defense	●●●●──
Power	●●●●●●●●
Accuracy	●●●──
Initiative	●●──
Movement	●●──

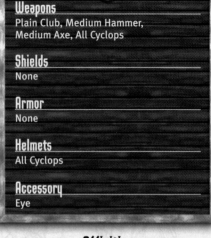

Weapons
Plain Club, Medium Hammer, Medium Axe, All Cyclops

Shields
None

Armor
None

Helmets
All Cyclops

Accessory
Eye

Affinities

Fire Water Earth Air Dark Light

➡ Skill			Description
Strike	0	0	Standard move to attack.
Punch	8	2	Quick, low power attack.

↘ Skill			Description
Eye Beam	4	1	Powerful range attack; damages all opponents directly in front of character.
Sweeping Attack	10	3	Two-handed attack that damages several squares in front of character.
Overhead Smash	12	3	Heavy damage attack that may stun opponent; does not effect animals.
Bungle Enemy	18	2	Effect: Reduce opponent's accuracy.
Destroy Shield	24	1	Successful attack may destroy opponent's shield.
Target Head	34	1	Effect: Reduce opponent's initiative.
Heavy Strike	40	5	Heavy damage, low accuracy attack.

✖ Skill			Description
Combo Attack 1	4	2	Two hit attack, slow speed.
Combo Attack 2	8	3	Three hit attack, slow speed.
Combo Attack 3	16	4	Four hit attack, slow speed.
Combo Attack 4	26	5	Five hit attack, slow speed.

✳ Skill			Description
Glower	0	1	Successful attack causes fear.
Knockback	0	1	Push opponent backward.
On Guard	20	0	Increase defense next turn.
Focus	22	2	Remove charm, stun, or confusion effects from ally.
High Guard	30	2	Increase defense next turn. *On Guard required.*
Devastating Glare	32	2	Successful attack causes long-lasting fear.
Supreme Guard	36	3	Massive increase defense next turn. *High Guard required.*
Penetrating Stare	38	3	Petrify opponents within range.

⬤ Skill			Description
Affinity Attack 1	4	40	Attack enhanced by the power of an affinity god.
Affinity Attack 2	10	60	Mighty attack enhanced by the power of an affinity god. *Affinity Attack 1 required.*
Affinity Attack 3	20	80	Mightiest attack enhanced by the power of an affinity god, has added effect. *Affinity Attack 2 required.*
Affinity Attack 4	36	100	Summon a servant of an affinity god to attack all opponents. *Affinity Attack 3 required.*

👤 Skill			Description
Parry	0	-	Standard defensive maneuver.
Heavy Handed	6	-	Increase melee attack damage.

DERVISH

TYPE: LIGHT

Weapons
Dervish Axe, Dervish Sword

Shields
None

Armor
Dervish Armor

Helmets
All Dervish

Accessory
Anklet

Character Class Statistics

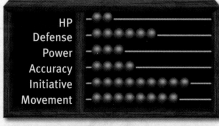

HP
Defense
Power
Accuracy
Initiative
Movement

Affinities

| Fire | Water | Earth | Air | Dark | Light |

→ Skill		◆	Description
Strike	0	0	Standard move to attack.
Surprise Attack	4	2	Target will not face when attacked.
Running Attack	12	1	Run across battlefield to attack (reduced damage and accuracy).

↘ Skill		◆	Description
Blood Letter	10	2	Heavy damage attack that may cause bleeding damage.
Blood Letter 2	20	4	Heavy damage attack that may cause bleeding damage.
Dust Devil 2	24	1	Damage surrounding opponents; reduce opponent initiative.
Bone Spray	34	3	Attack causes bleeding damage in nearby enemies.
Slicing Attack	40	4	Heavy damage attack that may cause bleeding damage.

✕ Skill		◆	Description
Combo Attack 1	6	2	Two hit attack, fast speed.
Combo Attack 2	12	3	Three hit attack, fast speed.
Combo Attack 3	22	4	Four hit attack, fast speed.
Combo Attack 4	34	5	Five hit attack, fast speed.

✦ Skill		◆	Description
Dust Devil	0	1	Reduce movement and initiative of surrounding opponents.
Wind Movement	0	3	Increase movement rate.
Whirlwind	18	3	Wind attack that knocks opponent down.
Whirlwind 2	36	5	Powerful wind attack that knocks opponent down and causes damage. *Whirlwind required.*

● Skill		◆	Description
Affinity Attack 1	4	40	Attack enhanced by the power of an affinity god.
Affinity Attack 2	10	60	Mighty attack enhanced by the power of an affinity god. *Affinity Attack 1 required.*
Affinity Attack 3	20	80	Mightiest attack enhanced by the power of an affinity god, has added effect. *Affinity Attack 2 required.*
Affinity Attack 4	36	100	Summon a servant of an affinity god to attack all opponents. *Affinity Attack 3 required.*

👤 Skill		◆	Description
Dodge	0	-	Standard defensive maneuver.
Adrenaline	6	-	Receive large damage bonus when Hit Points are low.
Air Protection	8	-	Increase resistance to Air Affinity attacks.
Evasion	22	-	More effective defensive maneuver.
Air Immunity	30	-	Immune to all Air Affinity attacks.
Lightning Reflexes	32	-	May reduce projectile range attacks.
Off Balance	38	-	Lowers opponent's defense if opponent misses attack.

Dervishes are the one light gladiator class that doesn't need to count on backstabbing and type-matching tricks to be a force in melee combat. Instead, their specialty is a variety of deadly techniques that do solid damage and cause bleeding or knock-backs. Many of these techniques can hit every adjacent enemy, even ones that are diagonal to the Dervish.

Many of the Dervish's techniques are interchangeable; **Bone Spray, Dust Devil 2**, and **Whirlwind 2** all do fundamentally the same thing. **Whirlwind 2** is probably the best for when your Dervish is surrounded, since knock-backs will prevent your foes from retaliating, but **Bone Spray** is great when you want to sneak in a cheap and deadly diagonal hit. **Surprise Attack** and **Adrenaline** are both cheap, must-have skills.

Dervishes are immune to all attacks that come from any unit equipped with an Air Affinity weapon. Even if the attack hits with a critical, it will deal 0 damage. This applies to everything from simple **Strike** attacks to Air Affinity attacks. If you're fighting against a Dervish, make sure your characters are equipped with anything but Air Affinity weapons.

In the thick of battle to be effective, Dervishes rarely last long in combat. The trick is to make sure they go out with a bang; if a Dervish can hit two or three guys with a single **Adrenaline**-fueled, effect-causing attack, then she's done her job.

GENERAL STRATEGY CHARACTER CLASSES WORLD ATLAS BONUS MATERIAL

TYPE: SUPPORT

GUNGNIR

Gungnirs, named for Odin's returning spear, are the javelin throwers of Nordagh. They excel at medium range attacks, offering both surprising power and good accuracy (assuming you can excel at rapid button pressing). They're best in medium-sized arenas, and are an excellent choice for taking out weakly armored light and arcane characters. A Gungnir who can take and hold high ground is a terror to behold.

However, Gungnirs take a great deal of skill to play correctly. The enemy AI knows that the best way to take out a Gungnir is to engage it in melee combat, denying it the line of sight it needs to hit other targets. Since Gungnirs, unlike Archers, can't move and do a ranged attack in the same turn, you'll then have to waste turns moving into ranged attack position or rely on your weak **Strike** attack. That's what **Bear Form** is for; it keeps your gladiator alive while giving them some reasonable melee attacks. Later in the game, **Bulls Eye** and **Powered Throw** provide other close range options.

Area attacks are always powerful, and **Exploding Javelin** is both cheap and effective. Don't waste job points buying every **Long Throw**, since they only increase in range incrementally. Saving up to buy **Unstoppable Throw**, which always hits, is a much better idea.

Character Class Statistics

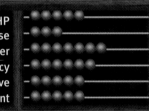

- HP
- Defense
- Power
- Accuracy
- Initiative
- Movement

Weapons
Plain Javelin, All Gungnir, Light Spear

Shields
Light Shield, Gungnir Shield, Peltast Shield

Armor
Barbarian Armor, Gungnir Armor

Helmets
All Gungnir, Hat Helmet, Helm Helmet

Accessory
Necklace

Affinities

Fire Water Earth Air Dark Light

→ Skill			Description
Strike	0	0	Standard move to attack.

↘ Skill			Description
Long Throw	0	1	Standard distance throwing attack.
Exploding Javelin	4	4	Exploding ranged attack, causes area damage.
Destroy Shield	6	2	Successful attack may destroy opponent's shield.
Bungle Enemy	10	2	Effect: Reduce opponent's accuracy.
Long Throw 2	12	2	Medium distance throwing attack.
Impale Leg	18	2	Effect: Reduce opponent's movement rate.
Long Throw 3	20	4	Long distance throwing attack.
Unstoppable Throw	24	4	Powerful javelin throw that damages multiple opponents in a line.
Bulls Eye	32	3	Close attack that bypasses opponent's defenses.
Pin Down	32	3	Aimed javelin throw pins opponent in place.
Powered Throw	34	4	Heavy damage attack for nearby opponents.
Long Throw 4	40	5	Extremely long distance throwing attack.

✖ Skill			Description
Combo Attack 1	4	2	Two hit attack, slow speed.
Combo Attack 2	8	3	Three hit attack, slow speed.
Combo Attack 3	16	4	Four hit attack, slow speed.
Combo Attack 4	26	5	Five hit attack, slow speed.

✚ Skill			Description
Bear Form 1	8	0	Shapeshift into a bear of lesser ability.
Cover Area	22	0	Automatically attack all opponents entering designated area.
Bear Form 2	36	1	Shapeshift into a bear. *Bear Form 1 required.*

⬤ Skill			Description
Affinity Attack 1	4	40	Attack enhanced by the power of an affinity god.
Affinity Attack 2	10	60	Mighty attack enhanced by the power of an affinity god. *Affinity Attack 1 required.*
Affinity Attack 3	20	80	Mightiest attack enhanced by the power of an affinity god, has added effect. *Affinity Attack 2 required.*
Affinity Attack 4	36	100	Summon a servant of an affinity god to attack all opponents. *Affinity Attack 3 required.*

🧍 Skill			Description
Dodge	0	-	Standard defensive maneuver.
Awareness	38	-	No bonus given to enemies when attacked from behind.

Left margin: GENERAL STRATEGY · CHARACTER CLASSES · WORLD ATLAS · BONUS MATERIAL

LEGIONNAIRE TYPE: MEDIUM

Weapons
Medium Axe, Medium Hammer, Medium Sword, All Legionnaire

Shields
Medium Shield, Legionnaire Shield

Armor
Medium Armor, Legionnaire Armor

Helmets
All Legionnaire, Military Helmet

Accessory
Medal

Character Class Statistics

HP	●●●●●
Defense	●●●●●●
Power	●●●●●●●●
Accuracy	●●●●●●●●●
Initiative	●●●
Movement	●●●

Attack
Precision Attack

Legionnaires aren't bad, they're just dull. Since your quest begins with two medium characters and you pick up two more in Chapter 2, you won't have a lot of space in your school for other medium weight characters. The solid stats and host of defensive skills Legionnaires offer just aren't as sexy as the Murmillo's shield shenanigans and silly hats, so they rarely make the cut. But the Legionnaire does have a few subtle strengths that should not be dismissed.

One is **Precision Attack,** a solid attack that has longer range than Strike and boosts your Accuracy significantly without affecting your Power much. **Destroy Shield** is another, a strong attack that costs only 1 skill point and can wipe the smug grin off a Murmillo's face. And **Riposte** is always great, especially on a class with a bunch of cheap defensive Innate skills.

Ludo fills this role in Valens' quest, but Ursula players may want to make some room for a Legionnaire in their school.

Affinities

Fire	Water	Earth	Air	Dark	Light

➡ Skill			Description
Strike	0	0	Standard move to attack.
Precision Attack	10	1	Quick, low power attack.

↘ Skill			Description
Target Leg	4	2	Medium damage, may reduce opponent's movement rate.
Bungle Enemy	18	2	Effect: Reduce opponent's accuracy.
Destroy Shield	24	1	Successful attack may destroy opponent's shield.
Target Head	34	1	Effect: Reduce opponent's initiative.
Overhead Cleave	40	4	Heavy overhead attack; may break opponent's helmet.

✖ Skill			Description
Combo Attack 1	6	2	Two hit attack, moderate speed.
Combo Attack 2	12	3	Three hit attack, moderate speed.
Combo Attack 3	22	4	Four hit attack, moderate speed.
Combo Attack 4	34	5	Five hit attack, moderate speed.

✳ Skill			Description
On Guard	6	0	Increase defense next turn.
High Guard	30	2	Increase defense next turn. *On Guard required.*

⬤ Skill			Description
Affinity Attack 1	4	40	Attack enhanced by the power of an affinity god.
Affinity Attack 2	10	60	Mighty attack enhanced by the power of an affinity god. *Affinity Attack 1 required.*
Affinity Attack 3	20	80	Mightiest attack enhanced by the power of an affinity god, has added effect. *Affinity Attack 2 required.*
Affinity Attack 4	36	100	Summon a servant of an affinity god to attack all opponents. *Affinity Attack 3 required.*

🚶 Skill			Description
Dodge	0	-	Standard defensive maneuver.
Shield Block	0	-	Standard defensive maneuver with shield.
Practiced Maneuvers	0	-	Increase initiative and movement when Legionnaires are within range.
Orders	8	-	Increase initiative when Centurion is within range.
Evasion	12	-	More effective defensive maneuver.
Indomitable Will	18	-	Immune to root, petrify, blindness and freeze.
Awareness	20	-	No bonus given to enemies when attacked from behind.
Riposte	22	-	Immediate counter attack when an opponent's attack misses.
Discipline	32	-	Immune to stun, confusion, charm and fear.
Off Balance	38	-	Lowers opponent's defense if opponent misses attack.

TYPE: HEAVY

MINOTAUR

Minotaurs are one of the most powerful classes in the game, but it's very difficult to get them to join your school (see side quest section). If you do manage to get them to join you, you'll find that they're powerhouse beaters with good Accuracy and better mobility than most heavy types."

It's hard to go wrong with the Minotaur's skills. Knock down attacks like **Rampage**, **Skewer**, and **Stampede** (which can hit two squares away) are great when you're ganging up on an opponent, since everyone else can get free hits while he's down. Once they're down, the **Trample** skill can finish them for good, although you won't get many opportunities to use it.

Running Attack is always great, and very cheap for Minotaurs. **Gore** is a very difficult attack to hit with, but it has decent range and does a lot of damage if it does hit. **Back Off!** is great when you're letting your opponent come to you, effectively giving you a free attack, and **Grunt** is another good way to kill a turn while you wait for your foes to show up.

Character Class Statistics

Stat	
HP	●●●●●●●●●
Defense	●●●●●●
Power	●●●●●●●
Accuracy	●●●●●●●
Initiative	●●●●●
Movement	●●●●●

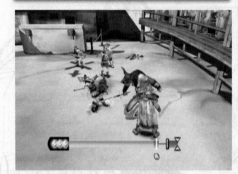

Weapons
Two Handed Sword, Two Handed Hammer, Two Handed Axe, All Minotaur

Shields
None

Armor
None

Helmets
All Minotaur

Accessory
Bullring

Affinities

●	●	●	●		
Fire	Water	Earth	Air	Dark	Light

➡ Skill		◆	Description
Strike	0	0	Standard move to attack.
Running Attack	6	2	Run across battlefield to attack (reduced damage and accuracy).
Gore	24	2	head butt attack; may stab opponent with horns.

✎ Skill		◆	Description
Rampage	0	2	Strong attack with low accuracy that may knock down opponent.
Skewer	18	3	Powerful attack that can knock an opponent down and stun them.
Stampede	22	1	Rush attack that knocks opponent down.
Trample	34	4	Prolonged stomping attack.
Overhead Cleave	38	4	Heavy overhead attack; may break opponent's helmet.
Heavy Strike	40	5	Heavy damage, low accuracy attack.

✕ Skill		◆	Description
Combo Attack 1	4	2	Two hit attack, slow speed.
Combo Attack 2	8	3	Three hit attack, slow speed.
Combo Attack 3	16	4	Four hit attack, slow speed.
Combo Attack 4	26	5	Five hit attack, slow speed.

❄ Skill		◆	Description
Maze	0	-	Successful attack causes confusion.
Back Off!	10	-	Immediately attack the next opponent that walks near.
Defend	20	-	Give up turn to reduce the damage received until next turn.
Grunt	32	2	Increase accuracy. *Defend required.*

● Skill		◆	Description
Affinity Attack 1	4	40	Attack enhanced by the power of an affinity god.
Affinity Attack 2	10	60	Mighty attack enhanced by the power of an affinity god. *Affinity Attack 1 required.*
Affinity Attack 3	20	80	Mightiest attack enhanced by the power of an affinity god, has added effect. *Affinity Attack 2 required.*
Affinity Attack 4	36	100	Summon a servant of an affinity god to attack all opponents. *Affinity Attack 3 required.*

♟ Skill		◆	Description
Parry	0	-	Standard defensive maneuver.
Bullheaded Resolve	0	-	Immune to stun.
Super Critical	0	-	Increase damage of all critical hits.
Labyrinth Senses	12	-	Immune to surprise or confusion.
Indomitable Will	18	-	Immune to root, petrify, blindness and freeze.
Riposte	30	1	Immediate counter attack when an incoming opponent attack misses.

MONGREL

TYPE: LIGHT

Weapons
Mongrel Club, Medium Hammer, Medium Axe, All Mongrel

Shields
None

Armor
Mongrel Armor

Helmets
All Mongrel

Accessory
Scalp

Character Class Statistics

HP	●● ●●
Defense	●●●●● ●●●
Power	●●● ●
Accuracy	●●●●● ●●
Initiative	●●●●● ●●●
Movement	●●●●● ●●

Time 2:50

ongrels tend to be a little stronger than Bandits, but lack the versatile skills that make their fellow light Gladiators so good. Essential light gladiator skills like **Backstabber** come at a higher price for Mongrels, and a few key abilities, like **Incapacitate Heavy**, are missing entirely.

Mongrels get a few exclusive skills in return, but nothing too interesting. **Kick** attacks are slightly stronger than regular **Strike**s. **Knuckle Buster** is an acceptable replacement for the Bandit's Slicing Attack, but **Hobble Leg** isn't worth much. The most interesting Mongrel skill is **Festering Claws**. The ability to poison on a successful hit is powerful, a fact that is, unfortunately, reflected in the job point cost.

Mongrels aren't terrible. With an item like the Mummy's Scalp, they can even rise from the dead. They are however, almost strictly inferior to Bandits, who are available cheaply and early in both Heroes' quests.

Affinities

Fire	Water	Earth	Air	Dark	Light
🜂	🜄	🜃	🜁		

➡ Skill			Description
Strike	0	0	Standard move to attack.
Running Attack	0	2	Run across battlefield to attack (reduced damage).
Kick 1	10	1	Standard kicking attack.
Kick 2	24	3	Powerful kicking attack.
Kick 3	34	5	Most powerful kicking attack.

✎ Skill			Description
Hobble Enemy	4	2	Medium damage attack that may reduce opponent's movement rate.
Knuckle Buster	40	3	Heavy damage attack that may cause bleeding damage.

✖ Skill			Description
Combo Attack 1	6	2	Two hit attack, fast speed.
Combo Attack 2	12	3	Three hit attack, fast speed.
Combo Attack 3	22	4	Four hit attack, fast speed.
Combo Attack 4	34	5	Five hit attack, fast speed.

✦ Skill			Description
On Guard	6	0	Increase defense next turn.
High Guard	30	0	Increase defense next turn. *On Guard required.*

⬤ Skill			Description
Affinity Attack 1	4	40	Attack enhanced by the power of an affinity god.
Affinity Attack 2	10	60	Mighty attack enhanced by the power of an affinity god. *Affinity Attack 1 required.*
Affinity Attack 3	20	80	Mightiest attack enhanced by the power of an affinity god, has added effect. *Affinity Attack 2 required.*
Affinity Attack 4	36	100	Summon a servant of an affinity god to attack all opponents. *Affinity Attack 3 required.*

♟ Skill			Description
Dodge	0	-	Standard defensive maneuver.
Driven	8	-	Initiative bonus received when Ogre is near.
Riposte	12	-	Counter attack when critically injured.
Backstabber	18	-	Damage doubled when attacking from behind.
Evasion	20	-	More effective defensive maneuver.
Riposte	22	-	Immediate counter attack when an opponent's attack misses.
Heightened Evasion	30	-	Most effective defensive maneuver.
Off Balance	36	-	Lowers opponent's defense if opponent misses attack.
Festering Claws	38	-	Successful attack causes poison damage.

GENERAL STRATEGY   CHARACTER CLASSES   WORLD ATLAS   BONUS MATERIA

TYPE: ARCANE

MONGREL SHAMAN

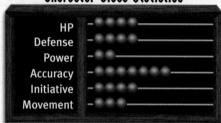

W hacking foes with a stick is the only way the Mongrel Shaman can gain Affinity Power, which puts him at a serious disadvantage compared to the other arcane classes. Sure, his combat stats are a little bit better than the Channeler and the Summoner, but the Mongrel Shaman is only as good as the Affinity Power of his weapon and accessories. If you can get those in the 20+ range, he can be reasonably effective, bopping foes one turn and dishing out decent Affinity techniques the next. But if you don't have the gear to get his Affinity Power above the 20 mark, he's just a bad version of the normal Mongrel.

At least the Mongrel Shaman's skills are cheap; **Freeze Enemy** and **Fungus Amongus** (which poisons all adjacent foes) are probably the best of his Affinity Attacks, and you can get both for just 16 job points. Throw in a few **Combo Attacks** (which, as affinity attacks, are medium range) and the Mongrel Shaman will be a decent mid-range spellcaster. But he'll never be as useful as the Channeler and Undead Summoner, who don't have to wade into combat and waste half their turns on ineffectual attacks to charge their abilities.

Character Class Statistics

HP	●●●●● ──
Defense	●●●● ───
Power	●● ─────
Accuracy	●●●●●●● ●
Initiative	●●● ────
Movement	●● ─────

Weapons
Plain Club, Plain Staff, All Mongrel, All Mongrel Shaman

Shields
None

Armor
Arcane Armor, Mongrel Armor

Helmets
All Mongrel Shaman, Diadem Helmet, Arcane Helmet

Accessory
Scalp

Affinities

Fire	Water	Earth	Air	Dark	Light
◐	◐	◐	◐		

➡ Skill		◆	Description
Strike	0	0	Standard move to attack.
Running Attack	6	1	Run across battlefield to attack (reduced damage).
Kick 1	10	1	Standard kicking attack.
Kick 2	24	3	Powerful kicking attack. *Kick 1 required.*
Kick 3	34	5	Most powerful kicking attack. *Kick 2 required.*

🗡 Skill		◆	Description
Knuckle Buster	40	3	Heavy damage attack that may cause bleeding damage.

❄ Skill		◆	Description
Distract	0	10	Reduce movement and initiative.
On Guard	22	0	Increase defense next turn.
High Guard	36	10	Increase defense next turn. *On Guard required.*

◐ Skill		◆	Description
Affinity Attack 1	4	40	Attack enhanced by the power of an affinity god.
Fungus Amongus	4	20	Area attack that causes lengthy poison damage.
Combo Attack 1	8	20	Two hit attack, slow speed.
Affinity Attack 2	10	60	Mighty attack enhanced by the power of an affinity god. *Affinity Attack 1 required.*
Freeze Enemy	14	20	Freeze opponent for a short time causing frost damage.
Combo Attack 2	16	40	Three hit attack, slow speed.
Affinity Attack 3	20	60	Mightiest attack enhanced by the power of an affinity god, has added effect. *Affinity Attack 2 required.*
Combo Attack 3	28	60	Four hit attack, slow speed.
Feverish Mind	32	30	Successful attack may cause weakness and confusion.
Affinity Attack 4	36	100	Summon a servant of an affinity god to attack all opponents. *Affinity Attack 3 required.*
Combo Attack 3	42	80	Five hit attack, slow speed.

🐾 Skill		◆	Description
Affinity Draw	0	-	Double Affinity power gained from any attack.
Dodge	0	-	Standard defensive maneuver.
Poison Resistance	6	-	Immune to poison.
Driven	10	-	Initiative bonus received when Ogre is near.
Evasion	20	-	More effective defensive maneuver.
Festering Claws	30	-	Kick attacks may cause poison damage.
Heightened Evasion	38	-	Most effective defensive maneuver. *Evasion required.*

MURMILLO

TYPE: MEDIUM

Weapons
Medium Sword, Medium Hammer, Medium Axe, All Murmillo

Shields
Medium Shield, Murmillo Shield

Armor
Medium Armor, Murmillo Armor

Helmets
All Murmillo

Accessory
Ring

Character Class Statistics

HP	●●●● ●
Defense	●●●●●●●●● ●
Power	●●●●●●
Accuracy	●●●●●●●
Initiative	●●●●
Movement	●●●●

Affinities

Fire	Water	Earth	Air	Dark	Light
●	●	●	●	●	●

With a shield-based fighting style that allows for good defense and a wide variety of attacks, Murmillos are certainly the most interesting of the Imperia fighters. They're missing a few fundamental medium type strengths like alternate movement skills. They make up for this shortcoming with their innate abilities and a bunch of reasonably priced attacks.

Throw Shield 3 is a great skill that makes Gungnirs and Peltasts obsolete by allowing Murmillos to toss their shields anywhere within line of sight (Throw Shield 1 only allows straight lines, while 2 adds diagonals). **Bull Rush** is a solid replacement for Running Attack and the like, since it can hit up to three squares away, in a straight line. **Shield Smash**, **Shield Ram**, and **Gut Basher** are all solid attacks for when you're locked in melee combat, and all three are affordable. The same can't be said for the Murmillo's assortment of defensive skills, which tend to be overpriced. The Murmillo's defensive skills cost so much because they're so effective, however. Pick up Shield Counter and Advanced Block as early as you can. If you enjoy using your Murmillo, save up for skills like Incoming, Off Balance, and Humiliate. All together these innate skills can allow a high level Murmillo to win a battle simply by blocking, counterattacking, and crippling an opponent's statistics.

➡ Skill		◆	Description
Strike	0	0	Standard move to attack.

↘ Skill		◆	Description
Throw Shield 1	0	3	Short range shield attack.
Gut Basher	10	1	Successful attack lowers opponent initiative.
Shield Smash	12	3	Shield attack that may knock back an opponent.
Throw Shield 2	18	4	Medium range shield attack.
Bull Rush	20	1	Shield-first charge to distant opponent.
Shield Ram	24	1	Shield attack that may knock opponent down.
Throw Shield 3	34	5	Long range shield attack.
Heavy Strike	40	5	Heavy damage, low accuracy attack.

✖ Skill		◆	Description
Combo Attack 1	6	2	Two hit attack, moderate speed.
Combo Attack 2	12	3	Three hit attack, moderate speed.
Combo Attack 3	22	4	Four hit attack, moderate speed.
Combo Attack 4	34	5	Five hit attack, moderate speed.

✳ Skill		◆	Description
On Guard	6	0	Increase defense next turn.
High Guard	32	2	Increase defense next turn. *On Guard required.*

◐ Skill		◆	Description
Affinity Attack 1	4	40	Attack enhanced by the power of an affinity god.
Affinity Attack 2	10	60	Mighty attack enhanced by the power of an affinity god. *Affinity Attack 1 required.*
Affinity Attack 3	20	80	Mightiest attack enhanced by the power of an affinity god, has added effect. *Affinity Attack 2 required.*
Affinity Attack 4	36	100	Summon a servant of an affinity god to attack all opponents. *Affinity Attack 3 required.*

👤 Skill		◆	Description
Parry	0	-	Standard defensive maneuver.
Shield Block	0	-	Standard defensive maneuver with shield.
Arrow Guard	6	-	May reduce damage from projectile range attacks.
Shield Mastery	8	-	Increase durability of shield.
Advanced Block	20	-	More effective defensive maneuver with shield.
Shield Counter	22	-	Damage opponent's shield if attack is blocked.
Incoming!	30	-	Increase evasion of ranged attacks for nearby allies.
Off Balance	36	-	Lowers opponent's defense if opponent misses attack.
Humiliate	38	-	A successfully defended attack lowers opponent's initiative.

GENERAL STRATEGY · CHARACTER CLASSES · WORLD ATLAS · BONUS MATERIAL

TYPE: HEAVY

OGRE

In many ways, Ogres are just slightly uglier Samnites. They have virtually identical stats, they use the same gear, and have a very similar selection of skills. But Ogres do have access to a few unique abilities, one of which ranks among the best skills in the game.

Broad Swing is a powerful attack that hits both its target and any poor chump who is directly left of him. **Uppercut** is a strong attack at a surprisingly cheap price. **Fearsome Funk** is similar to the Samnite's Befoul Area, but it's always funny to watch an Ogre fart, and the crowd seems to appreciate it.

Those are all solid techniques, but where are Blind Spot Attack, Forward Thrust and Bulldoze? Alas, the Ogre misses out on the best of the Samnite's utility attacks, but he does have a fantastic Innate Skill the Samnite would eagerly trade his favorite roll of fat for: **Counterattack**. The ability to counter any attack would be amazing on any character, but on a heavy character it's simply ludicrous. An Ogre who has learned this often ends up doing more damage during opponents' turns than his own! Does Counterattack make Ogres better than Samnites? Well... Considering its cost, probably not. But it's close.

Character Class Statistics

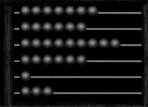

HP	●●●●●●●●●
Defense	●●●●●
Power	●●●●●●●●●
Accuracy	●●●●●●
Initiative	●●
Movement	●●●

Attack
Running Attack

Time 2:29

Weapons
Heavy Sword, Heavy Hammer, Two Handed Axe, All Ogre

Shields
Heavy Shield, Ogre Shield

Armor
None

Helmets
All Ogre, Gladiatorial Helmet

Accessory
Scalp

Affinities

Fire	Water	Earth	Air	Dark	Light
🔥	🌀	⬡	◎		

➡ Skill			Description
Strike	0	0	Standard move to attack.
Running Attack	6	2	Run across battlefield to attack (reduced damage and accuracy).

↘ Skill			Description
Charging Attack	0	4	Wind up and deliver distance attack.
Broad Swing	10	1	Sweeping attack that damages multiple opponents in front of character.
Uppercut	18	5	Heavy damage that may stun opponent; does not effect animals.
Destroy Shield	24	1	Successful attack may destroy opponent's shield.
Overhead Cleave	40	4	Heavy overhead attack; may break opponent's helmet.

✕ Skill			Description
Combo Attack 1	4	2	Two hit attack, slow speed.
Combo Attack 2	8	3	Three hit attack, slow speed.
Combo Attack 3	16	4	Four hit attack, slow speed.
Combo Attack 4	26	5	Five hit attack, slow speed.

✱ Skill			Description
Purge	0	2	Remove negative status effects.
Huddle	8	1	Give up turn to reduce the damage received until next turn.
Fearsome Funk	20	3	Adjacent units may become petrified.
Lecherous Grin	22	2	Lower opponent defense temporarily.
Stench	30	2	Opponents within range retreat.
Bulwark	32	2	Give up turn to reduce the damage received until next turn. *Huddle required.*

● Skill			Description
Affinity Attack 1	4	40	Attack enhanced by the power of an affinity god.
Affinity Attack 2	10	60	Mighty attack enhanced by the power of an affinity god. *Affinity Attack 1 required.*
Affinity Attack 3	20	80	Mightiest attack enhanced by the power of an affinity god, has added effect. *Affinity Attack 2 required.*
Affinity Attack 4	36	100	Summon a servant of an affinity god to attack all opponents. *Affinity Attack 3 required.*

⚔ Skill			Description
Parry	0	-	Standard defensive maneuver.
Deliberate Nature	12	-	Immune to stun and confusion.
Indomitable Will	18	-	Immune to root, petrify, blindness and freeze.
Awareness	34	-	No bonus given to enemies when attacked from behind.
Counterattack	38	-	Deliver counter attack.

PELTAST

TYPE: SUPPORT

Weapons
Plain Javelin, All Peltast, Light Spear

Shields
Light Shield, Peltast Shield

Armor
Light Armor, Peltast Armor

Helmets
All Peltast, Helm Helmet, Military Helmet

Accessory
Necklace

Character Class Statistics

HP	••• •••
Defense	••• ••• ••• ••
Power	••• ••
Accuracy	••• •••
Initiative	•••
Movement	•••

Affinities

Fire	Water	Earth	Air	Dark	Light

Peltasts are the Imperia version of Gungnirs, medium range spear throwers that are accurate, powerful, and have excellent defense, but require a clear line of sight that can be difficult to maintain. Peltasts are best against light and arcane characters, which are fairly rare in Imperia. Nevertheless, long range attackers are rare early in the game, and a Peltast always makes a reliable early recruit.

Peltasts lack the shape-shifting abilities of their Nordagh cousins, leaving them vulnerable on defense and hopeless on offense when engaged at close range. **Powered Throw** may be extremely expensive, but you should save up and get it as soon as possible, to give you a strong option for melee combat. Another must have is **Indirect Fire**, a Peltast exclusive that almost makes up for the lack of the Gungnir's Bear Form. This skill allows you to hit a foe anywhere within Long Throw 3 range, regardless of obstacles in the way. It doesn't do much damage, but the ability to hit anyone, anywhere, can be priceless when a brink-of-death foe has a turn approaching and no one else can get there in time.

➡ Skill			Description
Strike	0	0	Standard move to attack.
Running Attack	8	1	Run across battlefield to attack (reduced damage).

↘ Skill			Description
Long Throw	0	0	Standard distance throwing attack.
Exploding Javelin	4	3	Exploding ranged attack, causes area damage.
Destroy Shield	6	0	Successful attack may destroy opponent's shield.
Bungle Enemy	10	2	Effect: Reduce opponent's accuracy.
Long Throw 2	12	1	Medium distance throwing attack.
Impale Leg	18	2	Effect: Reduce opponent's movement rate.
Long Throw 3	20	2	Long distance throwing attack.
Unstoppable Throw	24	4	Powerful javelin throw that damages multiple opponents in a line.
Indirect Fire	30	3	Ranged attack that travels over obstructions.
Bulls Eye	32	3	Close attack that bypasses opponent's defenses.
Pin Down	34	3	Aimed javelin throw pins opponent in place.
Powered Throw	36	4	Heavy damage attack for nearby opponents.
Long Throw 4	40	3	Extremely long distance throwing attack.

✕ Skill			Description
Combo Attack 1	4	2	Two hit attack, slow speed.
Combo Attack 2	8	3	Three hit attack, slow speed.
Combo Attack 3	16	4	Four hit attack, slow speed.
Combo Attack 4	26	5	Five hit attack, slow speed.

✴ Skill			Description
On Guard	6	0	Increase defense next turn.
Cover Area	22	2	Automatically attack all opponents entering designated area.

◯ Skill			Description
Affinity Attack 1	4	40	Attack enhanced by the power of an affinity god.
Affinity Attack 2	10	60	Mighty attack enhanced by the power of an affinity god. *Affinity Attack 1 required.*
Affinity Attack 3	20	80	Mightiest attack enhanced by the power of an affinity god, has added effect. *Affinity Attack 2 required.*
Affinity Attack 4	36	100	Summon a servant of an affinity god to attack all opponents. *Affinity Attack 3 required.*

♟ Skill			Description
Dodge	0	-	Standard defensive maneuver.
Awareness	38	-	No bonus given to enemies when attacked from behind.

GENERAL STRATEGY · CHARACTER CLASSES · WORLD ATLAS · BONUS MATERIAL

TYPE: BEAST

PLAINSCAT

Plainscats have a skill selection that's similar to Bears, but trade the Bears' strong Defense and bottomless Hit Points for vastly increased Initiative and Mobility. Plainscats aren't as hard to kill as their ursine schoolmates, but they're a far better choice for large arenas where they excel at quickly reaching vulnerable foes and ripping them to shreds with powerful attacks.

If your Plainscat doesn't come with **Running Attack** and **Riposte** pre-installed, you'll want to pick them up early. After that, pick up a powerful and low cost attack like **Swipe** and Slash. **Growl** is a nice tool to have in your belt, in case things go wrong and you end up surrounded.

Because Plainscats have an innate Air Affinity, don't send your cat up against a Dervish. Their attacks will always miss, regardless of how you perform on the Swing Meter.

Character Class Statistics

- HP
- Defense
- Power
- Accuracy
- Initiative
- Movement

Weapons
None

Shields
None

Armor
None

Helmets
None

Accessory
Collar

Affinities

Fire　Water　Earth　Air　Dark　Light

Skill			Description
Claw	0	1	Standard move to attack.
Running Attack	6	2	Run across battlefield to attack (reduced damage).
Precision Attack	10	1	Quick, low power attack.

Skill			Description
Bite	4	3	High power attack with low accuracy.
Swipe	18	2	Medium damage, may reduce opponent's movement rate.
Pull Down	24	4	Prolonged stomping attack.
Slash	18	3	More powerful attack. *Swipe required.*
Raking Attack	36	4	Heavy damage claw attack that causes bleeding damage.
Slicing Attack	40	5	Heavy damage attack that may cause bleeding damage.

Skill			Description
Combo Attack 1	4	2	Two hit attack, slow speed.
Combo Attack 2	8	3	Three hit attack, slow speed.
Combo Attack 3	16	4	Four hit attack, slow speed.
Combo Attack 4	26	5	Five hit attack, slow speed.

Skill			Description
Growl	8	2	Successful attack petrifies nearby opponents.
On Guard	12	0	Increase defense next turn.
High Guard	30	2	Increase defense next turn. *On Guard required.*
Roar	32	4	Successful attack petrifies nearby opponents for a long duration..

Skill			Description
Affinity Attack 1	4	40	Attack enhanced by the power of an affinity god.
Affinity Attack 2	10	60	Mighty attack enhanced by the power of an affinity god. *Affinity Attack 1 required.*
Affinity Attack 3	20	80	Mightiest attack enhanced by the power of an affinity god, has added effect. *Affinity Attack 2 required.*
Affinity Attack 4	36	100	Summon a servant of an affinity god to attack all opponents. *Affinity Attack 3 required.*

Skill			Description
Dodge	0	-	Standard defensive maneuver.
Leap	0	-	You can move to higher positions.
Evasion	20	-	More effective defensive maneuver.
Riposte	22	-	Immediate counter attack when an opponent's attack misses.
Reflexes	38	-	Immune to counter attacks.

SAMNITE

TYPE: HEAVY

Weapons
Two Handed Axe, Heavy Spear, Heavy Sword, All Samnite

Shields
Heavy Shield, Samnite Shield

Armor
Heavy Armor, Samnite Armor

Helmets
All Samnite, Gladiatorial Helmet

Accessory
Ring

Character Class Statistics

HP	●●●●●●●●
Defense	●●●●●●
Power	●●●●●●●●●—
Accuracy	●●●●●●
Initiative	●—
Movement	●●—

Attack
Power Bulldoze

Affinities

❂	❂	❂	❂		
Fire	Water	Earth	Air	Dark	Light

Samnites are one of the most offense-oriented characters in the game. They hit hard, they have a strong attack option for any conceivable situation, and if equipped carefully, can be surprisingly accurate for a heavy gladiator. The only problem is that they're as slow as they look, and by the time these heavy hitters shamble over to the battle, it's sometimes too late.

For that reason, you need to take **Running Attack**, even though Samnites have to pay almost triple its normal price to get it. After that, forget the overpriced defensive skills and try to pick up a versatile set of attacks. **Sweeping Attack** lets you hit the opponent directly in front of you as well as anyone directly to his left or right. **Blind Spot Attack** lets you hit one foe in front, and one foe behind; a poetic payback for backstabbers. If you're surrounded on all sides, **Squat** and **Befoul Area** will damage everyone and send them back a square, giving you a little breathing room. Samnites also specialize in movement attacks, which are useful when you need to get out of a tight spot or set up your foes for an area attack from an ally. **Overrun** lets you rush past someone in front of you, and **Power Bulldoze** lets you take their square while knocking them back. Both attacks also deal damage, and never miss!

→ Skill	🗡	◆	Description
Strike	0	0	Standard move to attack.
Running Attack	22	2	Run across battlefield to attack (reduced damage).

↘ Skill	🗡	◆	Description
Overrun	4	2	Wind up and deliver distance attack.
Power Bulldoze	8	2	Push opponent backward, move into the previously occupied square, and cause damage.
Forward Thrust	10	2	Successful attack damages two squares in front.
Blind Spot Attack	18	2	Character attacks square in front and behind.
Sweeping Attack	20	2	Two handed attack that damages several squares in front of character.
Squat	32	4	Attack that knocks surrounding opponents back.
Befoul Area	34	4	Push back and damage all units in adjacent squares.
Heavy Strike	40	5	Heavy damage, low accuracy attack.

✕ Skill	🗡	◆	Description
Combo Attack 1	4	2	Two hit attack, slow speed.
Combo Attack 2	8	3	Three hit attack, slow speed.
Combo Attack 3	16	4	Four hit attack, slow speed.
Combo Attack 4	26	5	Five hit attack, slow speed.

✴ Skill	🗡	◆	Description
Bulldoze	0	1	Push an opponent backward and move into the previously occupied square.
Bulwark	6	0	Give up turn to reduce the damage received until next turn.
Befoul Area	24	3	Push back all units in adjacent squares.
On Guard	30	0	Increase defense next turn.

◐ Skill	🗡	◆	Description
Affinity Attack 1	4	40	Attack enhanced by the power of an affinity god.
Affinity Attack 2	10	60	Mighty attack enhanced by the power of an affinity god. *Affinity Attack 1 required.*
Affinity Attack 3	20	80	Mightiest attack enhanced by the power of an affinity god, has added effect. *Affinity Attack 2 required.*
Affinity Attack 4	36	100	Summon a servant of an affinity god to attack all opponents. *Affinity Attack 3 required.*

🧍 Skill	🗡	◆	Description
Parry	0	-	Standard defensive maneuver.
Shield Block	0	-	Standard defensive maneuver with shield.
Heightened Parry	12	-	More effective defensive maneuver.
Indomitable Will	18	-	Immune to root, petrify, blindness and freeze.
Off Balance	38	-	Lowers opponent's defense if opponent misses attack.

GENERAL STRATEGY · CHARACTER CLASSES · WORLD ATLAS · BO

TYPE: LIGHT

SATYR

Satyrs may be able to hold their liquor, but they sure can't take a hit. These lovable rascals have lots of neat tricks up their sleeves, but they're at the wrong end of the HP bell curve. While many of their skills can be used to good effect from a safe corner of the battlefield, all of their attacks require the Satyr to approach the front lines, where he won't last long.

Inexplicably, the audience loves lecherous, alcoholic man-goats, and Satyrs have made an art out of playing to the crowd. A turn one **Merry Jig** is a great way to start a battle with a troop-wide initiative boost, and a turn two **Crowd Pleaser** (or its enhanced form, **Crowd Charmer**) will win over easily entertained audiences to effectively give your entire troop significant boosts in several other stats. **Ridicule** and **Taunt** will further delight the crowd while lowering your foe's initiative, but since they are innate counters that requires your Satyr to actually survive an attack, you'll want to drop some job points into boosting **Evade** all the way to **Heightened Evasion**.

Jug Throw has a limited range, and **Jug Bonk** rarely hits, but they're as good as Satyr attacks get until late in the game, when you can afford solid area effects like **Exploding Breath** and **Kablooey**.

Character Class Statistics

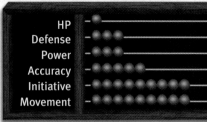

HP	
Defense	
Power	
Accuracy	
Initiative	
Movement	

Weapons
All Satyr

Shields
None

Armor
None

Helmets
None

Accessory
Poem

Affinities

Fire	Water	Earth	Air	Dark	Light

→ Skill	🍃	♦	Description
Strike	0	0	Standard move to attack.
Running Attack	0	2	Run across battlefield to attack (reduced damage).

↘ Skill	🍃	♦	Description
Merry Jig	0	1	Increase nearby allies' initiative.
Flammable Breath	4	1	Flaming spirits burn opponent.
Jug Bonk	10	1	Successful attack knocks opponent down.
Jug Throw	18	3	Standard range attack.
Exploding Breath	34	3	Flaming spirits burn multiple opponents.
Kablooey	40	5	Area attack of flaming spirits burns all opponents within range. *Exploding Breath required.*

✕ Skill	🍃	♦	Description
Combo Attack 1	6	2	Two hit attack, fast speed.
Combo Attack 2	12	3	Three hit attack, fast speed.
Combo Attack 3	22	4	Four hit attack, fast speed.
Combo Attack 4	34	5	Five hit attack, fast speed.

✳ Skill	🍃	♦	Description
Merry Jig	0	1	Increase nearby allies' initiative.
Crowd Pleaser	8	1	Crowd favors team with Satyr.
On Guard	12	0	Increase defense next turn.
Hair Of The Dog	22	0	May remove all negative status effects.
Invigorating Spirits	32	3	Recover Hit Points.
Crowd Charmer	36	5	Crowd heavily favors team with Satyr.
High Guard	38	2	Increase defense next turn. *On Guard required.*

◐ Skill	🍃	♦	Description
Affinity Attack 1	4	40	Attack enhanced by the power of an affinity god.
Affinity Attack 2	10	60	Mighty attack enhanced by the power of an affinity god. *Affinity Attack 1 required.*
Affinity Attack 3	20	80	Mightiest attack enhanced by the power of an affinity god, has added effect. *Affinity Attack 2 required.*
Affinity Attack 4	36	100	Summon a servant of an affinity god to attack all opponents. *Affinity Attack 3 required.*

🚶 Skill	🍃	♦	Description
Evade	0	-	Standard defensive maneuver.
Ridicule	8	-	Taunt opponent; crowd reacts positively.
Evasion	20	-	More effective defensive maneuver.
Taunt	24	-	Taunt opponent; crowd goes wild! *Ridicule required.*
Heightened Evasion	30	-	Most effective defensive maneuver. *Evasion required.*

SCARAB

TYPE: BEAST

Weapons
None

Shields
None

Armor
None

Helmets
None

Accessory
Jewel

Character Class Statistics

HP	●●●●●●●●●●——
Defense	●●●●————————
Power	●●●—————————
Accuracy	●●●—————————
Initiative	●●●—————————
Movement	●●——————————

Affinities

Fire	Water	Earth	Air	Dark	Light

→ Skill	◢	◆	Description
Bite	0	0	Standard move to attack.

↘ Skill	◢	◆	Description
Fiery Spittle	0	0	Fiery range attack.
Gas Cloud	10	0	Reduce initiative of opponents within range.
Carapace Ram	12	3	Successful attack may stun opponent.
Mandible Swipe	18	2	Successful attack damages three opponents.
Contamination	20	0	Gas cloud damages opponents and allies.
Tunnel	24	4	Tunnel to a distant point and attack, possibly knocking opponents back.
Poison Spittle	30	3	Ranged attack that may poison opponent.
Crippling Blow	34	5	Heavy damage attack that may stun opponent; does not effect animals.
Heavy Strike	40	4	Heavy damage, low accuracy attack.

✖ Skill	◢	◆	Description
Combo Attack 1	6	2	Two hit attack, slow speed.
Combo Attack 2	12	3	Three hit attack, slow speed.
Combo Attack 3	22	4	Four hit attack, slow speed.
Combo Attack 4	34	5	Five hit attack, slow speed.

✤ Skill	◢	◆	Description
Burrow	0	3	Tunnel under all units to a distant point.
Defend	8	0	Give up turn to reduce damage received until next turn.
Fortified Defense	36	2	Give up turn to reduce damage received until next turn.

◔ Skill	◢	◆	Description
Affinity Attack 1	4	40	Attack enhanced by the power of an affinity god.
Affinity Attack 2	10	60	Mighty attack enhanced by the power of an affinity god. *Affinity Attack 1 required.*
Affinity Attack 3	20	80	Mightiest attack enhanced by the power of an affinity god, has added effect. *Affinity Attack 2 required.*
Affinity Attack 4	36	100	Summon a servant of an affinity god to attack all opponents. *Affinity Attack 3 required.*

⚐ Skill	◢	◆	Description
Dodge	0	-	Standard defensive maneuver.
Gas Immunity	2	-	Immune to poison.
Weathered Chitin	6	-	Increase defense.
Fire Affinity Bonus	22	-	Resistant to Fire Affinity attacks; weak against Water Affinity attacks.
Toughened Chitin	32	-	Greatly increase defense.
Riposte	38	-	Immediate counter attack when an opponent's attack misses.

Scarabs are strange little creatures. Their stats are generally unimpressive (at least by beast standards), but don't be fooled by low Power and Movement scores; these creatures have a number of strong attacks and a series of Special skills that make them the most mobile class in the game.

The mobility skill is **Burrow**, which lets a Scarab dig down and pop up almost anywhere. This is a great way to slip behind a character and enable an ally to backstab or take out an enemy caster or archer who is hiding in the rear. The powered-up version of this skill, **Tunnel**, allows you to do damage to any adjacent character when you pop up, as well as knock them back a square. Very useful stuff.

Tunnel is the Scarab's best trick, but it's not the only one. **Mandible Swipe** is an effective version of the Samnite's Sweeping Attack, and **Fiery Spittle** is a good medium range attack, especially since it's won't cost you any skill or job points. After you pick up a good beater like **Crippling Blow**, you'll probably want to skip most of the other attacks and concentrate on **Toughened Chitin** and **Weathered Chitin**, since Scarabs have pretty lousy defense. **Riposte** never hurts, either.

TYPE: BEAST

SCORPION

L ike Scarabs, Scorpions are giant chitinous insects that suddenly begin to appear in droves in the Southern Expanse. They have horrible defense (**Weathered Chitin** helps a bit), and lack the mobility of the Scarab's Burrow and Tunnel (despite the descriptions, the **Skittering Attacks** aren't really any better than Running Attack), but do excel at powerful poison attacks.

Yep, **Poison Flick**, **Envenom**, and **Tail Whip** are great ways to turn your opponents green while doing solid damage in the process, but that won't stop them from crushing your Scorpion like the bug that he is while they're dying. That's why Fortified Defense and Riposte are top priorities for any Scorpion handler. **Fortified Defense** will negate virtually all of the damage while **Riposte** and lingering poison effects finish off your foes.

It's a fun little combo, but to put in bluntly, the Scarab is by far the better bug.

Character Class Statistics

HP	●●●●●●●●●
Defense	●
Power	●●●
Accuracy	●●●
Initiative	●●●
Movement	●●●

Weapons
None

Shields
None

Armor
None

Helmets
None

Accessory
Jewel

Affinities

Fire	Water	Earth	Air	Dark	Light

→ Skill	🗡	◆	Description
Bite	0	0	Standard move to attack.
Precision Attack	10	1	Quick, low power attack.
Skittering Attack	10	1	Run across battlefield to attack; reduced damage.
Skittering Attack 2	22	2	Run a greater distance across battlefield to attack.

🗡 Skill	🗡	◆	Description
Pincher Attacks	0	1	Light damage attack; cannot be blocked or evaded.
Envenom	10	3	Vicious tail attack that may poison opponent.
Poison Flick	18	2	Ranged attack that may poison opponent.
Shield Snip	24	3	Destroy shield by cutting it in half.
Hurricane	34	3	Tail attack that damages all opponents in adjacent squares.
Tail Whip	40	2	Quick attack that may poison opponent.

✗ Skill	🗡	◆	Description
Combo Attack 1	6	2	Two hit attack, slow speed.
Combo Attack 2	12	3	Three hit attack, slow speed.
Combo Attack 3	22	4	Four hit attack, slow speed.
Combo Attack 4	34	5	Five hit attack, slow speed.

✦ Skill	🗡	◆	Description
Defend	6	0	Give up turn to reduce damage received until next turn.
Fortified Defense	32	3	Give up turn to greatly reduce damage received until next turn. *Defend required.*

◐ Skill	🗡	◆	Description
Affinity Attack 1	4	40	Attack enhanced by the power of an affinity god.
Affinity Attack 2	10	60	Mighty attack enhanced by the power of an affinity god. *Affinity Attack 1 required.*
Affinity Attack 3	20	80	Mightiest attack enhanced by the power of an affinity god, has added effect. *Affinity Attack 2 required.*
Affinity Attack 4	36	100	Summon a servant of an affinity god to attack all opponents. *Affinity Attack 3 required.*

🐾 Skill	🗡	◆	Description
Beast Dodge	0	-	Standard defensive maneuver.
Fire Resistance	6	-	Resistant to Fire Affinity attacks; weak against Water Affinity attacks.
Weathered Chitin	12	-	Increase defense.
Poison Resistance	20	-	Immune to poison.
Riposte	30	-	Immediate counter attack when an opponent's attack misses.
Awareness	36	-	No bonus given to enemies when attacked from behind.
Evasion	38	-	More effective defensive maneuver.

GENERAL STRATEGY · CHARACTER CLASSES · WORLD ATLAS · BONUS MATERIAL

SECUTOR

TYPE: LIGHT

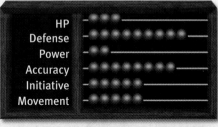

Weapons
Light Axe, Light Sword Light Spear,
All Secutor

Shields
Light Shield

Armor
Light Armor, Secutor Armor

Helmets
All Secutor, Gladiatorial Helmet

Accessory
Ring

Character Class Statistics

HP
Defense
Power
Accuracy
Initiative
Movement

Attack
Surprise Attack

Secutors are not quite as quick or accurate as Bandits, but do have a more combat-oriented skill selection, and a few neat tricks that are unavailable to their light type colleagues. The two classes fill the same role in your school, but you probably have room for both.

Like most light gladiators, the Secutor's first priority is the all-important **Backstabber** skill, which combos nicely with the Secutor's **Surprise Attack**. Follow that up with a few new attacks that will be useful in the heavily armored Imperia leagues: **Remove Shield**, a reliable way of destroying an opponent's shield and **Shield Bypass**, a solid, almost unblockable hit.

Instead of Riposte, Secutors counter successful attacks with **Taunt** and its enhanced form, **Deride**. These lower the attackers Initiative while boosting your Crowd Favor, and are well worth their job point cost.

Affinities

| Fire | Water | Earth | Air | Dark | Light |

Skill			Description
Strike	0	0	Standard move to attack.
Running Attack	0	1	Run across battlefield to attack (reduced damage and accuracy).
Surprise Attack	6	2	Target will not face when attacked.
Sprint Attack	36	2?	Run a greater distance across the battlefield to attack.

Skill			Description
Spear Attack	0	0	Attack from the diagonal using the spear's extended reach.
Trip	18	4	Successful attack knocks down opponent.
Remove Shield	24	0	Successful attack may remove opponent's shield.
Shield Bypass	32	1	Opponent cannot use shield to block attacks.
Target Head	34	1	Effect: Reduce opponent's initiative.
Slicing Attack	40	5	Heavy damage attack that may cause bleeding damage.

Skill			Description
Combo Attack 1	6	2	Two hit attack, fast speed.
Combo Attack 2	12	3	Three hit attack, fast speed.
Combo Attack 3	22	4	Four hit attack, fast speed.
Combo Attack 4	34	5	Five hit attack, fast speed.

Skill			Description
Sand Toss	2	1	Successful toss may blind opponent.
On Guard	12	0	Increase defense next turn.

Skill			Description
Affinity Attack 1	4	40	Attack enhanced by the power of an affinity god.
Affinity Attack 2	10	60	Mighty attack enhanced by the power of an affinity god. *Affinity Attack 1 required.*
Affinity Attack 3	20	80	Mightiest attack enhanced by the power of an affinity god, has added effect. *Affinity Attack 2 required.*
Affinity Attack 4	36	100	Summon a servant of an affinity god to attack all opponents. *Affinity Attack 3 required.*

Skill			Description
Dodge	0	-	Standard defensive maneuver.
Shield Block	0	-	Standard defensive maneuver with shield.
Taunt	8	-	Taunt opponent; crowd reacts positively.
Backstabber	10	-	Damage doubled when attacking from behind.
Evasion	20	-	More effective defensive maneuver.
Deride	22	-	Taunt opponent; crowd goes wild! *Taunt required.*
Heightened Evasion	30	-	Most effective defensive maneuver.
Off Balance	38	-	Lowers opponent's defense if opponent misses attack.

General Strategy Character Classes World Atlas Bonus Material

TYPE: ARCANE

SUMMONER

Summoners pull Affinity out of the sky, summon powerful allies for virtually nothing, and then sit back and pick away at their foes with medium range spells while Affinity Beasts do their dirty work. If you get the opportunity to recruit a Summoner, don't let it pass you by!

In battle, Summoners practically play themselves. First they use **Summon Power** to give themselves around 60 AP for free. After a quick recovery, they'll summon something, usually an Affinity Beast. All four beasts have basically the same stats, and differ only in appearance and the stat that they buff for your team. The **Air Beast** boosts Initiative, the **Earth Beast** boosts Defense, the **Fire Beast** boosts Power, and the **Water Beast** boosts Accuracy. The Dark version of each beast is the same (although often cooler looking), except that it lowers the appropriate stat for your opponents instead of boosting it for you. (They're also cheaper to summon, but require more job points to buy). Be warned though: when a Summoner is killed, his summond creature is removed from the arena.

Since you can only summon one beast at a time, your Summoner will spend the rest of his turns nailing foes with long distance Affinity Attacks. **Far Strike,** a medium range line of sight attack, is your best damage-for-Affinity value, dealing solid damage for only 20 AP per usage.

Character Class Statistics

HP	●●
Defense	●●●●
Power	●
Accuracy	●●●●●
Initiative	●●●●●
Movement	●●●●

Weapons
Plain Staff, All Summoner

Shields
None

Armor
Arcane Armor, Summoner Armor

Helmets
All Summoner, Diadem Helmet, Arcane Helmet

Accessory
Charm

Affinities

Fire	Water	Earth	Air	Dark	Light

➡ Skill			Description
Strike	0	0	Standard move to attack.

✷ Skill			Description
Summon Power	0	4	Summon Affinity power directly from the Affinity gods.
Air Beast	2	20	Summon a servant of the Air Affinity God.
Skeleton 1	2	10	Summon undead warrior.
Earth Beast	4	10	Summon a servant of the Earth Affinity God.
Fire Beast	6	20	Summon a servant of the Fire Affinity God.
Water Beast	8	10	Summon a servant of the Fire Affinity God.
Incapacitate Heavy	10	10	Successful attack may Petrify a heavy opponent for a short time.
Tornado	12	0	Teleport all within range to random location.
On Guard	18	0	Increase defense next turn.
Scarab	24	10	Summon a Scarab.
Skeleton 2	24	20	Summon a more powerful Skeleton. *Skeleton 1 required.*
Dark Air Beast	30	10	Summon a tainted servant of the Air Affinity God.
Dark Earth Beast	32	10	Summon a tainted servant of the Earth Affinity God.
Dark Fire Beast	34	10	Summon a tainted servant of the Fire Affinity God.
Dark Water Beast	36	10	Summon a tainted servant of the Water Affinity God.
Magic Guard	42	20	Greatly increase defense next turn. *On Guard required.*
Scorpion	44	10	Summon a Scorpion.

⬤ Skill			Description
Affinity Attack 1	4	40	Attack enhanced by the power of an affinity god.
Combo Attack 1	8	20	Two hit attack, slow speed.
Affinity Attack 2	10	60	Mighty attack enhanced by the power of an affinity god. *Affinity Attack 1 required.*
Combo Attack 2	16	40	Three hit attack, slow speed.
Affinity Attack 3	20	80	Mightiest attack enhanced by the power of an affinity god, has added effect. *Affinity Attack 2 required.*
Combo Attack 3	28	60	Four hit attack, slow speed.
Far Strike	28	20	More powerful attack.
Affinity Attack 4	36	100	Summon a servant of an affinity god to attack all opponents. *Affinity Attack 3 required.*
Combo Attack 4	42	80	Five hit attack, slow speed.

🜂 Skill			Description
Dodge	0	-	Standard defensive maneuver.

UNDEAD LEGIONNAIRE TYPE: MEDIUM

Weapons
Medium Axe, Medium Hammer, Medium Sword, All Legionnaire, All Undead

Shields
Medium Shield, Legionnaire Shield, Undead Shield

Armor
Medium Armor, Legionnaire Armor, Undead Armor

Helmets
All Legionnaire, All Undead, Military Helmet

Accessory
Medal

Affinities

Fire	Water	Earth	Air	Dark	Light

Character Class Statistics

HP	●●●●● —
Defense	●●●●● —
Power	●●●● —
Accuracy	●●●●●● —
Initiative	●● —
Movement	●●● —

Grave Rot Poisoned
POISON -2hp Move
Orders for Lakhaan

If you can earn the Talisman of Unlife from the second Mördare shopkeeper quest, you can summon an Undead Legionnaire at any gravestone in the game. While Undead Legionnaires have the same stats as living Legionnaires, they have a better skill selection, and one special trait that no other class has: They're expendable. When an Undead Legionnaire dies in a wilderness battle, you can just find a gravestone and get another. This makes them an ideal choice for the risky wilderness fights that can be a part of certain side quests.

Of course, if you trade in your Undead Legionnaires frequently, you won't be able to guide their development. This is a shame, because they have some great abilities. **Grave Rot** and **Knit Bones** are strong innate abilities, as well as the faithful **Riposte**. **Scare Attack** and **Fear of Death** have their place, although the Rot attacks are pretty dull, since they take so long to work.

The Undead Legionnaire's **Dark Affinity** attacks aren't really any different from other affinity attacks, but they're more reliable, because no enemies have Light Affinity armor equipped to block it. Unfortunately, since Dark Affinity weapons are incredibly difficult to find, it can be hard to exploit this feature.

➜ Skill	🪙	♦	Description
Strike	0	0	Standard move to attack.

➘ Skill	🪙	♦	Description
Scare Attack	4	2	Successful attack may cause opponent to retreat.
Fear of Death	10	3	Target may become panicked.
Rot Helmet	24	4	Attack that damages opponent's helmet.
Rotting Touch	24	3	Attack that damages opponent's shield.
Target Head	34	1	Effect: Reduce opponent's initiative.
Heavy Strike	40	5	Heavy damage, low accuracy attack.

✕ Skill	🪙	♦	Description
Combo Attack 1	6	2	Two hit attack, moderte speed.
Combo Attack 2	12	3	Three hit attack, moderte speed.
Combo Attack 3	22	4	Four hit attack, moderte speed.
Combo Attack 4	34	5	Five hit attack, moderte speed.

� Skill	🪙	♦	Description
Grave Laughter	8	1	Scare and lower opponents' initiatve.
Defend	22	0	Give up turn to reduce damage received until next turn.
Scared Stiff	32	4	Successful attack may petrify opponent.
Heightened Defense	36	0	Give up turn to greatly reduce damage received until next turn. *Defend required.*

● Skill	🪙	♦	Description
Affinity Attack 1	4	40	Attack enhanced by the power of the Dark Affinity God.
Affinity Attack 2	10	60	Mighty attack enhanced by the power of the Dark Affinity God. *Affinity Attack 1 required.*
Affinity Attack 3	20	80	Mightiest attack enhanced by the power of the Dark Affinity God, temporarily poisons opponent. *Affinity Attack 2 required.*

⚘ Skill	🪙	♦	Description
Dodge	0	-	Standard defensive maneuver.
Shield Block	0	-	Standard defensive maneuver with shield.
Afterlife	0	-	Resistance to worldly damage but weakness against affinity.
Fleshless Target	0	-	Resistant to projectile range attacks.
Sickly Marrow	12	-	When this Gladiator is defeated, an area effect cloud causes poison damage.
Grave Ròt	20	-	Critical hit causes poison damage.
Riposte	30	1	Immediate counter attack when an opponent's attack misses.
Knit Bones	38	-	Regenerate Hit Points.

TYPE: ARCANE UNDEAD SUMMONER

The worth of arcane classes is determined less by what they can do with their Affinity Power, and more by how they get it. In that respect, Undead Summoners are the best arcane gladiators in the game. That's generally bad news, since you'll be facing them as opponents frequently, but you can recruit one of your own if you clear the Dead of Night league in Mördare's Den.

The key to Undead Summoners is **Darkness From Life**, a skill that turns their own Hit Points into Affinity Power, and usually allows the Undead Summoner to take a second action immediately afterward. Don't worry about the Hit Points–you won't be in the front lines anyway. And you can always get them back with **Covet Life** or the **Knit Bones** innate skill.

The best use for this Affinity Power is the **Summon Skeleton** series of Special attacks. You can only have one skeleton at a time, so after that you'll have to rely on Affinity skills like **Covet Life**, **Splintering Bones**, **Fire Cloud** and **Fire Storm**. None of these are particularly strong, but all can be used from a safe distance of up to four squares away. It's also worth noting that the Undead Summoner is the rare caster of Dark Affinity attacks. You'll need a Dark Affinity weapon to use the Affinity attacks, of course, so keep an eye out for the **Death's Head** staff which is won in the Altahrun Tournament. It is the Undead Summoner's best weapon.

Character Class Statistics

HP
Defense
Power
Accuracy
Initiative
Movement

Weapons
Plain Staff, All Undead Summoner

Shields
None

Armor
Arcane Armor, Undead Summoner Armor

Helmets
All Undead Summoner, All Summoner, Diadem Helmet, Arcane Helmet

Accessory
Charm

Affinities
Fire Water Earth Air Dark Light

Skill			Description
Strike	0	0	Standard move to attack.
Steal Life	0	0	Steal the life force of teammates.

Skill			Description
Darkness From Life	0	4	Convert some of your life force into Affinity power.

Skill			Description
Summon Skeleton	0	10	Summon undead warrior.
Summon Skeleton 2	22	30	Summon a more powerful undead warrior.
Tornado	22	0	Teleport all within range to random location.
Teleport	30	30	Teleport a short distance on the battlefield.
Defend	32	0	Give up turn to reduce damage until next turn.
Reaper	40	100	Opponent is cursed to die in several turns, unless caster is killed first.
Summon Skeleton 3	42	70	Summon a very powerful undead warrior.

Skill			Description
Splintering Bones	0	30	Long range spell attack that can cause an enemy to retreat.
Affinity Attack 1	4	40	Attack enhanced by the power of an affinity god.
Combo Attack 1	8	20	Two hit attack, slow speed.
Affinity Attack 2	10	60	Mighty attack enhanced by the power of an affinity god. *Affinity Attack 1 required.*
Covet Life	10	80	Steal the life force of an opponent.
Fire Cloud	10	10	Attack that causes fire damage.
Combo Attack 2	16	40	Three hit attack, slow speed.
Affinity Attack 3	20	80	Mightiest attack enhanced by the power of an affinity god, has added effect. *Affinity Attack 2 required.*
Fire Storm	24	30	Powerful attack that causes intense fire damage.
Rotting Touch	24	30	Attack that damages opponent's shield.
Combo Attack 3	28	60	Four hit attack, slow speed.
Death Blast	38	30	More powerful attack.
Combo Attack 4	42	80	Five hit attack, slow speed.

Skill			Description
Dark Resistance	0	-	Resistant to Dark Affinity attack.
Parry	0	-	Standard defensive maneuver.
Fleshless Target	0	-	Resistant to projectile range attacks.
Sickly Marrow	12	-	When this gladiator is defeated, an area effect cloud causes poison damage.
Knit Bones	38	-	Regenerate Hit Points.

WOLF

TYPE: BEAST

Weapons
None

Shields
None

Armor
None

Helmets
None

Accessory
Collar

Character Class Statistics

HP	
Defense	
Power	
Accuracy	
Initiative	
Movement	

Wolves excel at mobility, scoring top marks in Initiative and Movement. They have average Power, and their low Defense is mostly mitigated by their abundance of Hit Points. Unfortunately, there isn't too much that a lone wolf can do with these strengths. The skill selection of Wolves is limited, and many require the presence of other Wolves to be effective.

A pack, on the other hand, can be brutal. Three or four wolves working together to isolate and surround opponents will find powerful advantages in the form of skills like **Pack Courage**, **Pack Mentality**, and **Area Lupus Call**. But few players will be willing to make room for more than one wolf in their school, and lone wolves have far fewer options: **Pull Down** and **Shred Throat** do big damage, and **Riposte** and **Tear Throat** are both solid and reasonably priced. Outside of that, there isn't much worth getting excited about. **Lupus Call** sounds promising, but it requires you to "crit" on the status meter, and the effect is often disappointing. Lone wolves are simply too underpowered to warrant a permanent slot in your school.

Affinities

Fire	Water	Earth	Air	Dark	Light

→ Skill			Description
Snap	0	0	Standard move to attack.
Nip	4	2	Weak running attack with high accuracy.

↘ Skill			Description
Target Leg	10	2	Medium damage, may reduce opponent's movement rate.
Tear Throat	18	4	Tearing attack that causes bleeding damage.
Bungle Enemy	24	2	Effect: Reduce opponent's accuracy.
Pull Down	34	4	Prolonged stomping attack.
Shred Throat	40	5	Tearing attack that causes extreme bleeding damage.

✗ Skill			Description
Combo Attack 1	4	2	Two hit attack, slow speed.
Combo Attack 2	8	3	Three hit attack, slow speed.
Combo Attack 3	16	4	Four hit attack, slow speed.
Combo Attack 4	26	5	Five hit attack, slow speed.

✴ Skill			Description
Lupus Call	6	3	Partially recover Hit Points of self.
On Guard	12	0	Increase defense next turn.
Fearful Snarl	20	2	Intimidate opponent and move them back one square.
Area Lupus Call	32	5	Partially recover Hit Points of allies within range.
Heightened Snarl	38	3	Intimidate opponents within range, causes them to retreat.

🌑 Skill			Description
Affinity Attack 1	4	40	Attack enhanced by the power of an affinity god.
Affinity Attack 2	10	60	Mighty attack enhanced by the power of an affinity god. *Affinity Attack 1 required.*
Affinity Attack 3	20	80	Mightiest attack enhanced by the power of an affinity god, has added effect. *Affinity Attack 2 required.*
Affinity Attack 4	36	100	Summon a servant of an affinity god to attack all opponents. *Affinity Attack 3 required.*

🧍 Skill			Description
Beast Dodge	0	-	Standard defensive maneuver.
Pack Courage	0	-	Increase movement and initiative when near other wolves.
Pack Mentality 1	8	-	Critical hit gives all wolves a free attack on targeted opponent.
Riposte	22	-	Immediate counter attack when an opponent's attack misses.
Evasion	30	-	More effective defensive maneuver.
Pack Mentality 2	36	-	Successful hit gives all wolves a free attack on targeted opponent.

General Strategy · Character Classes · World Atlas · Bonus Material

TYPE: HEAVY

YETI

I f you clear the Trial of the Elders league in Vargen, you'll be allowed to recruit Iaar the Yeti for free. Iaar's attitude says a lot about his class; Yeti aren't versatile, or fancy, or clever, they just like to whack things with sticks. In short: Yeti smash, and they're pretty good at it.

Unable to wear armor, Yeti are a little more mobile and a lot weaker on defense than their heavy brethren from Imperia. But when they can find a good weapon, they're number 1 at brute strength. Offense-oriented skills like **Cry of Anger,** (which is stackable and a devistating compliment to the Centurion's Motivate)**Heavy Claw,** and the Affinity-charging, stat-lowering **Numbing Blows** ensure that a successful Yeti attack usually results in a shattered rib cage for a medium weight defender. The catch is that Yeti tend to have a little trouble connecting with their targets, so you may want to select your weapons based more on Accuracy than Power. No Yeti skills boost Accuracy, but a successful **Ice Breath** will set you up for a free hit next round. Before you get that, though, shore up Iaar's defensive weaknesses by picking up **Thick Hide** as soon as possible.

Yeti are far from the best in their weight class, but in the land of medium-weights, Nordagh, Iaar is the only heavyweight Ursula players will be able to get in Chapter 1.

Character Class Statistics

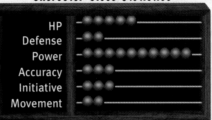

HP	●●●●●
Defense	●●
Power	●●●●●●●●●●—
Accuracy	●●●
Initiative	●●●
Movement	●●

Weapons
All Yeti, Two Handed Hammer

Shields
None

Armor
None

Helmets
None

Accessory
Teeth

Affinities

Fire	Water	Earth	Air	Dark	Light

➜ Skill			Description
Strike	0	0	Standard move to attack.
Running Attack	4	2	Run across battlefield to attack (reduced damage).
Fierce Backhand	34	4	Open handed attack that causes heavy damage.

❧ Skill			Description
Heavy Claw	10	2	Heavy damage attack
Numbing Blows	18	5	Series of hits causing cold damage, reduces movement and initiative.
Heavy Strike	40	5	Heavy damage, low accuracy attack

✖ Skill			Description
Combo Attack 1	4	2	Two hit attack, slow speed.
Combo Attack 2	8	3	Three hit attack, slow speed.
Combo Attack 3	16	4	Four hit attack, slow speed.
Combo Attack 4	26	5	Five hit attack, slow speed.

❄ Skill			Description
Cry of Anger	0	3	Increase attack damage for several turns.
Defend	8	0	Give up turn to reduce damage until next turn.
Back Off!	20	0	Immediately attack the next opponent that walks near.
Fearsome Yell	22	3	Adjacent opponents will retreat.
Ice Breath	24	3	Cold breath that can freeze opponents.
Hibernation	30	3	Give up turn to regain Hit Points.
Smack Back	36	3	Heavy attack that can knock an opponent back.

◐ Skill			Description
Affinity Attack 1	4	40	Attack enhanced by the power of an affinity god.
Affinity Attack 2	10	60	Mighty attack enhanced by the power of an affinity god. *Affinity Attack 1 required.*
Affinity Attack 3	20	80	Mightiest attack enhanced by the power of an affinity god, has added effect. *Affinity Attack 2 required.*
Affinity Attack 4	36	100	Summon a servant of an affinity god to attack all opponents. *Affinity Attack 3 required.*

⚔ Skill			Description
Parry	0	-	Standard defensive maneuver.
Deliberate Nature	6	-	Immune to stun.
Thick Hide	12	-	Reduce damage received.
Indomitable Will	19	-	Immune to root, petrify, blindness and freeze.

CHAPTER I

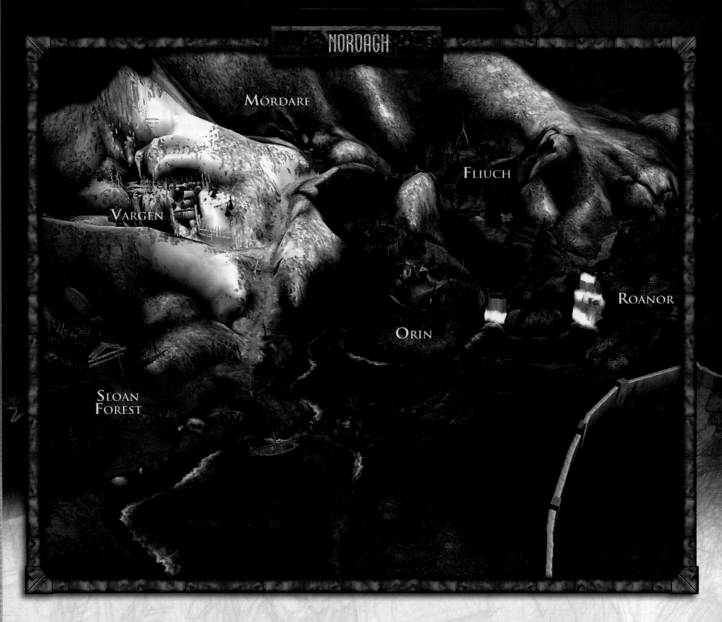

NORDAGH

HISTORY

Home of the mighty Barbarians, their land is harsh and rugged, filled with deep forests and snow covered mountains. The culture of the Barbarians has a deep history of magic, and for generations the Barbarian kings have taken serious counsel from the order of Galdr witches who live at the far northern reaches of the kingdom. It also is rumored that some warriors from the kingdom have been granted strange powers.

Nordagh fought for many years with Imperia, losing large amounts of lowlands to them. The harrowing events of the Great War finally stopped Imperia's northern advance. Imperia's army pulled back and a huge earthen wall some 40 miles long was erected at the border of the two kingdoms. A strained truce has existed between the two lands for the past few decades, and trade between them is just beginning.

Nordagh's involvement in the gladiator games has been increasing in recent years and the people of both lands have become more comfortable with their "peaceful" co-existence. But a simmering antagonism still exists for many northerners who wait for the day that Imperia will return to his violent past.

FLIUCH

THE FEN

THE FEN IS LITTLE MORE THAN A GLOOMY, SMELLY, DANK MUDPIT THAT COULD JUST AS READILY BE USED AS A PIG PEN (AND OFTEN IS DURING THE OFF SEASON), AS FOR FIGHTING. WEATHERED WOODEN PLANKS RING THE ARENA AND ALSO DEFINE ITS SHAPE, WHICH CHANGES FROM YEAR TO YEAR. THE PLANKS ARE THERE LESS TO PREVENT THE FIGHTERS FROM ESCAPING THAN TO KEEP THE CROWD FROM JOINING IN. THE MUD IN THE ARENA IS ALWAYS WET WITH BLOOD AND RAIN, AND IT'S NOT SURPRISING TO FIND ROCKS AND BONES STICKING UP FROM THE PACKED EARTH BELOW THE LAYER OF DREDGE.

LEAGUE STRATEGY

EARNING YOUR CERTIFICATION

You only need 6 Battle Points here, so you can skip all the Certification matches and go straight to the Final Exam if you already know what you're doing. However, you can earn easy money and experience from the five training bouts, so you may want to do them anyway.

To clear the Final Exam, you'll need to take and hold the high ground. Select the highest crates directly before you and you should be able to get to the top before your opponents. Quickly dispatch the poor chump who climbed to the spot between you, then use your height advantage to do as much damage to the Samnite as possible. You may lose Urlan to the Samnite, but not before doing enough damage to allow Ursula

to take her out next turn.

THE LEAGUE OF REDEMPTION

After earning your Certification, this is the first league that will be open to Ursula. The majority of the foes here are Bandits, and as light units, are at a natural disadvantage when facing medium-type Ursula and Urlan. For the first two fights, enlist a Gungnir as your third, since they're very effective against the lightly armored Bandits. The final battle is a repeat of your Arena Certification Final Exam, but should be easier due to the lack of Heavy units... Just don't let the Bandits get a clear shot at your back. Clearing this league should earn you enough Popularity to compete in the Contest of the Free Peoples and Lightning Circuit, and a healthy Mastery bonus. (continued on page 58)

Ursula: This is where Ursula's quest begins. After Kjell's speech, you'll automatcally be taken to the Leagues to compete for your Arena Certification. But before you enter, you can back out, head to Recruiting, and draft a new member for your school. By doing it now, the new recruit will be able to earn some second-hand EXP from the Arena Certification battles.

There are two strong recruits that are usually available from the beginning; Iain the Bandit and Jeanne the Gungnir. The Gungnir is a little more useful in the early fights, but you'll want to draft both before you continue on to Roanor.

CHARACTER RECRUITMENT

Name	Classification	PRM	SNG
Bestla	Wolf	1000	250
Cowan	Barbarian	750	150
Daithi	Barbarian	1000	250
Freyda	Barbarian	950	250
Grace	Bandit	750	150
Iain	Bandit	1500	100
Ishi	Wolf	750	150
Jeanne	Gungnir	1500	100
Lowry	Gungnir	750	150
Seumas	Bandit	750	150

NOTE: Cost is per recruitable character level.

PRM=Cost for permanent recruitment
SNG=Cost for single battle

SHOP: THE STOPOVER

FLIUCH HISTORY

Fliuch is and always has been Nordagh's most prosperous city, even if its citizens are a bit rough around the edges. Fliuch was established as a trade town, but as more people moved into the city, fewer outsiders breached its walls, carrying out their business just outside of the borders. Fliuch has become a marsh town, and is surrounded by bogs and lakes. Bridges and walkways were built through the dense moors in order to keep the trade routes open. The bridges allow the people of Fliuch to keep track of everyone who comes and goes. Because of this, Fliuch has never felt the pain of war like so many other cities in Nordagh.

CONTEST OF THE FREE PEOPLES

This league serves as an introduction to many of the special battles in Gladius, where the objective is earning points instead of killing your opponents. The Vandal Battle is all about destroying more barrels than your opponents. Since barrels have a decent amount of Hit Points, they take a few hits before they go down... Support characters like Gungnirs can take advantage of this by targeting distant barrels that your opponents have whittled down, stealing the point.

The Rival Nations battle here is easy, since if you hold the three lowest crates (after your Gungnir takes a higher post) you'll be blocking the only route to your statue. Your foes will have to try to punch through your defenders, who will be at a significant height advantage. The Points Battle will require all your standard type-matching and facing tricks, as well as a few new ones. Since the game doesn't care who you're doing damage to, you can score a ton of points by hurling an Exploding Javelins

ARENA CERTIFICATION

Req:	0%			None
Prize:	100-300D	Item: Nordagh Talisman		
Prize:	N/A	Item: N/A		

Battle Name	Points	Entry Fee	Teams(VS)	Prize (Ursula)	Prize (Valens)	Requirement / Restriction
Certification 1	(1)	0D	2 2	100-300D	N/A	None
Certification 2	(1)	0D	2 2	100-300D	N/A	None
Certification 3	(1)	0D	2 2	100-300D	N/A	None
Certification 4	(1)	0D	2 2	100-300D	N/A	None
Certification 5	(1)	0D	1 2	0D	N/A	None
Final Exam	(5)	0D	2 3	100-300D	N/A	None

LEAGUE OF REDEMPTION

Req:	0%			None
Prize:	200-400D	Item: Main Gauche		
Prize:	750-2250D	Item: Sickle, Francisca, Stone Axe, Leg Brace		

Battle Name	Points	Entry Fee	Teams(VS)	Prize (Ursula)	Prize (Valens)	Requirement / Restriction
Atonement 1	(1)	0D	3 3	100-300D	500-1500D	None
Atonement 2	(2)	0D	3 4	200-500D	500-1500D	None
Atonement 3	(3)	0D	2 3	100-300D	500-1500D	None

CONTEST OF THE FREE PEOPLES

Req:	15%			None
Prize:	200-700D	Item: Free Peoples Badge, Banded Shield, Fur Hat, Jackal Pelt, Small Sword		
Prize:	1000-3000D	Item: Free Peoples Badge, Horn Hammer, Night's Guardian, Ring of Fangs, Heavy Leather		

Battle Name	Points	Entry Fee	Teams(VS)	Prize (Ursula)	Prize (Valens)	Requirement / Restriction
Vandal Battle	(2)	25D	3 3	100-300D	500-1500D	None
Rival Nations	(2)	25D	4 4	100-300D	500-1500D	None
Freedom Fight 1	(3)	25D	3 3	100-300D	500-1500D	None
King of the Hill	(3)	25D	3 3	100-300D	500-1500D	None
Freedom Fight 2	(2)	25D	4 4	100-300D	500-1500D	None
Points Battle	(4)	25D	4 4	100-300D	500-1500D	None

LIGHTNING CIRCUIT

Req:	15%			None
Prize:	200-700D	Item: Iron Buckler, Hand Axe, Patched Cape, Spiculum		
Prize:	1000-3000D	Item: Wooden Shield, Fur Hat, Mountain Lion Hide, Berkana		

Battle Name	Points	Entry Fee	Teams(VS)	Prize (Ursula)	Prize (Valens)	Requirement / Restriction
Thunderhead 1	(2)	25D	3 3	500-2500D*	500-1500D	Light and Support Only.
Thunderhead 2	(2)	25D	2 2 2 2	500-2500D*	500-1500D	Light and Support Only.
Lord of the Clouds	(2)	25D	2 2 2	100-300D	500-1500D	Light and Support Only.
Thunderhead 3	(2)	25D	3 3	100-300D	500-1500D	Light and Support Only.
Thunderhead 4	(2)	25D	3 3	100-300D	500-1500D	Light and Support Only.
Fast Money	(2)	25D	3 3	100-300D	500-1500D	Light and Support Only.

*Additional prizes: Quaddara, Death's Head Cup, Hooded Cloak, Cudgel

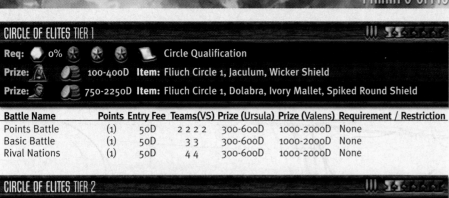

CIRCLE OF ELITES TIER 1

Req: 0% | Circle Qualification
Prize: 100-400D **Item:** Fliuch Circle 1, Jaculum, Wicker Shield
Prize: 750-2250D **Item:** Fliuch Circle 1, Dolabra, Ivory Mallet, Spiked Round Shield

Battle Name	Points	Entry Fee	Teams(VS)	Prize (Ursula)	Prize (Valens)	Requirement / Restriction
Points Battle	(1)	50D	2 2 2 2	300-600D	1000-2000D	None
Basic Battle	(1)	50D	3 3	300-600D	1000-2000D	None
Rival Nations	(1)	50D	4 4	300-600D	1000-2000D	None

CIRCLE OF ELITES TIER 2

Req: 0% | Mördare Circle 1, Fliuch Circle 1, Sloan Forest Circle 1, Vargen Circle 1
Prize: 500-100D **Item:** Fliuch Circle 2
Prize: 1000-2000D **Item:** Fliuch Circle 2

Battle Name	Points	Entry Fee	Teams(VS)	Prize (Ursula)	Prize (Valens)	Requirement / Restriction
Points Battle	(1)	200D	2 2 2 3	100-300D	500-1500D	None
Basic Battle	(1)	200D	4 4	1000-2000D	1200-2400D	None
King of the Hill	(1)	200D	4 4	300-900D	1200-2400D	None

IV — THE OTHER LEAGUES

into a crowd of foes and allies alike. Ursula players probably won't have enough light and support types to clear the **Lightning Circuit** league on their first visit to Fliuch, but if you have both a Bandit and a Gungnir you can enter the Thunderhead 2 fight and earn an unusually fat purse. It's an easy fight, too—with four teams on the field, you can hang back and let the other three teams kill each other. When you have the right units, make sure to do some looting in the Fast Money battle as well.

You won't be able to enter the **Circle of Elites Tier 1** league until you've earned the Circle Qualification badge at Roanor, and you won't be able to enter the **Circle of Elites Tier 2** league until you've cleared all the Tier 1's. Note that these leagues are optional; when you have a third light or support character you can come back to clear the Lightning Circuit and unlock the tournament without setting foot into the Circle of Elites.

TOURNAMENT: FREEDOM TOURNEY

Entry Fee: 200D
Teams(VS): 4 vs. 4
Requirement: 6 cups

Ursula
Prize: 500-1500D
Items: Maul, Cured Leather Shield, Suwilo

Valens
Prize: 1000-4000D
Items: Fuscina, Heavy Bronze Shield, Ring of Fangs, Lauguz

A lot of the strategy in this tournament is in selecting your characters' starting placements. The arena has been filled with a ring of crates, and you're allowed to put two characters inside the ring and two characters outside. Check out where your opponent has made its placements, and react accordingly. If they have Gungnirs outside the wall, put your in-ring fighters near them so they can jump over and get them, then put your own support characters outside the wall so they can pick off the opponents in the ring. If you don't have ranged attackers to worry about, have your two characters in the ring surround a vulnerable foe so you can take him out early.

GENERAL STRATEGY CHARACTER CLASSES WORLD ATLAS BONUS MATERIAL

ROANOR

Valens: This is where Valens' quest begin in Nordagh. Before you can explore Nordagh further, you'll need to earn the Nordagh Talisman in a simple 2-on-2 challenge that is exclusive to his quest. After that, you can enter Mixed Pairs and the Circle of Elites Qualifier, or simply be on your way.

When you do leave, you'll come upon Ursula and Urlan, beset by four Galdrs just outside of town. Help them win, and they'll lead you to Orin's Keep, where Ursula will join your school. After that, you'll be free to visit the cities of Nordagh in any order you chose.

CHARACTER RECRUITMENT

Name	Classification	PRM	SNG
Atorgh	Barbarian	850	800
Bain	Bandit	1000	200
Camrinn	Bandit	1100	250
Cassidea	Gungnir	1000	200
Doireann	Bandit	750	100
Grim	Barbarian	950	200
Kayne	Gungnir	750	100
Lamont	Gungnir	650	275
Shivawn	Barbarian	1100	250
Zod	Bear	1000	250

NOTE: Cost is per recruitable character level.

PRM=Cost for permanent recruitment
SNG=Cost for single battle

SHOP: "UNNA'S"

Ursula: The Mixed Pairs and Circle of Elites Qualifer are your only options here. All the other leagues will require the Kingdom Open Badge, which you must earn in King Orin. Before you head there, pop into the Recruiting Office, where you may find a Bear named Zod that would make a fine recruit. (You'll have other opportunities to recruit bears in Sloan Forest.)

General: From time to time, you'll run into a man with a cart just outside of Roanor, near the bridge to King Orin. This is the only place in Nordagh where you can buy a wide variety of accessories.

THE PIT

THE PIT IS THE SMALLEST SRENA IN NORDAGH, PERHAPS THE SMALLEST IN THE WORLD. EVENTS TEND TO BE SHORT AND VICIOUS.

STEALING ACCESSORIES

There's a little trick Ursula will be able to start doing in the recruitment office here. Keep an eye out for low-level Barbarians like Grim and Shivawn that have an affinity power of 10 or higher in both offense and defense. That's a giveaway that the character has a rare affinity-boosting accessory, which perhaps Urlan or Ursula might enjoy. If you'd like to steal it, "permanently" recruit them, unequip all their items, and expel them from your school (or keep them around, if you prefer). You can usually recoup their recruitment cost by selling the items they have equipped, and keep the runestone accessory for your own use. If you want to get really brazen, you can make a habit out of saving your game and searching the inventories of all the characters in all the recruitment offices.

ROANOR HISTORY

Roanor is on one side of the Nordagh-Imperia wall, while Belfort is on the other. After the war people who wanted to be in Imperia began waiting at the Nordagh side of the wall, but eentually they just settled there and founded a city. Some residents now make money by smuggling items from Imperia, while others serve in the army to protect Nordagh from Imperia.

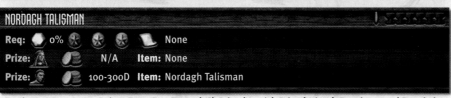

NORDAGH TALISMAN

Req:	0%					None
Prize:		N/A	**Item:** None			
Prize:		100-300D	**Item:** Nordagh Talisman			

Battle Name	Points	Entry Fee	Teams(VS)	Prize (Ursula)	Prize (Valens)	Requirement / Restriction
Talisman Challenge	(1)	0D	2 2	-		None

CIRCLE OF ELITES QUALIFIER

Req:	0%					None
Prize:		100-200D	**Item:** Circle Qualification			
Prize:		500-1000D	**Item:** Circle Qualification			

Battle Name	Points	Entry Fee	Teams(VS)	Prize (Ursula)	Prize (Valens)	Requirement / Restriction
Points Battle	(1)	100D	2 2	300-600D	1000-2000D	None
King of the Hill	(1)	100D	2 2	300-600D	1000-2000D	None
Basic Battle	(1)	100D	2 2	300-600D	1000-2000D	None

MIXED PAIRS

Req:	0%					None
Prize:		0D	**Item:** None			
Prize:		0D	**Item:** None			

Battle Name	Points	Entry Fee	Teams(VS)	Prize (Ursula)	Prize (Valens)	Requirement / Restriction
Play Together	(1)	50D	2 2	100-300D	500-1500D	Human: 1 Male, 1 Female
Stay Together	(1)	50D	2 2	100-300D	500-1500D	Human: 1 Male, 1 Female
Live Together	(2)	50D	2 2	100-300D	500-1500D	Human: 1 Male, 1 Female
Die Together	(2)	50D	2 2	100-300D	500-1500D	Human: 1 Male, 1 Female

LAST ONE STANDING

Req:	0%					Kingdom Open Badge
Prize:		300-900D	**Item:** Praecido, Banded Shield, Jackal Pelt			
Prize:		1000-3000D	**Item:** Flamberge, Iron Targe, Heavy Fur Skirt			

Battle Name	Points	Entry Fee	Teams(VS)	Prize (Ursula)	Prize (Valens)	Requirement / Restriction
King of the Hill	(1)	100D	1 1 1 1	100-300D	500-1500D	None
Survival	(2)	100D	1 1 1 1	200-600D	500-1500D	None
Points Battle	(3)	200D	1 1 1 1	500-1500D	1000-3000D	None

ONE AGAINST MANY

Req:	0%					Kingdom Open Badge
Prize:		200-500D	**Item:** None			
Prize:		500-1500D	**Item:** None			

Battle Name	Points	Entry Fee	Teams(VS)	Prize (Ursula)	Prize (Valens)	Requirement / Restriction
Endurance Series		500D	-	-	-	None
Battle 1	(1)	-	1 1	100-300D	500-1500D	None
Battle 2	(1)	-	1 1	200-600D	500-1500D	None
Battle 3	(1)	-	1 1	500-1500D	1000-3000D	None

LEAGUE STRATEGY

THE MIXED PAIRS LEAGUE

Ursula and Urlan work well as a "couple" (creepy as that may be), but at times you'll want to mix things up with characters from your bench instead. Most of the foes here are medium and light types, like Barbarians, Berserkers, and Bandits, but occasional Samnites can be a dangerous surprise. If you see a heavy type character, bring in the light types, or back out and make the computer randomly choose a new foe. In the first few fights, you'll have the opportunity to chose a starting position that lets you immediately surround and take out one of your opponents, so don't miss the opportunity to tilt the odds in your favor.

THE CIRCLE OF ELITES

The Circle of Elites is an entirely optional side quest that will probably require about ten hours to complete. It all starts here in Roanor; victory in the Circle of Elites qualifier will open up Circle of Elites Tier 1 tournaments in Fliuch, Mördare, Vargen, and Sloan Forest. Clear all those, and you can enter the Tier 2 tournaments in the same towns. Once you've added the Tier 2 badges to your collection, you'll be eligible for the Tournament Championships in Orin. The qualifier here will give you a good idea of what to expect from the rest of the Circle of Elites leagues. In general, you'll be competing in a variety of games like King of the Hill and Vandal Battles, instead of standard battles. Your foes will usually be a level or two above you, but clever strategists should be able to claim victory by outsmarting their opponents.

In the qualifier, the Points Battle should be easy if you're good at type matching and scoring crits, and the Basic Battle is on terrain that lends itself well to Gungnir sniping. For King of the Hill, you have the option of placing a unit one square in front of the hill (in the dead center of the map), so pick your heartiest unit to take and hold the hill, and a Bandit to backstab your opponents when they try to stop him.

THE KINGDOM OPEN LEAGUES

After earning the Kingdom Open badge in Orin, you'll be able to enter the Last One Standing, The Duel, and One Against Many leagues. All three have one thing in common; they're for one character only. **The Duel** is the easiest of the fights, since type matching and terrain advantages should lead to fairly easy victories.

In **Last One Standing**, you can usually play defensively and let your opponents kill each other in the Survival battle. This King of the Hill is difficult, though; since the other three will always attack the "king", no one stays on the hill for long. Let your opponents take the hill and die, gaining a few points each, and then take your turn near the end when the opposition is weakened and the point values double.

Finally, there's **One Against Many**. Pick a strong character with good combos and good Affinity Attacks to enter, and equip him or her with the best gear money can buy. In the first two waves, alternate between combos and affinity attacks to dish out the maximum damage possible. The Greater Bear in Round 3 is virtually impossible to beat, but you only need two battle points to earn the cup anyway.

THE DUEL

Req:	5%		Kingdom Open Badge	
Prize:	500-1500D	**Item:** Flamberge, Fur Hat		
Prize:	500-1500D	**Item:** Flamberge, Fur Hat		

Battle Name	Points	Entry Fee	Teams(VS)	Prize (Ursula)	Prize (Valens)	Prohibited
Duel 1	(1)	50D	1 1	100-300D	500-1500D	Arcane & Support
Duel 2	(1)	100D	1 1	200-600D	1000-3000D	Arcane & Support
Duel 3	(2)	100D	1 1	200-600D	1000-3000D	Arcane & Support
Duel 4	(3)	200D	1 1	500-1599D	1000-3000D	Arcane & Support

LORDS OF THE PIT

Req:	100%		None	
Prize:	2000-6000D	**Item:** None		
Prize:	2000-6000D	**Item:** None		

Battle Name	Points	Entry Fee	Teams(VS)	Prize	Requirement / Restriction
Basic Battle	(1)	1000D	2 2	2000-6000D	None
Basic Battle	(1)	1000D	2 2	2000-6000D	None
Basic Battle	(1)	1000D	2 2	2000-6000D	None

TOURNAMENT: ROANOR TOURNAMENT

Entry Fee: 500D
Teams(VS): 2 vs. 2
Requirement: 4 Cups

Ursula
Prize: 500-1500D
Items: Uruz, Shielded Ridge Helm

Valens
Prize: 2000-5000D
Items: Bazo, Digladio, Wing Hat, Braced Armor

This is a simple 2-on-2 fight, but the pit has been filled with a strange mesh of crates. You start on the highest level of crates, and if you position your team at the bottom and second-to-the-top of the available starting places, you'll have blocked off the route to your row of crates. In order to hit you with melee attacks, your foes will have to stand beneath you, yielding the height advantage to you. If you're facing Gungnirs or Berserkers, choose your best support character as one of your entrants, in case your foes hold back and try to use ranged attacks.

ORIN

ORIN'S KEEP

THE KEEP IS ONE OF THE MOST POPULAR ARENAS IN NORDAGH, WITH ITS STONE AMPHITHEATRE-SEATING AND A CAVE FOR HOLDING DANGEROUS BEASTS. PLUS, THE LOCALS LOVE TO SEE THE KING AND HIS FAMILY ENJOY THE GAMES. WHILE ORIN'S KEEP IS THE MOST MODERN ARENA IN NORDAGH, ITS PROXIMITY TO THE SEAT OF GOVERNMENT PREVENTS IT FROM SEEING TOO MUCH USE.

There's no place like home! Head due west across the bridges to get from Roanor to Orin, where you can enter the Kingdom Open league and earn the badge that will unlock the rest of the Roanor Leagues. This is also the home of the Circle Championships and the Nordagh Regional Championships, but those won't come into play for a while. For now, focus on earning the Kingdom Open Badge.

Orin's Recruitment Office will probably be the first place you see recruitable Berserkers. If you're a desperate for another light unit, you might want to give them a shot, but they're not one of the stronger light gladiators in Nordagh.

CHARACTER RECRUITMENT

Name	Classification	PRM	SNG
Briana	Gungnir	1000	100
Cano	Gungnir	750	200
Daryn	Gungnir	1050	225
Fearghall	Barbarian	1000	600
Hald	Berserker	1000	100
Kael	Berserker	900	100
Merna	Barbarian	1000	110
Sheyna	Barbarian	600	300
Tadgh	Berserker	750	75
Uallas	Barbarian	950	150

NOTE: Cost is per recruitable character level.

PRM=Cost for permanent recruitment
SNG=Cost for single battle

SHOP: ORIN'S ARMORY

LEAGUE STRATEGY

KINGDOM OPEN LEAGUE

There are a few interesting battles in this league. Tax Relief in particular should not be missed; what's not to love about looting treasure chests while the two other teams kill each other? You'll find a few grand worth of weapons here, including many that are hard to find in the local shops.
This league will probably also be your first experience with a Dominance battle. Divide your guys into two teams of two, one who holds the hot spot (ideally a Gungnir) and another who defends them. Use quick troops and spread them out, and you should be able to take two of the three hot spots without much trouble.

Hilltop Kingdom and Dominance are easy wins, since you can position your characters to give your team a major advantage. In Hilltop Kingdom, from the lower left corner of the placeable area, go two squares to the right and three squares up to find the top of the hill. Drop a character there and you'll be "king" from the get-go. You can't start directly on the hot spots in Dominance, but you can start near them; they're in the top-middle and the two lower corners.

LEAGUE OF NORTHERN PRIDE

Tired of Berserkers, Barbarians, and Gungnirs yet? Well, that's all you'll find here. Ursula and Urlan will do well here, but to complete this league you'll need another pair of Nordagh natives. These include Barbarians, Gungnirs, Satyrs, and Mongrel Shamans. You can either rely on the favorable type match-ups to best your (continued on page 64)

ORIN HISTORY

Built years ago by the past Barbarian Kings of Nordagh, Orin's Keep was originally a training ground for the King's most elite warriors. But as the gladiator games grew in popularity this camp also began to house the King's own gladiator school. Now that it is a time of peace, the Keep is primarily focused on training gladiators.

There isn't much of a town here; everything around these parts is just to support the king and the royal family. The royal family and the king's court stay within the castle walls, while the servants, the guards, the cooks, the blacksmiths, and all the rest of those not lucky enough to be on the inner circle stay in a village in the nearby woods.

General Strategy ♦ Character Classes ♦ World Atlas ♦ Bonus Material

Knock Back

foes in the simple Contests of Honor, or try to outmaneuver your foes at Rival Nations and the "Sack of Belfort" Vandal Battle. Either way, the first battle is a freebie; just hold back and let the two teams kill each other.

KINGDOM OPEN

Req: 0% None

Prize: 500D-1500D **Item:** Kingdom Open Badge, Spiculum, Patched Cape, Death's Head Cap, Wicker Shield

Prize: ???-????D **Item:** Kingdom Open Badge, Light Pick, Reinforced Targe, Confortari, Cured Leather Armor

Battle Name	Points	Entry Fee	Teams(VS)	Prize (Ursula)	Prize (Valens)	Requirement / Restriction
Clash of Kings	(1)	100D	4 4	500-1500D	500-1500D	None
Hilltop Kingdom	(1)	100D	3 3 3	500-1500D	500-1500D	None
Tax Relief	(1)	100D	3 3 3	150-450D	300-900D	None
Dominance	(2)	150D	4 4	200-600D	600-1800D	None
Royal Tally	(2)	150D	2 2 2 2	500-1500D	100-300D	None
Rival Nations	(3)	250D	4 4	300-600D	1000-2000D	None

LEAGUE OF THE NORTHERN PRIDE

Req: 0% None

Prize: 600D-1800D **Item:** Jaculum, Wolf Cowl, Jackal Pelt, Berkana

Prize: 1200D-3600D **Item:** Hercules Club, Mountain Lion Hide, Ring of Fangs, Ansuz

Battle Name	Points	Entry Fee	Teams(VS)	Prize (Ursula)	Prize (Valens)	Requirement / Restriction
Contest of Honor 1	(2)	100D	3 3 3	200-500D	200-500D	Req: From Nordagh only
Contest of Honor 2	(2)	100D	4 4	200-500D	500-1500D	Req: From Nordagh only
Rival Nations	(2)	200D	4 4	100-300D	500-1500D	Req: From Nordagh only
Contest of Honor 3	(2)	200D	4 4	200-600D	600-1800D	Req: From Nordagh only
The Sack of Belfort	(2)	200D	4 4	200-600D	600-1800D	Req: From Nordagh only

CIRCLE CHAMPIONSHIP

Req: 0% Fliuch Circle 2, Mördare Circle 2, Sloan Forest Circle 2, Vargen Circle 2

Prize: 2000-4000D **Item:** Eow, Gebo, Ingwaz, Uruz

Prize: 2000-4000D **Item:** Eow, Gebo, Ingwaz, Uruz

Battle Name	Points	Entry Fee	Teams(VS)	Prize (Ursula)	Prize (Valens)	Requirement / Restriction
Championship	(1)	500D	4 4	300-900D	1200-3600D	None

TOURNAMENT: ORIN TOURNAMENT

Entry Fee: 500D
Teams(VS): 4 vs. 4
Required: 4 Cups

Ursula
Prize: 300-900D
Items: Lignator, Fur Hat, Shoulder Brace, Leather Armband
Valens
Prize: 750-2250D
Items: Lignator, Fur Hat, Shoulder Brace, Leather Armband

This is a simple four-on-four fight with a random league that could be anything from local Barbarians and Gungnirs to Imperial Samnites and Murmillos. If you don't like the one you get, back out and try again; this league is as easy or hard as your random opponents.

CHAMPIONSHIP

Entry Fee: 100D
Teams(VS): 3 vs. 3
Required (Badges): All Regional Badges, Kingdom Open, Free Peoples, Dreas Open

Ursula
Prize: 2000-6000D, Nordagh Championship
Items: Flamerge, Fur Hat, Wolf Cowl, Wolfskin
Valens
Prize: 4000-12000D, All Nordagh Badges
Items: Bone Axe, Reinforced Targe, Iron Campana, War Hammer

When you've earned the tournament badges from Nordagh's six towns, the Championship battle will be open to you. This is your final battle in Nordagh, but don't expect anything special; it's your typical three-on-three battle, versus simple Nordagh natives like Barbarians, Berserkers and Gungnirs.

After claiming an easy victory, leave King Orin and head towards Roanor, which will cause Usus to pop up and ask if you're ready to move on. If you have other business in Nordagh, tell Usus and take care of it now. If not, tell Usus "Yes, I can't wait," and after a few intermissions, your new adventure will begin.

SLOAN FOREST

STADIUM DREAS

STADIUM DREAS IS LOCATED JUST INSIDE THE SLOAN FOREST IN THE CAVITY LEFT BEHIND WHEN THE FAMOUS TAVOAICH TREE FELL DURING THE STORM OF THE AGES. THE TAVOAICH TREE WAS THE TALLEST TREE IN THE SLOAN FOREST AND MARKED THE BORDER TO THE UNEXPLORED REGION OF THE IMMENSE WOODED AREA. ONCE THE TREE HAD FALLEN, TALES OF GREAT DESTRUCTIVE POWERS FROM DEEP WITHIN THE FOREST MADE THEIR WAY INTO NORDAGH LORE AND PEOPLE STARTED TO EXPLORE THE REGION, SEARCHING FOR THIS POWER. AS THE POPULACE BEGAN TO INHABIT THE FOREST, THE REMAINS OF THE TREE WERE USED FOR BUILDING HOUSES AND TEMPLES, IN HOPES THAT THE STRENGTH WITHIN THE WOOD WOULD WARD OFF EVIL SPIRITS. TWO SEEDS WERE TAKEN FROM THE TREE AND PLANTED IN THE RECESS MADE BY ITS COLLAPSE. UNTIL THOSE TREES ENVELOPE THE HOLE, GLADIATORIAL COMBAT WILL TAKE PLACE IN THE CAVITY OF THE MIGHTY TAVOAICH TREE, BETWEEN THE TWO CENTURY-OLD SAPLINGS.

Southwest of Roanor you'll find Sloan Forest, where you'll meet the Galdr in combat for the first time. They appear in the first battle of the Dreas Open League, which you must complete before the other leagues open up.

There are a lot of interesting recruitment opportunities here. Bears and Wolves are easy to find, and you may need to recruit one or two in order to meet the entrance requirements of certain leagues. You can also find Satyrs, hard-drinking light-type utility characters that are beloved by audiences everywhere, and Mongrel Shamans, who are underpowered but interesting arcane-type gladiators.

CHARACTER RECRUITMENT

Name	Classification	PRM	SNG
Badud	Mongrel Shaman	1000	100
Bevan	Satyr	825	100
Buri	Bear	900	100
Laertes	Satyr	750	150
Mandar	Wolf	800	100
Nemesis	Bear	950	100
Odin	Wolf	900	125
Quinn	Satyr	1100	100
Sim	Satyr	750	150
Snoog	Mongrel Shaman	1000	125

NOTE: Cost is per recruitable character level.

PRM=Cost for permanent recruitment
SNG=Cost for single battle

SHOP: RAGNOROK'S KEEP

LEAGUE STRATEGY

DREAS OPEN LEAGUE

The Sylvan Skirmish battle of the Dreas Open League always features a pair of Galdrs on your opponent's side. Galdrs specialize in spells that boost their teammates, but aren't too effective by themselves. So focus your attacks on their two allies and save the Galdrs for last. The Galdrs are very good at dodging, so when it's time to hunt them down you'll want to rely on accurate attacks and always go for critical hits.

After the Sylvan Skirmish you'll be able to enter the other leagues, but you might as well finish off the Dreas Open League. Standard tactics will be effective in Point Battles and Rival Nations, but the King of the Hill battle is a little unusual. There are four paths up the hill, and you'll want to secure two of them. That way you'll have a good chance of taking the hill when the "king" dies, and you can prevent your own king from being surrounded once you do.

BATTLING THE BEASTS

The three leagues that are unique to Stadium Dreas all revolve around beasts. You'll need at least two beasts of your own to enter the Man and Beast league, but anyone can enter the short but deadly **To The Wolves** and **Fight the Bear** leagues.

Bears are resilient fighters that only heavy gladiators can easily punch through, so Valens will want to register a roster of Centurions and Samnites in the Fight the Bear League. Ursula will have a difficult time with this league, since heavies are so (continued on page 66)

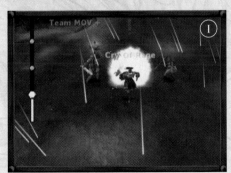

SLOAN FOREST HISTORY

The Sloan Forest is always the first image to come to mind when speaking of Nordagh. Shrouding more than a third of the region with dense covering of trees, the Sloan Forest is the home of the Galdr witches, and therefore, much intrigue. There are hundreds of settlements throughout the forest, including the King's hunting residence, but nothing big enough to be considered a proper city.

The forest has small rivers and creeks flowing throughout, with watermills and canals supplying homes with constant fresh water. Just inside the forest lies Stadium Dreas, a favorite arena in Nordagh.

rare in Nordagh. If you don't have Iaar the Yeti yet, you may want to pass on this league until after you recruit him in Vargen.

The wolves in To The Wolves will always strive to surround a single foe and slaughter them with non-stop Group Attacks, a skill that allows each adjacent Wolf to get a free hit when one gets a shot in. The key to countering this deadly strategy is positioning. In Wolf Battle 1, fall directly back to the arena wall where there's an alcove with only three squares. Position your characters at either side, backs to the wall, with an empty spot between them. This will force one wolf to move into the surrounded square between you, where you can quickly eliminate him with deadly combos. After that, your combatants can engage the remaining wolves one on one.

There's an even better spot in Wolf Battle 2, where you start on top of the hill. Have two beaters stand diagonal to each other beside the lower tree, with a character who can hit diagonals (like a spear-wielding Bandit) in between. This will force the Wolves to line up to get slaughtered three-on-one in the single square left to them.

TOURNAMENT: FOREST KINGS

Entry Fee: 0D
Teams(VS): 3 vs. 3
Required: 6 Cups

Ursula
Prize: 200-500D
Items: None
Valens
Prize: 500-1500D
Items: None

You begin this fight right on top of your foes, so bring a Bandit or Secutor and chose your starting positions carefully for a free backstab. Make sure everyone is in place for an attack on the backstabber's target on their first turn, and you'll be enjoying 3-on-2 odds on turn 2. For the Masters of the Glade, things should go downhill rapidly from there.

DREAS OPEN LEAGUE

Req: 0%   None
Prize: 750-2250 Item: Dreas Open Badge, Banded Shield, Jaculum, Horned Band, Full Moon
Prize: 2000-6000 Item: Dreas Open Badge, Egchos, Hard Leather Shield, Wood Armored Hat, Heavy Leather

Battle Name	Points	Entry Fee	Teams(VS)	Prize (Ursula)	Prize (Valens)	Requirement / Restriction
Sylvan Skirmish	(1)	100D	4 4	200-500D	500-1500D	None
King of the Hill	(1)	100D	3 3 3	100-300D	500-1500D	Req: 3 and higher
Points Battle	(1)	100D	2 2 2 2	100-300D	500-1500D	Req: 3 and higher
Rival Nations	(1)	100D	4 4	100-300D	500-1500D	Req: 3 and higher

FIGHT THE BEAR

Req: 0%   None
Prize: 350-1050 Item: Wolf Cowl, Battle Collar, Crook, Beast's Shield
Prize: 2000-6000 Item: Francisca, Reinforced Targe, Chain Collar, Arm Brace

Battle Name	Points	Entry Fee	Teams(VS)	Prize (Ursula)	Prize (Valens)	Requirement / Restriction
Bear Battle 1	(1)	100D	2 2	200-500D	500-1500D	Req: 3 and higher
Bear Battle 2	(1)	100D	2 2	200-500D	500-1500D	Req: 3 and higher
Bear on the Hill	(2)	100D	3 3	100-300D	500-1500D	Req: 3 and higher
Dominating Bears	(2)	100D	3 3	200-500D	500-1500D	Req: 3 and higher
Bear Battle 3	(3)	100D	2 1	200-500D	500-1500D	Req: 3 and higher

MAN AND BEAST

Req: 0%   None
Prize: 500-1500 Item: Wolfskin, Cured Leather Shield, Pike, Collar of Force
Prize: 2000-6000 Item: Pole Axe, Wooden Shield, Ring of Fangs, Mountain Lion Hide

Battle Name	Points	Entry Fee	Teams(VS)	Prize (Ursula)	Prize (Valens)	Requirement / Restriction
Rival Nations	(1)	200D	4 4	100-300D	500-1500D	Req: 2 Human, 2 Beast
Interspecies Effort 1	(1)	200D	4 4	200-500D	500-1500D	Req: 2 Human, 2 Beast
Points Battle	(2)	200D	2 2 2 2	200-500D	500-1500D	Req: 1 Human, 1 Beast
Interspecies Effort 2	(2)	200D	2 2 2 2	200-500D	500-1500D	Req: 1 Human, 1 Beast
King of the Hill	(3)	200D	3 3 3	100-300D	500-1500D	Req: 1 Human, 2 Beast

TO THE WOLVES

Req: 0%   None
Prize: 400-1200 Item: Bone Club, Iron Choker, Collared Cloak, Woven Collar
Prize: 2000-6000 Item: Horn Hammer, Spiked Round Shield, Confortari, Iron Choker

Battle Name	Points	Entry Fee	Teams(VS)	Prize (Ursula)	Prize (Valens)	Requirement / Restriction
Wolf Battle 1	(1)	100D	2 3	200-500D	500-1500D	Req: 3 and higher
Wolf Battle 2	(2)	100D	3 5	200-500D	1000-2000D	Req: 3 and higher
Wolf Battle 3	(3)	100D	3 4	200-500D	500-1500D	Req: 3 and higher

CIRCLE OF ELITES TIER 1

Req: 0%   Circle Qualification
Prize: 500-1500 Item: Sloan Forest Circle 1
Prize: 2000-6000 Item: Sloan Forest Circle 1

Battle Name	Points	Entry Fee	Teams(VS)	Prize (Ursula)	Prize (Valens)	Requirement / Restriction
Dominance	(1)	200D	2 2 2 2	200-500D	500-1500D	Req: 3 and higher
King of the Hill	(1)	200D	3 3 3	300-600D	1000-2000D	Req: 3 and higher
Rival Nations	(1)	200D	4 4	100-300D	500-1500D	Req: 3 and higher

CIRCLE OF ELITES TIER 2

Req: 0%   Mördare Circle 1, Fliuch Circle 1, Sloan Forest Circle 1, Vargen Circle 1
Prize: 750-2250 Item: Sloan Forest Circle 2
Prize: 2000-6000 Item: Sloan Forest Circle 2

Battle Name	Points	Entry Fee	Teams(VS)	Prize (Ursula)	Prize (Valens)	Requirement / Restriction
Points Battle	(1)	200D	2 2 2 2	100-300D	500-1500D	None
Basic Battle	(1)	200D	3 3 3	100-300D	500-1500D	None
Dominance	(1)	200D	4 4	200-500D	500-1500D	None

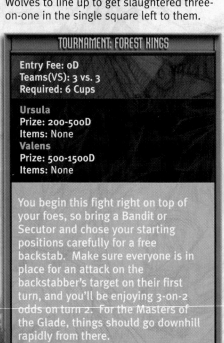

VARGEN

FJORD OF THE FALLEN

THE FJORD OF THE FALLEN ISN'T REALLY WHAT YOU'D CALL A "TRADITIONAL" ARENA. ALL OF THE GLADIATORIAL COMBAT IS HELD ON THE SURFACE OF THE GARDRED LAKE. THIS LAKE HAS NEVER THAWED—ALTHOUGH WATER DOES FLOW UNDER THE FROZEN SURFACE, SUPPLYING VARGEN WITH ALL OF ITS WATER. THE ARENA IS NAMED THE FJORD OF THE FALLEN, BECAUSE THIS IS WHERE THE ANCIENT WAR OF THE GIANTS BEGAN LONG AGO.

You'll find the icy town of Vargen north of Sloan Forest. You must defeat at least the first two battles of the Ahead of the Pack endurance series before the other Leagues open up.

In the recruiting office, you'll occasionally run into a Peltast named Agata. The opportunity to recruit an Imperial is a rare one for Ursula players, but Peltasts are virtually identical to Gungnirs, and are hardly worth getting excited about. A far more exciting recruit is Iaar the Yeti, but he won't be available until you complete the Trial of Elders league.

CHARACTER RECRUITMENT

Name	Classification	PRM	SNG
Agata	Peltast	750	75
Breeya	Barbarian	750	75
Dermott	Gungnir	1100	110
Dorothy	Gungnir	1000	100
Ergein	Berserker	1100	110
Fial	Berserker	1000	100
Jareth	Wolf	950	95
Kacea	Gungnir	900	90
Luna	Wolf	1000	100
Mavis	Berserker	900	90
Neel	Barbarian	750	75
Roark	Barbarian	850	100
Iaar	Yeti	0*	-
Rugh	Yeti	-	100*

*Accessable after completing the Trial of Elders.
NOTE: Cost is per recruitable character level.

PRM=Cost for permanent recruitment
SNG=Cost for single battle

SHOP: BIFROST

LEAGUE STRATEGY

AHEAD OF THE PACK

Series fights can be difficult, but you should be a few levels above your opponents in this one. Urlan, Ursula and a Gungnir make the best team, if you've mastered the art of positioning Gungnirs correctly (if the wolves rush her, remember that her Bear Form is very effective against Wolves in melee combat). In early rounds, keep Urlan and Ursula close together so they can reap the benefits of Older Brother and Sibling Rivalry skills, but space them out against the Greater Wolf in the final round, since she has the ability to hit two adjacent characters in one swing. That final battle can be rough if you've been heavily damaged in the early rounds, but you only need to beat the first two to conquer this league.

TRIAL OF THE ELDERS

If I were a Yeti, I'd insist on fighting Ursula too; as a medium character, she's at a significant type disadvantage against the heavy Yeti in the final battle. Fortunately, you can choose your roster in the first two battles, so load up on light gladiators and Gungnirs, who can get a few free turns worth of attacks as the Yeti lumber over. In Ursula's final one-on-one fight, taking the high ground is the only way to overcome the type mismatch, so claim it at all costs.

As an additional prize for winning this league, you'll be able to recruit Iaar the Yeti for free! As the only heavy gladiator in Nordagh, he's a must-recruit for Ursula players. Don't forget to equip your Bear Tooth prize in his accessory slot, and make him even deadlier. *(continued on page 68)*

VARGEN HISTORY

Vargen is both an ancient and new city. The top of this mountain was a very spiritual place for the elders of the distant past. The people of Vargen, then called Varghallen, were said to have lived among The Gods. But long ago, man's propensity for violence turned them against The Gods and they were forced off the mountain. Thus began The War of The Giants, which lasted for more than a century. After the war ended, the few humans that remained were given the charge of rebuilding this city in the name of peace between Heaven and Earth.

VARGEN'S OTHER LEAGUES

The **Hordes of the North** is a difficult series battle, especially for Valens players who may not have four good Nordagh recruits (remember, you can always get temporary recruits for the series). This league is primarily Berserkers and Barbarians, with a few Gungnirs thrown in, so you'll want to use primarily medium weight characters. Iaar the Yeti will start earning his keep in the **Mile-High Circuit**, where his Maul can score large numbers in the Points Battle. Rival Nations is another easy win, since the enemy team tends to divide its forces between offense and defense. Plant a Gungnir on one of the hills and places the rest of your forces in the center of the arena to meet and eliminate your opponents a few at a time.

TOURNAMENT: MASTERS OF ICE

Entry Fee: 0D
Teams(VS): 4 vs. 4
Requirement: 6 Cups

Ursula
Prize: 750-2250D
Items: Light Wrap, Banded Shield, Iron Pendant, Eow
Valens
Prize: 2000-6000D
Items: Sickle, Reinforced Targe, Confortari, Cured Leather Armor

The foes here are the usual locals: Barbarians, Berserkers, and Gungnirs. Taking the high ground seems like the key to this fight, but sometimes they start closer to it than you are, and are usually quicker. In that situation, hold your ground, get your Gungnir in a good sniping position, and start beefing up your own troops with skills like Empower Self and Crowd Pleaser (if you have them). Instead of using the icy boulders as terrain advantage, use them as a barrier between your squad and their Gungnirs.

AHEAD OF THE PACK

Req: 0% None
Prize: 300-900D Item: Pike, Bone Club, Wolfskin, Wolf Cowl
Prize: 1600-4800D Item: Egchos, Bamboo Shield, Confortari, Hooded Wrap

Battle Name	Points	Entry Fee	Teams(VS)	Prize (Ursula)	Prize (Valens)	Requirement / Restriction
Series		800D	-	-	-	-
Wolf Battle 1	(1)	-	3 3	200-500D	500-1500D	From Nordagh only
Wolf Battle 2	(1)	-	1-3 3	200-500D	500-1500D	From Nordagh only
Wolf Battle 3	(1)	-	2-3 3	200-500D	500-1500D	From Nordagh only

HORDES OF THE NORTH

Req: 0% None
Prize: 500-1500D Item: Fur Hat, Lignator, Wolfskin, Flamberge
Prize: 2000-6000D Item: Horn Hammer, Warlord's Shield, Bronze Italic, Leg Brace

Battle Name	Points	Entry Fee	Teams(VS)	Prize (Ursula)	Prize (Valens)	Requirement / Restriction
Series		1000D	-	-	-	-
They Come	(1)	-	4 4	200-500D	500-1500D	From Nordagh only
Can't Hold Out	(1)	-	1-4 4	200-500D	500-1500D	From Nordagh only
How Many Are There?!	(1)	-	1-4 4	200-500D	500-1500D	From Nordagh only

MILEHIGH CIRCUIT

Req: 0% None
Prize: 500-1500D Item: Mannaz, Wolfskin, Fur Hat, Jaculum
Prize: 1000-3000D Item: Francisca, Reinforced Targe, Wood Armored Hat, Mountain Lion Hide

Battle Name	Points	Entry Fee	Teams(VS)	Prize (Ursula)	Prize (Valens)	Requirement / Restriction
Vandal Battle	(2)	150D	3 3	200-500D	500-1500D	None
Thin Air 1	(2)	150D	3 3	200-500D	500-1500D	Req: 3 and higher
Thin Air 2	(2)	150D	4 4	200-500D	500-1500D	Req: 3 and higher
Points Battle	(3)	300D	2 2 2 2	100-300D	500-1500D	None
Rival Nations	(3)	300D	4-4	100-300D	500-1500D	None
Thin Air 3	(4)	500D	3-3	200-500D	500-1500D	None

TRIAL OF THE ELDERS

Req: 0% None
Prize: 500-1500D Item: Dabus, Bear Tooth, Wolfskin, Wicker Shield
Prize: 2000-6000D Item: Boar Tooth, Stone Club, Hercules Club, Lion Tooth

Battle Name	Points	Entry Fee	Teams(VS)	Prize (Ursula)	Prize (Valens)	Requirement / Restriction
Basic Trial	(1)	300D	3 2	250-750D	250-750D	Req: 3 and higher
Strict Trial	(1)	300D	2 2	250-750D	250-750D	Req: 3 and higher
Adverse Trial	(1)	300D	1 1	250-750D	250-750D	Restriction: Ursula only

CIRCLE OF ELITES TIER 1

Req: 0% None
Prize: 400-1200D Item: Vargen Circle 1, Dabus, Jaculum, Cured Leather Shield, Dark Band
Prize: 2000-6000D Item: Vargen Circle 1, Carnificina, Lacquired Shield, Rimmed Thracian, Braced Armor

Battle Name	Points	Entry Fee	Teams(VS)	Prize (Ursula)	Prize (Valens)	Requirement / Restriction
King of the Hill	(1)	300D	3 3 3	100-300D	500-1500D	None
Dominance	(1)	300D	2 2 2 2	200-500D	500-1500D	None
Points Battle	(1)	300D	4 4	100-300D	500-1500D	None

CIRCLE OF ELITES TIER 2

Req: 0% Mördare C1, Fliuch C1, Sloan Forest C1, Vargen C1
Prize: 750-2250D Item: Vargen Circle 2, Kard, Banded Shield, Horned Band, Leather Cape
Prize: 750-2250D Item: Vargen Circle 2, Heavy Spear, Wooden Shield, Wood Armored Hat, Ringmail Guard

Battle Name	Points	Entry Fee	Teams(VS)	Prize (Ursula)	Prize (Valens)	Requirement / Restriction
Basic Battle	(1)	500D	3 3 3	200-500D	500-1500D	None
King of the Hill	(1)	500D	2 2 2 2	100-300D	500-1500D	None
Vandal Battle	(1)	500D	4 4	200-500D	500-1500D	None

MÖRDARE

MÖRDARE'S DEN

This arena is situated inside the den of the long deceased dragon, Mördare. It is a cold, dark, and damp place for combat, with deep unexplored recesses hidden in the shadows beyond the light of the torches that ring the arena. In the center rests an imposing sight, the remains of the former resident. Most notably Mördare's giant skull is half imbedded in the side of the arena. Stretching entirely underneath the arena floor, the corpse of the mighty beast is exposed from a giant femur protruding from the ground to the lattice of a ribcage cascading from the packed earth. Spectators stand on the edge of this sunken grave, excavated too long ago to remember, to throw insults, and whatever else they can find, down upon the combatants.

F urther north of Vargen is Mördare, where you can choose from a number of unusual leagues after you clear the first battle of Test of the Tribes. The Dead of Night is a difficult league, but if you win you'll earn the right to enlist Taithleach, the only recruitable Undead Summoner in the game. If you're doing the Circle of Elites, you can pick up your third Tier 1 badge here and head east to Fliuch to get the last one and start on Tier 2. If you're not, you can pick up your last tournament badge and head back to Orin for the Nordagh Championships.

CHARACTER RECRUITMENT

Name	Classification	PRM	SNG
Anika	Bear	975	100
Asaeunn	Berserker	900	70
Bermork	Berserker	1000	100
Ceat	Berserker	900	75
Eva	Berserker	800	100
Kro Chack	Mongrel Shaman	950	110
Raini	Wolf	1000	100
Wiploc	Mongrel Shaman	1000	95
Zach	Satyr	1150	115
Zeebo	Mongrel Shaman	1100	110
Taithleach	Undead Summoner	0*	-

*After completing the Dead of Night league only.
NOTE: Cost is per recruitable character level.

PRM=Cost for permanent recruitment
SNG=Cost for single battle

SHOP: THE DRAGONSLAYER

SHOPKEEPER QUEST

Mördare is home to two shopkeeper quests, so make sure to have a lengthy conversation with the proprietor of the Dragonslayer before you leave. If you accept the quest he offers, he'll send you to search for Sigi, a Galdr who has gone missing. You'll find her about one screen northeast of the city of Roanor, where you'll be pulled into a battle between Sigi and a pack of Mongrel Shamans. Don't worry about Sigi-she's level 15, so she can dodge enemy attacks all day. So take it slowly, and overwhelm and eliminate the Shamans one or two at a time. After all, this is a random encounter, and deaths are permanent.

After your victory, return to the Dragonslayer where Sigi will gift you with the Signet of the Valkyrie and Xandl will toss in Flamberge and Tschehouta weapons. The Signet of the Valkyrie does nothing by itself, but is the first piece of the puzzle of the Hell's Gate side quest. *(see Secrets)*

SHOPKEEPER QUEST II

After you begin the Dead of Night league, Sorcha will refer your questions about the Unliving to Xandl. Ask him for advice, listen to his story, then leave, re-enter, and ask him again. He'll tell you about a small hill just south of Fliuch, marked with a tombstone, where the dead rise at night.

You know what comes next. When night falls, visit the hill and you'll end up in a battle with a vicious pack of... Tombstones? They're stationary, but far from harmless, as each tombstone can summon its own skeleton warrior. Ignore the skeletons, which will immediately return to life if they *(continued on page 70)*

MÖRDARE HISTORY

Mordare is a town fraught with intrigue. For hundreds of years, it was known as the humble village of Riwigo, slave to the whims of a giant forest dragon named Mordare, who lived just outside the city walls. Riwigo was founded as a small farming community, but eventually expanded on Mordare's territory. Slowly, the farming community died off and was replaced by dragon hunters, berserkers, and other thrill seekers. These new inhabitants referred to the town only as the home of a dragon. Today, the locals fight among the dried bones of the famous monster's carcass in the very den where it met its untimely demise.

School | Amateur | 38613D

School | Rest | Semi-Pro | 29151D

die, and concentrate on the graves themselves. When each tombstone dies, so will its skeleton. Victory will earn you the Talisman of Unlife badge, which will let you summon Undead Legionnaires to join your school at tombstones (you'll find one in Imperia, just south of Caltha).

LEAGUE STRATEGY

TEST OF THE TRIBES

You'll fight nothing but Berserkers in this league, which should pose no problem for a party with strong medium-type heroes and a Gungnir or two. The only thing that makes the Berserkers dangerous is their Adrenaline skill, which powers them up when they're low on health. It's always a good idea to single out foes and kill them one at a time, but against Berserkers, that strategy is crucial. If you spread the damage around equally, you risk a bloody reversal when their Adrenaline hits.

Adrenaline

DRAGONHEART OPEN

This league is one of the first where you'll run into a wide mix of types. Heavy, Medium, Light and Support are all well represented here, and in an arena with thin passages and no terrain effects, careful type-matching is the only edge you'll have. The most interesting battle is the Dragon's Hoard; the chests are full of weapons (roughly equal to your level) and small amounts of cash. It's easy enough to send three tough characters to take out the foes while a lone Bandit snags the loot.

TEST OF THE TRIBES

Req:	0%			None	
Prize:	500-1500D	**Item:** Lignator, Kard, Algiz, Igwaz			
Prize:	2000-6000D	**Item:** Francisca, Sickle, Wunjo, Uruz			

Battle Name	Points	Entry Fee	Teams(VS)	Prize (Ursula)	Prize (Valens)	Requirement / Restriction
Sacred Battle	(1)	100D	3 4	200-500D	500-1500D	Req: L3 and higher
Sacred Battle	(1)	100D	2 3	200-500D	500-1500D	Req: L3 and higher
Sacred Battle	(1)	200D	2 4	500-1500D	500-1500D	Req: L3 and higher

DRAGONHEART OPEN

Req:	0%			None	
Prize:	800-2400D	**Item:** Crowbill, Plated Band, Jackal Pelt, Kenaz			
Prize:	3000-8000D	**Item:** Mug, Spiked Round Shield, Wood Armored Hat, Heavy Leather			

Battle Name	Points	Entry Fee	Teams(VS)	Prize (Ursula)	Prize (Valens)	Requirement / Restriction
Wyrmbelly Brawl 1	(1)	100D	4 4	200-500D	500-1500D	None
Dragon's Hoard	(1)	100D	4 4	200-500D	500-1500D	Required: 3 and Higher
Wyrmbelly Brawl 2	(1)	500D	3 3	200-500D	1000-3000D	Required: 3 and Higher
Vandal Battle	(2)	100D	3 3	200-500D	500-1500D	Required: 3 and Higher
Wyrmbelly Brawl 3	(1)	100D	3 3 3	200-500D	500-1500D	None
Dragon's Fury	(2)	100D	3 3 3	100-300D	500-1500D	Required: 3 and Higher

THE WYRO

Req:	0%			None	
Prize:	500-1500D	**Item:** Chain Collar, Soldier's Scalp, Owl Beak, Flask			
Prize:	2000-4000D	**Item:** Mug, Stone Club, Leather Cloak, Rabbit Pelt			

Battle Name	Points	Entry Fee	Teams(VS)	Prize (Ursula)	Prize (Valens)	Requirement / Restriction
Peculiar Pillage	(2)	100D	2 2	200-500D	500-1500D	Req: L3 & higher, NoHumans
Strange Fray 1	(1)	100D	3 3	200-500D	500-1500D	Req: L3 & higher, NoHumans
Strange Fray 2	(1)	100D	2 2 2	200-500D	500-1500D	Req: L3 & higher, NoHumans
Strange Fray 3	(1)	100D	3 3	200-500D	500-1500D	Req: L3 & higher, NoHumans
Strange Fray 4	(1)	100D	3 3	200-500D	500-1500D	Req: L3 & higher, NoHumans
Weird Reckoning	(2)	100D	3 3	100-300D	500-1500D	Req: L3 & higher, NoHumans

THE DEAD OF NIGHT

Req:	0%			*Night Only Series	
Prize:	500-2500D	**Item:** Quaddara, Death's Head Cap, Hooded Cloak, Cudgel			
Prize:	500-2500D	**Item:** Quaddara, Death's Head Cap, Hooded Cloak, Cudgel			

Battle Name	Points	Entry Fee	Teams(VS)	Prize (Ursula)	Prize (Valens)	Requirement / Restriction
Series		1000D	-	-	-	-
Sun's Withdrawl	(1)	-	4 4	200-500D	500-1500D	Required: 3 and Higher
Midnight	(1)	-	1-4 4	200-500D	500-1500D	Required: 3 and Higher
False Dawn	(1)	-	1-4 4	200-500D	500-1500D	Required: 3 and Higher

CIRCLE OF ELITES TIER 1

Req:	0%					Circle Qualification

| Prize: | 500-1500D | Item: Mördare Circle 1, Jackal Pelt, Framea, Confortari, Banded Shield |
| Prize: | 2000-6000D | Item: Mördare Circle 1, Francisca, Gladius, Heavy Bronze Shield, Confortari |

Battle Name	Points	Entry Fee	Teams(VS)	Prize (Ursula)	Prize (Valens)	Requirement / Restriction
Points Battle	(1)	100D	3 3	100-300D	500-1500D	None
Basic Battle	(1)	100D	3 3	200-500D	500-1500D	None
Rival Nations	(1)	100D	4 4	100-300D	500-1500D	None

CIRCLE OF ELITES TIER 2

Req:	0%					Fliuch Circle 1, Mördare Circle 1, Sloan Forest Circle 1, Vargen Circle 1

| Prize: | 500-2500D | Item: Banded Shield, Pike, Fur Hat, Soldier's Armband |
| Prize: | 2000-6000D | Item: Hak, Wooden Shield, Confortari, Heavy Leather |

Battle Name	Points	Entry Fee	Teams(VS)	Prize (Ursula)	Prize (Valens)	Requirement / Restriction
Vandal Battle	(1)	350D	3 3	300-900D	1200-2400D	None
Basic Battle	(1)	350D	3 3 3	300-900D	1200-2400D	None
Points Battle	(1)	350D	4 4	300-900D	1200-2400D	None

THE DEAD OF NIGHT

This night-only league is Mördare's greatest challenge, but it's worth every bit of the trouble required to conquer it. A victory here will earn you the right to recruit Taithleach the Undead Summoner for free. Undead Summoners are the game's second-best arcane class, so this is an opportunity you don't want to miss.

Conquering this league, however, is easier said than done. Skeletons are virtually immune to projectiles, they poison everyone nearby when they're killed, and they can summon more of their number at will. Ugh. The only good news is that they're weak to Affinity attacks, and are very vulnerable to heavy type classes, but both weaknesses are hard to exploit early in the game. So leave the Gungnirs on the bench, don't crowd around when one's about to die (ideally, finish them from a distance with Ursula's ranged skills, like Energy Blast), and kill them as quickly as humanly possible, before they can replenish their ranks.

TOURNAMENT: HEART OF THE DRAGON

Entry Fee: 0D
Teams(VS): 3 vs. 3
Requirement: 8 Cups

Ursula
Prize: 750-2250D
Items: Shoulder Brace, Cured Leather Shield, Framea, Attic Duras
Valens
Prize: 3000-9000D
Items: Doloire, Throwing Hoplite, Ring of Fangs, Leather Armor

The Heart of the Dragon is a conventional three-on-three battle versus foes who tend to be around the same level as the rest of your party. A number of schools participate here, so you can end up battling difficult Samnites and Gungnirs, or another roster full of Berserkers. If you've managed to get this far, this battle should cause little trouble for your school.

CHAPTER II

IMPERIA

PIRGOS

BELFORT

CALTHA

ORUS

CRO BESKA

SYRNA

TRIKATA

HISTORY Imperia, the central land in Gladius, extends across the fertile central valley to the golden coast of the Aeonis Sea. During the expansion years Imperia used its large standing army and strong agricultural economy to become the leading government and culture. All trade routes ran through Imperia, and many prospered as Imperial culture extended its reach to its current borders.

The conquering power of Imperia remained unchallenged by all lands except one, Nordagh. This barbarian land from the north fought Imperia to a standstill during the Great War. After the war an enormous wall was constructed to separate the rivals and travel between the lands was regulated. During the peaceful time since the Great War, Imperia's Emperor and the ruling senate re-instituted the national games that pit schools of warriors against one another. So now the great military strength of Imperia is put to use as entertainment.

As of late the other lands across the world of Gladius have begun taking part in the games, and even schools from Nordagh can now be found competing in the Imperial Championships. The fierce competition of the games has entertained the masses and kept the various lands of Gladius in peace for many decades.

PIRGOS

PIRGOS ARENA

PIRGOS ARENA AFTER SUCCESSFULLY LEADING THE PIRGOS REVOLUTION, THE GREAT LAMETICUS STOOD IN THE CENTER OF THE NEWLY LIBERATED TOWN AND WITH GREAT AUTHORITY DECLARED IT FREE FROM THE TYRANNICAL RULE OF THE LOCAL DESPOT. THE INTENSITY OF THESE FEW SILENT MOMENTS OF GLORY WAS IMMEDIATELY SHATTERED WHEN A DELUSIONAL COUNTER-REVOLUTIONARY PLACED A GLADIUS THROUGH THE SPINE OF THE GREAT LEADER. IN HIS LAST EFFORT THE DYING LAMETICUS SWUNG ABOUT, DREW HIS SWORD AND SLEW THE HAPLESS DEVIANT WITH A SINGLE BLOW. A MONUMENT WAS ERECTED ON THE SPOT WHERE LAMETICUS FELL, AND THE SQUARE EVENTUALLY BECAME KNOWN AS A PLACE TO SETTLE DISPUTES. THE MORE FIGHTS AND ARGUMENTS, THE MORE PEOPLE STOPPED TO WATCH, AND SOON LARGE CROWDS GATHERED TO WATCH STRANGERS ENGAGE EACH OTHER IN COMBAT. MANY FIGHTS LATER, A FEW AMBITIOUS ENTREPRENEURS ERECTED WALLS AROUND THE SQUARE AND BEGAN CHARGING SMALL ADMISSION FEES TO COVER THE COST OF CONSTRUCTION. CENTURIES LATER THE PIRGOS OPEN ARENA IS NO LONGER USED FOR THE SETTLEMENT OF ARGUMENTS BUT IT IS NOW A MAJOR VENUE FOR ENTIRE GLADIATORIAL LEAGUES AND CHAMPIONSHIPS..

Valens: Your quest begins here in Pirgos, where you'll have to earn your Certification. After that, you're free to leave, but once you take a few steps out of town you'll automatically be marched to Belfort. So if you'd like to squeeze some cash for recruits and some solid experience out of Pirgos, try a few battles in the Civilis league and Pirgos Comminus before you head to the World Map.

CHARACTER RECRUITMENT

Name	Classification	PRM	SNG
Anatola	Channeler	1200	100
Artemij	Bandit	1000	200
Barbeeleen	Channeler	1100	200
Bryer	Bandit	450	45
Chryseida	Bandit	450	50
Drosis	Centurion	900	150
Galia	Legionnaire	950	95
Katre	Peltast	950	85
Quirinis	Peltast	1200	250
Serwacy	Secutor	1200	120
Sylwester	Peltast	2000	275
Velia	Peltast	850	100

NOTE: Cost is per recruitable character level.

PRM=Cost for permanent recruitment
SNG=Cost for single battle

SHOP: LEGENDARY BARTONUS

SHOPKEEPER QUEST

Listen to Cresus' long, tragic tale of his history, and he'll send you on the "Save Cresus' Father" quest. You'll find his father, Acrisius, in the Saraa Izel region of the Southern Expanse, but that's several chapters away.

PIRGOS HISTORY

Pirgos may seem like a small, old-fashioned agricultural town to outsiders, and for the settlers from Caltha who chose to move there for a quieter existence, this is true. Overall, the city has a very calm and peaceful air about it. But once you delve deeper into Pirgos you find it was founded on a strong sense of the arts and all the finer things in life, gladiatorial combat being no exception. The Pirgos Open Arena is more about showing off your skills than about bloodshed.

LEAGUE STRATEGY

 EARNING YOUR CERTIFICATION

You only need 6 Battle Points here, so you can skip all the Certification matches and go straight to the Final Exam if you already know what you're doing. However, the easy experience you can earn from the Training Battles will put you more than halfway to level 2, so you may want to do them anyway.

To clear the Final Exam, you'll need to take and hold the high ground. Select the highest crates directly before you and you should be able to get to the top before your opponents. Ignore the Centurion as you take out the weaker foes, then have Ludo fall back to lure the Centurion over to Valens, while Valens takes the opportunity to use Empower Self. Even if you lose Ludo, (continued on page 74)

General: Many of the recruits here will expect a certain amount of popularity, or a minimum level of experience from your school. You may have trouble finding worthy prospects at first, but check back as you gain experience and popularity and you'll be able to enlist some good ones.

an empowered Valens on the high ground should be able to take out the Centurion.

THE CIVILIS LEAGUE

In this anything-goes league, your foes could be anything from Citizens to Samnites. The numerical odds get progressively worse as the roman numerals rise, but the levels of your foes can fluctuate wildly. To avoid wasting time on unbeatable fights, peek into the enemy roster and back out if it's a bad type match-up. Starting positions are also random, so to tilt the odds on fair fights, you can back out and reenter until your enemies end up positioned far apart from each other. Then place your guys to surround one of them, and take them out one at a time. These fights are free to enter and pay well, so they're ideal for training your party.

ARCANE TEMPEST

(Ursula Only) Ursula will be forced into this all-Channeler league as soon as you finish the Civilis League, but you don't need to complete it to return to the normal league screen. The odds are fairly difficult, and as a series, you must complete each and every battle of the league, in a row. Fortunately, there are some weaknesses in the all-Channeler strategy you can exploit.

Characters with no affinity (or very low affinity) in their weapons are the best choice, because they force the Channelers to attack and steal from each other. You also want to make sure to choose high mobility characters and support characters whenever possible, since Channelers love to cast Tornado and scatter everyone's placements on the field. Bandits who can immediately Running Attack their way back to the fight are invaluable.

Battle II, in which you're stuck with only your two storyline characters, is the hardest, so make sure to seize the high ground for a strong but short-lived advantage. In Battles III and IV, you have more flexibility in selecting your roster, and your foes won't get any tougher.

Victory earns you the Host of the Arcane badge, which unlocks the Arcane-only Magic and Mysticism league in Trikata.

PIRGOS TRAINING

Req:	0%				None
Prize:		100-300D	**Item:** N/A		
Prize:		N/A	**Item:** Imperia Talisman		

Battle Name	Points	Entry Fee	Teams(VS)	Prize (Valens)	Prize (Ursula)	Prohibited
1st Training Battle	(1)	0D	2 2	100-300D	-	None
2nd Training Battle	(1)	0D	2 2	100-300D	-	None
3rd Training Battle	(1)	0D	2 2	100-300D	-	None
4th Training Battle	(1)	0D	2 2	100-300D	-	None
5th Training Battle	(1)	0D	1 2	0D	-	None
Training Exam	(5)	0D	2 3	100-300D	-	None

CIVILIS LEAGUE OF PIRGOS

Req:	0%				None
Prize:		1000-1150D	**Item:** None		
Prize:		500-625D	**Item:** None		

Battle Name	Points	Entry Fee	Teams(VS)	Prize (Valens)	Prize (Ursula)	Prohibited
Open Battle I	(1)	0D	4 4	500-550D	1000-1500D	Summoner, Undead Caster
Open Battle II	(1)	0D	4 3	500-550D	1000-1500D	Summoner, Undead Caster
Open Battle III	(2)	0D	2-4 4	500-550D	1000-1500D	Summoner, Undead Caster
Open Battle IV	(2)	0D	3 3	1000-1500D	1000-1500D	Summoner, Undead Caster
Open Battle V	(3)	0D	2 2	1000-1500D	1000-1500D	Summoner, Undead Caster
Open Battle VI	(3)	0D	3 4	1000-1500D	1000-1500D	Summoner, Undead Caster

ARCANE TEMPEST

Req:	0%				None
Prize:		N/A	**Item:** N/A		
Prize:		3000D	**Item:** Host of the Arcane badge		

Battle Name	Points	Entry Fee	Teams(VS)	Prize (Valens)	Prize (Ursula)	Prohibited
Arcane Series	-	0D	2-4 4	-	3000D	Summoner, Undead Caster
Battle I	(2)	-	2-4 4	-	-	Summoner, Undead Caster
Battle II	(2)	-	2 4	-	-	Summoner, Undead Caster
Battle III	(2)	-	1-3 4	-	-	Summoner, Undead Caster
Battle IV	(2)	-	1-2 4	-	-	Summoner, Undead Caster

PIRGOS COMMINUS

Req:	10%				None
Prize:		1500-1750D	**Item:** Plated Circlet		
Prize:		2000-2550D	**Item:** None		

Battle Name	Points	Entry Fee	Teams(VS)	Prize (Valens)	Prize (Ursula)	Required / Prohibited*
Tirocinium	(1)	0D	2-3 3	500-550D	500-550D	None
Lameticus	(1)	50D	2-4 4	500-550D	500-550D	One Heavy unit
Brutus Atrox	(2)	100D	2-4 4	500-550D	500-550D	*Beast, Arcane, Support
Eminus	(2)	200D	2-4 5	500-550D	500-550D	*Beast, Arcane, Support
Arcanum	(3)	300D	3-4 4	1000-1500D	1000-1500D	*Beast, Arcane, Support
Ludus	(3)	400D	4 6	5000-7500D	5000-7500D	*Beast, Arcane, Support

PIRGOS COMMINUS

It's hard to clear this league early in the game for Valens, but getting the four points necessary to earn the cup is a snap. Since your party consists of medium-weight Valens and Ludo at this point, as well as a few light-weight Secutors and Bandits, you'll do great in the Tirocinium fight, which consists entirely of light opponents. After that, challenge the Eminus and Arcanum battles. Eminus is all Peltasts, who can be

SATURNO'S FOLLY (VALENS)

Req:	0%				None
Prize:		2000-2500D	**Item:** Badge of Perpetuity		
Prize:		N/A	**Item:** N/A		

Battle Name	Points	Entry Fee	Teams(VS)	Prize (Valens)	Prize (Ursula)	Prohibited
Saturnos Folly	-	0D	-	-	-	-
Series I	(2)	-	4 4	500-550D	-	Summoner, Undead Caster
Series II	(2)	-	3 4	500-550D	-	Summoner, Undead Caster
Series III	(2)	-	3 4	500-550D	-	Summoner, Undead Caster

AGONY OF SATURNO (URSULA)

Req:	0%				None
Prize:		N/A	**Item:** N/A		
Prize:		2000-2500D	**Item:** Badge of Perpetuity		

Battle Name	Points	Entry Fee	Teams(VS)	Prize (Valens)	Prize (Ursula)	Prohibited
Trial of Saturno	-	0D	1-6 3	-	-	-
Stage I	(2)	-	1-6 3	-	1000-1500D	Summoner, Undead Caster
Stage II	(2)	-	1-6 4	-	1000-1500D	Summoner, Undead Caster
Stage III	(2)	-	1-6 3	-	500-550D	Summoner, Undead Caster
Stage IV	(2)	-	1-6 4	-	500-550D	Summoner, Undead Caster

THE SHIELD & THE SPEAR

Req:	45%			Pro Tier Only
Prize:		-	**Item:** None	
Prize:		-	**Item:** None	

Battle Name	Points	Entry Fee	Teams(VS)	Prize (Valens)	Prize (Ursula)	Required
Target Practice	(1)	500D	2-4 3	5000-5300D	5000-5300D	Support only
Anchor Point	(1)	500D	4 4	5000-5300D	5000-5300D	Support only
Quarrelsome Fight	(1)	500D	4 3	5000-5300D	5000-5300D	Support only
Dead Release	(1)	500D	2 4	5000-5450D	5000-5450D	Support only
Take Aim	(1)	500D	3 4	2500-2950D	2500-2950D	Support only
Follow Through	(1)	500D	2 2	6000-6350D	6000-6350D	Support only

shut down if you position your men so they're each engaging one Peltast in melee combat (preventing them from getting a good line-of-sight shot at your guys). Arcanum is entirely Channelers, who simply can't beat a party of aggressive fighters without some heavy support.

When you have a wider selection of gladiators, you can come back and challenge Lameticus (Bandits and Legionnaires), Brutus Atrox (Bandits and Centurions) and Ludus (Legionnaires and Centurions).

SATURNO'S FOLLY (VALENS)

(Valens Only) Fortunately, Saturno's Folly isn't a true series. You'll be back at full health before each fight, and can even choose a different roster. But you do have to do all three battles in a row, so the pressure is high. There's a crate structure in the first series that can give you some height advantage if you start in the middle, but the odds should be in your favor until the third series. Then you'll have to rely on proper type-matching and the numerical advantage you can gain by placing your characters so as to quickly eliminate whatever foes are furthest from the rest of the group.

VI AGONY OF SATURNO (URSULA)

(Ursula Only) Ursula will find a very different Agony of Saturno, a true series in which your six best fighters (including at least two that are between levels 7 and 8) must go against 14 foes in four rounds (only three of which are needed to claim the Badge). In general, you'll begin a great distance away from your opponents, allowing you to form a strong defense and play to the crowd while they make their way to your side of the arena.

TOURNAMENT: PIRGOS TOURNAMENT

Entry Fee: 1000D
Teams(VS): 5 vs. 5
Requirement: None

Valens
Prize: 3000-3500D
Items: Keys to Pirgos badge, Heavy Bronze Shield
Ursula
Prize: 3000-3500D
Items: Keys to Pirgos badge, Heavy Bronze Shield

Your opponents in this Tournament always consist of a pair of Peltasts, a Pair of Centurions, and one random Imperial surprise. Your units begin in a ring in the center of the arena, while the enemy placements are random. Place your faster characters so they're able to run at the Peltasts and block their line-of-sight. The other three characters can take out the enemy in the center of the ring (if there is one) or simply prepare a good defensive position for when your opponents rush in.

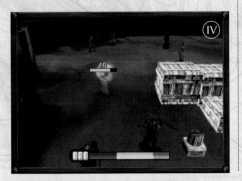

BELFORT

Ursula: Belfort is where Ursula's school begins its adventures in Imperia. To progress, you'll need to complete Talisman Challenge (an easy battle versus lower level opponents) and then one other league of your choice. After that, you will automatically depart to Syrna. Make sure to hit the Recruitment Office before that trip, so you can enlist a few Centurions. These powerful gladiators will fill the heavy-type hole in your current line up.

Valens: As soon as you leave Pirgos, you'll automatically go to Belfort. It's a good idea to complete a league or two before moving on.

BELFORT ARENA

THE MARKETPLACE IN THE CENTER OF BELFORT WAS A BUSY, BUSTLING MEETING PLACE FOR ALL IMPERIALS TRAVELING THE LAND. BUT THOSE WHO BUILT IT DIDN'T KNOW THAT IT WAS CONSTRUCTED ON UNSTABLE SOIL, CONCEALING THE RUINS OF AN ANCIENT CITY BURIED BY THE SANDS OF TIME, JUST METERS BELOW. AFTER THE CITY CENTER COLLAPSED MANY YEARS AGO, IT WAS TURNED INTO A GLADIATORIAL ARENA, INSPIRED BY THE WALLS OF THE RUINS IT REVEALED. MINIMAL WORK WAS DONE TO MAKE THIS LOCALE PRIME TERRITORY FOR THE FIGHTS, AS THE ANCIENT FOUNDATIONS CREATED AN EXCELLENT FIGHTING SPACE ON THEIR OWN. GATES WERE BUILT OVER CAVERNS AND BEASTS WERE KEPT HUNGRY AND THIRSTY FOR BLOOD BEHIND THEM. THE RIM OF THE ARENA WAS LINED WITH SPIKES MORE FOR DECORATION THAT FOR PRACTICAL USE, BECAUSE THE WALLS WERE SO SHEER THAT IT WAS NEARLY IMPOSSIBLE TO CLIMB OUT OF THE ARENA. A WOODEN FENCE NOW LINES THE PRECIPICE, HOLDING AT BAY A JEERING AND EXCITED CROWD. NEARLY AROUND THE CLOCK, THE NOISE OF THE CROWDS CAN BE HEARD, AS THIS CITY-SPONSORED ARENA IS IN ALMOST CONSTANT USE.

CHARACTER RECRUITMENT

Name	Classification	PRM	SNG
Ageliasa	Bandit	850	75
Alexander	Centurion	1500	500
Amphritritis	Centurion	900	80
Blaise	Legionnaire	1000	100
Cole	Bandit	400	45
Craiga	Centurion	1000	175
Deireoe	Centurion	1100	175
Furdain	Legionnaire	750	75
Imaus	Wolf	700	75
Jehan	Centurion	1000	175
Syprian	Bandit	800	80

NOTE: Cost is per recruitable character level.

PRM=Cost for permanent recruitment
SNG=Cost for single battle

SHOP: THE LOYALIST

The Challenge of Lykos and Regimental Challenge are the only ones initially available, but you'll gain popularity rapidly and be able to enter the Glory of Imperia and Best of Belfort after just a fight or two. If you haven't already recruited a pair of Centurions make sure to grab some here, as they're good against wolves and amazing against the many medium-type gladiators you'll meet in Belfort.

General: There are no less than three badges to be won here in Belfort. In fact, every league has one except for the Regimental Challenge. You don't need to earn them all, but you won't be able to enter all of Imperia's other leagues without them.

BELFORT HISTORY

Originally a military stronghold against the north, Belfort was built along a wall bordering Nordagh. It was founded by soldiers who where left behind to serve Imperia and protect it from invasion by those across the border. About the same size as Pirgos, the citizens are anything but refined. There is a distinct class separation in Belfort with descendants of famous Centurions, Legionnaires, and other war heroes living the high life while everyone else struggles just to get by. Fighting for entertainment has always been a staple in Belfort and continues to this day. The arena in Belfort is located in the center of town and frequented by commoners and those from the north who've made it across the border, legally or otherwise.

CHALLENGE OF LYKOS

This is a difficult league, but with solid strategy and a handful of Centurions, you have a good chance of victory. Don't let the wolves isolate individual characters; the first priority in this league is always to circle the wagons and form a tight group defense. Use as many Centurions as you have, and take advantage of their Coordinated Attack and Garrison skills while you're clustered. Surrounding is especially important against the Great Wolves-make sure you're hitting them from all four sides to maximize damage and prevent the wolf from getting two-in-ones on his own attacks. Finally, make sure to check out your opponents' stats before the battle. You'll often encounter a single Wolf who is much higher level than the others. Try to start as far away as possible from him, and kill most of the lesser Wolves first.

GOAL AWARDED

KEY BADGE
GLORY OF IMPERIA

OK

TALISMAN CHALLANGE

Req: ⬡ 0% ✦ ✦ ✦ 📜 None
Prize: 👤 💰 N/A N/A
Prize: 🏛 💰 100-300D **Item:** Imperia Talisman

Battle Name	Points	Entry Fee	Teams(VS)	Prize (Valens)	Prize (Ursula)	Required
Talisman of Imperia	(1)	0D	2-5 4	-	0D	None

CHALLENGE OF LYKOS

Req: ⬡ 0% ✦ ✦ ✦ 📜 None
Prize: 👤 💰 250-300D **Item:** Lupus' Master Badge
Prize: 🏛 💰 250-300D **Item:** Lupus' Master Badge

Battle Name	Points	Entry Fee	Teams(VS)	Prize (Valens)	Prize (Ursula)	Prohibited
Dinner Time	(3)	0D	1-4 6	500-750D	1000-1500D	Archer, Gungnir, Peltast
Dinner Time II	(3)	0D	1-4 4	500-750D	1000-1500D	Archer, Gungnir, Peltast
Pack Mentality	(4)	225D	1-4 4	500-750D	1000-1500D	Archer, Gungnir, Peltast
Dark Moon	(4)	300D	1-4 4	500-750D	1000-1500D	Archer, Gungnir, Peltast
The Fray	(4)	300D	4 6	1000-1500D	1000-1500D	Amazon, Archer, Gungnir, Peltast

REGIMENTAL CHALLENGE

Req: ⬡ 0% ✦ ✦ ✦ 📜 None
Prize: 👤 💰 1000-1030D **Item:** None
Prize: 🏛 💰 500-750D **Item:** None

Battle Name	Points	Entry Fee	Teams(VS)	Prize (Valens)	Prize (Ursula)	Prohibited
Classic Battle I	(2)	0D	1-5 3	500-750D	1000-1500D	Archer, Gungnir, Peltast
Classic Battle II	(2)	0D	1-3 3	500-750D	1000-1500D	Archer, Gungnir, Peltast
Classic Battle III	(2)	25D	1-4 4	500-750D	1000-1500D	Archer, Gungnir, Peltast
Classic Battle IV	(3)	50D	1-3 3	1000-1500D	2000-2500D	Archer, Gungnir, Peltast
Classic Battle V	(3)	50D	1-3 5	1000-1500D	2000-2500D	Archer, Gungnir, Peltast
Classic Battle VI	(3)	50D	1-3 5	1000-1500D	2000-2500D	Archer, Gungnir, Peltast

BEST OF BELFORT

Req: ⬡ 10% ✦ ✦ ✦ 📜 None
Prize: 👤 💰 1500-1750D **Item:** Badge of Belfort, Regal Cape
Prize: 🏛 💰 2000-2200D **Item:** Badge of Belfort

Battle Name	Points	Entry Fee	Teams(VS)	Prize (Valens)	Prize (Ursula)	Prohibited
Active Duty	(2)	200D	1-5 4	1000-1500D	1000-1500D	Archer, Gungnir, Peltast
Damage Control	(2)	200D	1-6 5	1000-1500D	1000-1500D	Archer, Gungnir, Peltast
Hostile Intent	(3)	300D	1-5 5	1000-1500D	1000-1500D	Archer, Gungnir, Peltast
Law of War	(3)	350D	1-5 5	1000-1500D	1000-1500D	Archer, Gungnir, Peltast
Packaged Forces	(4)	400D	1-6 6	5000-5050D	5000-5050D	Archer, Gungnir, Peltast
Tactical Control	(4)	450D	1-3 6	1000-1500D	1000-1500D	Archer, Gungnir, Peltast

THE BEST OF BELFORT

The Best of Belfort consist entirely of Centurions and Legionnaires. Bring in a mix of Bandits and Centurions and carefully check your enemy placements so you can start each gladiator where it can do the most damage. Many of your foes have moronically chosen spots at the bottom of pits, so you can walk right up and slaughter them within a turn or two from the high ground. Note that while all of these fights pay well, Packaged Forces has an eye-popping 5,000 dinar purse. The first round of that fight is four Centurions, so don't attempt this unless you have at least a pair of capable light characters.

GLORY OF IMPERIA (VALENS)

(Valens Only) The Glory of Imperia is one of the easier leagues Valens will encounter. Your foes will be primarily Barbarians and Berserkers, so it's easy to counter-program your offense. Check out the enemy placements, drop your Centurions near the Barbarians, and Ludo and Valens near the Berserkers. The foes do get tougher for Only the Strong, but effective type-matching will still lead to an easy victory, and the Glory of Imperia key badge.

TRIBAL WARFARE (URSULA)

(Ursula Only) You'll fight nothing but Legionnaires and Centurions in Ursula's version of this league, which does not make for a favorable match-up for primarily medium weight Nordagh natives (that bandit of yours might be an Imperial). That makes Bears, Yetis and Gungnirs the best choices for companions for Ursula's team.

You need to beat four battles to earn the key badge, and the final four give you the best opportunity to overcome your type mismatches with clever strategy. In those fights, you only need to take out the Centurion (or two), and if you carefully place your characters, you should be able to make it to the Centurion and take him out before your troop is chopped entirely to bits. If you start far away from your quarry, wait until you can see the Centurion's movement arrows, and then mobilize your force for a deadly ambush.

TRIBAL WARFARE (URSULA)

Req: 🔹 15% ✸ ✸ 👟 None
Prize: 👤 🪙 N/A   **Item:** N/A
Prize: 🧍 🪙 2500-2650D   **Item:** Glory of Imperia badge

Battle Name	Points	Entry Fee	Teams(VS)	Prize (Valens)	Prize (Ursula)	Required
No Diathan Leibh	(3)	625D	4 5	-	500-750D	From Nordagh
Bedhens Yndellma	(3)	625D	4 5	-	500-750D	From Nordagh
Osclaitear Na Geatai	(3)	625D	4 4	-	500-750D	From Nordagh
Clagh Billey	(3)	625D	4 5	-	500-750D	From Nordagh
Teine Coisrigte	(4)	625D	3 4	-	500-750D	From Nordagh
An Rud Seo	(4)	625D	4 7	-	500-750D	From Nordagh

GLORY OF IMPERIA (VALENS)

Req: 🔹 5% ✸ ✸ 👟 None
Prize: 👤 🪙 2500-2650D   **Item:** Glory of Imperia badge
Prize: 🧍 🪙 N/A   **Item:** N/A

Battle Name	Points	Entry Fee	Teams(VS)	Prize (Valens)	Prize (Ursula)	Required
Ancestan Challenge	(2)	500D	4 4	500-750D	-	From Imperia
Blood of Boreas	(2)	500D	4 4	500-750D	-	From Imperia
Fire in the Gullet	(2)	500D	3 3	500-750D	-	From Imperia
Yield to None	(2)	500D	3 3	500-750D	-	From Imperia
Only the Strong	(2)	500D	4 4	500-750D	-	From Imperia
Retribution of the Sword	(2)	500D	4 3	1000-1500D	-	From Imperia

TRIAL OF ARMADUS

Req: 🔹 30% ✸ 👟 None
Prize: 👤 🪙 -   **Item:** None
Prize: 🧍 🪙 -   **Item:** None

Battle Name	Points	Entry Fee	Teams(VS)	Prize (Valens)	Prize (Ursula)	Required
Trial of Armadus		1250D	-	-	-	-
First Wave	(2)	-	1 1	-	-	-
Second Wave	(2)	-	1 2	-	-	-
Third Wave	(2)	-	1 1	-	-	-
Fourth Wave	(2)	-	1 1	-	-	-
Fifth Wave	(2)	-	1 1	-	-	-

TOURNAMENT: BEAST MASTERY

Entry Fee: 1000D
Teams(VS): 1-4 vs. 6
Battle Points: 5
Requirement: 3 Cups

Valens
Prize: 1000-1500D
Items: None

Ursula
Prize: 2000-2500D
Items: None

This one should remind you of all the fun you had in the later fights of Challenge of Lykos. Fortunately, the same strategies still work; play a Murmillo, Peltast Gungnir, get everyone into the area to the North with the smaller entrances. The Greater wolves cannot chase after you here, so you can use your unit's long range attacks to safely whittle down their life, and easily dispatch the wolves that appear here.

TOURNAMENT: BELFORT CONQUEST

Entry Fee: 1000D
Teams(VS): 2-4 vs. 5
Battle Points: 5
Requirement: 3 Cups

Valens
Prize: 1000-1500D
Items: None

Ursula
Prize: 2000-2500D
Items: None

Well, this one's fair... Four guys versus two Legionnaires, two Centurions, and a Samnite, all at your level. Oh, and did I mention you have to waste two of your slots on your seriously type-disadvantaged storyline characters? Yep, the odds are against you, but you have a pretty big edge: To win this fight you only need to kill the pair of Centurions. If you feel like cheating, feel free to back out and re-enter until you can find four open placements slots near one of the Centurions. Focus your hate on him, and hopefully you'll have enough life left over to track down and kill his buddy.

TRIKATA

BLOODY HALO

NESTLED IN THE CENTER OF THE BUSTLING BUSINESS DISTRICT OF TRIKATA IS A SIMPLE ARENA KNOWN FOR ITS INTENSE BATTLES INSTEAD OF THE SPECTACLE OF ITS ARCHITECTURE. ORIGINALLY NAMED AFTER ITS BENEFACTOR, MAXIMO ABAVUS, ONE OF THE MOST PROMINENT MERCHANTS IN THE EARLY DAYS OF TRIKATA, THIS ARENA IS NOW KNOWN ONLY BY ITS NICKNAME, THE BLOODY HALO. ABAVUS' ONLY REMAINING LEGACY IS THE WELL ORGANIZED, AND EXTREMELY PROFITABLE, BETTING WINDOW THAT HE OPENED TO TRY TO MAKE BACK THE MONEY HE SPENT CONSTRUCTING THE ARENA. UPON FIRST GLANCE, MANY VISITORS MAY WONDER WHAT MAKES THIS SMALL, UNADORNED CIRCULAR ARENA SUCH A FAN FAVORITE. BUT ONCE THE WARRIORS TAKE THEIR PLACE IN THE ARENA AND THE WEAPONS BEGIN FLYING, NEWCOMERS SOON UNDERSTAND THE ATTRACTION OF THE UNPRETENTIOUS PRESENTATION OF THE BLOODY HALO. FANS GET CLOSER TO THE ACTION IN THIS ARENA MAKING THE CLASH OF SWORDS OR A FALLEN HERO EVEN MORE IMPRESSIVE. AND THE FACT THAT WARRIORS OF ALL SKILL LEVELS ARE ENCOURAGED TO TAKE PART IN THE GAMES AT TRIKATA BRINGS AN IMMENSE DIVERSITY TO WHAT FANS MIGHT SEE. IT'S THE COMBINATION OF ALMOST BEING PART OF THE ACTION AND NEVER KNOWING WHAT TO EXPECT NEXT THAT MAKES THE BLOODY HALO AN UNFORGETTABLE EXPERIENCE.

When Valens is done in Belfort and Ursula concludes her business in Syrna, you'll be free to go anywhere in Imperia you choose. Trikata isn't the first place you'll come across when you head south over the river past Caltha (a town where you can do nothing but watch games at this point), but it is the most interesting choice available to you right now. Stay on the main road as you pass two paths on your left; the first leads to Orus, the second to Cro Beska. Trikata will be the next town you see.

CHARACTER RECRUITMENT

Name	Classification	PRM	SNG
Arviragus	Centurion	2000	280
Callisto	Legionnaire	500	55
Dorota	Peltast	900	85
Dukker	Samnite	900	90
Eldred	Murmillo	1200	100
Georgius	Murmillo	1100	100
Ladislaus	Murmillo	1150	100
Leentje	Murmillo	1000	100
Maillie	Channeler	1200	100
Obelia	Legionnaire	800	80
Rea	Bandit	700	50

NOTE: Cost is per recruitable character level.

PRM=Cost for permanent recruitment
SNG=Cost for single battle

SHOP: VIA DOMUS

TRIKATA HISTORY

Unlike its sister city of Caltha, the coastal town of Trikata is strictly a working class metropolis. It's arena, the Bloody Halo, is a reflection of the city's attitude of straight-forward common sense, which is in direct contrast to the opulent Arena at Caltha. Warriors of all skill levels come to take place in the brutish games at the Halo, making it one of the most popular arenas in all of Imperia. The games bring tourists not only from the rest of Imperia, but also from other lands, as Trikata is Imperia's main harbor on the coast of the Aeonis Sea. Now a booming metropolis, Trikata was founded as a trade town, but soon outgrew its humble beginnings. Those who didn't fancy the big city life moved up the coast and founded the city of Pirgos.

SHOPKEEPER QUEST

Introduce yourself to Caryatis at Via Domus and force yourself to express an interest in her family and wellbeing. After a long conversation, she'll start pouring out her heart, and ask you to seek vengeance on her brother's killer. You can find the killer, a high level Murmillo named Priam, walking along the beach between Trikata and Syrna at night, within the next few days. This is a one-on-one fight with a Murmillo who is a few levels above you, so you'll need to risk your best heavy gladiator to take him down. Murmillos have tough defense, so focus on critical hits and affinity attacks. After he dies, you'll get a high level Murmillo sword, the Blade of Tides.

Caryatis will pay for the hit with a guilt trip and a bunch more Murmillo gear, (continued on page 80)

Here you'll be able to recruit a Murmillo, surely the coolest of the medium-type gladiators, and a Samnite, probably the strongest of the heavies. After boosting your popularity in the People's League of Trikata, you can enter the Hammer of Justice, where you'll earn a badge that will be crucial in your Imperial travels. The Survive Trikata league offers a key badge that you'll need to enter the Imperial championship. The Arcane-only Magic and Mysticism league offers accessories for Arcane types, but is only available to Ursula at this point.

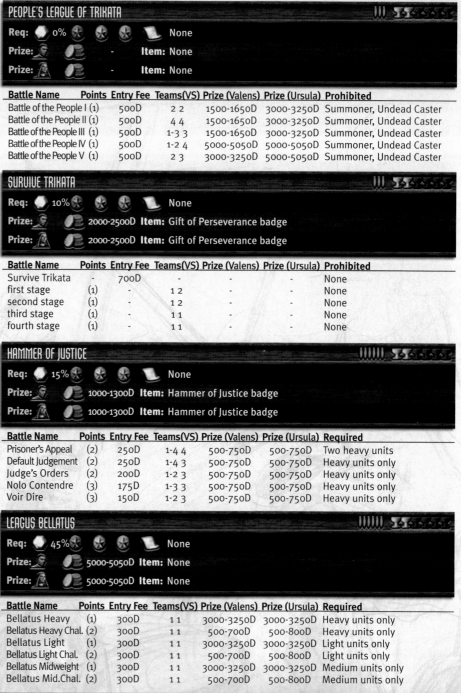

including a Teres Moles throwing shield, a Latticed Skirt, an Iron Capana helmet. If this is your first visit to Imperia, you won't yet be high enough level to use any of it, but it will come in handy one day.

PEOPLE'S LEAGUE OF TRIKATA

There's no avoiding this league-you'll need to earn a few rounds worth of popularity here to open up anything else in Trikata. Fortunately, battles I-III are quite easy. You can choose your roster to exploit your opponents' weaknesses, and with so many placement spots, you can start all of your characters right where they'll do the most damage.

If you choose to continue, you'll find Battle of the People IV offers a huge cash purse, but you'll have to overcome 2-on-4 odds to get it. Fortunately, your opponents start at the far corners of the ring, so if you place your gladiators to surround the character who is furthest from their heaviest (and slowest) fighter, you can take them out quickly, battle the next two in a two-on-two fight, and hopefully have a clear field and a reasonable amount of strength left to double team the heavy straggler.

PEOPLE'S LEAGUE OF TRIKATA

Req: 0% None
Prize: - Item: None
Prize: - Item: None

Battle Name	Points	Entry Fee	Teams(VS)	Prize (Valens)	Prize (Ursula)	Prohibited
Battle of the People I (1)	500D	2 2	1500-1650D	3000-3250D	Summoner, Undead Caster
Battle of the People II (1)	500D	4 4	1500-1650D	3000-3250D	Summoner, Undead Caster
Battle of the People III (1)	500D	1-3 3	1500-1650D	3000-3250D	Summoner, Undead Caster
Battle of the People IV (1)	500D	1-2 4	5000-5050D	5000-5050D	Summoner, Undead Caster
Battle of the People V (1)	500D	2 3	3000-3250D	5000-5050D	Summoner, Undead Caster

SURVIVE TRIKATA

Req: 10% None
Prize: 2000-2500D Item: Gift of Perseverance badge
Prize: 2000-2500D Item: Gift of Perseverance badge

Battle Name	Points	Entry Fee	Teams(VS)	Prize (Valens)	Prize (Ursula)	Prohibited
Survive Trikata	-	700D	-	-	-	None
first stage	(1)	-	1 2	-	-	None
second stage	(1)	-	1 2	-	-	None
third stage	(1)	-	1 1	-	-	None
fourth stage	(1)	-	1 1	-	-	None

HAMMER OF JUSTICE

Req: 15% None
Prize: 1000-1300D Item: Hammer of Justice badge
Prize: 1000-1300D Item: Hammer of Justice badge

Battle Name	Points	Entry Fee	Teams(VS)	Prize (Valens)	Prize (Ursula)	Required
Prisoner's Appeal	(2)	250D	1-4 4	500-750D	500-750D	Two heavy units
Default Judgement	(2)	250D	1-4 3	500-750D	500-750D	Heavy units only
Judge's Orders	(2)	200D	1-2 3	500-750D	500-750D	Heavy units only
Nolo Contendre	(3)	175D	1-3 3	500-750D	500-750D	Heavy units only
Voir Dire	(3)	150D	1-2 3	500-750D	500-750D	Heavy units only

LEAGUS BELLATUS

Req: 45% None
Prize: 5000-5050D Item: None
Prize: 5000-5050D Item: None

Battle Name	Points	Entry Fee	Teams(VS)	Prize (Valens)	Prize (Ursula)	Required
Bellatus Heavy	(1)	300D	1 1	3000-3250D	3000-3250D	Heavy units only
Bellatus Heavy Chal.	(2)	300D	1 1	500-700D	500-800D	Heavy units only
Bellatus Light	(1)	300D	1 1	3000-3250D	3000-3250D	Light units only
Bellatus Light Chal.	(2)	300D	1 1	500-700D	500-800D	Light units only
Bellatus Midweight	(1)	300D	1 1	3000-3250D	3000-3250D	Medium units only
Bellatus Mid.Chal.	(2)	300D	1 1	500-700D	500-800D	Medium units only

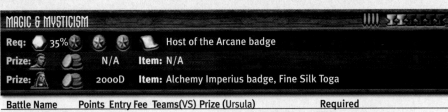

MAGIC & MYSTICISM

Req:	35%					Host of the Arcane badge	
Prize:		N/A		Item: N/A			
Prize:		2000D		Item: Alchemy Imperius badge, Fine Silk Toga			

Battle Name	Points	Entry Fee	Teams(VS)	Prize (Ursula)	Required
6 Minute Battle	(2)	500D	1-3 33	3000-4000D, Lucky Charm	Arcane units only
5 Minute Battle	(2)	500D	1-2 3	3000-4000D, Heart Star	Arcane units only
4 Minute Battle	(2)	500D	1-3 3	3000-4000D	Arcane units only
3 Minute Battle	(2)	500D	4 4	3000-5000D, Sceptrum	Arcane units only

CIRCUS INHUMANUS

Req:	20%			Circus Antiquitus badge	
Prize:		-		Item: None	
Prize:		-		Item: None	

Battle Name	Points	Entry Fee	Teams(VS)	Prize	Prohibited
Roll Out the Barrels	(2)	0D	4 3 3	-	Summoner and Undead Caster
Break the Kegs	(2)	0D	4 4	-	Summoner and Undead Caster
Dash the Course	(2)	500D	2 2 2	-	Summoner and Undead Caster
Prop Smasher	(2)	500D	2 3	-	Summoner and Undead Caster
Finish Line	(2)	500D	2 2	-	Summoner and Undead Caster

THE HAMMER OF JUSTICE

This one looks like a repeat of Nordagh's simple League of Redemption, but there's a nasty twist; after the first fight, you can only use heavy gladiators. Your opponents here are all Bandits, so the type advantage will always be theirs.

Of course, the main benefit that Bandits enjoy when battling heavy units is a significant accuracy boost for them and a serious accuracy penalty for you. But even when you only have a 5% chance of scoring a normal hit, you can't miss with a critical. So good reflexes and carefully chosen attacks (you want ones with an easy critical zone, like Strike and Combo Attack) can overcome the type mismatch here.

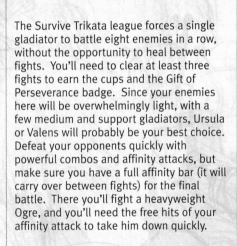

SURVIVE TRIKATA LEAGUE

The Survive Trikata league forces a single gladiator to battle eight enemies in a row, without the opportunity to heal between fights. You'll need to clear at least three fights to earn the cups and the Gift of Perseverance badge. Since your enemies here will be overwhelmingly light, with a few medium and support gladiators, Ursula or Valens will probably be your best choice. Defeat your opponents quickly with powerful combos and affinity attacks, but make sure you have a full affinity bar (it will carry over between fights) for the final battle. There you'll fight a heavyweight Ogre, and you'll need the free hits of your affinity attack to take him down quickly.

TOURNAMENT: BLOODY HALO FINALS I

Entry Fee: 2000D
Teams(VS): 4 vs. 4
Battle Points: 5
Requirement: 4 Cups
Prohibited: Summoner, Undead Caster

TOURNAMENT: BLOODY HALO FINALS II

Entry Fee: 2000D
Teams(VS): 5 vs. 5
Battle Points: 5
Requirement: 4 Cups
Prohibited: Summoner, Undead Caster

Valens
Prize: 2000-6000D per tournament
Items: None
Ursula
Prize: 2000-6000D per tournament
Items: None

The first Bloody Halo Finals is one of the easier tournaments in the game; it's a simple 4 on 4 fight, and with carefully type matching, the odds will be on your side.

The second is a bit less conventional, however. A strange structure of crates cuts through this arena, dividing the arena into four small rooms. Fortunately, it does create an opportunity for little tricks; you can set up an easy ambush near the starting point (for the majority of your party) by placing your guys in a ring near the single-crate opening. Impatient enemies will come rushing in to find themselves surrounded on three sides.

SYRNA

Ursula: Attempt to leave shortly after you arrive to trigger the event where you'll meet Valens for the first time. After that event, you'll find the Leagues have opened when you return to Theatre Antiquitis. Whether you choose to compete now or not, you'll find another event waiting when you attempt to leave town: An ambush by a pair of Summoners. Don't waste time with their summoned skeletons, instead take out the Summoners as rapidly as possible. After the first turn, a friend will appear on the scene to help... and invite you to visit his home afterwards.

CHARACTER RECRUITMENT

Name	Classification	PRM	SNG
Akil	Murmillo	1200	220
Cathistra	Legionnaire	600	75
Kaethe	Amazon	-	160
Laina	Centurion	700	75
Madlen	Legionnaire	600	55
Myrscila	Secutor	800	85
Nerita	Secutor	800	75
Ovid	Legionnaire	2000	280
Rusi	Legionnaire	600	75
Sindel	Legionnaire	650	75
Sylwan	Centurion	1200	100
Trofim	Secutor	2000	200
Venutius	Samnite	800	90
Vindicis	Secutor	825	100
Virgil	Secutor	1000	100
Waleryjan	Murmillo	775	90
Zenon	Secutor	800	85

NOTE: Cost is per recruitable character level.

PRM=Cost for permanent recruitment
SNG=Cost for single battle

SHOP: TRINKETS

General: Continue back up the path that took you to Trikata, and you'll end up in Syrna. Here you can recruit Samnites, Secutors, and perhaps a Murmillo. You can also recruit a bow-wielding Amazon, but only temporarily. With your newly received Hammer of Justice badge, you can enter the Tribunal of Brutality and earn the Justice of Syrna badge, the last prerequisite for the final "Justice" leagues in Orus and Cro Beska. This is also where you'll battle in the Imperia Championships, when you've beaten all the regional Tournaments.

It's often here, just outside of Syrna, where Althaag sets up his Accessory Shop. When you get some extra cash, pay him a visit and shop for a wide array of useful accessories.

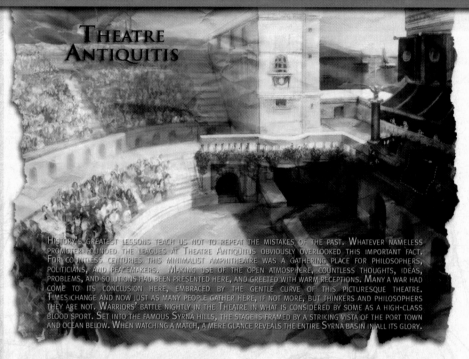

THEATRE ANTIQUITIS

HISTORY'S GREATEST LESSONS TEACH US NOT TO REPEAT THE MISTAKES OF THE PAST. WHATEVER NAMELESS PROMOTER FOUNDED THE LEAGUES AT THEATRE ANTIQUITUS OBVIOUSLY OVERLOOKED THIS IMPORTANT FACT. FOR COUNTLESS CENTURIES THIS MINIMALIST AMPHITHEATRE WAS A GATHERING PLACE FOR PHILOSOPHERS, POLITICIANS, AND PEACEMAKERS. MAKING USE OF THE OPEN ATMOSPHERE, COUNTLESS THOUGHTS, IDEAS, PROBLEMS, AND SOLUTIONS HAD BEEN PRESENTED HERE, AND GREETED WITH WARM RECEPTIONS. MANY A WAR HAD COME TO ITS CONCLUSION HERE, EMBRACED BY THE GENTLE CURVE OF THIS PICTURESQUE THEATRE. TIMES CHANGE AND NOW JUST AS MANY PEOPLE GATHER HERE, IF NOT MORE, BUT THINKERS AND PHILOSOPHERS THEY ARE NOT. WARRIORS' BATTLE NIGHTLY IN THE THEATRE IN WHAT IS CONSIDERED BY SOME AS A HIGH-CLASS BLOOD SPORT. SET INTO THE FAMOUS SYRNA HILLS, THE STAGE IS FRAMED BY A STRIKING VISTA OF THE PORT TOWN AND OCEAN BELOW. WHEN WATCHING A MATCH, A MERE GLANCE REVEALS THE ENTIRE SYRNA BASIN IN ALL ITS GLORY.

SYRNA HISTORY

Syrna is located on the western shore of Imperia between Trikata and the border with Nordagh. It is an upscale village and the summer home to many of Imperia's Senators and other wealthy families.

LEAGUE STRATEGY

CIVILIS ANTIQUITIS

With only six battle points required for victory, you can afford to pick and choose your fights. Ursula players will have the best luck versus Femina Formosos, which tends to be full of light, arcane, and support classes that your medium-heavy school can easily best. A roster full of light and arcane gladiators are your best bet versus the heavy Flabios Avengers, and a female and beast-heavy team will leave the all-Amazons School of Antonio with no targets for their male-charming tricks. The other schools have more diverse rosters, consisting mainly of Centurions, Legionnaires, and Secutors.

CIVILIS ANTIQUITIS

Req: 0% None
Prize: 1500-1650D **Item:** None
Prize: 3000-3250D **Item:** None

Battle Name	Points	Entry Fee	Teams(VS)	Prize (Valens)	Prize (Ursula)	Prohibited
Cultus Ocularis	(1)	500D	1-5 5	1500-1650D	3000-3250D	Summoner & Undead Caster
Femina Formosos	(1)	500D	1-3 3	1500-1650D	3000-3250D	Summoner & Undead Caster
Flabios Avengers	(2)	500D	1-3 4	1500-1650D	3000-3250D	Summoner & Undead Caster
Heralds of Certo	(2)	500D	1-4 6	1500-1650D	3000-3250D	Summoner & Undead Caster
School of Antonio	(3)	500D	3 5	1500-1650D	3000-3250D	Summoner & Undead Caster
Brutus Ferinus	(3)	500D	1-4 4	1500-1650D	3000-3250D	Summoner & Undead Caster

SPIRIT OF THE VALKYRIE

Req: 0% None
Prize: 6000-6500D **Item:** Honor of the Valkyrie badge, Leather Bikini, Amazon's Braceletz
Prize: 6000-6500D **Item:** Honor of the Valkyrie badge, Leather Bikini, Amazon's Bracelet

Battle Name	Points	Entry Fee	Teams(VS)	Prize (Valens)	Prize (Ursula)	Restricted
Eyes of the Valkyrie	(3)	1000D	1-3 3	1500-1650D	3000-3250D	Female only
Fists of the Valkyrie	(3)	1000D	1-3 3	1500-1650D	3000-3250D	Female only
Cunning of the Valkyrie	(3)	1000D	1-3 3	1500-1650D	1000-1100D	Female only
Force of the Valkyrie	(4)	1000D	1-3 4	1000-1300D	1000-1100D	Female only
Heart of the Valkyrie	(4)	1000D	1-4 4	1000-1100D	5000-7500D	Female only

STRENGTH OF AFFINITY

Req: 15% None
Prize: 1000-1500D **Item:** Xiphos, Visigoth Shield (x2), Praetorian Italic
Prize: 1000-1500D **Item:** Xiphos, Visigoth Shield (x2), Praetorian Italic

Battle Name	Points	Entry Fee	Teams(VS)	Prize (Valens)	Prize (Ursula)	Required
Aerus vs. Exuro	(2)	1500D	1-3 3	1000-1500D	1000-1500D	Air Affinity
Solum vs. Maritimus	(2)	1500D	1-3 5	1000-1500D	1000-1500D	Earth Affinity
Exuro vs. Aeris	(2)	1500D	1-3 4	1000-1500D	1000-1500D	Fire Affinity
Maritimus vs. Solum	(2)	1500D	1-3 2	1000-1500D	1000-1500D	Water Affinity

TRIBUNAL OF BRUTALITY

Req: 20% None
Prize: 2000-2200D **Item:** Justice of Syrna Badge
Prize: 2000-2200D **Item:** Justice of Syrna Badge

Battle Name	Points	Entry Fee	Teams(VS)	Prize (Valens)	Prize (Ursula)	Required
Syrna Tribunal	-	0D	-	-	-	Summoner & Undead Caster
first circuit	(1)	-	4 3	-	-	None
second circuit	(1)	-	1-4 3	-	-	None
third circuit	(1)	-	1-4 2	-	-	None
fourth circuit	(1)	-	1-4 3	-	-	None
final circuit	(1)	-	1-4 3	-	-	None

SYRNA'S FAVOR

Req: 10% None
Prize: N/A **Item:** N/A
Prize: 1000-1500D **Item:** None

Battle Name	Points	Entry Fee	Teams(VS)	Prize (Valens)	Prize (Ursula)	Requirement / *Prohibited
Ceteris Paribus	(2)	1000D	1-3 3	-	5000-5050D	*Summoner & Undead Caster
Ad Honorem	(2)	1500D	4 3	-	5000-5050D	*Summoner & Undead Caster
Vita Brevis	(2)	2000D	3 3	-	5000-5050D	*Summoner & Undead Caster
Docendo Discimus	(3)	2500D	4 3	-	5000-5050D	Secutor 2 or higher
Festina Lente	(3)	3000D	1-4 4	-	5000-5050D	Secutor 2 or higher
Vino Intrante	(3)	3000D	2-3 3	-	5000-5050D	Secutor 2 or higher

SPIRIT OF THE VALKYRIE

Only females can enter this league, and the maximum level cap makes coming back later in the game difficult. Ursula players should have no problem meeting the requirements by this point, but Valens may need to make an unscheduled tour of Imperia's recruiting offices. Temporarily recruiting the Amazon in Syrna's office may be tempting, but your inability to control her directly may interfere with your strategy. You're better off shopping around for female recruits that are worthy of a permanent slot in your school. A Murmillo would be ideal, since they have skills that protect them from the ranged attacks of the Amazons that you'll encounter frequently.

You'll fight all kinds of female foes in this league, but that certainly won't make it easy. In the "Eyes" and "Cunning" battles, try to claim the high ground and prepare ambushes near the few routes up to give your side a tactical advantage. Winning this league earns you some great prizes including a necessary key badge, a mountain of gold, and some equipment that will come in handy if manage to recruit an Amazon later in the game.

CIRCUS ANITQUITUS

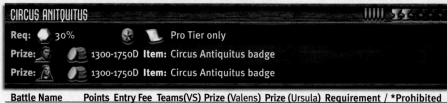

Req:	30%		Pro Tier only	
Prize:	1300-1750D	Item:	Circus Antiquitus badge	
Prize:	1300-1750D	Item:	Circus Antiquitus badge	

Battle Name	Points	Entry Fee	Teams(VS)	Prize (Valens)	Prize (Ursula)	Requirement / *Prohibited
Barrel of Fun	(2)	0D	2-3 3	3000-3250D	3000-3250D	None
Double Barreled	(2)	0D	2-3 3	3000-3250D	3000-3250D	None
Cask Task	(3)	0D	3 3	5000-5550D	5000-5550D	None
Barrel Run	(3)	0D	3 4	5000-5700D	5000-5700D	None
Mystical Hand	(3)	0D	3 3	5000-5700D	5000-5700D	None

OTHER LEAGUES

The hardest part about the **Strength of Affinity** league is meeting the entrance requirements. Of course, changing your affinity is as easy as changing your weapons, so if you have a wide variety of gear in your school's storehouse, that shouldn't be a problem. You don't actually have to use the appropriate Affinity Attacks to win.

Syrna's Favor is an all Secutor league, but it's not as easy as it sounds. There are two routes to victory: Kill all the Secutors in the first three battles, or out-Secutor your opponents in the final three. Since no one wants a roster full of Secutors (one or two are fine, but four?), we suggest the former. Your best medium fighters can take their Secutors, but only if you can prevent the Secutors from flanking you. Fall back to the wall or make an ambush spot around one of the ramps to the higher ground.

The **Tribunal of Brutality** is part of Imperia's ongoing series of Justice-themed leagues. In this series, you have to clear all five fights in a row to conquer the league and earn your badge. Fortunately, your foes consist entirely of Bandits and Citizens that will be no match for your hero and a few medium and support class friends. Use the terrain to prevent backstabs and take the Bandits out first for an easy series victory.

TOURNAMENT: SYRNA CHAMPIONSHIP

Entry Fee: 500D
Teams(VS): 3-5 vs. 4
Battle Points: 5
Required: 4 Cups
Prize: 5000-5500D
Prohibited: None

Valens
Prize: 5000-5500D
Items: None
Ursula
Prize: 5000-6000D
Items: None

Your opponents in Syrna's final tournament are exclusively Secutors. That may sound easy, but... Well, no, you're right. If you have a couple extra medium types on your team, the outnumbered Secutors won't have much of a chance. Put a Peltast on the low crate, make sure your fighters don't expose their backs, and this one is as good as done.

CHAMPIONSHIP: GRAND IMPERIA

Entry Fee: 5000D
Teams(VS): 4-6 vs. 4
Battle Points: None
Required (Badges): All Regional Championships, Glory of Imperia, Honor of the Valkyrie, & Gift of Perseverance
Prohibited: Summoner, Undead Caster

CHAMPIONSHIP: SINISTER FORCES

Entry Fee: 5000D
Teams(VS): 6 vs. 3
Battle Points: 3
Required (Badges): All Regional Championships, Glory of Imperia, Honor of the Valkyrie, & Gift of Perseverance
Prohibited: Summoner, Undead Caster

Valens
Prize: 5000-7500D per battle
Items: None
Ursula
Prize: 5000-7500D per battle
Items: None

Championship battles tend to be easier than the tournaments that preceed them, and this one is certainly no exception. If you've hit the level cap, you'll be higher level than the foes in Grand Imperia, and you already outnumber them. Position your troops to take out the Channeler, and the rest will follow.

In Sinister Forces, you do battles with a Mongrel, Ogre, and Minotaur. Bring in all the light types you can to help defeat the heavies, but even if you can't get the type advantage, your numerical advantage should lead to an easy victory. When you are ready, leave Syrna and tell Usus that you want to move on.

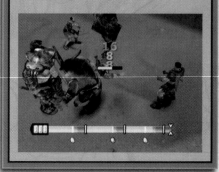

CRO BESKA

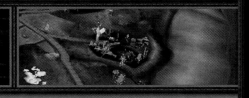

MONGREL'S MAW

THE MONGREL'S MAW WAS BUILT BY THE MONGRELS, WHO ARE ALSO ITS PRIMARY AUDIENCE. IT WAS BUILD TO MIMIC WHAT THE MONGRELS GLIMPSED OF THE CIVILIZED WORLD, BUT ANY FAME THAT THE MAW HAS GOTTEN IS PURELY FOR DISRESPECTFUL REASONS. IT WAS LAUNCHED INTO INFAMY ON THE DAY THAT 100 SLAVES WERE DECIMATED BY AN OGRE, BEFORE THE OGRE FINALLY GOT BORED AND FELL ASLEEP IN THE MIDDLE OF THE ARENA. THE REMAINING SLAVES WERE GIVEN TO FAMILIES OF MONGRELS, TO DO WITH AS THEY PLEASED. AFTER THIS EVENT, THE ARENA WAS DOOMED TO CARRY WITH IT AN UNWHOLESOME REPUTATION.

Cro Beska is the Mongrel headquarters of Imperia, and you'll run into a lot of them in the local leagues, as well as their daunting allies, the Ogres. You can't recruit Ogres (yet), but Mongrels are available for recruitment here.

If you come back for the Historians League (after beating the Mongrel Siege and then hearing about it from the shopkeeper) you can get a rare crack at enlisting a Satyr or Minotaur.

LEAGUE STRATEGY

QUARREL IN THE MAW

You can't go wrong with this league. The battles are all simple one-on-one point battles, which you should have no trouble winning if you're good at scoring critical hits and choosing optimal attacks. You only need to win one battle to take the whole league, and every battle you win gains the victor some cool class gear in addition to the cash prize.

MONGRELS UNTAMED

If you acquired the Lupus' Master badge from the Challenge of Lykos league in Belfort, you'll be able to enter the **Imperia Untamed** league. These are pretty typical beast battles, but they'll probably be your first introduction to Plainscats and Scarabs. Plainscats mix the power of Bears with the mobility of Wolves, but are low on Defense, so make them your priority targets. Scarabs have a variety of strange abilities, including the ability to dig up to almost any point on the field.

Victory at Imperia Untamed will fulfill the requirements to get into the **Mongrel Siege** league. You'll fight exclusively Mongrels and Ogres here, which is a hard combination to type-match. Backstabbing is a popular tactic here (and well loved by the

crowd), so if you start near the bottom of the arena and the terrain isn't in your favor, just fall back to the wall of the pit and let them come to you. It will deprive your foes of both the terrain advantage and the ability to stab you in the back.

THE HISTORIANS LEAGUE

After earning the Mongrel Butcher badge, head back to Scotia's and ask the Shopkeeper if there are any interesting leagues here. She'll tell you about the Historians League, which will be visiting Cro Beska seven days later. Mark down the day and remember to come back then, because if you miss it, you miss it.

The Mythic Invasion forces your four best troops to go against a pair of Minotaurs and three Satyrs. The point is not simply to kill them, but to save the three Citizens who are in the middle of the battlefield. You'll need to run your quickest units, or the Citizens will get promptly slaughtered by the speedy Satyrs. If you can beat this difficult league, you'll get a bunch of Satyr and Minotaur gear, and one of the combatants will offer to join your school if you have an open slot for them. If you don't get a Minotaur (Satyrs are easily recruitable in Nordagh), you can either try later in Syrna when you're Pro tier, or reload and battle in the Historian's League again for an even chance of getting him. (continued on page 86)

CHARACTER RECRUITMENT

Name	Classification	PRM	SNG
Aegir	Wolf	300	75
Bertha	Centurion	1000	175
Farwuq	Mongrel	500	200
Frias	Mongrel	800	250
Gioll	Bandit	750	125
Goff	Mongrel	500	500
Hagan	Samnite	650	100
Haws	Mongrel	1200	450
Liaka	Wolf	750	250
Madair	Dervish	-	250
Rima	Wolf	450	100
Toulta	Dervish	-	250
Zuzene	Dervish	-	400

NOTE: Cost is per recruitable character level.

PRM=Cost for permanent recruitment
SNG=Cost for single battle

SHOP: SCOTIA'S

CRO BESKA HISTORY

Cro Beska is the only known city in all of Imperia that the Mongrels call home. After its discovery, most Imperials stopped exploring the surrounding region due to the violent nature of the Mongrels. The only Imperials that stayed were the ones brave enough to set up a trade system with the creatures. Mongrels don't understand the wealth contained within their mines, so local humans who live on the outskirts of town trade with them what they don't want and end up living very richly because of it.

IV — CONDEMNED HOPE

This is the culmination of the "justice leagues" and is home to some of the most interesting battles in Imperia. Each of the barrels that dot the battlefield is the key to releasing a Bandit, who will fight by your side if you smash his symbolic prison. In early battles you can simply run down the weaker Mongrels, but in later fights you begin sharply outnumbered, and will need the allies to win.

Theoretically, in the later fights, the Mongrels and Ogres can destroy the barrels to prevent this, but they don't show much interest in this strategy. Soak up their relentless attacks, and concentrate on barrel removal. With enough allies, you can win even if your side only has one survivor. As much fun as this league is, it costs good money and offers nothing in return.

TOURNAMENT OF PAIN: ROUND 1

Entry Fee: 5000D
Teams(VS): 4 vs. 4
Battle Points: 2
Requirement: 4 Cups
Prohibited: Summoner, Undead Caster

TOURNAMENT OF PAIN: ROUND 2

Entry Fee: None
Teams(VS): 1-4 vs. 3
Battle Points: 2
Requirement: 4 Cups
Prohibited: Summoner, Undead Caster

TOURNAMENT OF PAIN: ROUND 3

Entry Fee: None
Teams(VS): 1-4 vs. 3
Battle Points: 2
Requirement: 4 Cups
Prohibited: Summoner, Undead Caster

Valens
Prize: 1000-1500D
Items: Stone Club, Tortoise's Scalp

Ursula
Prize: 1000-1500D
Items: Stone Club, Tortoise's Scalp

This is a three round Survival Series against ten opponents: Light units in round 1, a variety of units in round 2, and a pair of Mongrels with a high level Ogre in the final battle. It sounds daunting, but there are a number of advantages you can claim on your side. Crowd meters carry over from round to round, and the crowd loves to see a good backstab. If you bring a Secutor along (ideally one with Surprise Attack), and have him pull a few backstabs on round one, you can enjoy a full crowd meter for the rest of the fight. I like to bring a Peltast as my fourth, and move him back against the wall of the lower pit on his first turn. The Peltast will make a tempting target for your opponent, setting you up for terrain advantages from the higher step.

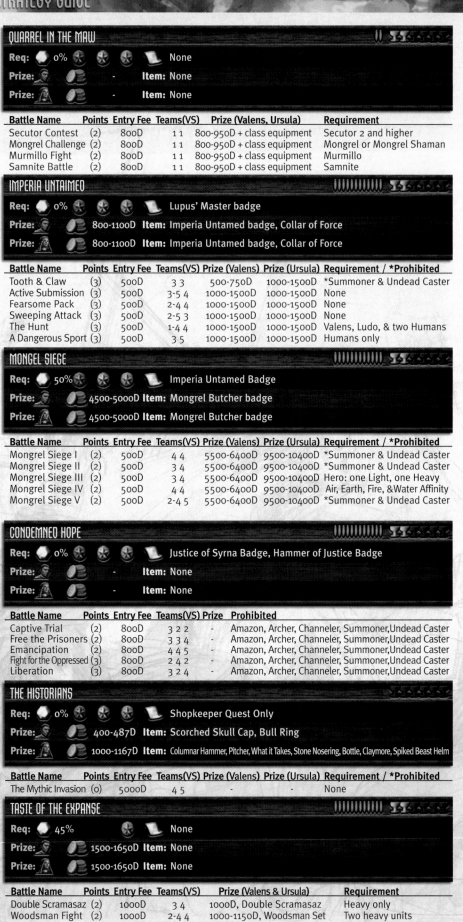

QUARREL IN THE MAW

Req:	0%						None
Prize:		-		Item: None			
Prize:		-		Item: None			

Battle Name	Points	Entry Fee	Teams(VS)	Prize (Valens, Ursula)	Requirement
Secutor Contest	(2)	800D	1 1	800-950D + class equipment	Secutor 2 and higher
Mongrel Challenge	(2)	800D	1 1	800-950D + class equipment	Mongrel or Mongrel Shaman
Murmillo Fight	(2)	800D	1 1	800-950D + class equipment	Murmillo
Samnite Battle	(2)	800D	1 1	800-950D + class equipment	Samnite

IMPERIA UNTAMED

Req:	0%					Lupus' Master badge
Prize:		800-1100D		Item: Imperia Untamed badge, Collar of Force		
Prize:		800-1100D		Item: Imperia Untamed badge, Collar of Force		

Battle Name	Points	Entry Fee	Teams(VS)	Prize (Valens)	Prize (Ursula)	Requirement / *Prohibited
Tooth & Claw	(3)	500D	3 3	500-750D	1000-1500D	*Summoner & Undead Caster
Active Submission	(3)	500D	3-5 4	1000-1500D	1000-1500D	None
Fearsome Pack	(3)	500D	2-4 4	1000-1500D	1000-1500D	None
Sweeping Attack	(3)	500D	2-5 3	1000-1500D	1000-1500D	None
The Hunt	(3)	500D	1-4 4	1000-1500D	1000-1500D	Valens, Ludo, & two Humans
A Dangerous Sport	(3)	500D	3 5	1000-1500D	1000-1500D	Humans only

MONGEL SIEGE

Req:	50%					Imperia Untamed Badge
Prize:		4500-5000D		Item: Mongrel Butcher badge		
Prize:		4500-5000D		Item: Mongrel Butcher badge		

Battle Name	Points	Entry Fee	Teams(VS)	Prize (Valens)	Prize (Ursula)	Requirement / *Prohibited
Mongrel Siege I	(2)	500D	4 4	5500-6400D	9500-10400D	*Summoner & Undead Caster
Mongrel Siege II	(2)	500D	3 4	5500-6400D	9500-10400D	*Summoner & Undead Caster
Mongrel Siege III	(2)	500D	3 4	5500-6400D	9500-10400D	Hero: one Light, one Heavy
Mongrel Siege IV	(2)	500D	4 4	5500-6400D	9500-10400D	Air, Earth, Fire, & Water Affinity
Mongrel Siege V	(2)	500D	2-4 5	5500-6400D	9500-10400D	*Summoner & Undead Caster

CONDEMNED HOPE

Req:	0%					Justice of Syrna Badge, Hammer of Justice Badge
Prize:		-		Item: None		
Prize:		-		Item: None		

Battle Name	Points	Entry Fee	Teams(VS)	Prize	Prohibited
Captive Trial	(2)	800D	3 2 2	-	Amazon, Archer, Channeler, Summoner, Undead Caster
Free the Prisoners	(2)	800D	3 3 4	-	Amazon, Archer, Channeler, Summoner, Undead Caster
Emancipation	(2)	800D	4 4 5	-	Amazon, Archer, Channeler, Summoner, Undead Caster
Fight for the Oppressed	(3)	800D	2 4 2	-	Amazon, Archer, Channeler, Summoner, Undead Caster
Liberation	(3)	800D	3 2 4	-	Amazon, Archer, Channeler, Summoner, Undead Caster

THE HISTORIANS

Req:	0%				Shopkeeper Quest Only
Prize:		400-487D		Item: Scorched Skull Cap, Bull Ring	
Prize:		1000-1167D		Item: Columnar Hammer, Pitcher, What it Takes, Stone Nosering, Bottle, Claymore, Spiked Beast Helm	

Battle Name	Points	Entry Fee	Teams(VS)	Prize (Valens)	Prize (Ursula)	Requirement / *Prohibited
The Mythic Invasion	(0)	5000D	4 5	-	-	None

TASTE OF THE EXPANSE

Req:	45%			None
Prize:		1500-1650D		Item: None
Prize:		1500-1650D		Item: None

Battle Name	Points	Entry Fee	Teams(VS)	Prize (Valens & Ursula)	Requirement
Double Scramasaz	(2)	1000D	3 4	1000D, Double Scramasaz	Heavy only
Woodsman Fight	(2)	1000D	2-4 4	1000-1150D, Woodsman Set	Two heavy units
Dual Pugio	(2)	1000D	1-4 4	1000-1150D, Dual Pugio	Dervish only
Cote Fez	(2)	1000D	1-2 3	1000-1150D, Cote Fez	Dervish only

ORUS

EXURO'S EYE IS PROBABLY THE MOST DANGEROUS ARENA IN IMPERIA—AND NOT JUST BECAUSE OF THE KINDS OF FIGHTS HELD IN IT. THE BATTLEFIELD OF THE EYE IS ACTUALLY NESTLED INSIDE THE CONE OF THE VOLCANO ADURO. ADURO HASN'T ERUPTED IN ABOUT 150 YEARS, BUT AS THE PEOPLE OF ORUS SAY, "KEEP YOUR EYE ON THE EYE." THROUGHOUT THE PLAYFIELD ARE FISSURES AND POOLS OF LAVA WHICH SOMETIMES SPEW FORTH FIRE AND LAVA ONTO THE GLADIATORS. AND EVEN THOUGH THEY'RE ABOUT TWO HEADS HIGHER THAN THE FLOOR OF THE ARENA, IT'S NOT UNCOMMON FOR THE AUDIENCE TO SOMETIMES BE HIT AS WELL.

EXURO'S EYE

You'll find the town of Orus over the bridge south of Caltha, and far to the east. Two leagues will be open to you on your first visit, but the other leagues here require two badges from other cities in Imperia. You can't enter the tournament without clearing at least one of these special leagues, so you probably shouldn't visit Orus until late in the chapter, when you'll have the badges you need.

CHARACTER RECRUITMENT

Name	Classification	PRM	SNG
Agyieus	Murmillo	1200	250
Bartorius	Secutor	1200	220
Donat	Samnite	1050	140
Evander	Legionnaire	1010	200
Gregorios	Samnite	1015	700
Juterna	Secutor	1010	200
Patulik	Mongrel	800	70
Tancorix	Murmillo	1300	200
Theophilius	Centurion	1075	750

NOTE: Cost is per recruitable character level.

PRM=Cost for permanent recruitment
SNG=Cost for single battle

SHOP: THE FORGE OF EXURO

LEAGUE STRATEGY

THE OPEN LEAGUES

The **Assembly of Imperia** features strange restrictions and preset enemies. If you have a wide selection of gladiators to choose from, it's easy to hammer out a victory by picking battles where your side has the type advantage. Brutus Atrox pits your heavy gladiators against their Legionnaires, and Mongrel Band will pit your best medium fighters against a pack of light Mongrels. Masters of the Arcane is a battle versus a group of Channelers, which is usually an easy win for an aggressive, mobile team.

The **Civilis League** is just a bunch of simple, random battles. You only need four battle points to win this league, so use type matching to score an easy victory in the one-on-one Civilis Orus V, and then beat any other battle for the cups.

THE SPECIAL LEAGUES

The culmination of the Beast leagues, **Fury & Flame** puts the numerical odds in your favor, as you battle against an exotic variety of enemies. If you can meet the requirements, you can probably win these fights, so they make good training bouts for your new recruits. Among the interesting match-ups are a 3 on 1 battle versus a Cyclops (Embers of Exuro), and a 2 on 1 fight against a Minotaur (Curses of Miscreation). Your own heavy units should easily overpower the Cyclops, while your light units will make short work of the Minotaur. *(continued on page 88)*

ORUS HISTORY

Orus is located high in the Cardis mountains, under the shadows of the volcano Aduro. The Eye is one attraction, but another draw to Orus is the hot springs at the base of the Volcano Aduro. There are many spas in Orus, so gladiators who are looking for some pampering after a hard battle can head to the base of the mountain and take a night in the spas. For these reasons, Orus became popular among the high class of Imperia, as well as rich foreigners traveling the region.

The **Fires of Justice** is another league that requires both justice badges. This one's a lot less interesting than Cro Beska's Condemned Hope; you fight nothing but high level Bandits. The twist is the entrance requirements, which make type-matching difficult. But as always, any mismatch can be overcome with a hearty series of critical hits.

The **Onslaught** requires the Badge of Perpetuity and the Gift of Perseverance, two hard-to-get series badges. Like Orus' tournament, this difficult Survival Series forces you to fight a series of enemies while unreachable Archers pelt you with arrows. Ursula players who have raised a Murmillo with Incoming! and recruited an Undead Legionnaire should use them for the natural defenses against projectiles. The best Valens can do is probably a Murmillo or two with Arrow Guard. Note that the Archers don't play favorites, so if you keep your enemies between you and them, your enemies will take the hits while you escape unscathed. Careful positioning is the key to this series.

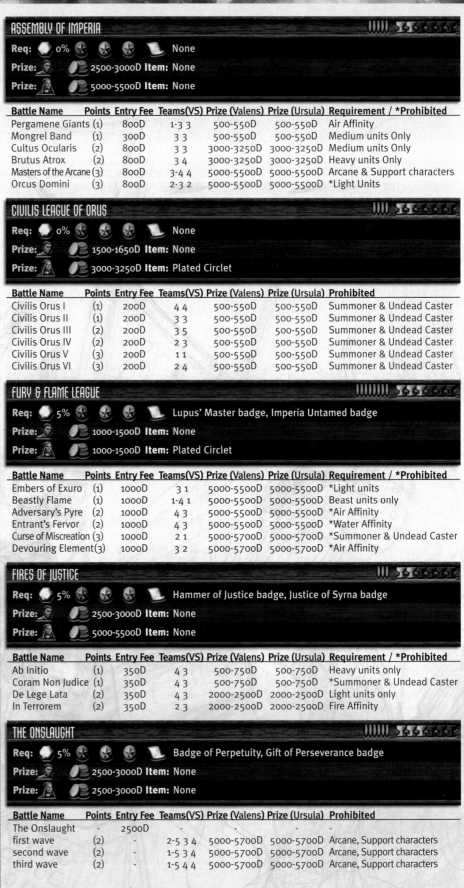

ASSEMBLY OF IMPERIA

Req:	0%			None
Prize:	2500-3000D	Item: None		
Prize:	5000-5500D	Item: None		

Battle Name	Points	Entry Fee	Teams(VS)	Prize (Valens)	Prize (Ursula)	Requirement / *Prohibited
Pergamene Giants (1)	800D	1-3 3		500-550D	500-550D	Air Affinity
Mongrel Band (1)	300D	3 3		500-550D	500-550D	Medium units Only
Cultus Ocularis (2)	800D	3 3		3000-3250D	3000-3250D	Medium units Only
Brutus Atrox (2)	800D	3 4		3000-3250D	3000-3250D	Heavy units Only
Masters of the Arcane (3)	800D	3-4 4		5000-5500D	5000-5500D	Arcane & Support characters
Orcus Domini (3)	800D	2-3 2		5000-5500D	5000-5500D	*Light Units

CIVILIS LEAGUE OF ORUS

Req:	0%			None
Prize:	1500-1650D	Item: None		
Prize:	3000-3250D	Item: Plated Circlet		

Battle Name	Points	Entry Fee	Teams(VS)	Prize (Valens)	Prize (Ursula)	Prohibited
Civilis Orus I	(1)	200D	4 4	500-550D	500-550D	Summoner & Undead Caster
Civilis Orus II	(1)	200D	3 3	500-550D	500-550D	Summoner & Undead Caster
Civilis Orus III	(2)	200D	3 5	500-550D	500-550D	Summoner & Undead Caster
Civilis Orus IV	(2)	200D	2 3	500-550D	500-550D	Summoner & Undead Caster
Civilis Orus V	(3)	200D	1 1	500-550D	500-550D	Summoner & Undead Caster
Civilis Orus VI	(3)	200D	2 4	500-550D	500-550D	Summoner & Undead Caster

FURY & FLAME LEAGUE

Req:	5%			Lupus' Master badge, Imperia Untamed badge
Prize:	1000-1500D	Item: None		
Prize:	1000-1500D	Item: Plated Circlet		

Battle Name	Points	Entry Fee	Teams(VS)	Prize (Valens)	Prize (Ursula)	Requirement / *Prohibited
Embers of Exuro	(1)	1000D	3 1	5000-5500D	5000-5500D	*Light units
Beastly Flame	(1)	1000D	1-4 1	5000-5500D	5000-5500D	Beast units only
Adversary's Pyre	(2)	1000D	4 3	5000-5500D	5000-5500D	*Air Affinity
Entrant's Fervor	(2)	1000D	4 3	5000-5500D	5000-5500D	*Water Affinity
Curse of Miscreation (3)		1000D	2 1	5000-5700D	5000-5700D	*Summoner & Undead Caster
Devouring Element (3)		1000D	3 2	5000-5700D	5000-5700D	*Air Affinity

FIRES OF JUSTICE

Req:	5%			Hammer of Justice badge, Justice of Syrna badge
Prize:	2500-3000D	Item: None		
Prize:	5000-5500D	Item: None		

Battle Name	Points	Entry Fee	Teams(VS)	Prize (Valens)	Prize (Ursula)	Requirement / *Prohibited
Ab Initio	(1)	350D	4 3	500-750D	500-750D	Heavy units only
Coram Non Judice (1)		350D	4 3	500-750D	500-750D	*Summoner & Undead Caster
De Lege Lata	(2)	350D	4 3	2000-2500D	2000-2500D	Light units only
In Terrorem	(2)	350D	2 3	2000-2500D	2000-2500D	Fire Affinity

THE ONSLAUGHT

Req:	5%			Badge of Perpetuity, Gift of Perseverance badge
Prize:	2500-3000D	Item: None		
Prize:	2500-3000D	Item: None		

Battle Name	Points	Entry Fee	Teams(VS)	Prize (Valens)	Prize (Ursula)	Prohibited
The Onslaught	-	2500D	-	-	-	-
first wave	(2)	-	2-5 3 4	5000-5700D	5000-5700D	Arcane, Support characters
second wave	(2)	-	1-5 3 4	5000-5700D	5000-5700D	Arcane, Support characters
third wave	(2)	-	1-5 4 4	5000-5700D	5000-5700D	Arcane, Support characters

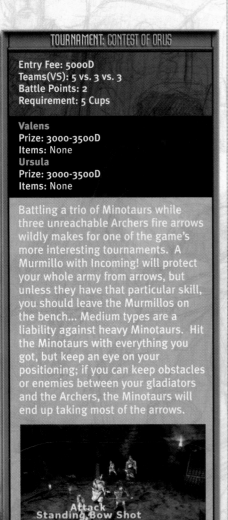

TOURNAMENT: CONTEST OF ORUS

Entry Fee: 5000D
Teams(VS): 5 vs. 3 vs. 3
Battle Points: 2
Requirement: 5 Cups

Valens
Prize: 3000-3500D
Items: None
Ursula
Prize: 3000-3500D
Items: None

Battling a trio of Minotaurs while three unreachable Archers fire arrows wildly makes for one of the game's more interesting tournaments. A Murmillo with Incoming! will protect your whole army from arrows, but unless they have that particular skill, you should leave the Murmillos on the bench... Medium types are a liability against heavy Minotaurs. Hit the Minotaurs with everything you got, but keep an eye on your positioning; if you can keep obstacles or enemies between your gladiators and the Archers, the Minotaurs will end up taking most of the arrows.

Attack
Standing Bow Shot

CHAPTER III

WINDWARD STEPPES

THE WASTES

ONONHAAR

ALTAHRUN

YUSET

THE WASTES
(VARIABLE)

HISTORY These barren and seemingly endless plains were virtually uninhabited for many years, but all that changed once a handful of brave adventurers carved trails through the imposing Baitan Mountains. This finally opened the rest of the lands to the massive plateau of the Windward Steppes. Unlike Nordagh and Imperia, however, the Steppes never became densely populated; instead, its citizens live in traveling tented communities. During the Imperial conquests, this vast land was the first to be subjugated by Imperia's massive army, because there was little organized resistance.

After the Great War, the Imperial military occupation retreated. The Windward Steppes is now the home of nomads and outcasts. It can be a dangerous place, filled with bandits and others who prey upon travelers for their way of life.

Now there is limited access to the Steppes through a few well-traveled mountain passes. And only adventure seekers and expertly trained gladiator schools spend their time wandering through these plains because the merchants here have access to goods from many far away lands. Strange and powerful weapons can be purchased in the Windward Steppes and these items have been showing up in the games in Imperia.

YUSET

ARENA SUREN

ARENA SUREN IS BUILT IN THE SHADOW OF ONE OF THE SIGNATURE TOWERING ROCK STRUCTURES FOUND THROUGHOUT THE WINDWARD STEPPES. ONE OF THE LARGER FORMATIONS, IT HAS A SERIES OF CAVES AT THE BOTTOM. LONG AGO, A BEAST-MASTER NAMED SUREN KEPT HIS PRIDE OF HIDEOUS MONSTERS IN THESE CAVES. AFTER HE DIED, A GROUP OF TRAVELING NOMADS FOUND THE GATED ENTRANCES TO THE CAVES AND DECIDED TO EXPLORE THE DEPTHS WITHIN. IN THE DARKNESS OF THE CAVES, THE BEASTS MADE QUICK WORK OF THE WANDERERS. DAYS LATER, A GROUP OF NOMADS FOUND ONE OF THE SURVIVORS, STAGGERING THROUGH THE WASTES IN A STATE OF SHOCK. AFTER HEARING THE TALES OF THE BEASTS, THE NOMADS DECIDED TO CAMP NEAR THE ROCK FORMATION IN ORDER TO INVESTIGATE THE CAVES. BUT THESE FIRST NOMADS NEVER BUILT UP THE COURAGE TO EXPLORE THE DANGEROUS CAVERNS. AS THE TALE OF THE MONSTERS SPREAD THROUGHOUT THE NOMAD COMMUNITY, MORE AND MORE PEOPLE SETTLED ON THE OUTSKIRTS OF YUSET, NEAR THE IMPOSING ROCK STRUCTURE AND CAVES. AFTER MANY YEARS THE TALL TALES OF THE BEASTS CONTAINED WITHIN THE CAVES HAD BEEN ELEVATED TO SUCH HEIGHTS THAT NOBODY DARED TO ENTER THE CAVERNS. IT WASN'T UNTIL A GROUP OF WARRIORS FROM IMPERIA CAME TO INVESTIGATE AND PROVE THEMSELVES AS HEROES, THAT A GROUP WAS FINALLY ORGANIZED TO EXPLORE THE CAVES. ALL THEY FOUND WERE THE REMAINS OF THE VICTIMS OF THE NOW LEGENDARY MONSTERS. UNABLE TO PROVE THEIR MIGHT BY SLAYING THE LEGENDARY BEASTS, THE WARRIORS DECIDED TO FENCE THE AREA OFF AND HOLD GLADIATORIAL FIGHTS UPON THE PLAIN AT THE FOOT OF THE ROCK WALL. THE GAMES HAVE BEEN A TRADITION HERE EVER SINCE.

A s soon as you arrive in Yuset, the locals will force you to enlist an Archer in your ranks. You'll find a promising recruit, Eiji, in the outskirts of town, but that's no reason not to recruit another, if you see a good one in the recruiting office. Eiji is more of an Amazon anyway, and doesn't have access to a lot of good Archer skills.

In addition to Archers, you can recruit an Ogre (a Samnite-esque heavy unit) and a pair of Plainscats here. When your troop is ready, enter the Archer Nya league and clear all three battles to earn your Talisman.

CHARACTER RECRUITMENT

Name	Classification	PRM	SNG
Bhetak	Bandit	900	90
Ekaterina	Plainscat	9000	90
Fjorgyn	Wolf	950	95
Heirax	Ogre	1100	110
Jhunago	Samnite	1100	110
Jogesh	Wolf	1150	115
Kassar	Archer	1050	105
Mehkari	Samnite	1050	105
Nukus	Plainscat	1000	100
Qhualo	Secutor	900	90
Qhurin	Bandit	850	85
Vakga	Ogre	1050	105

NOTE: Cost is per recruitable character level.

PRM=Cost for permanent recruitment
SNG=Cost for single battle

SHOP: OUGER'S IMPORTS

After that, you'll have to attempt the Featherweight Fight battle of the King of the Hill Ke, before the other leagues open up. (The Heavyweight league won't appear until you complete the Lightweight league in the Wastes.)

You have almost no freedom in choosing your path in the Steppes. Each town's Tournament prize is a prerequisite for each other town's leagues, so you'll need to complete the towns in the following order: Yuset, Altahrun, The Wastes and Ononhaar.

YUSET HISTORY

The biggest city in the Steppes, Yuset has been partially stripped of its heritage after its occupation by the Imperial army. One remnant of its past is the giant archway at the city's end, where a constant nomad presence resides. As one group of nomads moves on, another moves in and the cycle continues in the hope that their ancient culture will not be totally forgotten. Other than being a nomad stronghold, Yuset is surrounded on both sides by the Baitan mountain range with rolling hills and cliffs alike. Yuset is not a very hospitable place for visitors from other lands, as the constant flow of nomads through the town gives the locals all they need to survive. But those who persevere will find that this unique town has much to offer that cannot be found elsewhere in the lands of Gladius .

LEAGUE STRATEGY

ARCHER NYA

Most of your opponents begin with a significant terrain advantage, so if your plan is to stay on the ground and trade projectiles, you're going to loose. Remember that Murmillos and Undead Legionnaires have skills that make them resistant to projectiles, and because you'll be seeing a lot of support characters from this point on, they'll be key players. Teach your Murmillo Arrow Guard (and Incoming! if possible), and have him or her lead the charge on the hill (accompanied by allies with high defense and mobility) in round 1.

The Peltast and Gungnir battles are a little easier, because you're usually safe from enemy-ranged attacks when you're at the foot of the hill.

ARCHER NYA

Req:	0%			None
Prize:		100-1000D	**Item:** Archer Nya Talisman, Flaming Bow, Tono
Prize:		100-1000D	**Item:** Archer Nya Talisman, Flaming Bow, Tono

Battle Name	Points	Entry Fee	Teams(VS)	Prize	Item	Prohibited
Archers Ke	(1)	0D	4 4	1000-1500D	War Hero	Summoner & Undead Caster
Imperia Peltasts Hyo	(1)	0D	5 5	1200-1800D	Ansuz	Summoner & Undead Caster
Nordagh Gungnir Ju	(1)	0D	6 6	1500-2300D	Master's Belt	Summoner & Undead Caster

KING OF THE HILL KE

Req:	0%			Archer Nya Talisman
Prize:		5000-15000D	**Item:** Sligi, Weighted Mallet, Beast's Shield, Worn Attic
Prize:		5000-15000D	**Item:** Sligi, Weighted Mallet, Beast's Shield, Worn Attic

Battle Name	Points	Entry Fee	Teams(VS)	Prize	Requirement /*Prohibited
Featherweight Threat	(2)	0D	4 4 4	2500D	Ursula, Valens, Urlan & Ludo only
Hilltopper Rywigo	(3)	0D	4 4 4	2500D	*Summoner & Undead Caster
Hilltopper Chi	(2)	0D	4 4 4	2500D	*Summoner & Undead Caster
Open Throne Gyo	(2)	0D	4 4 4	2500D	*Summoner & Undead Caster
Moving Mountains Kwo	(2)	0D	4 4 4	2500D	*Summoner & Undead Caster

BEAST ZA

Req:	0%			Archer Nya Talisman
Prize:		250-2750D	**Item:** Leather Collar, Jade, Silken Collar
Prize:		250-2750D	**Item:** Leather Collar, Jade, Silken Collar

Battle Name	Points	Entry Fee	Teams(VS)	Prize	Requirement
Circus Bears	(2)	0D	2-4 4	100-500D	Barbarian, Gungnir, Urlan only.
Frisky Cats	(2)	0D	2-4 4	100-500D	Barbarian, Gungnir, Urlan only.
Greater Beasts Chi	(3)	0D	2-4 2	100-500D	Barbarian, Gungnir, Urlan only.
Weary Wolves	(2)	0D	2-4 4	100-500D	Barbarian, Gungnir, Urlan only.
Wild Beasts	(2)	0D	2-3 2 3 2	100-500D	Barbarian, Gungnir, Urlan only.

INFLATIONARY EGOS SU

Req:	15%			Archer Nya Talisman
Prize:		250-2750D	**Item:** Inflationary Egos Su badge, Lion's Pride, The Cat's Claw
Prize:		250-2750D	**Item:** Inflationary Egos Su badge, Lion's Pride, The Cat's Claw

Battle Name	Points	Entry Fee	Teams(VS)	Prize	Prohibited
Heavy Hitters Ra	(3)	0D	3 3 3	200-1000D	Summoner & Undead Caster
Limelight Ni	(1)	0D	3 3	200-1000D	Summoner & Undead Caster
Vandal Tu	(2)	0D	3 3	200-1000D	Summoner & Undead Caster
Vandal Zo	(2)	0D	2 3	200-1000D	Summoner & Undead Caster
Confrontation Mu	(1)	0D	3 3 3	200-1000D	Summoner & Undead Caster

HEAVYWEIGHT GVU

Req:	0%			Lightweight badge
Prize:		200-5000D	**Item:** Crescent Moon, Horned Shield, Horned Thracian, Dervish's Scalp
Prize:		200-5000D	**Item:** Crescent Moon, Horned Shield, Horned Thracian, Dervish's Scalp

Battle Name	Points	Entry Fee	Teams(VS)	Prize	Item
Monster Mayhem	(1)	0D	5 5	-	Horned Shield, Strength Armor Prohibited: Summoner & Undead Caster
Open Season Bya	(2)	0D	3 3 3 3	300-4000D	Armored Suit, Tou-Fung Prohibited: Summoner & Undead Caster
Ssimas Toys Gwa	(1)	0D	5 5	-	Decorated Iron Plate, Casus Prohibited: Summoner & Undead Caster

Bring some heavies to the Nordagh Gungnir Ju fight, because the Gungnirs will turn into bears as soon as they lose their line-of-sight.

KING OF THE HILL KE

A hill with eight spots makes for some strange King of the Hill battles. You want to get as many of your guys on the hill as possible, positioned so they can attack and kill hillmates from opposing teams. Characters with access to ranged abilities are good here, and make sure to focus your attack on the weakest link of whatever team is doing best. If you can get three tough fighters on the hill, and take out one or two of your opponents, you'll be in good shape. In later bouts, where enemies get heavier and tougher, you might want to change your strategy and simply try to score points by getting there first and using skills like On Guard to run down the clock. Note that in addition to the cash prizes, each of these battles awards the winning team with a random piece of equipment.

INFLATIONARY EGOS SU

This league offers two standard battles, two Vandal battles and a Points Battle. Completing it is a necessity, since the Inflationary Egos Su badge is one of the prerequisites to enter the Steppes Championship.

The Points Battle is worth three battle points, so it's well worth the difficulty of jousting with two heavy gladiator-filled teams. Use heavies of your own, especially ones who can hit multiple foes with skills like Sweeping Attack. You might also want to use Ursula, whose Spell Blast can be an instant win, or any Archers who know the Volley skill. Note that hit points are unlimited here, so don't worry about losing your heavy hitters. Protect Ursula from the heavies' powerful strikes and let her unleash spells from a distance.

In the Vandal Battles, Archers make great teammates, for their ability to smash barrels from a long distance away. Target the ones closest to your opponents first to slow their plans down.

SINGH LIS THAN TOURNAMENT: ATTACK OF THE BEASTS
Entry Fee: 0D
Teams(VS): 5 vs. 4
Battle Points: 2
Requirement: 2 Cups
Prohibited: Summoner, Undead Caster

SINGH LIS THAN TOURNAMENT: ARROWS OF FIRE
Entry Fee: 5000D
Teams(VS): 1-5 vs. 5
Battle Points: 1
Requirement: 2 Cups
Prohibited: Summoner, Undead Caster

SINGH LIS THAN TOURNAMENT: QO'AI-MARAEL PROS
Entry Fee: 5000D
Teams(VS): 1-5 vs. 5
Battle Points: 1
Requirement: 2 Cups
Prohibited: Summoner, Undead Caster

SINGH LIS THAN TOURNAMENT: BLAZING INFERNO
Entry Fee: 5000D
Teams(VS): 1-5 vs. 5
Battle Points: 1
Requirement: 2 Cups
Prohibited: Summoner, Undead Caster

Ursula / Valens
Prize: 500-10000D
Items: Legacy of Singh Iis Than, Half Moon, Silk Cap, Ingwaz, Dadao

In this grueling Endurance battle, you have to slog your way through four rounds and 19 total enemies. Round 1 is a variety of beasts and often the hardest battle. Take out the Plainscats first, then the Bears, as they represent the deadliest combatants. Round two is heavy on Archers and Secutors, some of which may begin on the hills. Take out the easy prey first, then send runners after the snipers. Round 3 is a mixed bag, featuring everything from Ogres to Channelers to Undead Legionnaires. Fortunately, you can win this tricky round instantly if you manage to defeat Ssima the Channeler. Your final opponents are a tough squad of Imperial warriors, heavy on the Samnites. Good luck, you'll definitely need it.

ALTAHRUN

ALTAHRUN RUINS

Follow the path from Yuset, and turn right at both forks to reach Altahrun. The Legacy of Singh Iis Than badge, won at the Yuset Tournament, is the key to entering the Jochi Affinity league. And, the Jochi Affinity Talisman you win there is the key to everything else in Altahrun (except the Mystical Zo league, which has no requirements). You need to win the Dreamcatcher badge from the tournaments here before you can enter any leagues in the Wastes, which is further east of Altahrun.

SHOPKEEPER QUEST

There is a shopkeeper quest of sorts here, although the only thing you win for it is grief. Talk to Tolui at the Crag after clearing the Jochi Affinity League, and ask her if there are any special battles going on. She'll schedule one for four days later, in the History of the Frontier league. It's called a "Ringer" battle, and the point is to kill each other team's leaders without losing yours. Stay far away from the two teams in the west, and concentrate on killing the leader of the nearby team, until one team loses on the other side of the field. Your only prize is the equipment you win from the battle, and a lot of backtalk from Tolui the next time you speak to her.

LEAGUE STRATEGY

JOCHI AFFINITY SERIES

Underneath all the purple electricity shenanigans, the Dark Legionnaires you face in the first round of this series aren't much different from regular Legionnaires. They don't do too much damage, but you'll need to use accurate attacks and score some critical hits to penetrate their strong armor. The second match-up is against a pack of beasts, so swap out the medium types and bring in the heavy hitters (and a support character or two). The same squad will be effective against the single Greater Plainscat in the third round.

In the final two rounds, you'll be battling against two teams of enemies. You start right in the middle, and there's no easy way (continued on page 94)

CHARACTER RECRUITMENT

Name	Classification	PRM	SNG
Andijon	Wolf	850	85
Grahbek	Mongrel	1050	105
Ihnku	Archer	1200	120
Jucha	Bandit	900	90
Khaidu	Secutor	1000	100
Kipqhua	Samnite	1150	115
Ohlimad	Mongrel Shaman	1100	110
Plexaura	Channeler	1100	110
Sahlu	Bear	950	95
Xokhu	Mongrel	900	90
Yhata	Mongrel Shaman	-	95

NOTE: Cost is per recruitable character level.

PRM=Cost for permanent recruitment
SNG=Cost for single battle

SHOP: THE CRAG

ALTAHRUN HISTORY

The Altahrun Ruins is the oldest site in all of the lands to host battles. The details of the construction of the arena are lost in the annals of time, but it is said that the cities here once rivaled those in Imperia.

of making them fight each other. If you try to start on the little log at the south end of the placeable area, you'll just end up with no room to maneuver when both teams come gunning for you. Suck it up and fight 'em both.

HISTORY OF THE FRONTIER

If you recruit a Cyclops into your school, you'll be glad you conquered this league. Everyone will have to do this league eventually, as the badge you receive is one of the prerequisites for entering the Championships.

The first battle is a standard brawl, at least as standard as any fight with the undead can be. Use your Affinity Specialists and blast them out of the game. The second fight adds a twist: statues that rotate around breathing fire on adjacent squares. They're easy to avoid if you keep an eye on them, and it can be fun to trap clueless opponents in their path. The other battles are pretty standard stuff, just form a strong defense and let your foes come for you.

JOCHI AFFINITY

Req:	0%			Legacy of Singh Iis Tahn
Prize:	250-7000D		**Item:** Jochi Affinity Talisman, Death's Head, Horn Hammer
Prize:	250-7000D		**Item:** Jochi Affinity Talisman, Death's Head, Horn Hammer

Battle Name	Points	Entry Fee	Teams(VS)	Prize	Requirement / Prohibited
Jochi Affinity Series	-	oD	-	-	-
Enter the Darkness	(1)	oD	1-4 4	-	None
Beasts Rule Mu	(1)	oD	1-4 4	-	None
Air Extra Tyo	(1)	oD	1-4 1	-	None
Lone Well He	(1)	oD	1-4 2 2	-	None
Darkness Rising	(1)	oD	1-4 2 2	-	None

MYSTICAL ZO

Req:	0%			Archer Nya Talisman
Prize:		oD	**Item:** Scorched Skull Cap, Warrior Del, Traveler's Verse
Prize:		oD	**Item:** Scorched Skull Cap, Warrior Del, Traveler's Verse

Battle Name	Points	Entry Fee	Teams(VS)	Prize	Requirement
Undead Spellcasters	(3)	oD	1-4 4	300-4300D	Arcane only
Galdr Spellcasters	(2)	oD	1-4 4	300-4300D	Arcane only
Mongrel Madness	(1)	oD	1-4 4	300-4300D	Arcane only
Summoners Styx	(3)	oD	1-4 4	300-4300D	Arcane only
Channeler Spellcasters	(2)	oD	1-4 4	300-4300D	Arcane level 10 only

HISTORY OF THE FRONTIER

Req:	5%			Jochi Affinity Talisman
Prize:		oD	**Item:** History of the Frontier badge, Scorched Skull Cap, Blindman's Eye
Prize:		oD	**Item:** History of the Frontier badge, Scorched Skull Cap, Blindman's Eye

Battle Name	Points	Entry Fee	Teams(VS)	Prize	Items
Battle for Habaas River	(1)	oD	5 5	700-4000D	Ivory Anklet, Scalemail Guard Silk Cap, Warlord's Shield **Prohibited:** Summoner, Undead Caster
Battle for Volcano Aduro	(1)	oD	5 5	350-5850D	Xan, Snakeskin Armband, Horned Shield **Prohibited:** Summoner, Undead Caster
Battle for Ultasan Gorge	(1)	oD	4 4	400-5000D	Full Del, Recurve Bow, Silk Cap **Prohibited:** Summoner, Undead Caster
Imperial Ringers	(o)	oD	3 3 2 3	400-500D	Horned Thracian, Liberation, Throwing Axe **Required:** From Imperia Only **Prohibited:** Summoner, Undead Caster
Nordagh Ringers	(o)	oD	3 3 2 3	400-500D	Horned Thracian, Liberation, Platemail Bikini **Required:** From Nordagh Only **Prohibited:** Summoner, Undead Caster
Repel the Yetis	(1)	oD	4 4	200-6000D	Poison Axe, Silk Fez, Jade, Hard Leather Shield **Prohibited:** Summoner, Undead Caster

MINIONS OF THE DARK GOD

Req:	5%			Jochi Affinity Talisman
Prize:		oD	**Item:** Warlord's Shield, Casus, Phoenix Feather
Prize:		oD	**Item:** Warlord's Shield, Casus, Phoenix Feather

Battle Name	Points	Entry Fee	Teams(VS)	Prize	Items
All His Children Ga	(1)	oD	5 5	250-2000D	Horse Tooth **Prohibited:** Summoner, Undead Caster
Dark Beasts Hyu	(1)	oD	4 4	350-3350D	Fang, Sligi, Rounded Axe, Flaming Bow **Prohibited:** Summoner, Undead Caster
Dark Militia Bu	(1)	oD	4 4	350-3350D	Fang, Sligi, Rounded Axe, Flaming Bow **Prohibited:** Summoner, Undead Caster
Dark Militia Ji	(1)	oD	5 5	350-3350D	Fang, Sligi, Rounded Axe, Flaming Bow **Prohibited:** Summoner, Undead Caster
Dark Militia Tya	(1)	oD	5 5	350-3350D	Fang, Sligi, Rounded Axe, Flaming Bow **Prohibited:** Summoner, Undead Caster
Mutations Wo	(1)	oD	4 3	350-3350D	Fang, Sligi, Rounded Axe, Flaming Bow **Prohibited:** Summoner, Undead Caster

OTHER LEAGUES

The **Minions of the Dark God** league is a rare (and disgusting) opportunity to see Dark Beasts. These foul creatures are as deadly as their non-evil counterparts, but with access to a few powerful techniques that can cause mass Affinity Drain and Petrification. The statues in the final battle cast Tornado every turn, scrambling the positions of everyone near them. Since you'll be using high mobility light characters against your heavy Cyclops foes, this can only work to your advantage.

You'll need at least a trio of Arcane characters to have a shot at **Mystical Zo**, but you won't lose out on much, prize-wise, if you skip it. If you do choose to challenge it, use as many Channelers as you can (they should be easy to recruit locally), and dominate your foes by using Steal Affinity to power yourself while simultaneously crippling the opposition.

DREAMCATCHER TOURNAMENT: CALL OF THE WILD PE
Entry Fee: 0D
Teams(VS): 4 vs. 4 vs. 4
Battle Points: 1
Requirement: 2 Cups
Prohibited: Summoner, Undead Caster

DREAMCATCHER TOURNAMENT: FREE OF THE DARK GOD PE
Entry Fee: 0D
Teams(VS): 4 vs. 4
Battle Points: 1
Requirement: 2 Cups
Prohibited: Summoner, Undead Caster

DREAMCATCHER TOURNAMENT: GOOD NEIGHBOR SYU
Entry Fee: 0D
Teams(VS): 5 vs. 5
Battle Points: 1
Requirement: 2 Cups
Prohibited: Summoner, Undead Caster

DREAMCATCHER TOURNAMENT: HUMAN TOUCH OYU
Entry Fee: 0D
Teams(VS): 5 vs. 6
Battle Points: 1
Requirement: 2 Cups
Prohibited: Summoner, Undead Caster

DREAMCATCHER TOURNAMENT: HUMAN TOUCH RI
Entry Fee: 0D
Teams(VS): 5 vs. 6
Battle Points: 1
Requirement: 2 Cups
Prohibited: Summoner, Undead Caster

DREAMCATCHER TOURNAMENT: UNDEAD CASTER ORIGINS
Entry Fee: 0D
Teams(VS): 3 vs. 3 vs. 3
Battle Points: 1
Requirement: 2 Cups
Prohibited: Summoner, Undead Caster

Ursula / Valens
Prize: 600-5600D
Items:Dreamcatcher badge, Xan, Nomad's Shield, Garuda Feather, Wing Hat

The first and last battles of this tournament are freebies for patient players, because it's easy to place your guys far from the action, let the opposing teams rip each other apart, and then wade in and clean up the survivors.

The second battle features a strange alliance of Cyclopes and Galdrs, but a good roster of light characters should be effective against both. Use your starting position to your advantage, by standing behind the columns and making the Cyclopes come between them, where they'll be surrounded.

There aren't many tricks you can use in the other fights, just careful type-matching and strong defensive starts.

MAGNA STEPPES CHAMPIONSHIP: OPEN MYA
Entry Fee: 0D
Teams(VS): 3 vs. 3 vs. 3 vs. 3
Battle Points: 1
Requirement (Badges): All tournament, Inflationary Ego Su, History of the Frontier, & Open Ghazan
Prohibited: Summoner, Undead Caster

MAGNA STEPPES CHAMPIONSHIP: OPEN SYU
Entry Fee: 0D
Teams(VS): 3 vs. 3 vs. 3 vs. 3
Battle Points: 1
Requirement (Badges): All tournament, Inflationary Ego Su, History of the Frontier, & Open Ghazan
Prohibited: Summoner, Undead Caster

MAGNA STEPPES CHAMPIONSHIP: OPEN GYU
Entry Fee: 0D
Teams(VS): 3 vs. 3 vs. 3 vs. 3
Battle Points: 1
Requirement (Badges): All tournament, Inflationary Ego Su, History of the Frontier, & Open Ghazan
Prohibited: Summoner, Undead Caster

DREAMCATCHER TOURNAMENT: HUMAN TOUCH OYU
Entry Fee: 0D
Teams(VS): 3 vs. 3 vs. 3
Battle Points: 1
Requirement (Badges): All tournament, Inflationary Ego Su, History of the Frontier, & Open Ghazan
Prohibited: Summoner, Undead Caster

MAGNA STEPPES CHAMPIONSHIP: OPEN WO
Entry Fee: 0D
Teams(VS): 3 vs. 3 vs. 3
Battle Points: 1
Requirement (Badges): All tournament, Inflationary Ego Su, History of the Frontier, & Open Ghazan
Prohibited: Summoner, Undead Caster

Ursula / Valens
Prize: 5000D per battle
Items:Prizes: Chopper, The Cat's Claw, Griffin Pelt, Scarlet Anklet

I know we've said it countless times before, but the best strategy when there are multiple teams is to fall back and let them kill each other. That's easy in Open Mya, when you can just send your guys to safety behind the wagon near your starting point and escape the notice of virtually all of your foes. It gets trickier in Open Syu. One or two enemies will pursue you, but if you fall back, you'll be able to deal with them without interference.

You start toward the bottom of the map in Open Gyu and Open Wo, but hiding is just as easy if you head toward the log bridge. Sure, you'll be in plain sight, but your foes would rather attack nearby targets than pursue you. Hiding and stalling don't seem like the most honorable of techniques, but they're the key to winning the regional championships.

GENERAL STRATEGY • CHARACTER CLASSES • WORLD ATLAS • BONUS MATERIAL

THE WASTES

T his small encampment is somewhere in the field north of where the east road ends, and can be a little tricky to find. The league selection is limited now, but as with most Windward Steppes towns, many new ones will be added in later chapters of your quest. You'll need to conquer the Amazon Tyu league to open up the other two, only one of which must be conquered to unlock the Tournament. Beating Amazon Tyu will also earn you the right to recruit Amazons from theRecruiting Office.

WANDERING SOUL

THE WANDERING SOUL IS PROBABLY THE HARDEST ARENA TO FIND IN ALL OF THE KNOWN LANDS. SINCE THE NOMADS ARE ALWAYS ON THE MOVE, THE PITCH OF THE WANDERING SOUL RARELY ENDS UP IN THE SAME PLACE TWICE. IN THE CENTER OF THE CAMP, A LARGE SECTION OF LAND IS RINGED OFF WITH CARTS AND FENCES TO MAKE THE ARENA. USUALLY WHEN THERE'S A FIGHT GOING ON, THERE ARE MERCHANTS WHO OPEN THEIR SHOPS AT A DISCOUNT AND THE PRIZES AWARDED IN THE PITCH ARE GENEROUS.

CHARACTER RECRUITMENT

Name	Classification	PRM	SNG
Ahnqe	Wolf	900	90
Dauhla	Samnite	1200	120
Enq	Plainscat	950	95
Ghen	Bandit	950	95
Horazm	Plainscat	1000	100
Jahkre	Amazon	1000	100
Jhaura	Amazon	1150	115
Naphu	Wolf	1100	110
Nehvna	Archer	1100	110
Qoyor	Archer	900	90
Sabha	Samnite	1100	110
Yheki	Bandit	900	90
Yujin	Secutor	1000	100
Zhurtak	Archer	1150	115

NOTE: Cost is per recruitable character level.

PRM=Cost for permanent recruitment
SNG=Cost for single battle

SHOP: THE TRAVELER

LEAGUE STRATEGY

AMAZON TYU

Your players in this league are limited to females, and … Ludo? No, Ludo doesn't have a dark secret to share, he or Urlan will have special storyline events in this league. If your party is lacking in strong females, you'll have no choice but to hit the recruitment offices. I hope you enlisted a female Murmillo in Imperia, because they're great here.

Don't get confused by the barrels in many of these fights. This isn't a Vandal Battle. The Barrels are explosive, and a well-placed arrow can do light damage to a number of your foes. Keep a safe distance from them because your foes will use the same trick.

OTHER LEAGUES

Earning your second cup should be a snap. If you have enough light units, you can enter the "Secular Secutors" battle of the **Lightweight** league and take it in one fight. If you don't have enough light units to win that fight, there's no point doing the rest of the league, because the other battles don't offer enough points to earn the cup. Once again, you can exploit the exploding barrels in the arena, if you have access to ranged attacks, like Throw Weapon. Beating this league will open up the **Heavyweight** league in Yuset.

If you're light on the lights, you have no choice but to fight all the way through the **Nomad Shu**. That isn't so tough, because you can always hang back and let the other teams fight amongst themselves.

THE WASTES HISTORY

The Nomads of the Wandering Soul have traversed the Wastes for hundreds of years. Even when rulers try to lay claim over their lands, the people of the Wastes remain Nomads. The Nomads are said to be as strong as the land upon which they live. Hunters and crafters make up most of the population, although they have very strong warriors as well.

If people are found wandering The Wastes without protection or an obvious purpose, the Nomads will take them. If those brought to the community try to escape, the Nomads will throw them in one of the battles in the arena. Usually after surviving a battle or so, these people come around and settle in to life as a Nomad.

AKAR AN

PALACE
IBLIIS

YEARS AGO, THE TYRANT KING RUFIIT LOVED ARENA COMBAT AND DECIDED TO HAVE A COURTYARD FROM WITHIN HIS VERY OWN PALACE CONVERTED FOR THE SPORT. HAVING ACCESS TO REGULAR MATCHES AT A WHIM WOULD MOMENTARILY QUENCH THE RULER'S THIRST FOR THE BLOODSHED. SEEING THIS, HIS MINISTERS EXPANDED THE OPERATION, HOPING THAT THE BRUTALITY IN THE ARENA WOULD DIMINISH RUFIIT'S OWN VIOLENCE AGAINST THE POPULACE. THIS CONTINUED UNTIL FINALLY AN ENTIRE WING OF THE PALACE WAS DEVOTED TO THE DAILY MATCHES. NOW, LONG AFTER RUFIIT'S DEATH, THE PALACE HAS BEEN HANDED TO IBLIIS, A PUPPET LEADER PLACED IN AKAR AN BY THE IMPERIALS. THE PALACE OF IBLIIS IS KNOWN AS THE PREMIER ARENA IN THE SOUTHERN EXPANSE. WITH IT'S BEAUTIFUL SETTING, HISTORY, AND UNIQUE CLIENTELE, MANY A HERO HAS BEEN MADE HERE. WITH MARBLE WALLS AND WALKWAYS AND ELABORATE CERAMIC MOSAIC WORK, THIS ARENA IS A SIGHT TO BEHOLD.

Trouble awaits as soon as you set foot on the parched earth of the Southern Expanse. When you rush in to thwart a local mugging, your storyline characters will come face to face with a quintet of Bandits and Dervishes. They're lower level than you are, but if everyone falls in this battle it's Game Over, so you have to take it seriously. To prevent potentially serious backstabs, have your team start together and stay together. Don't worry about Gwazi, because the Bandits will forget about him when you appear on the scene. After the fight, Gwazi will join your party. He's a light gladiator with mostly Secutor skills, but has very poor Accuracy. Avoid using him when you don't have to.

CHARACTER RECRUITMENT

Name	Classification	PRM	SNG
Amenti	Channeler	1150	115
Banenre	Samnite	1200	120
Beketaten	Dervish	1150	115
Ikuk	Cyclops	1300	130
Inalchuk	Channeler	1100	110
Karoatjet	Samnite	1250	125
Kozma	Cyclops	1300	130
Luzige	Dervish	1100	110
Nari	Plainscat	950	95
Sutekh	Summoner	1300	130*
Ulugh	Plainscat	1050	105

*Accessable after visiting Saraa Izel
NOTE: Cost is per recruitable character level.

PRM=Cost for permanent recruitment
SNG=Cost for single battle

SHOP: THE OASIS

AKAR AN HISTORY

Akar An is a bustling river city situated near the bordering Windward Steppes and therefore does some trading with the nomads of the East. Akar An's anger with Imperia runs deep as the royal families of the city were imprisoned or killed during the war with the North. It not only ended Akar An's royal lineage, but changed the entire city forever. Now, Akar An's royal palace is used to train warriors in the graceful ways of the Dervish. Those who graduate from the Palace Academy are viewed as elite warriors, the closest thing to royalty that still exists in Akar An.

SHOPKEEPERS QUEST

At the Oasis, you'll find a shopkeeper who loves to gab. Ask him about the Dervishes, and he'll set up the Test of the Underclass league for seven days later. This is a single, tough battle that pits four of your best against six Dervishes. Victory earns you, among other things, Royal Garb armor that is fantastic for Dervishes.

Win or lose, talk to Nazin the shopkeeper twice more, and he'll set up the Test of the Midclass in Qaa Rah five days later. That's a three-on-three fight, and you can set your starting positions to give your group a three-on-two advantage while the third wanders in, making it a little easier than the last fight. But don't surround your foes too closely, or they'll be able to hurt you all with their Whirlwind skills.
(continued on page 102)

Akar An, your first stop, is just to the north. Here you can recruit exotic classes, like the Dervish and Cyclops, and earn the first of two Southern Expanse badges. The shop here is the starting point for a long side quest, and stocks a wide variety of weapons and armor, specializing in goods for light classes. You can also find a number of rare accessories at Althaag's, which has set up shop just outside of town.

Running Attack

Whirlwind

When you report that victory, Nazin will set up the final battle for three days later in the lost city of Saraa Izel. You can only reach this town after completing the tournament in Qaa Rah, so plan accordingly. This is a one-on-one fight against a Dervish who is much higher level than you are. Start far from your opponent, buff yourself with whatever tactics you have, and try to finish the Dervish with an all-crit Combo Attack 4. Even your heartiest character won't survive more than two turns, so make sure you're capable of winning in that time frame.

Your prize is Nazin's respect. Don't spend it all in one place.

OPEN AFFINITY PHI

Not to sound like a broken record, but the fall-back-and-let-them-kill-each-other strategy is as useful as ever in the first and fourth battles of this essential league. Another classic favorite, camping out diagonally to the statues, works like a charm at evening the odds in Enter the Darkness Tsu and the other straight fights.

SUMMONERS ENDURANCE

In this Endurance series, you battle one Summoner and a pair of permanently summoned Affinity Beasts in each of the first rounds and a single high-level Summoner in the last. In case that's not funky enough, scattered statues freeze any characters within two squares in front of them, and the Summoners are fond of using Tornado to scatter character placements and drop them in front of the statues' icy glare.

The Summoner is your primary target. Killing him won't make the beasts go away, but it will kill anything else he

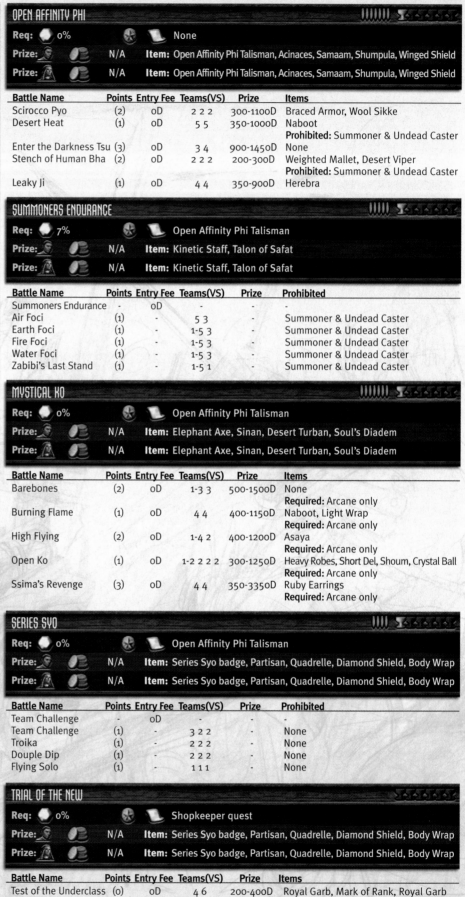

OPEN AFFINITY PHI

Req: 0% None

Prize: N/A Item: Open Affinity Phi Talisman, Acinaces, Samaam, Shumpula, Winged Shield

Prize: N/A Item: Open Affinity Phi Talisman, Acinaces, Samaam, Shumpula, Winged Shield

Battle Name	Points	Entry Fee	Teams(VS)	Prize	Items
Scirocco Pyo	(2)	0D	2 2 2	300-1100D	Braced Armor, Wool Sikke
Desert Heat	(1)	0D	5 5	350-1000D	Naboot
					Prohibited: Summoner & Undead Caster
Enter the Darkness Tsu	(3)	0D	3 4	900-1450D	None
Stench of Human Bha	(2)	0D	2 2 2	200-300D	Weighted Mallet, Desert Viper
					Prohibited: Summoner & Undead Caster
Leaky Ji	(1)	0D	4 4	350-900D	Herebra

SUMMONERS ENDURANCE

Req: 7% Open Affinity Phi Talisman

Prize: N/A Item: Kinetic Staff, Talon of Safat

Prize: N/A Item: Kinetic Staff, Talon of Safat

Battle Name	Points	Entry Fee	Teams(VS)	Prize	Prohibited
Summoners Endurance	-	0D	-	-	
Air Foci	(1)	-	5 3		Summoner & Undead Caster
Earth Foci	(1)	-	1-5 3		Summoner & Undead Caster
Fire Foci	(1)	-	1-5 3		Summoner & Undead Caster
Water Foci	(1)	-	1-5 3		Summoner & Undead Caster
Zabibi's Last Stand	(1)	-	1-5 1		Summoner & Undead Caster

MYSTICAL KO

Req: 0% Open Affinity Phi Talisman

Prize: N/A Item: Elephant Axe, Sinan, Desert Turban, Soul's Diadem

Prize: N/A Item: Elephant Axe, Sinan, Desert Turban, Soul's Diadem

Battle Name	Points	Entry Fee	Teams(VS)	Prize	Items
Barebones	(2)	0D	1-3 3	500-1500D	None
					Required: Arcane only
Burning Flame	(1)	0D	4 4	400-1150D	Naboot, Light Wrap
					Required: Arcane only
High Flying	(2)	0D	1-4 2	400-1200D	Asaya
					Required: Arcane only
Open Ko	(1)	0D	1-2 2 2 2	300-1250D	Heavy Robes, Short Del, Shoum, Crystal Ball
					Required: Arcane only
Ssima's Revenge	(3)	0D	4 4	350-3350D	Ruby Earrings
					Required: Arcane only

SERIES SYO

Req: 0% Open Affinity Phi Talisman

Prize: N/A Item: Series Syo badge, Partisan, Quadrelle, Diamond Shield, Body Wrap

Prize: N/A Item: Series Syo badge, Partisan, Quadrelle, Diamond Shield, Body Wrap

Battle Name	Points	Entry Fee	Teams(VS)	Prize	Prohibited
Team Challenge	-	0D	-	-	-
Team Challenge	(1)	-	3 2 2		None
Troika	(1)	-	2 2 2		None
Douple Dip	(1)	-	2 2 2		None
Flying Solo	(1)	-	1 1 1		None

TRIAL OF THE NEW

Req: 0% Shopkeeper quest

Prize: N/A Item: Series Syo badge, Partisan, Quadrelle, Diamond Shield, Body Wrap

Prize: N/A Item: Series Syo badge, Partisan, Quadrelle, Diamond Shield, Body Wrap

Battle Name	Points	Entry Fee	Teams(VS)	Prize	Items
Test of the Underclass	(0)	0D	4 6	200-400D	Royal Garb, Mark of Rank, Royal Garb

summons (usually Skeletons) and stop his Tornado shenanigans. If you haven't fought with Affinity Beasts before, you should know that they boost the stats of everyone on their team: the Air Beast boosts Initiative, the Earth Beast boosts Defense, the Fire Beast boosts Power and the Water Beast boosts Accuracy. Fortunately, they're not very powerful on offense, and are generally restricted to simple attack skills. They can be hard to hit, so Affinity Attacks, critical hits and can't-miss techniques, like Bulls Eye, will serve you well.

OTHER LEAGUES

After completing the Open Affinity Phi and Summoners Endurance leagues, you'll have the two cups you need for the regional Tournament. But two new leagues will also appear, and you'll have to complete Series Syo to get one of the badges needed for the Southern Expanse Championships. The **Series Syo** fights always feature three teams, and while there are no places to hide, you can run up the stairs to the upper area. The other teams won't pursue distant targets, and will usually end up fighting amongst themselves. An all support party works great here, because your Archers can opportunistically shoot into the fray from their higher vantage point.

The **Mystical Ko** league, a sequel of sorts to Mystical Zo from the Steppes, will also appear after Summoners Endurance. You'll need four Arcane characters to meet the entrance requirements of some of the battles and take the cup. These are similar to past Arcane-on-Arcane battles, but a few feature heavy gladiators to defeat and all feature several spell-casting statues to contend with.

MIRAGE TOURNAMENT: FIRE AND ICE KYO

Entry Fee: 0D
Teams(VS): 2 vs. 2
Battle Points: 1
Requirement: 2 Cups
Prohibited: None

MIRAGE TOURNAMENT: BLEEDING HEARTS

Entry Fee: 0D
Teams(VS): 2 vs. 2
Battle Points: 1
Requirement: 2 Cups
Prohibited: None

MIRAGE TOURNAMENT: MOTION SICKNESS

Entry Fee: 0D
Teams(VS): 2 vs. 2
Battle Points: 1
Requirement: 2 Cups
Prohibited: None

MIRAGE TOURNAMENT: SIGHT FOR SORE EYES

Entry Fee: 0D
Teams(VS): 2 vs. 3
Battle Points: 1
Requirement: 2 Cups
Prohibited: None

Ursula / Valens
Prize: 1500-16500D
Items: Mirage badge, Sapara, Shank, Oiled Pelt, Shisa Vika

There are no less than eight statues in these two-on-two fights, and while exploiting the outer statues remains a good strategy, it's not the only one. If you back up and use the terrain advantage to place your characters on the high ground between the stairs and the birdbaths, you'll have great terrain advantage, and it will be difficult for your opponents to surround you. (Just remember that Dervishes have several diagonal attack options that may thwart your plans.) If you run into support characters, use your own and exploit the high ground advantage your opponent rarely bothers with. It's a far safer strategy than running the gauntlet of statues.

EXPANSE THRONE CHAMPIONSHIP: OPEN SYU

Entry Fee: 0D
Teams(VS): 2 vs. 2 vs. 2
Battle Points: 1
Requirement (Badges): All tournament, Series Syo, Barn Burner, & Open Affinity Phi Talisman

EXPANSE THRONE CHAMPIONSHIP: OPEN ZYO

Entry Fee: 0D
Teams(VS): 2 vs. 2 vs. 2
Battle Points: 1
Requirement (Badges): All tournament, Series Syo, Barn Burner, & Open Affinity Phi Talisman

EXPANSE THRONE CHAMPIONSHIP: OPEN NYA

Entry Fee: 0D
Teams(VS): 2 vs. 2 vs. 2
Battle Points: 1
Requirement (Badges): All tournament, Series Syo, Barn Burner, & Open Affinity Phi Talisman

EXPANSE THRONE CHAMPIONSHIP: OPEN KWA

Entry Fee: 0D
Teams(VS): 2 vs. 2 vs. 1 vs. 2
Battle Points: 1
Requirement (Badges): All tournament, Series Syo, Barn Burner, & Open Affinity Phi Talisman

Ursula / Valens
Prize: 5000-15000D per battle
Items: Kheten, The Steel Skull, Mighty Gear, Sphinx Feather

This is a championship that even a pacifist can win. With three opposing teams and a field full of statues, you can clear these battles while your swords rust in their scabbards. If you'd like to do something more than pass every turn, use support or arcane characters and pluck at the weaklings from the safety of the arena's higher level. But active participation in this league isn't necessary. They'll kill each other if you let 'em, and you can hold back and finish the bleeding survivors while your team is at full health.

QAA RAH

At the other end of the path that took you to Akar An, you'll find Qaa Rah. You can gamble for big money in the Cash Money Gwa league, and if you've earned the Mirage badge in Akar An, you can get started earning the Southern Expanse's second championship badge (the Barn Burner) and tournament victory.

This is the only place where you can recruit Scorpion and Scarab beasts, but they won't appear in the Recruiting Office until you complete the Insect Ze league.

There's another interesting event that takes place in the desert of the Expanse. Walk towards the circling vultures, and you'll find a Dervish dying of thirst. Locate a nearby bottle of water, buried in the sand, and bring it to her. If you refuse her reward, she'll teach your hero the Dervish Faith skill, which makes Ursula or Valens immune to bleeding while a Dervish is on the battlefield.

SCORCHED OASIS

THIS ONCE DESERTED OASIS IS HAUNTED WITH THE GHOSTS OF LOST TRAVELERS THAT NEVER FOUND THEIR WAY OUT OF THE UNFORGIVING DESERT. THE TAR PITS ARE RUMORED TO HOUSE THE SKELETONS OF THESE POOR SOULS.

CHARACTER RECRUITMENT

Name	Classification	PRM	SNG
Azchk-Ykuk*	Scorpion	1100	110
Chachik*	Scorpion	1150	115
Djenutymes	Samnite	1300	130
Fayrouz	Dervish	1000	100
Gahji	Dervish	1100	110
Kallipides	Cyclops	1200	120
Keket	Channeler	1250	125
Mehykhati	Samnite	1250	125
Nebetawy	Channeler	1100	110
Nisus	Cyclops	1300	130
Ookutyk*	Scarab	1200	120
Vktuktruk*	Scarab	1150	115

*Accessable after completing Insect Ze League.
NOTE: Cost is per recruitable character level.

PRM=Cost for permanent recruitment
SNG=Cost for single battle

SHOP: NONE

QAA RAH HISTORY

All you'll find in Qaa Rah are lost souls. It is a deserted oasis that is a burial ground for unfortunate desert travelers.

LEAGUE STRATEGY

 **CASH MONEY GWA**

This league is all about the money. There are no prizes or cups to be won. To enter each battle you pay a steep upfront fee, and then do battle with three other teams on a field full of loaded treasure chests. Each chest contains around 20,000 Dinars, so you'll need to hit at least two or three to recoup your investment.

Unless the chests are scattered in distant corners, you can't afford to fall back and let your foes kill each other. Your opponents won't actively pursue the chests, but they'll take the loot if they're in the neighborhood. To maximize your earnings, you'll need to immediately grab all the chests near your starting position before regrouping to battle your foes, and then leave one or two alive

while you hit chests in distant corners.

 TREASURE TROVE

Each Treasure Trove battle begins with your foes on the central island, guarding a single treasure chest. You start on the outside, and have a wonderful opportunity to set an ambush in the three squares around the mouth of the bridge. Because your opponents will only be able to cross one at a time, a support character or two can pepper those on the bridge and island with arrows while the ambushed character gets cut to pieces.

Lure out the last survivor, and then send someone to slip behind him and grab the chest. The chests typically contain equipment and accessories with the Dark Affinity, which are a rare and valuable find for Undead Summoners.

CASH MONEY GWA

Req:	0%		None	
Prize:		N/A	**Item:** None	
Prize:		N/A	**Item:** None	

Battle Name	Points	Entry Fee	Teams(VS)	Prize	Requirement
Break the Bank Open	(1)	60000D	1-3 3 3 3	-	None
Bulk of Hulk	(1)	45000D	1-3 3 3 3	-	Heavy only.
Elementals Po	(1)	35000D	1-3 3 3 3	-	Arcane only.
Lightweights	(1)	20000D	1-3 3 3 3	20000-30000D	Light only.
Ranged Combat Rya	(1)	25000D	1-3 3 3 3	-	Support only.

TREASURE TROVE

Req:	0%		Mirage badge	
Prize:		1500D	**Item:** Treasure Trove Talisman	
Prize:		1500D	**Item:** Treasure Trove Talisman	

Battle Name	Points	Entry Fee	Teams(VS)	Prize	Requirement
Mongrel Mash	(1)	0D	4 4	-	None
Quarry Break	(2)	0D	4 4	-	None
Summoner's Gwa	(2)	0D	4 2	-	None
The Morgue	(3)	0D	4 4	-	None

INSECT ZE

Req:	10%		Treasure Trove Talisman	
Prize:		2000-17000D	**Item:** Moonstone, Quartz	
Prize:		2000-17000D	**Item:** Moonstone, Quartz	

Battle Name	Points	Entry Fee	Teams(VS)	Prize	Prohibited
Insect Ze	-	0D	-	-	-
Wave Nyo	(1)	-	4 3	-	None
Wave Tyu	(1)	-	1-4 4	-	None
Wave Zya	(1)	-	1-4 4	-	None
Wave Kyo	(1)	-	1-4 4	-	None
Wave Ryu	(1)	-	1-4 4	-	None

BARN BURNER

Req:	0%		Treasure Trove Talisman	
Prize:		3000-16000D	**Item:** Barn Burner badge, Hooked Ridge Helm, Leather Bikini, Bazo, Medal of Stature	
Prize:		3000-16000D	**Item:** Barn Burner badge, Hooked Ridge Helm, Leather Bikini, Bazo, Medal of Stature	

Battle Name	Points	Entry Fee	Teams(VS)	Prize	Items
Open Barn Burner	(1)	0D	1-3 3 3 3	700-1900D	Bronze Gear, Lorica Segmentata **Required:** Fire Affinity only
Phoenix Flames	(3)	0D	1-4 2	-	Scarab Beetle **Required:** Fire Affinity only
Red Eye Nya	(2)	0D	1-4 4	750-2000D	Quadrelle **Required:** Fire Affinity only
Toasted Roaches	(2)	0D	1-5 5	650-1900D	Quartz **Required:** Fire Affinity only

LEVIATHAN

Req:	20%		Treasure Trove Talisman	
Prize:		5000-15000D	**Item:** Leviathan badge, Dalima, Poison Barb Shield, Jeweled Diadem, Turtlebone Armor	
Prize:		5000-15000D	**Item:** Leviathan badge, Dalima, Poison Barb Shield, Jeweled Diadem, Turtlebone Armor	

Battle Name	Points	Entry Fee	Teams(VS)	Prize	Required
Heavyweight Mya	(2)	0D	1-5 5	2000D	Water Affinity only
Liquid Swords Zya	(1)	0D	1-5 5	2000D	Water Affinity only
Mystics Po	(3)	0D	1-4 4 2	2000D	Water Affinity only
Oasis Vagrants	(1)	0D	1-3 3 1 3	2000D	Water Affinity only
One On One Du	(2)	0D	1 1 1 1	2000D	Water Affinity level 12 only

Five battle points will earn you the Treasure Trove Talisman, and the right to compete in the Scorched Oasis's other leagues.

OTHER LEAGUES

The **Insect Ze** league is a difficult five-round Endurance Series versus a series of Scarabs and Scorpions. You'll need to pursue an aggressive strategy in this league, because playing defense will tend to get you a face full of poisonous Scarab spit. After clearing this league, you'll be able to recruit Scarabs and Scorpions of your own in the Recruiting Office.

If you have four or five Fire Affinity units (counting your new Scarab friend), you won't have too much trouble with the **Barn Burner** league. Round 1 is a simple free-for-all, and round 2 lets you get an aggressive jump on the two Summoner foes. Round 3 features a head-to-head brawl with four Cyclopes, while your foes in round 4 are Scorpions and Scarabs. You only need to win one of the last two leagues, so do whichever will be easiest. If worst comes to worst you can always just equip a bunch of fire affinity weapons to your light gladiators. (continued on page 106)

(continued on page 106)

Your reward for clearing this league is the Barn Burner badge — the last of the key badges in the Expanse.

Victory at Barn Burner will also open up the **Leviathan** league. This is basically the same as Barn Burner, but it's a league for Water units only.

Finally, after clearing the Qaa Rah Tournament, the **Pro Citizen Byu** league will appear. In this strange league, the objective is to save a single citizen from being murdered by the opposing team. The opponents will target your troops if they're closer, so make sure they're a more convenient target than the citizen. The final battle against four Summoners is a difficult one, but the Robe of Rebirth prize is worth it if you have a Summoner in your ranks.

PRO CITIZEN BYU

Req:	0%		Endless Horizons badge
Prize:		-	Item: None
Prize:		-	Item: None

Battle Name	Points	Entry Fee	Teams(VS)	Prize	Items
Rescue Hentutwedjeb	(1)	0D	4 6	2000-12000D	Wing of Safat
Rescue Ashuruballit	(1)	0D	4 4	1700-11700D	Snakeskin Bow
Rescue Sedjefkare	(1)	0D	4 4	1500-11500D	Collar of Spite
Rescue Hentutwedjeb	(1)	0D	4 4	10000-20000D	Robe of Rebirth

TRIAL OF THE NEW

Req:	0%		Shopkeeper quest
Prize:		-	Item: None
Prize:		-	Item: None

Battle Name	Points	Entry Fee	Teams(VS)	Prize	Items / *Prohibited
Test of the Midclass	(0)	0D	3 3	400-800D	Tekuja Sikke, Myth of the Sands *Summoner & Undead Summoner

ENDLESS HORIZONS TOURNAMENT: BESERKER SHI

Entry Fee: 0D
Teams(VS): 1 vs. 1
Battle Points: 1
Requirement: 2 Cups
Item: Liberation

ENDLESS HORIZONS TOURNAMENT: CYLCOPS ZU

Entry Fee: 0D
Teams(VS): 1 vs. 1
Battle Points: 1
Requirement: 2 Cups
Item: Turtlebone Armor

ENDLESS HORIZONS TOURNAMENT: DERVISH RO

Entry Fee: 0D
Teams(VS): 1 vs. 1
Battle Points: 1
Requirement: 2 Cups
Item: Veiled Sikke

ENDLESS HORIZONS TOURNAMENT: SAMNITE TSU

Entry Fee: 0D
Teams(VS): 1 vs. 1
Battle Points: 1
Requirement: 2 Cups
Item: Vicious Blade

ENDLESS HORIZONS TOURNAMENT: SUMMONER KWA

Entry Fee: 0D
Teams(VS): 1 vs. 1
Battle Points: 1
Requirement: 2 Cups
Item: Eye of the Gods

ENDLESS HORIZONS TOURNAMENT: UNDEAD CASTER WO

Entry Fee: 0D
Teams(VS): 1 vs. 1
Battle Points: 1
Requirement: 2 Cups
Item: Interment Robes

Ursula / Valens
Prize: 6000-30000D
Items: Listed individually above

In these simple one-on-one battles you start toe to toe with a single enemy and battle it out till one gladiator drops. Your foes are around your level, so if you choose a good type match, the advantage is clearly yours for the first four fights. In the final two, you battle Summoners who can summon allies to help in the fight. Pick a good medium fighter (so they can't Incapacitate you), and get in their faces immediately, before they can summon a creature in the space between you. The creature will end up behind you, but you should be able to take the caster out before his pet can be a factor.

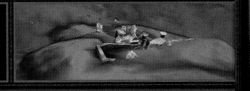

SARAA IZEL

THE OFFERING PLATE

THE OFFERING PLATE IS A SACRIFICIAL ALTAR WHERE OFFERINGS ARE MADE TO ALL SIX OF THE GODS. AS NEWS OF THE GLADIATORIAL GAMES CAME FROM THE ROYAL PALACE, THE OFFERING PLATE STARTED DOUBLING AS AN ARENA WHERE THE ARCANE COULD CHALLENGE ONE ANOTHER IN DUELS TO THE DEATH. THE NEXT STEP WAS TO START HOSTING DARING BATTLES FOR THOSE WILLING TO BRAVE THE MISTS OF IZEL. FASHIONED FROM FLAWLESS MARBLE AND POLISHED TO A BRILLIANT SHEEN, THIS CIRCULAR ARENA IS A PERFECT SHAPE TO CALL, HOLD AND RELEASE ENERGY. THE NEXUS IS AS MYSTERIOUS TO THOSE WHO LIVE WITHIN IT AS THE MISTS OF IZEL ARE TO WIDE-EYED TRAVELERS.

You can only visit Saraa Izel after you've completed the tournament in Qaa Rah, and then you'll have no other choice. As you leave town, an event will occur, and Gwazi will lead you to the lost city, where a battle with a group of Summoners awaits. Focus your group's attacks on a single target and take them down one-by-one.

Remember that this is a wilderness battle, if your hero dies it's Game Over.

SARAA IZEL HISTORY

Most of the people who live in Saraa Izel are Summoners or Channelers, or those hoping to learn their ways. Its residents live quietly, enjoying the spiritual energy that flows from the nexus in the center of town. People have been known to fall ill simply by being so close to such raw power. Others find it amazingly therapeutic. A permanent fog looms over the city, adding to Saraa Izel's mysterious reputation. It is said that the power of the Gods is what keeps the fog from evaporating. Rumors of powerful magic and the fog cause most travelers to give this entire area a wide berth when traveling through the Southern Expanse.

SHOPKEEPER QUEST

Remember way back in Imperia, when Cresus asked you to find his father? Well, you found him. Talk to the people who wait at the entrance to the city and ask to see "A man named Acrisius." The queen will give you one day to prepare for a special battle: your four Channelers versus her four Summoners. Don't have four Channelers? Better hit the Recruiting Offices. ... No less than four will do.

The Summoners tend to have the level advantage, but the Channelers' Steal Affinity and Drain Affinity skills are very affective against Summoners. Let your enemies Summon Power, steal the power, and then have all four Channelers focus their Affinity hate on blowing the Summoners out of the fight one by one. *(continued on page 108)*

CHARACTER RECRUITMENT

Name	Classification	PRM	SNG
N/A	N/A	N/A	N/A

NOTE: Cost is per recruitable character level.

PRM=Cost for permanent recruitment
SNG=Cost for single battle

SHOP: BAZAAR AZIZA

After the battle, return to Akar An to trigger another event, and you'll then be free to return here to shop at Bazaar Aziza, which carries a small selection of rare and powerful items (including accessories). Do a few shopkeeper quests and battle in the final Trial of the New league, when the time comes.

Once the four Summoners are defeated, four of their Undead brethren will join the fray. If you diligently steal and drain their power, they'll have to resort to ineffective physical attacks.

The prizes for the battle are a Crown of Darkness and the Death's Head, two pieces of equipment that will make your Undead Summoner obscenely powerful.

TRIAL OF THE NEW

Req:	0%		Shopkeeper quest
Prize:	-	**Item:**	None
Prize:	-	**Item:**	None

Battle Name	Points	Entry Fee	Teams(VS)	Prize	Prohibited
Test of the Overclass	(0)	0D	1 1	600-1200D	Summoner & Undead Summoner

SHOPKEEPER QUEST

Saraa Izel is the smallest town in the game, but Aziza has a region's worth of quests for you. To trigger the first, ask Aziza to tell you about herself and follow the conversation until she asks you to kill a Desert Yeti that's wandering the Expanse. Wander around the Expanse until you find it in a random encounter (be sure to look everywhere), and Ursula and Valens will have to battle a single Yeti that's a few levels higher than they are. Defeat him, bring his head to Aziza, and move on to the next quest.

SHOPKEEPER QUEST

Once you've earned the Barn Burner badge, ask Aziza for gossip, and then ask if she has any jobs for you. She'll ask you to deliver a mysterious tablet to a man named Sarenenutet. You'll find him if you wander the dunes in the desert south east of Qaa Rah. But before you set out after him, take a moment to read the Mysterious Tablet, now located in your Accessories list. Talk to the man imprisoned within it, then fulfill your quest as promised to Aziza.

SHOPKEEPER QUEST

In the final quest, ask if there's anything exciting going on, and she'll send you to find Sarenenutet again — this time to kill him. You'll find him in one of many fixed positions on the world map, and despite all the build-up, he's a pretty easy kill. The skeletons he summons are deadly so don't even attack them, unless you want to get counter-attacked and poisoned. Instead, focus on Sarenenutet, but watch out for Hell's Fury, a deadly skill he may use. Have a Channeler or two steal his affinity and blast him with it while your best medium units surround him and dish out their best attacks. You'll recover the Mysterious Tablet, which you can return to Aziza for a reward.

CHAPTER V

Usus is in a tizzy to get to Caltha, but once you enter the final battle there's no going back. Before you do that, you may want to complete some of the leagues you haven't finished yet, many of which have new prizes. Most shops have updated stock, including high level items that will be useful in the final challenges. There are also a few new leagues and side quests available, which are listed below.

IMPERIA

I BELFORT

SHOPKEEPER QUEST

Ask Agamede how her shop's doing, and she'll tell you of a recent burglary she suffered. The burglars haven't gone far, just to the woods slightly east of Belfort. The Bandits and their Nordagh allies are high level opponents, so be cautious in the battle that ensues. Your reward from Agamede is Rhino Spangenhelm headgear, usable by the Ur-twins or any other Barbarian.

 **TRIAL OF ARMADUS**

Belfort's final league is now open to you, although the only prize is cash and, presumably, glory. The Trial of Armadus is an endurance battle for a single character, who will have to face six opponents, mostly heavy types. The trick is to move your fighter to the edge of a pit, so your opponent's most direct route will put them beneath him, perfect for easily slaughtering.

II CRO BESKA

SHOPKEEPER QUEST

If you battled in the Historian's League in Cro Beska the last time you were in Imperia, visit Scotia's shop again and the shopkeeper will tell you about a new Historian's League, this time in Syrna, 7 days later. If you win, maybe you'll finally get that Minotaur...

 **THE HISTORIANS**

The Historians League gets even harder on the second try, now that your foes are higher level and a Cyclops has joined the mix. If you manage to pull out a victory by saving the outnumbered and surrounded Citizens, one of the combatants (including the Cyclops) will offer to join your team.

III PIRGOS

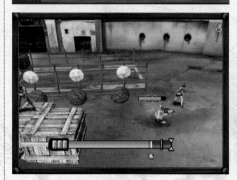

THE SHIELD & THE SPEAR

You can only enter Support characters in this battle, but some of the battles have you facing melee fighters as well as enemy Archers and Peltasts. When facing a mixed group, choose a good starting position and shoot down anyone who approaches. If you're only facing other Support characters, you'll need the advantage that comes from holding the high ground. Most battles feature a random piece of Archer or Peltast equipment, as well as a hearty cash prize.

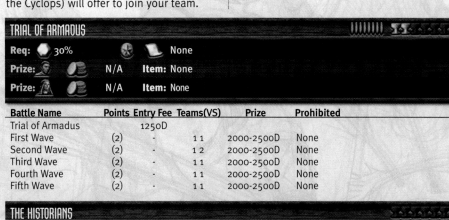

TRIAL OF ARMADUS

Req: 30%		None	
Prize:	N/A	Item: None	
Prize:	N/A	Item: None	

Battle Name	Points	Entry Fee	Teams(VS)	Prize	Prohibited
Trial of Armadus		1250D			
First Wave	(2)	-	1 1	2000-2500D	None
Second Wave	(2)	-	1 2	2000-2500D	None
Third Wave	(2)	-	1 1	2000-2500D	None
Fourth Wave	(2)	-	1 1	2000-2500D	None
Fifth Wave	(2)	-	1 1	2000-2500D	None

THE HISTORIANS

Req: 0%		From Imperia only	
Prize:	N/A	Item: N/A	
Prize:	10000-10212D	Item: Serrated Bone Club, Declamatio, Carafe, Cycloptic Corinthian	

Battle Name	Points	Entry Fee	Teams(VS)	Prize	Prohibited
The Mythic Invasion	(0)	7500D	4 6	-	None

IV SYRNA & TRIKATA

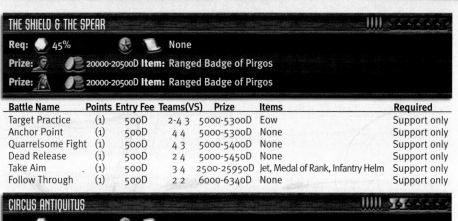

IV CIRCUS ANTIQUITUS/INHUMANUS

In these two Pro-tier only battles, your fighters need to evade a group of Satyrs to smash their barrels. In some Circus Antiquitus fights, you actually need to kill Satyrs to make the barrels appear, and in Circus Inhumanus you usually need to cut through the Satyrs to reach the targets. So what all these fights basically amount to is your best medium type fighters thrashing a bunch of Satyrs. They aren't difficult, but they do get tedious, and you get virtually nothing for it.

THE SHIELD & THE SPEAR

Req: 45%   None

Prize: 20000-20500D Item: Ranged Badge of Pirgos

Prize: 20000-20500D Item: Ranged Badge of Pirgos

Battle Name	Points	Entry Fee	Teams(VS)	Prize	Items	Required
Target Practice	(1)	500D	2-4 3	5000-5300D	Eow	Support only
Anchor Point	(1)	500D	4 4	5000-5300D	None	Support only
Quarrelsome Fight	(1)	500D	4 3	5000-5400D	None	Support only
Dead Release	(1)	500D	2 4	5000-5450D	None	Support only
Take Aim	(1)	500D	3 4	2500-25950D	Jet, Medal of Rank, Infantry Helm	Support only
Follow Through	(1)	500D	2 2	6000-6340D	None	Support only

CIRCUS ANTIQUITUS

Req: 30%   None

Prize: 1300-1750D Item: Circus Antiquitus badge

Prize: 1300-1750D Item: Circus Antiquitus badge

Battle Name	Points	Entry Fee	Teams(VS)	Prize	Prohibited
Barrel of Fun	(2)	0D	2-3 3	3000-3250D	None
Double Barreled	(2)	0D	2-3 3	3000-3250D	None
Cask Task	(3)	0D	3 3	5000-5550D	None
Barrel Run	(3)	0D	3 4	5000-5700D	None
Mystical Hand	(3)	0D	3 3	5000-5700D	None

CIRCUS INHUMANUS

Req: 20%   Circus Antiquitus badge

Prize: N/A Item: None

Prize: N/A Item: None

Battle Name	Points	Entry Fee	Teams(VS)	Prize	Prohibited
Roll Out the Barrels	(2)	0D	4 3 3	-	Summoner and Undead Caster
Break the Kegs	(2)	0D	4 4	-	Summoner and Undead Caster
Dash the Course	(2)	500D	2 2 2	-	Summoner and Undead Caster
Prop Smasher	(2)	500D	2 3	-	Summoner and Undead Caster
Finish Line	(2)	500D	2 2	-	Summoner and Undead Caster

NORDAGH

WINDWARD STEPPES

V ROANOR

SHOPKEEPER QUEST

Now that it's remotely possible to kill the Greater Bear at the end of the One Against Many league, try to take him down with your strongest heavy type fighter. If you win, visit Unna at the shop for a bunch of grief on how hard it is to find good bears. If you want to make a bit of money, agree to help her out and head to the woods south of Sloan Forest to find another.

To win, you need to reduce the bear to 1/4 of its health without killing it, which is a minor detail compared to the extreme difficulty of even surviving an encounter with a high level Greater Bear in the first place. Use expendable troops like summoned creatures and Undead Legionnaires to draw his wrath while you attack from behind.

V LORDS OF THE PIT

There's only one new league in all of Nordagh, and that's the Lords of the Pit league in Roanor. Your opponents in these simple two-on-two battles are all members of Gladius's QA team, hence the "bug" on the league poster. If you don't feel Chuck and the gang have suffered enough, feel free to beat on them here.

VI YUSET

SHOPKEEPER QUEST

When you "chew the fat" with Duger now, he'll have a few new things to say. One is that an Amazon named Qorin is looking for Eiji, and can now be found in The Wastes. If you then go to The Wastes, you'll find a new league called Wandering Souls, with only a single fight where your heroes battle a bunch of Amazons and light fighters. You may need to recruit some more Support characters to meet the entrance requirements, but it's worth it. In the end, Qorin, a high level Amazon will join your school.

SHOPKEEPER QUEST

If you ask Duger about fighting tips in Yuset, and have completed the Beast Za league, he'll tell you about a new fight being held in that league one day later. There's only one Greater Plainscat to fight in the Attack the Plains Cat battle, but it's supported by seven unreachable Archers who hail arrows on your team. Use Murmillos and the Undead for their natural defenses, and throw everyone at the cat. Your prize for victory is 2000D, The Cat's Claw shield, a Cat's Eye charm, and Dragon Hide armor. Duger will also give you a cut of his gambling winnings if you visit him afterwards.

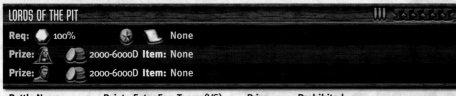

LORDS OF THE PIT

Req:	🔷 100%	⚙ 📜 None		
Prize:	💰 2000-6000D	Item: None		
Prize:	💰 2000-6000D	Item: None		

Battle Name	Points	Entry Fee	Teams(VS)	Prize	Prohibited
Basic Battle	(1)	1000D	2 2	2000-6000D	None
Basic Battle	(1)	1000D	2 2	2000-6000D	None
Basic Battle	(1)	1000D	2 2	2000-6000D	None

CALTHA

CALTHA ARENA

NEARLY 2000 SLAVES DIED IN THE MAKING OF THE CALTHA ARENA, AND 400 BEASTS AND SEVERAL SMALL VILLAGES ALSO PERISHED IN THE WAKE OF ITS CONSTRUCTION. AT THE TIME, BUILDING RESOURCES WERE SO SCARCE IN IMPERIA THAT SOME SAY THE MASSIVE CAMPAIGNS AGAINST NORDAGH WERE INITIALLY MOTIVATED OUT OF THE NEED FOR MORE STONE AND WOOD, SIMPLY TO COMPLETE THE ARENA. EVEN WITH SO MUCH BLOOD ALREADY STAINING THE COLISEUM, THE POPULACE WAS MORE THAN READY TO SUPPORT THE BLOOD-SPORT WITHIN AND THE ARENA AT CALTHA HAS BECOME THE JEWEL IN THE CROWN OF THE IMPERIAL EMPIRE.

When you're ready for the biggest battle of all, return to Caltha in Imperia. There are no leagues or tournaments here, just the final Championship bout. You can't leave during the series of battles that follows, so make sure everyone's skills are in order, and that you've spent every last dime improving your gladiators' equipment. Caltha offers one final shop, the Emperor's Annex, where you can find a few nice items.

CHARACTER RECRUITMENT

Name	Classification	PRM	SNG
N/A	N/A	N/A	N/A

PRM=Cost for permanent recruitment
SNG=Cost for single battle

SHOP: EMPEROR'S ANNEX

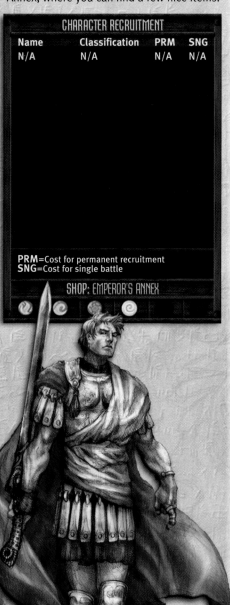

CALTHA HISTORY

Since Caltha is located on the Hatteus River, it started out as a port town, exporting olives. Hundreds of years old, the Senate of Caltha was founded by the wealthiest farmers of the area. Interested in getting more money in their pockets, they negotiated trade agreements with those as close as the other fledgling cities of Imperia, and as far away as the booming mine towns of the Southern Expanse. Over time, the Senate moved out of the countryside and into the city center. They had less and less to do with farming and eventually fell into power over the people of Caltha. The people have prospered under the Senate's governance now for nearly 1000 years, and Caltha benefits from this prosperity more than any other city.

School | Professional | 300000D

IMPERIAL HIGH CHAMPIONSHIP: CULTUS OCULARIS

Entry Fee: 9464D
Teams(VS): 5 vs. 5
Battle Points: 2
Required: All regional championship victories

IMPERIAL HIGH CHAMPIONSHIP: HIGH KRIGARE SCHOOL

Entry Fee: N/A
Teams(VS): 0-5 vs. 4
Battle Points: 2
Required: All regional championship victories

IMPERIAL HIGH CHAMPIONSHIP: RWINGO ARROWHEADS

Entry Fee: N/A
Teams(VS): 0-5 vs. 5
Battle Points: 2
Required: All regional championship victories

IMPERIAL HIGH CHAMPIONSHIP: DESERT OASIS

Entry Fee: N/A
Teams(VS): 0-5 vs. 4
Battle Points: 2
Required: All regional championship victories

IMPERIAL HIGH CHAMPIONSHIP: SCHOOL OF MUTUUS

Entry Fee: N/A
Teams(VS): 0-5 vs. 5
Battle Points: 2
Required: All regional championship victories
Items: Tidal Guard, Boar's Head, Heavy Scutum, Ramshead Bow
Prize: 50000-51000D

This is the relatively easy kind of series, where you heal up and can choose a new roster between rounds, so you only need to think one fight ahead when you choose your team. There are no restrictions on any of these fights, so use your Summoners (undead and otherwise) to great advantage. Since most of the battles start out with the two teams in a row, facing each other, dropping a skeleton or affinity beast behind the enemy lines will throw them into disarray and set you up for an unlimited supply of backstabs.

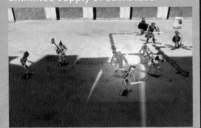

In the first round, you'll be fighting a Centurion-lead squad of Imperial Legionnaires. Your best heavies will make short work of them. In the second, light and medium Nordagh natives are your opponents, and while they're slightly higher level than you, the numerical advantage should make it an easy victory. Round three is primarily Archers and Amazons, an easy battle to type match with your Murmillos and Undead. Round four is the hardest to type match: Four Scorpions and Scarabs. Heavy units are best for bug smashing, but only use ones with long range attacks (like Cyclopes) or Running Attack (like Samnites and Ogres), in case the bugs decide to hang back and spit poison. In the final round, you face Ludo and his army of Dark Legionnaires. They're higher level than you are, but what are they going to do against your best heavy units? If you remember to choose ones with high Accuracy (since Legionnaires have good defense), you'll stand a good chance of victory. In situations like this, a Cyclops with a Blindman's Eye accessory is the best gladiator in the game. Ludo's defense is particularly high, so save up the affinity you earn from beating his henchmen and unleash it all on him.

But Then...
The game generously gives you several nanoseconds to savor your victory before everything goes horribly wrong. Now begins the game's true finale... You didn't really think it would be that easy, did you? In the battles that follow, there are no healers, and all deaths are permanent, except for story characters Ursula, Valens, Urlan, and Eiji (although the loss of your main character is still game over).

Usus: Hurry, we must get to safety. Follow me!

URSULA'S FINALE

I The Battle for Orin's Keep

Prize: Dark Gear, The Carnivore, Crown of Darkness, Death's Head

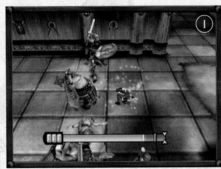

In this first challenge, Ursula, Valens, Urlan, and Eiji are forced to battle a behemoth of a man named Galverg, and his two Ogre henchmen. Three heavy types versus your three mediums, plus Eiji... match ups don't get much worse than that. Fortunately, despite what Usus said, anyone who dies here will come back for the next battle, except for Ursula.

Galverg can counter almost anything, so use Affinity Attacks, Ursula's magic abilities, and critical hits to take him down. Don't risk a combo, because if you fail to get all criticals, Galverg could kill you with a series of counter-attacks. Try to work up some affinity beating up on the Ogres, use earth or air Affinity Attack 3 to disable Galverg (the Ogres are immune to immobilizing status effects), and then take down the Ogres two on one. Gain some more Affinity in the

process, and use that and backstabs to finish off big G.

In the intermission after this battle, Urlan receives his father's gear: Orin's Axe, King's Armor, and the Barbarian Pride helm. These items grant him the Affinity Charge Up ability (among others), but no affinity on which to use it. Equip an Affinity Runestone to put this ability to good use.

II The Last of the Valkyrie

Prize: None

o Ursula, Urlan, and Valens will have to fight their way through a pair of Galdr to reach the witches' stronghold, but that's an easy battle that requires no explanation. The Galdrs will send you to the Lost City of the Valkyrie, but you'll be waylaid by an army of undead warriors before you get there. Take out the Summoner first, then use Affinity Attacks and Ursula techniques like Heavenly Light and Spell Blast to soften up the other Legionnaires.

Remember that the Undead are weak to Affinity, so a few uses of Affinity Attack 4 will wipe the board in this fight.

III   King Cyclops's Challenge

Prize: Spine Staff, Slate Axe, Gungnir, Piercing Hammer

The first wave of Cyclopes is an easy one. They're dangerous foes, sure, but at least they take plenty of damage when you slice 'em. Treat the first few to a couple good Combo Attacks, and then give their friends the best wishes of the Affinity Gods.

In future rounds, you'll be facing two Cyclopes and a single giant Affinity Beast. Despite their size, these beasts are only slightly more dangerous than regular Affinity Beasts. But they can be very difficult to kill; each is weak to weapons and attacks of opposing affinities, and virtually immune to weapons and attacks of its own kind.. Since you won't know which one you're facing beforehand, you have to make sure you have characters with decent Affinity Attacks (and ways to charge them) in at least of three of the four Affinities.

You get three free slots, so use them wisely; Channelers and Summoners are best.

Check each Affinity Beast's stats to see what its weaknesses are (they're listed as Innate Skills), and send the appropriate characters to take it down, while the others stay on Cyclops duty. You'll have to defeat all four beasts before the Cyclops King will enter the fight personally. Beware his devastating heavy strike and area attacks. You can cripple him from a distance with status effects, then charge him, surround him, and thrash him before he comes to his senses and begins winnowing your ranks.

Victory will earn you a variety of weapons, as well as new gear for Ursula: Feighona's Sword, Fendeil, Treanid, and Iolair. She'll also learn the Icarus Wings skill, and Heavenly Blast, a light affinity spell.

IV   Final Reckoning of Ludo & Mutuus

Prize: Phalanx, Clypeus

On your way to Roanor, you'll run into Ludo and a pair of his Dark Legionnaire henchmen. You've beaten them before, and the newly empowered Ur-Twins are stronger than ever. Ursula can charge her new Light Affinity bar with other techniques, like Spell Blast, and that should prove particularly devastating to the Dark Legionnaires.

The odds are worse when you get to Roanor: Your same four storyline characters versus Mutuus (a heavy unit similar to a Centurion) and four Dark Legionnaires. Ursula will be the key here, as her new armor makes her virtually indestructible, and her Light Affinity defense can negate Dark Affinity attacks. Have her wade into the center of battle, and your foes will surround her. She'll survive fine in the mush pot (if her hit points get low, she can always teleport away with Icarus Wings), and Urlan and Valens can get backstab bonuses by going after the distracted legionnaires.

VALENS'S FINALE

I The Temple of the Channelers

Prize: Dark Gear, The Carnivore, Crown of Darkness, Death's Head

In this first battle, Ursula, Valens, Urlan, and Eiji must defeat a behemoth of a man named Galverg and three Dark Legionnaires. This is a tough battle, but despite what Usus said, deaths on your side are not permanent (except for Valens, which is game over).

Galverg can counter almost anything, so use affinity attacks, Ursula's magic abilities, and critical hits to take him down. Don't risk a combo, because if you fail to get all criticals, Galverg could kill you with a series of counterattacks. Try to work up some Affinity beating up on the Dark Legionnaires, use earth or air Affinity Attack 3 to disable Galverg (the Dark Legionnaires are immune to immobilizing status effects), and then take down the Dark Legionnaires

two on one. Gain some more Affinity in the process, and use that and backstabs to finish off big G.

II The Test of Affinity Gods

Prize: Feathered Pike, Arcane Mallet, Andimaru, Brimmed Corinthian

Outside of the Hall of the Titans, you'll encounter an army of Undead Legionnaires lead by an Undead Summoner. Take out the Summoner first, then use Affinity Attacks and Ursula techniques like Heavenly Light and Spell Blast to soften up the other Legionnaires. Remember that the Undead are weak to Affinity, so a few uses of Affinity Attack 4 will wipe the board in this fight.

In each of the four rounds that follow, you'll battle a giant Affinity Beast summoned by an Affinity "Titan" and a pair of Channelers. Despite their size, these beasts are only slightly more dangerous than regular Affinity Beasts. But they can be very difficult to kill; each is weak to weapons and attacks of opposing affinities, and virtually immune to weapons and attacks of its own kind. The Fire Affinity beast in the first round is weak to earth and fire, the Air Affinity beast in the second is weak to air and earth, the Water Affinity beast in the third is weak to fire and water, and the final Earth Affinity beast is weak to air and earth. Dispatch your two best affinity specialists of the appropriate types to deal with the beasts, and fill your other slots with quick and deadly fighters (like Dervishes and Secutors) to kill the Channelers.

After the battle, don't forget to check out all of Valens' new gear. Not only do Munio's Sword, Shield, Armor, and Helmet provide stat boosts well beyond anything Valens could otherwise have, but they also gift him with a ton of innate abilities. Note that while the sword has Affinity Charge Up, it has no affinity itself, so you'll need to equip an affinity boosting badge if you want to continue to use affinity attacks.

III Final Reckoning of Ludo & Mutuus

Prize: Spine Staff, Slate Axe, Gungnir, Piercing Hammer

On your way to the Belfort gates you'll run into Ludo and a pair of his Dark Legionnaire henchmen. You've beat them before, and Valens is more than a match for his old friend now that he's packing Munio's gear. But don't get cocky about it; since Valens begins closer to Ludo than your other fighters, he'll quickly become surrounded. Have him fight defensively while Ursula and Urlan get free backstabs on the Dark Legionnaires. When they're finished, all three fighters can take Ludo down together.

Next up is Mutuus, who has brought four Dark Legionnaires to his battle with the same four characters that fought Ludo. Mutuus is a heavy gladiator, similar to a Centurion, so you'll want to concentrate on eliminating his henchmen first. Head up the steps for a bit of terrain advantage (especially useful to Eiji), and build up powerful Affinity Attacks with Combo Attacks. An early Affinity Attack 4 will make this battle significantly easier.

THE FINAL BATTLE

The first round of this battle is the most difficult, so you'll need to choose your roster carefully. An ideal character has a fairly cheap attack that can be used from two squares away, so Gungnirs, Peltasts, and Channelers are among the best, although you won't want more than two of them.

The Dark Knights that surround the Dragon have a very strong Wide Swing attack that can hit diagonally and does heavy damage, but they can't hurt you if there's an empty square between you. The danger in long range tactics comes from the Dragon itself, which fireblasts one side of the arena each turn. The dragon turns like clockwork, so if you time it carefully and move in to attack before your region gets blasted, you can avoid the inferno and only get attacked by the knights occasionally.

Dark Knights have high defense, and can take a beating, so Affinity Attacks are your best bet when you're in melee range. Start your characters far apart, since there is no effective way to team up against the knights (double teaming them will just result in taking extra damage from the Wide Swing attacks).

The key to defeating the Dark Knights is to exploit the safe point that opens up whenever one is killed. If you position a character diagonal to the dead Knight (on the side where there is no other knight), they'll be safe from everything. A Gungnir, Peltast, or Channeler (among others) can then safely kill the rest of the Knights on the two sides she's diagonal to. It's a cheap trick, but in this fight, you need it.

The second round is much easier. Just start a brawler in each of the four corners, and have them rush to the diagonal spots between the two faces. Bash the faces from each side (focus on two on opposite sides), and when they die, just turn and start fighting the other two. As long as you can survive their summoned creatures (which will die when they do), you'll be fine.

In the final round, choose strong characters who have a decent Running Attack. The key to victory is getting into melee with the dragon and pounding it silly, but its wing attack will knock characters back, so you'll spend a lot of time moving back into position. There will be casualties in this battle, but if you can get enough damage in, the final victory will be yours.

SAMPLE ENTRY

CLASS	NAME	Item Level LEVEL	Power PWR	Accuracy ACC	Defense DEF	Affinity Power AFF PWR	⚀	⚁	⚂	⚃	✦	✧	+ ABILITIES
Item Class	Item Name	10	10	10	10	10	●	●	●	●	●	●	Any Added Abilities

Brief description about the item.

WEAPONS

AXES

Light Axes are used only by Bandits, Berserkers, and Secutors, while most medium classes (as well as Cyclops and Mongrels) can use Medium Axes. Powerful Two Handed Axes can be used by heavy types like the Minotaur and Ogre.

CLASS	NAME	LEVEL	PWR	ACC	DEF	AFF PWR	⚀	⚁	⚂	⚃	✦	✧	+ ABILITIES
Light	Hatchet	1	3	4	-1	0							N/A
Light	Light Hatchet	2	6	4	-2	6	●	●	●	●			N/A
Light	Securis	2	6	4	-2	0							N/A
Light	Hand Axe	3	9	4	-2	6	●	●	●	●			N/A
Light	Ascia	4	12	4	-3	6	●	●	●	●			N/A
Light	Lignator	5	15	4	-4	6	●	●	●	●			N/A
Light	Francisca	6	18	6	-5	6				●			N/A
Light	Stone Axe	6	18	6	-5	4	●	●	●	●			N/A
Light	Pickaxe	7	21	6	-5	4	●	●	●	●			N/A
Light	Dolabra	8	24	6	-5	6	●	●	●	●			N/A
Light	Hunter's Axe	9	27	6	-6	6	●	●	●	●			N/A
Light	Bone Axe	10	30	6	-6	8			●				N/A
Light	Miner's Axe	10	30	6	-6	8				●			N/A
Light	Rounded Axe	12	36	8	-7	8	●	●	●	●			N/A
Light	Poison Axe	13	39	8	-7	10		●					Poisoned Blade
Light	Throwing Axe	14	42	8	-8	10				●			N/A
Light	Bladed War Axe	15	45	8	-8	0							N/A
Light	Inhero	15	45	8	-8	12	●	●	●	●			N/A
Light	Cleaver	16	48	10	-9	0							N/A
Light	The Bonesplitter	17	51	10	-9	14				●			N/A
Light	Golden Axe	18	54	10	-9	16			●				N/A

Hatchet — The Hatchet is a small axe with a heavy head, generally used in one hand. They are made quickly and shoddily, but are very inexpensive.

Light Hatchet — The Light Hatchet is a short handled tool used for chopping small game throughout the Windward Steppes. It is used as a weapon only because it has a blade.

Securis — The Securis is a sturdy, well made hatchet found throughout Imperia. Nearly every household has one.

Hand Axe — This is a basic small axe used in one hand. More for handy-men, this axe is usually used as a tool rather than a weapon.

Ascia — The Ascia is a carpenter's axe and normally isn't used for much more than chopping smaller pieces of wood. It loses its edge fairly quickly in battle.

Lignator — This small woodcutter's axe is relatively heavy for its size. It was first brought into the gladiatorial games as a challenge to disfavored fighters.

Francisca — The Francisca is a small, well-weighted axe designed to be thrown. In Nordagh, it is little more than an amusement and less of a weapon.

Stone Axe — This robust short axe is of crude construction but since it's heavier than most, it can be very effective in battle.

Pickaxe — More of a miner's pick than an axe, this light one-handed axe has a very small blade on one side and a long pick on the other.

Dolabra — The Dolabra is a standard issue weapon used by Legionnaires in the Imperial army for both combat and hunting.

Hunter's Axe — The Hunter's Axe has a pick on one side of the shaft and a long, thin, barbed blade on the other side. One who has hunted with this axe before is often a very powerful opponent in the arena.

Bone Axe — The strong stone blade of this axe is wedged in the crook of an old bone and carries enough weight behind it to do decent damage even through armor.

Miner's Axe — The Miner's Axe has a socketed iron head fastened onto a strong iron-reinforced wooden handle. The blade is more for cleaving than cutting, and therefore, isn't too sharp.

Rounded Axe — The rounded blade of this axe is sharpened into a very fine, almost razor sharp blade. Additionally, it has some weight to it allowing fairly heavy damage for a light axe.

Poison Axe — Alchemists have glazed the blade of this axe with a fine layer of poisonous crystal. When it cuts deep enough, it poisons the attacked.

Throwing Axe — This uniquely designed axe is very lightweight and has blades on both the top and the bottom of the handle.

Bladed War Axe — The Bladed War Axe, rather than having one axe blade, has many sword-like blades sticking out of the handle in a fan. This is a good weapon for piercing armor.

Inhero — The inhero is a heavy one-handed axe used by hunters to cleave apart fallen game. Its obvious connotation is what brought it into the gladiatorial games.

Cleaver — A very unique crafting, this axe has three blades that extend from the hilt outward at different angles, almost making it a bladed mace.

The Bonesplitter — The Bonesplitter is a strange looking light axe made to cut through bones with ease. The weight of this axe and the shape make it a very dangerous weapon.

Golden Axe — The Golden Axe is made from one piece of solid gold, hilt and all. Although originally meant for show, this axe's weight has brought it into the arena as a weapon.

CLASS	NAME	LEVEL	PWR	ACC	DEF	AFF PWR	🜁	🜂	🜃	🜄	✦	✧	+ ABILITIES
Light	**Ceremonial Axe**	19	57	10	-10	18			●				N/A
	This jewel encrusted axe is often used by clerics of the Southern Expanse during ceremonies honoring the earth god Solum. This Ceremonial Axe is a strong one handed weapon.												
Medium	**Broad Axe**	1	6	4	-1	0							N/A
	This is a tall war axe having a crudely forged broad edge on one side and a smaller blade opposite. It is the low end of medium ranking axes.												
Medium	**Epsilon Axe**	2	9	4	-2	0							N/A
	Crafted by amateur blacksmiths in the Southern Expanse, this axe has an uncharacteristically broad bronze head for an Expanse weapon.												
Medium	**Masakari**	3	13	4	-2	8	●	●	●	●			N/A
	This strong battle-axe has a very heavy metal head with a point opposite the blade. Its weight makes it both strong, yet difficult to wield.												
Medium	**Praecido**	4	15	4	-3	6	●	●	●	●			N/A
	The blades of this double-sided axe usually aren't very sharp, as most of the power comes from the combined weight of its blades and the harness which holds them to the hilt.												
Medium	**Bazo**	5	18	4	-4	6	●	●	●	●			N/A
	The Bazo is a traditional war axe whose variations have been used throughout history in the Expanse. It is often considered an old standby.												
Medium	**Vermillion Axe**	8	27	6	-5	6	●						N/A
	The Vermillion Axe is a standard medium axe in every way, except for the vivid reddish-orange enamel on its blade and hilt, giving it a fiery appearance.												
Medium	**Carnificina**	9	30	6	-6	0							N/A
	The Carnificina is a very basic double-bladed executioner's axe with a heavy hilt. The blades are large and a bit unwieldy in battle.												
Medium	**Slayer**	12	39	8	-7	8	●		●	●			N/A
	The Slayer is a shorter heavy axe whose enormous blades make it quite powerful, hence its name.												
Medium	**The Crusher**	13	42	8	-7	8	●	●	●	●			N/A
	Unlike most typical battle axes, The Crusher has only one blade, opposite which is a heavy metal ball adding a lot of weight and power to this weapon, hence its name.												
Medium	**Hook Axe**	14	45	8	-8	10	●	●	●	●			N/A
	The hook axe has standard blades on both sides of the hilt, except the tips of these blades are barbed, making it look all the more fierce.												
Medium	**Sparte**	16	51	10	-9	0							N/A
	This large axe was used for felling trees in the Sloan Forest before the dragon Riwigo was brought down at the blade of one, changing this axe from a tool to a weapon.												
Medium	**Spiked Battle Axe**	17	54	10	-9	10	●	●	●	●			N/A
	This axe has an elongated blade that extends above the end of the handle. On the opposite side is a long, wavy spike, making it effective when held forward or backward.												
Medium	**Thrusting Axe**	18	57	10	-9	12	●	●	●	●			N/A
	This axe has two very sharp, angular blades on either side of the shaft and a long blade sticking out from the tip of the shaft.												
Medium	**The Carnivore**	19	60	10	-10	12			●				N/A
	The Carnivore has a tall razor sharp blade on one side of the handle and a long toothed blade on the other side of the handle.												
Medium	**Altan**	20	63	10	-10	16	●	●	●	●			N/A
	The Altan is a very powerful Nordagh axe with legendary might. It takes two blacksmiths to forge this awesome war axe.												
Two Handed	**Great Axe**	1	8	4	-1	6	●	●	●	●			N/A
	The Great Axe was used to cut down the enormous trees of the Sloan Forest until Imperia and Nordagh started threatening each other at which point people took these to arms.												
Two Handed	**Bearded War Axe**	2	12	4	-2	6	●	●	●	●			N/A
	The Bearded War Axe gets its name from how the blade extends down to nearly where the wielder's hands are. For a two-handed weapon, its handle is fairly short, however.												
Two Handed	**Doloire**	5	24	4	-4	6	●	●	●	●			N/A
	This axe has a heavy blade that can be removed and put on a new handle. Since the blade is so heavy, the handles often crack under the stress and are reinforced with leather wraps.												
Two Handed	**Elephant Axe**	13	56	8	-7	6	●	●	●	●			N/A
	This large and long Southern Expanse axe was used to hunt elephants. Its long handle kept the hunter safely away from the dangerous tusks of their prey.												
Two Handed	**Kheten**	16	68	10	-9	8	●	●	●	●			N/A
	This is an ancient axe used by the noble guards of the kings of old throughout the Expanse. Light but huge, these double-handed axes are very intimidating.												
Two Handed	**Tekuja Axe**	20	84	10	-10	16	●	●	●	●			N/A
	Every now and again, the weapons of the revered Tekuja statues will show up for sale to be used in the arena. The Tekuja Axe symbolizes a great conquerer.												
Barbarian	**Riveted Battle Axe**	20	84	10	-10	0							N/A
	The Riveted Battle Axe's blades are replaceable once they've dulled from battle. The shaft and blade housing are made of a strong metal giving this axe a long lifespan.												
Berserker	**Slate Axe**	18	54	10	-9	0							N/A
	In a rare moment of calm, this axe was meticulously crafted from slate by the largest clan of Berserkers in Nordagh. It is rumored that there are women among the group.												
Berserker	**Jagged Stone Axe**	19	57	10	-10	14			●				N/A
	As the peoples of Nordagh are more in tune with the Earth affinity than any other region, this crude but very strong axe also has very strong ties to Solum.												
Dervish	**Hatchet Set**	2	6	4	-2	0							N/A
	This is a set of two Hatchets wielded by the dervish simultaneously. This low-end weapon is a good beginner's axe set, as it is very inexpensive.												
Dervish	**Light Hatchet Set**	4	12	4	-3	6	●	●	●	●			N/A
	While the Light Hatchet alone isn't too threatening, while in the hands of a dervish, two of them can be lethal. It is a light weapon set and easy for the dervish to use.												
Dervish	**Double Fist**	6	18	6	-5	4	●	●	●	●			N/A
	The Double Fist is what the dervishes call a pair of hand axes when they wield these "primitive" weapons from Nordagh.												
Dervish	**Axes Conseco**	8	24	6	-5	8	●	●	●	●			N/A
	Axes Conseco, literally meaning "dismembering axes" is simply a pair of Lignators wielded simultaneously. The Lignator is weighted so well that it is a perfect choice for the dervish.												
Dervish	**Pickaxes**	14	42	8	-8	8	●	●	●	●			N/A
	This is a pair of Pickaxes sold as a set to dervishes. Their light weight makes it easy to wield two of them simultaneously.												

CLASS	NAME	LEVEL	PWR	ACC	DEF	AFF PWR							+ ABILITIES
Dervish	**Crude Axes**	15	45	8	-8	12			●				N/A

A pair made of one Bone Axe and one Stone Axe, this weapon set allows for heavier attacks as well as lighter ones.

| Dervish | **Hunter's Axe Set** | 17 | 51 | 10 | -9 | 12 | ● | ● | ● | ● | | | N/A |

The Hunter's Axe Set is about the heaviest set of weapons that a dervish will wield. Generally inexperienced dervishes use this set.

| Dervish | **Woodsman Set** | 18 | 54 | 10 | -9 | 14 | | | ● | | | | N/A |

This axe set consists of an Ascia and an Inhero. Imperials use them alone--one for chopping wood and one for cleaving game--the dervish, however, are able to wield them simultaneously.

| Dervish | **Venomous Pair** | 22 | 66 | 12 | -10 | 20 | | ● | | | | | Poisonous Blade |

The Venomous Pair consists of two Poison Axes wielded simultaneously by the Dervish. Doubling the chances of successfully poisoning someone.

| Minotaur | **Declamatio** | 18 | 76 | 10 | -9 | 8 | ● | ● | ● | ● | | | N/A |

This brutal looking, yet finely crafted weapon is made by beastmasters for their minotaurs. The mouth on the face of this axe makes a screaming sound when swung through the air.

| Ogre | **Cultellus** | 20 | 84 | 10 | -10 | 12 | | | ● | | | | N/A |

A crude weapon forged by the beastly ogres, the Cultellus is little more than a huge meat cleaver. The strength of this weapon is nothing to be considered lightly.

| Undead | **The Carnivore** | 19 | 60 | 10 | -10 | 12 | | | | | ● | | N/A |

The Carnivore has a tall razor sharp blade on one side of the handle and a long toothed blade on the other side of the handle.

| Urlan | **Orin's Axe** | 20 | 84 | 10 | -10 | 0 | | | | | | | Affinity Charge Up |

Bequeathed upon Urlan, this axe was of his father's design, forged at the legendary Amtower Smithy, whose work remains, even to this day, unparalleled among all the known regions.

| Dark Legion | **Carnificina** | 9 | 30 | 6 | -6 | 6 | | | | | ● | | N/A |

The Carnificina is a very basic double-bladed executioner's axe with a heavy hilt. The blades are large and a bit unwieldy in battle.

BOWS

Only Amazons, Archers and Eiji can use Bows. Bows do less damage than spear-throwers' javelins, but have longer range and allow you to move and shoot in the same turn.

CLASS	NAME	LEVEL	PWR	ACC	DEF	AFF PWR							+ ABILITIES
Plain	**Bow**	1	3	0	-1	0							N/A

This is a standard beginner's bow made from a light wood with little or no embellishments whatsoever.

| Plain | **Short Bow** | 3 | 9 | 0 | -2 | 0 | | | | | | | N/A |

The Short Bow is an average bow that is often used while on horseback. It has decent accuracy and is easy to wield.

| Plain | **Hunter's Bow** | 6 | 18 | 0 | -5 | 6 | ● | ● | ● | ● | | | N/A |

The Hunter's Bow is an average, but sturdy and reliable bow. It's a rugged looking implement with small trophies of past kills dangling from it, such as feathers and fangs.

| Plain | **Silver Bow** | 10 | 30 | 0 | -6 | 8 | ● | ● | ● | ● | | | N/A |

This bow is made from the tough, pliable wood of the cypress tree with silver embellishments. It's not uncommon for this bow to have a small, silver sight just above the hand-guard.

| Plain | **Flaming Bow** | 11 | 33 | 0 | -7 | 10 | ● | | | | | | N/A |

This orange and red lacquered bow gives the illusion that the wielder is holding a bow of flame. It has a light, hollow construction and was historically used on horseback.

| Plain | **Recurve Bow** | 13 | 39 | 0 | -7 | 10 | ● | ● | ● | ● | | | N/A |

The ancient design of the Recurve Bow uses horn and sinew, taking the bowyers who made such weapons months to form into the unique double-curve shape.

| Plain | **Coral Bow** | 14 | 42 | 0 | -8 | 12 | | ● | | | | | N/A |

This bow is decorated with coral from the reefs of Southern Imperia. Those whose livelihood is hunting fish use this bow exclusively, adorning it with treasures found inside their catch.

| Plain | **Snakeskin Bow** | 16 | 48 | 0 | -9 | 12 | ● | ● | ● | ● | | | Poisoned Blade |

The Snakeskin Bow curves like the body of a snake and is coated with the skin of the vicious desert Black Adder. This bow adds poison to any arrow fired from it.

| Plain | **Black Bow** | 17 | 51 | 0 | -9 | 12 | | | | ● | | | Range Up |

Made of a darkly stained hardwood, this bow has amazing power, and is capable of extending an archer's range greatly. It is a good bow for covering your team.

| Amazon | **The Androktone** | 19 | 57 | 0 | -10 | 0 | | | | | | | Woman's Strength |

The Androktone, or "male killer" is a precision bow. In the hands of a skilled warrior, an attack from this bow does more harm to men than it does to women.

| Amazon | **Amazon's Bow** | 20 | 60 | 0 | -10 | 0 | | | | | | | N/A |

This elegant bow has been mastered by the leaders of the Amazons. They have been perfecting this bow type for generations and there is not a better bow in all the world.

| Archer | **Sniper's Bow** | 20 | 60 | 5 | -10 | 0 | | | | | | | Range Up |

The Sniper's Bow is a professional assassin's choice of weaponry. Its long shaft allows for increased range and fatal precision when aiming.

| Eiji | **Ramshead Bow** | 20 | 60 | 0 | -10 | 0 | ● | ● | ● | ● | | | N/A |

The Ramshead bow is a simplistic compound bow of uniquely ornate crafting. Instead of being attached directly to the bow's skeleton, the cord is held in the grip of miniture ram's heads.

CARAFES

Carafes are the only weapons Satyrs can use. Bottles of liquor don't make for particularly powerful weapons, but it's the only option for cloven-hoofed gladiators.

CLASS	NAME	LEVEL	PWR	ACC	DEF	AFF PWR							+ ABILITIES
Satyr	**Hip Flask**	1	3	4	-1	6	●	●	●	●			N/A

The Hip Flask is an ideal companion whilst away from home. Easily concealable, the Hip Flask can carry a small snifter of spirit to be savored when the Satyr needs it most.

| Satyr | **Flagon** | 3 | 9 | 4 | -2 | 6 | ● | ● | ● | ● | | | N/A |

The bulb at the bottom of this bottle packs quite a punch when the Satyr uses this item as a weapon. Keeping this bottle full is the key to maximum damage.

| Satyr | **Flask** | 5 | 15 | 4 | -4 | 6 | | | | ● | | | N/A |

This big round Flask holds in it a brew of the Satyr's own concocting. Either using it to hit someone with or to drink out of, the Satyr is very proficient with its uses.

| Satyr | **Cruet** | 6 | 18 | 6 | -5 | 7 | ● | ● | ● | ● | | | N/A |

This seemingly delicate bottle is cast in thick, nearly unbreakable glass. Due to the thickness of the glass, the volume of spirits within is sub-standard to most Satyrs.

CLASS	NAME	LEVEL	PWR	ACC	DEF	AFF PWR	◐	◑	●	◓	✦	✧	+ ABILITIES
Satyr	Phial	7	21	6	-5	8	●	●	●	●			N/A

The Phial has a solid base to accomodate for the rowdy nature of the Satyrs. Less spirit on the floor means more spirit among guests.

| Satyr | Mug | 8 | 24 | 6 | -5 | 9 | ● | | | | | | N/A |

This mug of mead is suitable for swinging madly in the air in an inebriated revalry, hitting whomever the satyr can.

| Satyr | Vial | 9 | 27 | 6 | -6 | 10 | ● | ● | ● | ● | | | N/A |

The Vial is typically used to keep medicinal spirits in. The base is much too small to be a reliable container for more recreational drink, as it is too easy to spill.

| Satyr | Bottle | 10 | 30 | 6 | -6 | 11 | | | ● | | | | N/A |

The Bottle, made from thick glass is a popular weapon for the satyr, as they're very easy to come by and once empty they don't have much worth other than that of a weapon.

| Satyr | Heavy Bottle | 11 | 33 | 8 | -7 | 12 | ● | ● | ● | ● | | | N/A |

The Heavy Bottle is a favorite among Satyrs in battle, as the base is solid glass. This bottle never spills.

| Satyr | Decanter | 12 | 36 | 8 | -7 | 0 | | | | | | | N/A |

The Decanter that the Satyr carries at his side is a source of bravery for the half human creature--or at least the liquid kept inside the Decanter is.

| Satyr | Crock | 14 | 42 | 8 | -8 | 15 | ● | ● | ● | ● | | | N/A |

Lighter than a jug, but much heavier than a bottle, this carafe holds an awful lot of mead. Only the toughest Satyrs can polish off the spirits within.

| Satyr | Pitcher | 15 | 45 | 8 | -8 | 16 | | | ● | | | | N/A |

This is a ceramic Pitcher used to bash people with or drink out of, depending on one's mood.

| Satyr | Jug | 17 | 51 | 10 | -9 | 17 | | | ● | | | | N/A |

This Jug is one of the heaviest weapons that the Satyr can equip. A hit on the head with this corked ceramic jug can deal major damage.

| Satyr | Decorated Bottle | 18 | 54 | 10 | -9 | 18 | ● | ● | ● | ● | | | N/A |

This Bottle is ribbed with sharp rings of glass. Even without the weight of the Satyr's spirits, this bottle packs quite a punch.

| Satyr | Canteen | 19 | 57 | 10 | -10 | 19 | ● | ● | ● | ● | | | N/A |

The Canteen is brought on long journeys by bands of Satyrs. Useful for transporting large amounts of wine and mead, it can also double as a weapon quite easily.

| Satyr | Carafe | 20 | 60 | 10 | -10 | 20 | ● | | | | | | N/A |

This heavy Carafe is filled with wine and keeps the Satyr's spirits high while in battle.

CLUBS

Plain clubs are simple weapons used only by Cyclops, Mongrel Shamans, and Yetis. They're not very accurate, and Yetis and Cyclops have access to more powerful options. High-affinity clubs are often the best bet for Arcane Mongrel Shamans, however.

CLASS	NAME	LEVEL	PWR	ACC	DEF	AFF PWR	◐	◑	●	◓	✦	✧	+ ABILITIES
Plain	Club	1	6	0	-1	0							N/A

This crude weapon is nothing more than a heavy piece of wood used to batter people, animals and things with.

| Plain | Wooden Bludgeon | 3 | 12 | 0 | -2 | 10 | | | | ● | | | N/A |

This is a basic wooden club. It is nothing more than a branch ripped from a hardwood tree.

| Plain | Bone Club | 5 | 18 | 0 | -4 | 10 | | | ● | | | | N/A |

The Bone Club is the most crude of the Mongrel weapons. It is nothing more than a large femur bone of a dead horse.

| Plain | Dabus | 5 | 18 | 0 | -4 | 10 | ● | ● | ● | ● | | | N/A |

The Dabus is basically a club with nails sticking out of it. It is a poor person's weapon and is better than nothing in the arena.

| Plain | Stone Club | 10 | 33 | 0 | -6 | 0 | | | | | | | N/A |

The Stone Club has been known to break after a lot of use, but generally is strong enough to smash most anything to a pulp, shields and helmets included.

| Plain | Crude Mace | 15 | 48 | 0 | -8 | 10 | ● | ● | ● | ● | | | N/A |

Inspired by their more civilized neighbors, the Mongrels fashioned this mace from raw metal and wood, pounding the metal spikes into a standard club to make this Crude Mace.

| Cyclops | Oracle Staff | 1 | 104 | 0 | -1 | 20 | | | | | ● | | N/A |

Said to be able to grant the Cyclops with a sixth sense, the Oracle Staff is used not only for arcane support, but is also a very powerful weapon.

| Cyclops | Serrated Bone Club | 19 | 60 | 0 | -10 | 18 | | | ● | | | | N/A |

Made from one of the wing bones of an immature dragon, the end of this club has the beginnings of the wing bones protruding from its end, forming a vicious edge.

| Mongrel | Petrified Bludgeon | 20 | 63 | 0 | -10 | 50 | | | ● | | | | N/A |

This club is made from wood that has long since turned to stone. It was found in caves as the Mongrels started excavating for their arena.

| Yeti | Horse Leg | 16 | 51 | 0 | -9 | 0 | ● | ● | ● | ● | | | N/A |

This weapon, suitable only for the Yeti is a gruesome testimony to the Yeti's strength. Ripped from a fallen warhorse, this "club" is left to dry until it's very rigid.

| Civilian | Stick | 1 | 12 | 0 | -1 | 0 | | | | | | | N/A |

This stick, ripped off of a nearby tree is all a civilian thrown into the arena can hope to be given to defend themselves with.

| Galverg | Pillar of Hate | 1 | 66 | 0 | -1 | 12 | | | | | ● | | N/A |

N/A

HAMMERS

Hammers are very powerful, but their Accuracy penalties make them a poor choice for heavy gladiators who already have low Accuracy. More accurate classes can put medium hammers to good use.

CLASS	NAME	LEVEL	PWR	ACC	DEF	AFF PWR	◐	◑	●	◓	✦	✧	+ ABILITIES
Medium	Jitte	3	13	0	-2	0							N/A

The Jitte, though considered a hammer, has no head. It is merely a shaft with a disarming hook at its base. This tool is used to keep prisoners in line throughout the Windward Steppes.

| Medium | Mallet | 4 | 17 | 0 | -3 | 6 | | | | | | | N/A |

The short handle of this hammer makes it possible to use the Mallet as a weapon at all, being that it has a very heavy metal head on the other end.

CLASS	NAME	LEVEL	PWR	ACC	DEF	AFF PWR							+ ABILITIES
Medium	**Crowbill**	5	20	0	-4	6	●	●	●	●			N/A

The Crowbill is more of a pick than a hammer, although if turned sideways, the harness for the pick blades could cause fair blunt damage.

| Medium | **Horn Hammer** | 6 | 23 | 0 | -5 | 8 | | ● | | ● | | | N/A |

The head of this weapon is made from the horns of oxen found throughout Nordagh. They are strapped to a handle wrapped in leather. The sharp horns can pierce some armors.

| Medium | **Light Pick** | 8 | 30 | 0 | -5 | 10 | ● | | | | | | N/A |

This pick was first used as a tool to bring ice down from the mountains. Now it has found its way into the gladiatorial games as a light and easy to wield weapon.

| Medium | **Weighted Mallet** | 9 | 33 | 0 | -6 | 10 | ● | ● | ● | ● | | | N/A |

The Weighted Mallet is an upgraded version of the Mallet. At the base of the head, there's a weight, making the weapon heavier.

| Medium | **Claw Hammer** | 10 | 36 | 0 | -6 | 0 | | | | | | | N/A |

The Claw Hammer is a carpenter's tool with a metal head fitted to a wooden handle. It is a powerful weapon for its size.

| Medium | **Fang** | 11 | 40 | 0 | -7 | 0 | | | | | | | N/A |

Made entirely of iron, shaft and blade alike, this weapon has a head with two blades sticking out of it at right angles to each other like shears.

| Medium | **Stone Hammer** | 13 | 46 | 0 | -7 | 12 | | | ● | | | | N/A |

Crafted much like the Horn Hammer, the Stone Hammer has a tapered stone bound to a shaft of wood. Heavier than the Horn Hammer, it is also more blunt.

| Medium | **Hoeroa** | 14 | 50 | 0 | -8 | 14 | ● | | | | | | N/A |

Made from a whale bone, this weapon has a curved handle with a double curved head sitting atop it.

| Medium | **Pernat** | 15 | 53 | 0 | -8 | 14 | ● | ● | ● | ● | | | N/A |

A simple mace, the Pernat consists of a large, round metal bead perched atop a medium-length stick. Made with functionality in mind, this mace is very powerful.

| Medium | **Clenched Fist** | 16 | 56 | 0 | -9 | 14 | ● | ● | ● | ● | | | N/A |

This hammer has a fist clenched in fury, cast in steel atop a medium length handle. It is heavy for a medium sized weapon.

| Medium | **Morningstar** | 18 | 63 | 0 | -9 | 16 | ● | ● | ● | ● | | | N/A |

This short-handled weapon has a round metal ball with spikes at its head. It is a fierce weapon wielded by Medium Class gladiators.

| Medium | **Studded Fist** | 19 | 66 | 0 | -10 | 16 | ● | ● | ● | ● | | | N/A |

The Studded Fist has a medium length handle with a cast iron head on it in the shape of a fist wearing jeweled rings. It is a pretentious weapon, but a crowd favorite nonetheless.

| Medium | **Lion's Fury** | 20 | 69 | 0 | -10 | 18 | ● | ● | ● | ● | | | N/A |

The Lion's Fury is a hammer with a head cast in heavy metal, to look like a pouncing lion. The head of this hammer is blunt, while the tail of it is semi-sharp.

| Heavy | **Miner's Pick** | 1 | 9 | 0 | -1 | 0 | | | | | | | N/A |

This is a heavy pick-axe used in the mines of the Qaa Rah Desert.

| Heavy | **Sledgehammer** | 3 | 18 | 0 | -2 | 6 | ● | ● | ● | | | | N/A |

This hammer is a convenient weapon found throughout the Windward Steppes. It is used to pound the stakes of the nomads' camps into the ground when pitching tents.

| Heavy | **Stone Maul** | 4 | 22 | 0 | -3 | 6 | | | ● | | | | N/A |

When the quarry workers in the Qaa Rah Desert discovered a new type of stone, they manufactured these crude hammers that sell in bazaars throughout the Southern Expanse.

| Heavy | **Tou-Fung** | 6 | 31 | 0 | -5 | 8 | ● | | | | | | N/A |

This heavy mace has a rigid shaft, upon which sits a forged cube of heavy metal. It is a crude weapon, though very effective.

| Heavy | **Ivory Mallet** | 8 | 40 | 0 | -5 | 0 | | | | | | | N/A |

The Ivory Mallet is an elephant's tusk taken from one of the great hunts strapped to an old tent stake. It is a crude, yet effective weapon in a bind.

| Heavy | **War Hammer** | 10 | 48 | 0 | -6 | 0 | | | | | | | N/A |

This is a standard war hammer with nothing too special about it. There's a spike on one side and a hammer head on the other.

| Heavy | **Quadrelle** | 11 | 53 | 0 | -7 | 0 | | | | | | | N/A |

This mace has four blades, or flanges, extending out from the center of the shaft at the top of the handle. It is a heavy brawler's weapon.

| Heavy | **Goupillon** | 13 | 62 | 0 | -7 | 12 | ● | ● | ● | ● | | | N/A |

The Goupillon is a steel, three pronged horseman's mace used by the queen's royal guard in Khorhu. It has a flat surface on its head so it can be stood on the ground easily.

| Heavy | **Samaam** | 14 | 66 | 0 | -8 | 12 | ● | ● | ● | ● | | | N/A |

The Samaam is a counterweighted hammer with a relatively small head for the weight of its handle. It can move extremely fast, building up a lot of force in its small head.

| Heavy | **Crusher** | 15 | 70 | 0 | -8 | 14 | ● | ● | ● | ● | | | N/A |

The Crusher is a smaller version of the Tenderizer, with two heavy mallet heads on either side of the shaft.

| Heavy | **Deletum** | 15 | 70 | 0 | -8 | 12 | ● | ● | ● | ● | | | N/A |

The head of this Maul fans out into a large flat square on one side and comes to a point on the other. Either way it is wielded brings about major damage.

| Heavy | **Dalima** | 18 | 84 | 0 | -9 | 16 | ● | | | | | | N/A |

The Dalima is a finely crafted war hammer cast of one solid piece of metal and polished to a sheen. Its dark blue color and simple elegance give it a fearsome visage.

| Heavy | **Curtus Saxum** | 19 | 88 | 0 | -10 | 12 | ● | | | | | | N/A |

This is a short handled war hammer with a sizeable metal head on the end, opposite a sizeable spike. It is capable of crushing someone's skull in a single hit if wielded with proficiency.

| Heavy | **Mjollnir** | 20 | 92 | 0 | -10 | 16 | ● | | | | | | N/A |

This mystic hammer of ancient myth carries with it an innate Fire Affinity charge and will sometimes burn an enemy. When thrown, this hammer always returns to its owner.

| Heavy | **The Tenderizer** | 20 | 92 | 0 | -10 | 18 | ● | ● | ● | ● | | | N/A |

The biggest of all mauls, The Tenderizer has a long, thick shaft and a mighty head. It is better to evade attacks from this maul than block them, as most shields won't survive the blow.

| Two Handed | **Maul** | 3 | 18 | 0 | -2 | 0 | | | | | | | N/A |

The Maul is a basic two-handed weapon found commonly throughout Nordagh. Its iron reinforced wooden head deals decent damage for a low end barbarian weapon.

| Two Handed | **Hercules Club** | 7 | 35 | 0 | -5 | 0 | | | | | | | N/A |

The Hercules Club is a huge two-handed wooden club adorned with metal studs. It is modeled after the ancient fables of Hercules, a hero of old.

CLASS	NAME	LEVEL	PWR	ACC	DEF	AFF PWR	◉	◉	◉	◉	◆	◉	+ ABILITIES
Two Handed	Plombee	9	44	0	-6	10	●	●	●	●			N/A

The Plombee is a wooden maul with lead reinforcing wrapped around the head to add both weight and skeletal support.

| Two Handed | Skullbasher | 14 | 66 | 0 | -8 | 12 | | | | ● | | | N/A |

This enormous hammer has a compact head of solid steel making it a very heavy and powerful weapon. Only the strongest barbarians can wield this weapon.

| Two Handed | Guardian's Mallet | 17 | 79 | 0 | -9 | 12 | ● | ● | ● | ● | | | N/A |

This heavy mallet from the Steppes was used in ancient times and therefore is fairly rare. It was wielded by barbarian slaves in the Steppes used as bodyguards while on long journeys.

| Two Handed | Tekuja Hammer | 20 | 92 | 0 | -10 | 16 | ● | ● | ● | ● | | | N/A |

The weapons wielded by the royal Tekuja statues depend upon how a particular monarch ruled in life. The Hammer is a symbol of unrelenting endurance.

| Barbarian | Piercing Hammer | 20 | 92 | 0 | -10 | 18 | | | ● | | | | N/A |

This barbarian hammer has a heavy head and is designed to break through armor. Made of strong iron mined within the Sloan Forest, this weapon holds a strong earth affinity.

| Centurion | Gavel | 18 | 84 | 0 | -9 | 16 | ● | ● | ● | ● | | | N/A |

A cerimonial hammer used in the courts of Imperia, the Gavel has made it into the gladiatorial games as if to illustrate judgement being passed on one's enemy. For Centurions only.

| Minotaur | Columnar Hammer | 16 | 75 | 0 | -9 | 16 | ● | ● | ● | ● | | | N/A |

This blunt-ended hammer is reminiscent of the architecture of Imperia. Wielding this weapon adds to the already fearsome appearance of a minotaur, making them seem invincible.

| Undead | Horn Hammer | 6 | 23 | 0 | -5 | 8 | | | | | ● | | N/A |

The head of this weapon is made from the horns of oxen found throughout Nordagh. The sharp horns can pierce some armors.

| Two Handed | Biathainne | 10 | 48 | 0 | -6 | 10 | | | | ● | | | N/A |

This mighty hammer is crafted and named after the hammer used by the Earth Titan to hunt Giant Boar; its shiny surface attracting the creatures to his ambush.

JAVELINS

Javelins are throwing spears, used exclusively by Gungnirs and Peltasts. Those classes can also use normal spears, but Javelins do more damage and tend to be more accurate, making them a superior choice.

CLASS	NAME	LEVEL	PWR	ACC	DEF	AFF PWR	◉	◉	◉	◉	◆	◉	+ ABILITIES
Plain	Aclys	1	6	0	-1	0							N/A

This is the most basic of all javelins as it is simply a piece of wood sharpened to a point at one end. About four feet long, it does very little damage.

| Plain | Tono | 2 | 9 | 0 | -2 | 0 | | | | | | | N/A |

This three-pronged spear has fierce barbed tips on each of its prongs. It is a unique looking weapon--a favorite among beginning peltasts and gungnirs.

| Plain | Spiculum | 3 | 15 | 0 | -2 | 6 | ● | ● | ● | ● | | | N/A |

The Spiculum has a thin, bladed point not unlike the Pilum, although shorter. There is very little weight to this spear and it is fairly easy to protect yourself from.

| Plain | Jaculum | 4 | 17 | 0 | -3 | 6 | ● | ● | ● | ● | | | N/A |

The Jaculum is a light Imperial Army issue javelin with a diamond-shaped steel head. It is fairly popular among peltasts as well as the gungnir.

| Plain | Egchos | 5 | 18 | 0 | -4 | 6 | ● | ● | ● | ● | | | N/A |

The Egchos is a reliable javelin with a heavy bronze tip designed to pierce most armors. The end of the javelin is also capped in bronze to prevent the wood from splitting.

| Plain | Sinan | 6 | 21 | 0 | -5 | 6 | | | | ● | | | N/A |

The Sinan is a blunt javelin made of solid gold, making this a heavy-hitting missile weapon. Only about four feet in length, when thrown hard, it can deal major damage.

| Plain | Spear | 8 | 27 | 0 | -5 | 6 | | | | ● | | | N/A |

This is a standard spear, longer than a lot of other javelins, it has no accents at all and is a basic, mass produced weapon, dealing average damage upon its target.

| Plain | Fuscina | 9 | 30 | 0 | -6 | 5 | ● | ● | ● | ● | | | N/A |

Although typically, tridents aren't thrown, this one is weighted such that it can be thrown short distances, causing major damage to the target.

| Plain | Gaesum | 13 | 42 | 0 | -7 | 0 | | | | | | | N/A |

The Gaesum is a light javelin made entirely of iron. These can be as long as ten feet, however, are much shorter when used in the arena.

| Plain | Javelin | 14 | 45 | 0 | -8 | 10 | | | | ● | | | N/A |

The Javelin is pointed on both ends of the spear and bends in the middle when winding up to throw it. It is extremely sharp and will penetrate nearly any armor.

| Plain | Pilum | 15 | 48 | 0 | -8 | 12 | ● | ● | ● | ● | | | N/A |

This is the standard issue javelin for the Imperial army. It has a long steel blade that extends from a pyramid shaped housing atop a round weight at the end of a long shaft.

| Plain | Koveh | 16 | 51 | 0 | -9 | 14 | ● | ● | ● | ● | | | N/A |

This spear from the Southern Expanse is weighted just heavily enough to pierce most armors, yet is light enough to carry many of. It has a barbed head causing extra damage upon removal.

| Plain | Falarica | 18 | 57 | 0 | -9 | 16 | ● | ● | ● | ● | | | N/A |

This heavy spear has a shaft of light metal with a weighted head of solid steel. It is meant to be either thrown or fired from a ballista.

| Gungnir | Gungnir | 19 | 60 | 99 | -10 | 14 | ● | ● | ● | ● | | | N/A |

The Gungnir is said to be one of the ancient mythical gods' javelins which always flies true, can never be deflected and returns to the thrower.

| Peltast | Feathered Pike | 19 | 60 | 0 | -10 | 15 | | | | ● | | | Bleeding |

The serrated blade on the end of this javelin can cause bleeding in opponents. It is a difficult to use javelin historically used by the Imperial cavalry, but was adopted by peltasts in the arena.

SPEARS

Light Spears can be thrown by Gungnirs or Peltasts, and used as a melee weapon by Bandits and Secutors. Heavy Spears can only be used in melee, and only by Centurions and Samnites.

CLASS	NAME	LEVEL	PWR	ACC	DEF	AFF PWR	◉	◉	◉	◉	◆	◉	+ ABILITIES
Light	Light Spear	1	3	3	-1	0							N/A

This small spear can only attack adjacent opponents, although it can also attack diagonally. Quick jabs are all it's good for. It's made of one piece of light metal, cast rather than assembled.

| Light | Contus | 2 | 5 | 3 | -2 | 0 | | | | | | | N/A |

The Contus is a light wooden polearm preferred by charioteers. Remarkably easy to use, it has recently found a home in the gladiatorial games.

CLASS	NAME	LEVEL	PWR	ACC	DEF	AFF PWR	◉	◉	◉	◉	✦	✦	+ ABILITIES
Light	Framea	3	8	3	-2	0							N/A
The Framea is nearly a lance rather than a bladed polearm. It is merely a thrusting weapon and not a slicing weapon.
Light	Pike	5	14	3	-4	0							N/A
The Pike is a standard polearm from the Windward Steppes consisting of a simple barbed blade at the top.
Light	Sligi	6	16	5	-5	6	●	●	●	●			N/A
Instead of a thrusting point traditional to other spears, this unique light spear actually has a long, single-edged blade at the end that tapers to a very sharp point.
Light	Ictus	7	19	5	-5	4	●	●	●	●			N/A
This short spear is made for thrusting rather than slashing. It has a small arrowhead-like tip on the end. Because of its size, it has short range for a spear.
Light	Keris	8	22	5	-5	8				●			N/A
The Keris has a teardrop shaped point, the heft of which is counterweighted by a golden orb on the far end of the shaft.
Light	Hak	10	27	5	-6	8	●	●	●	●			N/A
This intimidating spear has a long, wavy blade at its end. This spear evolved when people started fastening used sword blades to the ends of their walking sticks for protection.
Light	Mongile	12	32	6	-7	10	●	●	●	●			N/A
This thrusting spear has a very sharp point on the end that is carved out of the same wood as the shaft and then encased in metal. At the base are two metal barbs.
Light	Half Moon	13	35	6	-7	12	●	●	●	●			N/A
This is an ages old traditional polearm found in the Steppes. It has a crescent-shaped blade at the tip, which is sharpened on both sides.
Light	Cuspis	14	38	6	-8	0							N/A
This spear is used mainly for slashing enemies at a distance rather than stabbing them, as the blade is too brittle to be used effectively against well armored warriors.
Light	Naginata	16	43	8	-9	16	●	●	●	●			N/A
The Naginata are used by the nomadic guards that patrol the camps of the Wastes in The Windward Steppes. They have a curved blade at the top, with a sword-like guard at its base.
Light	Spetum	18	49	8	-9	0							N/A
An interesting trident-type spear, this thin polearm forks at the top with a double-sided blade surrounded by long thin spikes.
Heavy	Rummh	3	14	3	-2	6	●	●	●	●			N/A
This thin polearm has an ornate grip in the middle of the shaft which gradually tapers to a point. The weights on this spear add strength to its thrusting power.
Heavy	Tschehouta	5	22	3	-4	6	●	●	●	●			N/A
This double pointed Spear is made of heavier wood and has a weight at each end, just beneath its spaded points.
Heavy	Pole Axe	8	32	5	-5	6	●	●	●	●			N/A
This long polearm has a large axe blade at the top with a long thin hammer opposite the blade.
Heavy	Heavy Spear	9	36	5	-6	6	●	●	●	●			N/A
This heavy spear can strike from very far away. It has a heavy weight at the foot of the shaft which acts as a counter-balance when the spear is thrust at maximum distance.
Heavy	Halberd	12	47	6	-7	8	●	●	●	●			N/A
Although technically a spear, the Halberd is nearly a battle axe, except the shaft is about seven feet long and it's only got a blade on one side of the staff.
Heavy	Romphaea	13	50	6	-7	10	●	●	●	●			N/A
This polearm has a long curved, double-edged blade atop its head adding at least two feet to an already sizeable weapon.
Heavy	Partisan	15	58	6	-8	12	●	●	●	●			N/A
The Partisan has a solid bronze blade at the top that fans out in an ornate fork-like design. It is a tall and intimidating weapon used for stabbing more than slicing.
Heavy	Tumpuling	16	61	8	-9	14	●	●	●	●			N/A
This spear has a uniquely bladed flat tip and is kept very sharp. It has a strong shaft made of a heavy wood and is stained with the blood of fallen foes.
Heavy	Assegai	18	68	8	-9	16	●	●	●	●			N/A
This tall spear has an exaggerated point, around the base of which stick out small barbs for added damage and even parrying when wielded by a true master.
Heavy	Tawuus	20	76	8	-10	8	●	●	●	●			N/A
This spear has six blades extending from the top. Each blade represents the power of one of The Gods. When using this weapon, The Heavens are at your command.
Samnite	Pierced Spear	19	76	8	-10	0							N/A
The incredible weaponsmiths of the Windward Steppes created the Pierced Spear based on the design of the Pierced Blade.
Javelin	Khonsu	10	33	0	-6	6					●		N/A
This mighty spear is crafted and named after the spear used by the Air Titan to hunt Hippogriffs. It can be thrown so fast that it becomes seemingly invisible.

STAFFS

Staffs are used by Channelers, Mongrel Shamans, Summoners, and Undead Summoners—arcane classes that have little use for attack power. Choose your staff based primarily on Affinity type and power.

CLASS	NAME	LEVEL	PWR	ACC	DEF	AFF PWR	◉	◉	◉	◉	✦	✦	+ ABILITIES
Plain	Escrima Stick	1	3	6	-1	0							N/A
The Escrima Stick, wielded as you would a sword, is for any class that cannot equip more traditional weapons. This is a beginner's weapon for arcane classes.
Plain	Crook	2	6	6	-2	10	●	●	●	●			N/A
This is a long, crooked walking stick adorned with jewelry and precious personal treasures. A hefty piece of wood, it is usually used for magical support rather than attack.
Plain	Cudgel	3	9	6	-2	10				●			N/A
Used by casters more in tune with the rough rather than the refined, the Cudgel is a shorter staff with a heavy head used to beat animals--and humans--into submission.
Plain	Naboot	4	12	6	-3	10	●						N/A
Used in the Qaa Rah Desert as a tool of punishment by beating. However, the basic style of this staff wouldn't give a warrior the upper hand if they didn't already have it.
Plain	Bo	5	15	6	-4	10					●		N/A
This long staff is the most basic of the long fighting staves. It is simply a round piece of flexible wood about six feet long.

CLASS	NAME	REQ LVL	PWR	ACC	DEF	AFF PWR	◉	◉	◉	◉	◉	◉	+ ABILITIES
Plain	Quarterstaff	6	18	9	-5	10	●	●	●	●			N/A

The Quarterstaff is a simple, straight piece of wood wielded as a weapon to keep melee attackers at bay. It is very similar to the Bo, found in the Windward Steppes.

| Plain | Shoum | 8 | 24 | 9 | -5 | 0 | | | | | | | N/A |

Like many staves of the Expanse, this one is more about providing physical protection than magical support. It is made of a strong wood and has knots all the way up the shaft.

| Plain | Sceptrum | 9 | 27 | 9 | -6 | 0 | | | | | | | N/A |

A politician's staff from Imperia made from cypress wood with precious metals and ivory, this staff has a heavy attack, but carries no affinity.

| Plain | Asa | 12 | 36 | 12 | -7 | 12 | ● | ● | ● | ● | | | N/A |

The Asa is a simple rod of wood topped with a crystal sphere held on by the will of the wielder alone. Once mastered, it's a formidable melee tool.

| Plain | Veneficus | 14 | 42 | 12 | -8 | 12 | | ● | | | | | Venom |

This staff carries the inherent ability to poison the victim of its blow. It casts a magical poison attack upon impact that cannot be cured by any antidote known.

| Plain | Asaya | 16 | 48 | 15 | -9 | 14 | | | | ● | | | Magic Attack Up |

The Asaya is a staff of gold with a jeweled sun atop, which glows in the strong desert sunlight. It is an essential tool for casters as it boosts the carrier's magic.

| Plain | Magus | 18 | 54 | 15 | 9 | 14 | ● | ● | ● | ● | | | Spell Range Up / Magic Defenses |

A mysterious looking staff that not only cuts the SP cost of spells greatly, but also surrounds its master with an aura of protection, increasing defense against magic attacks.

| Plain | Earth Staff | 20 | 60 | 15 | -10 | 18 | | | ● | | | | N/A |

Dug up from the mire of the bogs of Fliuch, this petrified root curves up from the base, forming a knotted head at the top. It is a heavy weapon blessed by Solum.

| Plain | Flame Staff | 20 | 60 | 15 | -10 | 18 | ● | | | | | | N/A |

The dark wood of the shaft of this staff and the flame-red phoenix feathers adorning it make this staff appear as if it is aflame. Blessed by Exuro.

| Plain | Staff of Air | 20 | 60 | 15 | -10 | 18 | | | | ● | | | N/A |

Aeris, the great warrior god of the sky, distributed his weapons down to earth so mortals who fought wars in his name could excel by his glory.

| Plain | Staff of Water | 20 | 60 | 15 | -10 | 18 | | ● | | | | | N/A |

Crafted out of steel, this staff assumes the shape of a fabled two-headed sea-monster inhabiting the Aeonis Sea. This weapon increases your Water Affinity.

| Channeler | Arcane Mallet | 19 | 57 | 15 | -10 | 16 | ● | ● | ● | ● | | | N/A |

The Arcane Mallet is a hybrid of an arcane staff and a traditional melee weapon. The floating jewel above the mallet head enhances one's affinity.

| Mongrel | Spine Staff | 18 | 54 | 15 | -9 | 20 | | | ● | | | | Blind |

This evil tool of the dark arts consists of a horse's spine; the skull acting as a receiver of the dark energy. It carries the ability to blind opponents.

| Summoner | Kinetic Staff | 19 | 57 | 15 | -10 | 12 | ● | ● | ● | ● | | | N/A |

The Kinetic Staff is a testament to the power of the mind. Held only by the willpower of the summoner's mind, this staff is stronger than most other arcane weapons.

| Undead Summoner | Death's Head | 20 | 60 | 15 | -10 | 10 | | | | | ● | | Death |

Made of an obsidian shaft, this staff is capable of killing someone in one hit, if wielded by a true master, serving under the Dark God.

| Plain | Sceptrum Fontis | 10 | 30 | 9 | -6 | 10 | | ● | | | | | N/A |

This mighty staff is crafted and named after the staff used by the Water Titan to control the tempers of the sea.

SWORDS

Swords are accurate, fairly powerful, and can be used by most classes. Bandits, Berserkers and Secutors use light swords; all medium classes (except Barbarians) use medium swords; and Centurions, Ogres, and Samnites wield heavy blades.

CLASS	NAME	LEVEL	PWR	ACC	DEF	AFF PWR	◉	◉	◉	◉	◉	◉	+ ABILITIES
Light	Dagger	1	3	6	-1	0							N/A

The Dagger is a basic beginner's weapon. It's reliable, although not too powerful.

| Light | Parazonium | 2 | 5 | 6 | -2 | 0 | | | | | | | N/A |

The Parazonium is an old, simple knife with no accents at all.

| Light | Main Gauche | 3 | 8 | 6 | -2 | 0 | | | | | | | N/A |

Typically, this kind of sword would have been used more for parrying, due to its long, curved quillons, but its heft has brought it into the arena as a light sword.

| Light | Kard | 4 | 11 | 6 | -3 | 0 | | | | | | | N/A |

The Kard is an ornate knife crafted from one piece of metal, hilt and blade of the same forging. The handle is engraved with religious scriptures and iconography.

| Light | Full Moon | 5 | 14 | 6 | -4 | 6 | ● | ● | ● | ● | | | N/A |

Used more for parrying than attacking, the Full Moon has a curved blade and a round orb on the end of the handle. Used well, it can cause serious damage as it is kept very sharp.

| Light | Pugio | 6 | 16 | 9 | -5 | 6 | ● | ● | ● | ● | | | N/A |

The Pugio is a straight, double-edged dagger. It looks fairly similar to the Gladius and is very popular among Imperials.

| Light | Acinaces | 8 | 22 | 9 | -5 | 8 | ● | ● | ● | ● | | | N/A |

Like the Kard, this weapon is forged from one solid piece of metal, however, its blade is sharpened on both sides, rather than one.

| Light | Scramasax | 9 | 24 | 9 | -6 | 0 | | | | | | | N/A |

The Scramasax is a strong sword not uncommon to the gladiatorial games, nor to full scale war. Since they are made with great care, buying a Scramasax is a wise investment.

| Light | Sickle | 9 | 24 | 9 | -6 | 8 | ● | ● | ● | ● | | | N/A |

This sword has a small, simple handle with a curved blade extending from it and is sharpened only on the inside of the nearly circular curve.

| Light | Chopper | 11 | 30 | 12 | -7 | 10 | ● | ● | ● | ● | | | N/A |

This executioner's tool is a broad, heavy-bladed light sword brought into the arena to cleave rather than slash or pierce.

| Light | Forester's Dagger | 12 | 32 | 12 | -7 | 12 | | | | ● | | | N/A |

The Forester's Dagger is meant to be carried for protection against wild animals and is always kept very sharp. It has a long, light blade with a slight curve to it.

| Light | Liberation | 14 | 38 | 12 | -8 | 0 | | | | | | | N/A |

Liberation is the official suicidal dagger used by the queens of the royal families should any enemy forces ever overtake their palace.

CLASS	NAME	LEVEL	PWR	ACC	DEF	AFF PWR	◐	◑	◒	◓	✦	⬡	+ ABILITIES
Light	Falx Supina	15	41	12	-8	14	●	●	●	●			N/A
Light	Croag	16	43	15	-9	16	●						N/A
Light	Leviathan	17	46	15	-9	16		●					N/A
Light	Harpe	20	54	15	-10	18	●	●	●	●			Deep Strike
Medium	Machera	1	5	6	-1	0							N/A
Medium	Small Sword	2	8	6	-2	0							N/A
Medium	Chereb	3	11	6	-2	6	●	●	●	●			N/A
Medium	Rising Sun	4	14	6	-3	6				●			N/A
Medium	Quaddara	5	16	6	-4	6	●		●	●			N/A
Medium	Sica	6	19	9	-5	8	●						N/A
Medium	Gladius	7	22	9	-5	0							N/A
Medium	Fazwan	8	24	9	-5	0							N/A
Medium	Xan	9	27	9	-6	10	●	●	●	●			N/A
Medium	Flyssa	10	30	9	-6	10	●	●	●	●			N/A
Medium	Caithain	11	32	12	-7	10	●	●	●	●			N/A
Medium	Saif	12	35	12	-7	10	●	●	●	●			N/A
Medium	Mainz	13	38	12	-7	12	●	●	●	●			N/A
Medium	Shamshir	14	41	12	-8	14				●			N/A
Medium	Falcatta	15	43	12	-8	14	●	●	●				N/A
Medium	Cor	16	46	15	-9	4	●	●	●	●			N/A
Medium	Trialabrum	16	46	15	-9	14	●	●	●	●			N/A
Medium	Zatoichi	19	54	15	-10	16	●	●	●	●			Cripple
Heavy	Estoc	1	7	6	-1	0							N/A
Heavy	Chemong	2	11	6	-2	0							N/A
Heavy	Zulf-I-Khar	4	18	6	-3	a64	●	●	●	●			N/A
Heavy	Falchion	5	22	6	-4	0							N/A
Heavy	Spatha	6	25	9	-5	0							N/A
Heavy	Yatagan	6	25	9	-5	8	●	●	●				N/A
Heavy	Herebra	7	29	9	-5	6		●					N/A
Heavy	Sapara	9	36	9	-6	6							N/A

Differing from the Sickle mainly by its weight, this Imperial weapon is curved and is sharpened only on the inside of the curve.

It is rumored that this light sword is made from polishing down and sharpening a dragon's fang, although it's more likely to be a boar's tusk.

This wavy-bladed dagger carries the affinity of the water god, Maritimus, and cuts through flesh as easily as a boat cuts through water.

The curved blade of this sword is said to pierce twice as deep. Mythology claims that exactly this type of knife was used to slay the cyclops king.

This sword is always kept sharp, but once it loses its edge, it's not very useful. This is a good short sword for one-on-one combat, but in a big battle it's not very practical.

Simple and easy to use, the Small Sword is rarely kept too sharp. Someone trained with this weapon usually uses thrusting attacks rather than slashing attacks.

This is a straight short, double-edged bronze sword usually used in holy rituals by the middle to lower class citizens.

The Rising Sun is a traditional nomadic weapon, light, with a subtly curving blade. The hilt pays homage to the god of life.

The Quaddara is one of the few straight-bladed swords used in the Southern Expanse. It has a central shaft down the middle where the blades originate from.

The Sica is a short Imperial sword favored by assassins. It's easy to conceal and light enough to carry great distances, while stalking the target.

The standard arena sword of Imperia, the Gladius, is a small double-sided straight bladed sword. These swords are mass produced, their quality suffers and they can be brittle.

The Fazwan is a simple, light, well crafted sword and is a favorite throughout the Southern Expanse. It has been known to be called the Gladius of the South.

The handle of the Xan is exactly as long as the blade and weighs as much. It is meant to be wielded one-handed.

This is the national weapon of choice of most upper class throughout the Expanse. It has a simple elegance which appeals to the schools of Akar An.

This is a rare Nordagh sword made with care over brute force. Its blade is strong and its handle, makes this sword not only deadly, but handsome.

The Saif is a curved sword from the Southern Expanse with a hooked pommel for easier swordplay acrobatics.

The Mainz is a step above the Gladius. It isn't mass produced and although the blade is thinner, it is wider and gives more during combat.

This is a medium length curved sword used in the school of Akar An to train would be Dervishes.

The Falcatta is a unique looking weapon with a hooked handle and a blade that is curved on its sharpened side, but straight on the dull side of the blade.

One of the heaviest medium swords, the Cor is forged deep in the forest by the roughest blacksmiths in the known world.

This is a short sword with a fat blade, sharpened on both sides. Its weight makes up for its length as it is very heavy for a one-handed weapon.

This is a true warrior's sword. It has no hand-guard and although light and seemingly easy to use, only the mighty can wield it with precision to killl.

The Estoc is a long sword designed for thrusting attacks more than for slicing attacks. Its blades aren't kept very sharp, but the bonus to accuracy one gets is great.

This sword is a heavier version of the short daggers that the nomads of the Steppes use as utility tools. It has a very sharp curved blade.

Because of its accuracy and history, this sword, modeled after that of the great prophets of the royal court of Ibliis is a rare commodity.

The Falchion is different from most Imperial swords, as it has a curved, double-edged blade that looks as if its design was inspired by the weaponry of the Southern Expanse.

The Spatha is a longer version of the Gladius, usually reserved for the Imperial Cavalry, but sometimes making its way into the gladiatorial arena.

Made for the holy war between the East and the South, this sword was meant to dispatch enemies of the gods. It has made its way into the games because of its intimidating history.

The blade of the Herebra is shaped like the rare, yet robust life-giving leaves of the trees of the Southern Expanse and carries an innate Water Affinity charge.

This ancient sword is crafted of bronze and was rumored to be the very same style of sword that Aeris fought with alongside the other gods in the Six Heavens War.

CLASS	NAME	LEVEL	PWR	ACC	DEF	AFF PWR						+ ABILITIES
Heavy	Xiphos	10	40	9	-6	8				●		N/A
This bronze sword has a straight, razor sharp blade on one side, upon which rest the heavenly shapes of clouds, inspiring visions of heaven.											
Heavy	Crescent Moon	11	43	12	-7	12	●	●	●	●		N/A
The Crescent Moon has a fat blade that curves to mimic the shape of the crescent moon above the plains of the Windward Steppes.											
Heavy	Scimitar	12	47	12	-7	10	●	●	●	●		N/A
The Scimitar is a one-handed sword used throughout the desert to protect royalty and the high-class. It has a curved blade, tapered toward the hilt which comes to a point at the fatter tip.											
Heavy	Dammar	15	58	12	-8	12	●	●	●	●		N/A
The Dammar is almost more of a cleaver than a sword. It only has one sharpened edge and could be thought of as a cross between the Cinquedea and the Dadao.											
Heavy	Runic Blade	15	58	12	-8	10	●	●	●	●		N/A
The Runic Blade is an ancient sword, older than most swords of Nordagh. It has a straight blade, that, if not for the runes inscribed along its length, would seem rather mundane.											
Heavy	Chagatai	16	61	15	-9	18		●	●	●		N/A
This sword is named after the blades the nomads use to protect their camp. They prop these blades around their camp to dissuade attacks. Eventually, they made them into swords.											
Heavy	Executioner's Sword	17	65	15	-9	0						Death
With no need for a point, the Executioner's Sword is used for beheading prisoners. The blade is sharp enough to kill with a single blow if a critical hit is achieved.											
Heavy	Cinquedea	18	68	15	-9	16			●			N/A
This heavy, Imperial themed version of the traditional dagger of the same name is a favorite among heavy classes and is one of the heaviest swords found in Imperia.											
Heavy	Dahshat	19	72	15	-10	14	●					N/A
The Dahshat is a long sword with a wavy blade and curved hilt. The mists of Saraa Izel have been blown into the jewel joining the blade to the handle, which can confuse an opponent.											
Heavy	Kuzhuk	20	76	15	-10	6						N/A
The Kuzuk is a legendary warrior's sword passed down through a warrior's family. It has a curved blade which mimics the winds that blow over the Windward Steppes.											
Heavy	Percello Gravis	20	76	15	-10	0						N/A
Available to the Samnite only, the Percello Simplex, like the Percello Gravis, is only used in the games.											
Two Handed	Flamberge	4	18	6	-3	8		●				N/A
This unique two-handed Flamberge has a slight bend to its blade and is kept relatively sharp even though its weight is the true reason to equip this weapon.											
Two Handed	Claymore	11	43	12	-7	12	●	●	●	●		N/A
The Claymore is a standard two-handed sword. The blade is relatively thin and totally straight. The length of this sword is very intimidating.											
Two Handed	Dadao	15	58	12	-8	16	●	●	●	●		N/A
This sword has a heavy one-sided blade that makes it feel very much like a cleaver, although it still comes to a sword-like point at the end.											
Two Handed	Caladcholg	18	68	15	-9	18	●	●	●	●		N/A
The Caladcholg is a regal sword with perfectly straight angles and a long blade. The base is covered with leather so the wielder can hold it by the blade as well as by the handle.											
Two Handed	Tekuja Sword	20	76	15	-10	16	●	●	●	●		N/A
Throughout the Expanse, giant statues are erected in honor of Kings and Queens past. The Tekuja Sword is a weapon stolen from these oracles. It is a very powerful weapon.											
Bandit	Shank	8	22	9	-5	0						N/A
Bandits will often craft small and crude daggers from scraps of metal. The Shank has a low attack, but can strike someone dead in one hit if used in a back attack.											
Barbarian	Pointed Broadsword	18	68	15	-9	16	●	●	●	●		N/A
The Pointed Broadsword has a long blade that comes to a diamond-shaped point at the end. The weight of this weapon is enormous.											
Centurion	Phalanx	19	16	15	-10	16						N/A
The Phalanx is a heavy Gladius wielded only by the strongest Centurions.											
Centurion	Emperor's Blade	20	76	15	-10	0						Crowd's Favor
The largest blade found in the Imperial Army, the Emperor's Blade is awarded to the best centurions serving the Emperor's glory. Wielding this weapon pleases the crowd.											
Dervish	Pair of Daggers	1	3	6	-1	0						N/A
Although this weapon is fairly weak when wielded as the primary weapon, a Dervish wielding two of them is a dangerous enemy to encounter.											
Dervish	Jambiya	10	27	9	-6	10	●	●	●	●		N/A
The Jambiya is a typical Expanse game-carving knife with a curved, double-edged blade used by apprentice Dervishes in Akar An.											
Dervish	Dual Pugio	12	32	12	-7	12	●	●	●	●		N/A
This is the closest a Dervish can come to feeling at home with a weapon while in Imperia. These light swords are a fairly good complement to a pair of light swords from the Southern Expanse.											
Dervish	Khanjar Set	13	35	12	-7	12	●	●	●	●		N/A
This widely used dagger set has a slightly double-curved blade and a curved grip. The Khanjar are rarely used by any class other than the dervish.											
Dervish	Double Scramasax	16	43	15	-9	0						N/A
These two swords have hardwood handles with brass pommels. This weapon has fallen out of favor with most gladiators and is a rare treat to find.											
Dervish	Twin Vipers	17	46	15	-9	12		●				Poisonous Blade
The Vipers are short swords with poisonous blades used by assassin Dervishes employed throughout the royal court in the Southern Expanse.											
Dervish	Double Hookblade	19	51	15	-10	16	●	●	●	●		N/A
Using the vicious hooks at the ends of these blades, the Dervish can keep their target close by, greatly increasing the accuracy of their attacks.											
Dervish	Hunter's Arsenal	19	51	15	-10	12	●					N/A
The Hunter's Arsenal is a natural choice for Dervishes traveling through Nordagh, as the Forester's Dagger and the Croag are weighted perfectly for their double-bladed skills.											
Dervish	Tsunami	20	54	15	-10	32		●				N/A
The Tsunami is simply what the dervish call it when they wield two Leviathans, a sword with strong water affinity.											
Dark God	Eleventh Hour	20	90	15	-10	200				●		N/A
N/A											

General Strategy · Character Classes · World Atlas · Bonus Material

CLASS	NAME	LEVEL	PWR	ACC	DEF	AFF PWR	◉	◉	◉	◉	◆	◉	+ ABILITIES
Gwazi	**Ram-Dao**	19	54	15	-10	16					●		N/A
A very powerful ore found only in the Southern Expanse. The refined metal of this ore is imbued with the dark affinity and as such, suits Gwazi well.													
Legionnaire	**Light Spatha**	16	46	15	-9	0							N/A
A shorter version of the Spatha. Although shorter, the weight of this sword is retained to a great extent, making it a powerful sword for the Legionnaire.													
Legionnaire	**Longblade Pugio**	17	49	15	-9	0							N/A
The Longblade Pugio is a sword version of its very popular Imperial dagger's namesake. Kept very sharp, even for a short sword, its damage rating is very high.													
Ludo	**Dark Blade**	1	54	15	-9	18					●		N/A
After leaving Valens' school, Ludo swore his life away to the Dark God. He uses this bastardized version of Valens' Machera charged with the dark affinity as his weapon.													
Murmillo	**Blade of Tides**	17	49	15	-9	18	●						Bleeding
The Blade of Tides is a cruel looking weapon based on the ferocity of the open sea. As many lives as the mighty waters have claimed, so shall this blade.													
Murmillo	**Caudal Blade**	18	51	15	-9	14	●						N/A
Nearly all the Murmillo honor Maritimus, the turtle god of water. The truly strong Murmillo wield weapons honoring Maritimus' glory. The Caudal Blade is one such weapon.													
Samnite	**Vicious Blade**	17	65	15	-9	8			●				N/A
The Vicious Blade is one of the few heavy swords from the Southern Expanse. The smiths of the South view the samnites as more barbaric and this sword reflects that point-of-view.													
Samnite	**Percello Simplex**	19	72	15	-10	0							N/A
Available to the Samnite only, the Percello Simplex, like the Percello Gravis, is only used in the games.													
Samnite	**Pierced Blade**	19	72	15	-10	0							N/A
The Pierced Blade makes a unique noise when clashing against armor due to the rings adorning the backside of the blade. Its sound has become synonomous with death.													
Secutor	**Razor Shard**	16	43	15	-9	0							Bleeding
Although crude looking, the razor sharp blade of this sword can cause bleeding in opponents.													
Secutor	**Andimaru**	18	49	15	-9	14	●	●	●	●			N/A
The Andimaru is a warrior's sword passed down through generations. The tassle at the end of the handle signifies the warrior's affinity by its color and their family status by its size.													
Valens	**Munio's Sword**	22	67	18	-10	0							Supreme Critical / Affinity Charge Up
Finding his father's sword, Valens feels empowered with a great strength. This legendary sword felled many a gladiator and soon, a Dark God.													
Valkyrie	**Feighona's Sword**	20	67	15	-8	30					●		Power Increase
The spirit of the fallen Valkyrie Queen, Feighona has descended from the heavens and manifested herself as a spear so powerful as to bring the Dark God to his knees.													
DarkLegion	**Sica**	6	16	9	-5	8					●		N/A
The Sica is a short Imperial sword favored by assassins. It's easy to conceal and light enough to carry great distances, while stalking the target.													
Mutuus	**Dragon Sword**	1	22	6	-1	20					●		N/A
The Dragon Sword is a manifest of the Dark God itself, crafted in the likeness of the god's true form. It has unmatched power when wielded by a slave of darkness.													
Heavy	**Qo'ai-marael**	10	40	9	-6	12	●						N/A
This mighty sword is crafted and named after the sword used by the Fire Titan in the Six Heavens War. Its extremely thick blade makes it suitable only for heavy gladiators.													

ARMOR

Most of a character's additional Hit Points come from their armor, although this bonus often comes at a penalty to their Initiative. They cost more than other armaments, but have the most significant effect on the wearer's stats.

CLASS	NAME	LEVEL	PWR	DEF	ACC	INI	AFF PWR	◉	◉	◉	◉	◆	◉	+ ABILITIES
Light	**Wrist Brace**	1	2	1	0	-1	0							N/A
This is nothing more than a light brace that covers the wrist.														
Light	**Chainmail Guard**	2	6	1	0	-2	4	●	●	●	●			N/A
This guard consists of a chainmail sleeve and pant leg. It is worn mainly to protect against slashing attacks and is not too strong against heavy blows or piercing attacks.														
Light	**Rough Greaves**	2	6	1	0	-2	6	●	●	●	●			N/A
The Rough Greaves are a used pair of light braces that strap onto the lower legs.														
Light	**Iron Bracer**	3	10	1	0	-2	0							N/A
The Iron Bracer is a small, light wristguard that protects the hand as well as the forearm.														
Light	**Bronze Bracer**	4	14	2	0	-3	4	●	●	●	●			N/A
Made of solid bronze, this is a medium weight piece of armor worn on the forearm, offering fair protection.														
Light	**Shoulder Brace**	5	18	2	0	-4	4	●	●	●	●			N/A
This is a standard medium weight metal brace strapped onto the shoulder.														
Light	**Arm Brace**	6	22	3	0	-5	6	●	●	●	●			N/A
The heaviest single-piece arm brace, this item covers the entire arm, offering the strongest arm protection you can get from a brace.														
Light	**Leg Brace**	7	26	3	0	-5	6	●	●	●	●			N/A
The heaviest single-piece leg brace, this item covers the entire leg, offering the strongest leg protection you can get from a brace.														
Light	**Ringmail Guard**	8	30	3	0	-5	8	●	●	●	●			N/A
The Ringmail Guard is a more robust arm and leg covering worn to protect from slashes and heavier blows. It's not too strong against piercing attacks.														
Light	**Scalemail Guard**	9	34	4	0	-8	8	●	●	●	●			N/A
This strong chainmail guard has metal scales attached, offering fair protection against any type of attack.														

CLASS	NAME	LEVEL	PWR	DEF	ACC	INI	AFF PWR	◉	◉	◉	◉	✦	◉	+ ABILITIES
Light	Steel Bracer	10	38	4	0	-8	10	●	●	●	●			N/A
The Steel Bracer is a medium sized, light weight shield that straps onto the forearm.														
Light	Silver Bracer	11	42	4	0	-4	10	●	●	●	●			N/A
This is a simple strap-on bracer made of strong silver.														
Light	Gold Bracer	12	46	5	0	-7	12	●	●	●	●			N/A
The Gold Bracer is a heavy piece of armor that straps onto the forearm and offers the best in light protection.														
Light	The Bloody Hide	13	50	5	0	-6	12	●	●	●	●			N/A
Inspired by the bloody coats of the desert jackals, this bronze gauntlet has rivlets of fur sculpted into it, making it thicker in some places and therefore stronger.														
Light	Segmented Guard	14	54	5	0	-7	14	●	●	●	●			N/A
The Segmented Guard is a fairly standard guard made of metal plates linked together with either chain or leather.														
Light	Studded Guard	15	58	5	0	-8	0							N/A
Designed to glance blows off of the armor rather than to absorb the blow, the Studded Guard is made of heavy metal scales chained together.														
Light	Spiked Guard	16	62	6	0	-9	0							N/A
This spiked guard covers the shoulder, knee, foot and forearm. Being hit while wearing this armor will sometimes damage your foe.														
Light	Bladed Guard	17	66	6	0	-9	14	●	●	●	●			N/A
Like the Spiked Guard, this guard has blades mounted on it and covers the shoulder, knee, foot and forearm and will sometimes deal damage upon your foe once attacked.														
Light	Weapon Rig Guard	18	70	6	4	-8	0							N/A
This standard guard has a brace at the wrist that fastens weapons tight to the wielder, making their weapon a virtual extension of their arm.														
Light	Sword Breaker Guard	19	74	6	0	-10	16	●	●	●	●			N/A
An odd looking guard, this arm and leg piece is designed with many grooves and catches on it, making it possible to break the attacker's weapon.														
Light	Acid Guard	20	78	6	0	-10	18			●				Retaliation
Made by an alchemist and a blacksmith, this guard has a thin layer of acid imbued into the finish. If knockback is used against the wearer, the armor will damage the attacker.														
Medium	Short Cape	1	3	1	0	-1	0							N/A
The Short Cape is a standard for beginning light infantry in Imperia.														
Medium	Woven Skirt	2	7	1	0	-2	4	●	●	●	●			N/A
This short cloth skirt yields standard low-end protection without much embellishment.														
Medium	Leather Cape	4	15	2	0	-3	4	●	●	●	●			N/A
Generally made from the hide of a relatively large animal, this cape is one piece of thick leather that hangs nearly an entire body's length.														
Medium	Heavy Fur Skirt	5	19	2	0	-4	4			●				N/A
Worn for camouflage, warmth and as armor, the Heavy Fur Skirt offers mid-range protection.														
Medium	Regal Cape	6	23	3	0	-5	4	●	●	●	●			N/A
The Regal Cape is made of double layered leather, with embellishments of fur and the crests of famous schools covering its surface.														
Medium	Leather Armor	7	27	3	0	-5	0							N/A
This is a standard, tanned and worked light leather armor.														
Medium	Heavy Leather Armor	8	31	3	0	-5	6	●	●	●	●			N/A
The Heavy Leather Armor is a well crafted, durable armor. Its weight makes it a popular choice for gladiators who would rather not wear heavy metal armor.														
Medium	Cured Leather Armor	9	35	4	0	-8	6	●	●	●				N/A
The Cured Leather Armor is a thick Leather, cured with oils and hardened through heat tempering.														
Medium	Leather Breastplate	10	39	4	0	-8	0							N/A
Worn close to the body, this armor conforms to the muscles of the wearer and allows for much ease of movement.														
Medium	Reinforced Leather Armor	10	39	4	0	-8	6	●						N/A
The Reinforced Leather armor is a standard Leather armor with rigid metal boning.														
Medium	Ivory-Stud Leather	11	43	4	0	-7	0							N/A
This armor from the Steppes is heavily imbued with Ivory studs crafted from the tusks of fallen tundra mammoths.														
Medium	Latticed Skirt	12	47	5	0	-8	8	●	●	●	●			N/A
This Imperial skirt is a testament to the aesthetics of combat as well as the functionality of armor. Metal plates hang from a leather belt.														
Medium	Chainmail Skirt	14	55	5	0	-4	10	●	●	●	●			N/A
The Chainmail Skirt is one of the heavier skirts worn in combat, and offers a great deal of protection.														
Medium	Lorica Segmentus	14	55	5	0	-9	10	●	●	●	●			N/A
Wrapped around the body, this armor latches in the front, down the middle of the chest. It's made up of many pieces of metal and therefore allows for decent movement.														
Medium	Bronze Studded Leather	15	59	5	0	-8	10	●	●	●	●			N/A
This studded armor is a standard Leather armor imbedded with numerous bronze studs.														
Medium	Bronze Breastplate	16	63	6	0	-9	12	●	●	●	●			N/A
One solid piece of Bronze, this medium-weight breastplate has muscular shapes formed into it, making the wearer seem stronger.														
Medium	Studded Breastplate	17	67	6	0	-10	12	●	●	●	●			N/A
The Studded Breastplate is a piece of armor designed to deflect blows as well as simply protect the wearer.														
Medium	Bronze Imperial Skirt	18	71	6	0	-9	12	●	●	●	●			N/A
A heavier version of the Latticed Skirt, the Bronze Imperial Skirt is the heaviest of the standard skirts and protects well while still allowing for easy movement.														
Medium	Dragon's Cape	19	75	6	0	-6	16	●						N/A
An extremely rare cape, the Dragon's Cape is made from the segmented leather of a dragon's belly.														

CLASS	NAME	LEVEL	PWR	DEF	ACC	INI	AFF PWR							+ ABILITIES
Medium	**Precious Cuirass**	20	79	6	0	-10	18			●				N/A
Heavy	**Heavy Gorget**	1	6	1	0	-1	0							N/A
Heavy	**Iron Gorget**	1	6	1	0	-1	0							N/A
Heavy	**Crude Iron Plate**	2	10	1	0	-2	0							N/A
Heavy	**Heavy Chain Gorget**	2	10	1	0	-2	4	●	●	●	●			N/A
Heavy	**Iron Gear**	3	15	1	0	-2	0							N/A
Heavy	**Bronze Plate**	4	19	2	0	-3	4	●	●	●	●			N/A
Heavy	**Metal Suit**	4	19	2	0	-3	4	●	●	●	●			N/A
Heavy	**Bronze Gear**	5	24	2	0	-4	6	●	●	●	●			N/A
Heavy	**Lorica Segmentata**	5	24	2	0	0	4	●	●	●	●			N/A
Heavy	**Layered Shell**	6	28	3	0	-5	6	●	●	●	●			N/A
Heavy	**Braced Armor**	7	33	3	0	-5	10				●			N/A
Heavy	**Plated Cuirass**	7	33	3	0	-5	8	●	●	●	●			N/A
Heavy	**Horned Shell**	8	37	3	0	-5	10	●	●	●	●			N/A
Heavy	**Scaled Gorget**	8	37	3	0	-5	0							N/A
Heavy	**Decorated Iron Plate**	9	42	4	0	-8	12	●	●	●	●			N/A
Heavy	**Brace Plate**	10	46	4	0	-8	12	●	●	●	●			N/A
Heavy	**Heavy Gear**	10	46	4	0	-8	0							N/A
Heavy	**Armored Suit**	11	51	4	0	-5	12	●	●	●	●			N/A
Heavy	**Strength Armor**	11	51	4	0	-5	12	●	●	●	●			N/A
Heavy	**The Ferratus**	12	55	5	0	-6	12	●	●	●	●			N/A
Heavy	**Dark Armor**	13	60	5	0	-8	0							N/A
Heavy	**Turtlebone Armor**	13	60	5	0	-8	14		●					N/A
Heavy	**Brave Armor**	14	64	5	0	-9	0							N/A
Heavy	**Mighty Gear**	14	64	5	0	-7	14	●	●	●	●			N/A
Heavy	**Suit of Flight**	15	69	5	0	-3	16		●					N/A
Heavy	**Golden Suit**	16	73	6	0	-10	16	●	●	●	●			N/A
Heavy	**Obsidian Shell**	17	78	6	0	-10	16	●	●	●	●			N/A
Heavy	**Legendary Suit**	18	82	6	0	-3	18				●			N/A
Heavy	**Robustus Gustos**	19	87	6	0	0	18			●				Heavy Retaliation

The Precious Cuirass is a breastplate made of solid Gold with iconic symbols carved into its front. Jewels adorn the edges, accentuating this armor's beauty.

The Heavy Gorget is made of a combination of strong metals, cast together into a stong, solid armor.

Simple and crude, this gorget is made of pure iron faces hinged together at the shoulder and neck with a leather reinforced body covering attached to the underside.

This is a cumbersome wrought-iron armor set that only the strongest warriors can wear. There are no embellishments. It is worn only for protection.

The heavy iron chainmail in this gorget is plated with gold, making it flow with the body and hinder movement less.

The most basic of all the "Gear" type armors, this is a heavy-weight package of armor made of forged iron.

The Bronze Plate is a basic plate that's quite affordable for how much protection it offers.

Simply made to fit around the leg, waist and arm, the Metal Suit leaves the chest to be defended by a shield instead of armor.

The Bronze Gear consists of bronze leg guards, shoulder guards and an upper chest plate.

The Lorica Segmentata is made of light metal bands wrapped around all the limbs and torso.

The Bronze Layered Shell is especially strong, as plates of bronze are joined together and layered, three deep.

The Braced Armor has a layer of air between two layers of metal, so that when one layer gets damaged, there's still another layer to go through.

The nickel plating on this bronze cuirass absorbs most of the damage, keeping wear and tear on the armor beneath to a minimum.

The Horned Shell is a piece of armor worn only by the strongest warriors. The knees, feet, elbows and shoulders have animal horns mounted on them to add extra protection.

This is a gorget made of heavy metal plates that hangs down to the stomach in the front and past the shoulder blades in the back.

This solid iron plate is reinforced and decorated with ribbings of steel in the visage of fearsome mythological animals.

The Brace Plate is only worn by the most powerful warriors. It is a steel plate worn against the body with steel "braces" hanging off the shoulders for extra protection.

The Heavy Gear has a full chestplate and nearly full covering of one arm and one leg.

The Armored Suit is the strongest suit there is without covering the body entirely.

The Strength Armor consists of a breastplate, shinguard and forearm, leaving the biceps and thighs exposed so the muscles aren't hindered by the armor.

The Ferratus is a piece of armor commandeered from the royal Imperial army. It is the strongest armor worn by the elite forces.

Images of skulls and bones are embossed and carved into this strong suit of unrefined Iron--a fearsome shell.

Modeled after the enormous shell of the mighty sea turtle, this steel reconstruction offers great protection from all physical attacks.

This armor is made of solid gold and engraved with fearsome enactments of past battles won. This intimidates opponents, increasing their chance of missing while attacking.

The Mighty Gear is made of only the finest reinforced metals, yet due to its masterful crafting still allows for agile movement.

A well kept Suit of Flight makes it easier to cross any terrain. There are hinges at every joint in the body, down to the toes and fingers.

Cast in the most precious metal, the Golden Suit is measured to fit each warrior individually, making it well worth the cost.

This shell is made of a legendary metal, polished down to a shiny black. The inside is made of leather, making it comfortable to wear, while still offering very strong protection.

Fashioned after the suit of armor worn by Aeris during the six-heavens war, this armor is light, yet offers strong protection.

Used by those who started the gladiatorial games. Made of a unique metal, it has no effect on movement. Shockwaves created by attacks may injure the opponent.

CLASS	NAME	LEVEL	PWR	DEF	ACC	INI	AFF PWR	◉	◉	◉	◉	◉	◉	+ ABILITIES
Heavy	Diamond Shell	20	91	6	0	-10	0							Defense Up

This shell is studded with hundreds of unbreakable diamonds that offer mighty protection, while making it harder for foes to land a hit, due to the sun reflecting off of its surface.

CLASS	NAME	LEVEL	PWR	DEF	ACC	INI	AFF PWR	◉	◉	◉	◉	◉	◉	+ ABILITIES
Amazon	Leather Bikini	3	10	1	0	-2	0							N/A

The Leather Bikini is the most basic protection found in a bikini garment.

| Amazon | Cured Bikini | 6 | 22 | 3 | 0 | -5 | 4 | ◉ | ◉ | ◉ | ◉ | | | N/A |

The Cured Bikini is very strong for leather. It is cured to a near rigid state and protects much better than standard leather.

| Amazon | Chainmail Bikini | 12 | 46 | 5 | 0 | 0 | 8 | ◉ | ◉ | ◉ | ◉ | | | N/A |

The Chainmail Bikini has a leather underpiece bound to a strong layer of chainmail. It offers fair protection against standard melee attacks.

| Amazon | Platemail Bikini | 13 | 50 | 5 | 0 | -2 | 8 | ◉ | ◉ | ◉ | ◉ | | | N/A |

Stronger than the Chainmail Bikini, the metal plates attached to this leather garment protect not only from standard slash attacks, but piercing ones as well.

| Amazon | Braided Metal Bikini | 18 | 78 | 6 | 0 | 0 | 16 | | | | | | | N/A |

The Braided Metal Bikini is a flexible piece of armor made of thin pieces of metal braided together.

| Amazon | Rigid Bikini | 18 | 70 | 6 | 0 | -7 | 14 | | | ◉ | | | | N/A |

The Rigid Bikini is made from one solid piece of Bronze and fastened on with leather buckles.

| Arcane | Burlap Wrap | 1 | 2 | 1 | 0 | -1 | 0 | | | | | | | N/A |

This wrap is merely a long swath of burlap wrapped around the body to protect mainly from the heat. Yet it is light enough to allow wind to pass through.

| Arcane | Canvas Robe | 1 | 2 | 1 | 0 | -1 | 0 | | | | | | | N/A |

This is a standard robe worn open in the front. It offers cheap protection from the elements.

| Arcane | Collared Cloak | 2 | 6 | 1 | 0 | -2 | 0 | | | | | | | N/A |

This cloak is made of a heavy fabric and has a tall firm collar to protect the neck.

| Arcane | Cotton Del | 2 | 6 | 1 | 0 | -2 | 0 | | | | | | | N/A |

The Cotton Del is a flimsy flowing robe usually worn during meditation exercises.

| Arcane | Cotton Toga | 3 | 10 | 1 | 0 | -2 | 0 | | | | | | | N/A |

The most basic of togas, the Cotton Toga, is a basic beginner's costume for arcane gladiators.

| Arcane | Woven Toga | 3 | 10 | 1 | 0 | -2 | 0 | | | | | | | N/A |

A fairly weak arcane covering, the Woven Toga is fashioned together from scraps of textile and offers little protection.

| Arcane | Hooded Cloak | 4 | 14 | 2 | 0 | -3 | 0 | | | | | | | N/A |

The Hooded Cloak is a basic cloak that offers added head protection.

| Arcane | Light Wrap | 4 | 14 | 2 | 0 | -3 | 10 | ◉ | ◉ | ◉ | ◉ | | | N/A |

The Light Wrap is nothing more than a swath of cotton wrapped around the body to offer protection from the elements as well as light physical attacks.

| Arcane | Short Del | 5 | 18 | 2 | 0 | -4 | 0 | | | | | | | N/A |

The Short Del is easily found throughout the desert as it is often the only covering worn by wandering nomads.

| Arcane | Velvet Robe | 6 | 22 | 3 | 0 | -5 | 12 | ◉ | ◉ | ◉ | ◉ | | | N/A |

This is an expensive arcane garment imbuing the wearer with confidence in the magic arts.

| Arcane | Fine Silk Toga | 7 | 26 | 3 | 0 | -5 | 14 | ◉ | ◉ | ◉ | ◉ | | | N/A |

Traditionally, the tightly woven Fine Silk Toga is worn to protect against water while still flowing naturally with the body.

| Arcane | Heavy Robes | 8 | 30 | 3 | 0 | -5 | 16 | ◉ | ◉ | ◉ | ◉ | | | N/A |

These fairly heavy robes are wrapped multiple times around the wearer, offering great protection from the elements.

| Arcane | Hooded Wrap | 8 | 30 | 3 | 0 | -5 | 14 | ◉ | ◉ | ◉ | ◉ | | | N/A |

A combination of different fabrics, this wrap covers the head as well, offering fair protection.

| Arcane | Leather Cloak | 9 | 34 | 4 | 0 | -8 | 16 | ◉ | ◉ | ◉ | ◉ | | | N/A |

This is a leather cloak that trails on the ground, hiding your footsteps as you travel, making it harder for people to track you.

| Arcane | Silk Del | 10 | 38 | 4 | 0 | -8 | 18 | ◉ | ◉ | ◉ | ◉ | | | N/A |

This medium length robe is a standard worn by villagers and wanderers all throughout the Windward Steppes.

| Arcane | Body Wrap | 11 | 42 | 4 | 0 | -1 | 18 | ◉ | ◉ | ◉ | ◉ | | | N/A |

The Body Wrap covers the legs, body, arms and head with one piece of fabric.

| Arcane | Dyed Cotton Toga | 12 | 46 | 5 | 0 | 0 | 18 | ◉ | ◉ | ◉ | ◉ | | | Beast Dodge |

This toga is woven from heavy cotton and dyed light brown making it harder for animals to discern its wearer as a target. It increases beast evasion.

| Arcane | Full Del | 13 | 50 | 5 | 0 | 0 | 20 | ◉ | ◉ | ◉ | ◉ | | | Frontal Defense |

This is a long-sleeved del that wraps around the wearer, offering double protection from frontal attacks.

| Arcane | Sequined Robe | 14 | 54 | 5 | 0 | -1 | 20 | ◉ | ◉ | ◉ | ◉ | | | N/A |

With heavy sequins on this robe of velvet, the wearer has a stronger confidence in the magic arts and decent protection from lighter weaponry.

| Arcane | Wizard's Cloak | 15 | 58 | 5 | 0 | 0 | 20 | ◉ | ◉ | ◉ | ◉ | | | Spell Range Up |

The wizard's cloak is a mysterious cloak that enhances magic wielded by the wearer, increasing the range of spell skills.

| Arcane | Belted Wrap | 16 | 62 | 6 | 0 | -2 | 22 | ◉ | ◉ | ◉ | ◉ | | | N/A |

The Belted Wrap is a basic wrap made from a heavy fabric. It is held on with a strong leather belt.

| Arcane | Cloak of the Heavens | 17 | 66 | 6 | 0 | -2 | 22 | ◉ | ◉ | ◉ | ◉ | | | Affinity Charger |

The Cloak of the Heavens honors all the Affinity Gods with iconic imagery embroidered into it. Wearing this cloak increases one's affinity charge rate.

| Arcane | Dragon Robe | 18 | 70 | 6 | 0 | 2 | 24 | ◉ | | | | | | N/A |

No other robe offers as much protection as the Dragon Robe. It is made from the webbing of a dragon's wing.

CLASS	NAME	LEVEL	PWR	DEF	ACC	INI	AFF PWR	●	●	●	●	✦	✦	+ ABILITIES
Arcane	**Padded Silk Toga**	19	74	6	0	0	24	●	●	●	●			N/A
	This is a sturdy silk toga with woolen batting on the inside, offering protection not only from the elements, but also from assault.													
Arcane	**Warrior Del**	20	78	6	0	-1	24	●						N/A
	This is a legendary garment worn by ancient warriors. Light metal plates adorn this double stitched silk del.													
Bandit	**Thief's Clothing**	12	46	5	10	10	0							Defense Up
	The lightness of the Thief's Clothing allow for swift movement and gives the bandit a much higher chance of evading attacks.													
Barbarian	**Lamb's Hide**	1	3	1	0	-1	0							N/A
	The Lamb's Hide is the most basic protection you can get. It's little more than a shirt made of sheepskin.													
Barbarian	**Patched Cape**	2	7	1	0	-2	4	●	●	●	●			N/A
	Made from various animal pelts sewn together, the patched cape is a heavier armor worn by beginners in Nordagh.													
Barbarian	**Jackal Pelt**	3	11	1	0	-2	8	●	●	●	●			N/A
	The Jackal Pelt is a light pelt worn for protection against the harsh winds of the Qaa Rah Desert.													
Barbarian	**Wolfskin**	5	19	2	0	-4	4	●	●	●	●			N/A
	The Wolfskin is a light and mobile hide to wear when traveling. It is a favorite among Gungnir, although others have been known to wear it as well.													
Barbarian	**Mountain Lion Hide**	7	27	3	0	-5	4	●	●	●	●			N/A
	This armor is nothing more than a short cape made from the hide of a mountain lion.													
Barbarian	**Leather Garb**	9	35	4	1	-8	0							N/A
	The Leather Garb feels a bit unusual for the Nordagh classes, as they are used to wearing pelts and furs, but when traveling, this is an adequate piece of armor.													
Barbarian	**Double Leather**	11	43	4	2	2	10	●	●	●	●			N/A
	As the name would suggest, the Double Leather is a heavier type of Leather Garb for the Nordagh classes. Although very fluid in movement, it offers decent protection.													
Barbarian	**Oiled Pelt**	13	49	5	0	0	8	●						Antidote
	This pelt is made from the hide of the elusive Desert Eels that dwell in the sands surrounding Saraa Izel. They have a natural oil which prevents the wearer from being poisoned.													
Barbarian	**Buffalo Hide**	15	55	5	0	-1	10	●	●	●	●			N/A
	The thick leather and dense fur of the buffalo offers much protection for a hide.													
Barbarian	**Griffin Pelt**	16	63	6	0	0	12					●		N/A
	Warriors who manage to fell a griffin often wear its pelt as a trophy. The Griffin Pelt has very dense fur and a thick, yet light, leather.													
Barbarian	**Chimera Pelt**	17	67	6	0	-1	14	●	●	●	●			N/A
	There is no better protection found in a fur garment than that found in the coat of the legendary Chimera.													
Barbarian	**Horse Hide**	18	71	6	0	-2	8	●	●	●	●			N/A
	This armor is the thick hide from fallen horse warriors treated and tanned and worn out of respect for the defeated.													
Barbarian	**Bear Pelt**	19	75	6	0	-1	6	●	●	●	●			N/A
	The large size of this pelt, along with the thick leather of the bear, offers good protection for a pelt armor.													
Barbarian	**Dragon Hide**	20	79	6	0	2	18	●						N/A
	This is nothing more than the hide of a dragon--about as strong as a light metal--fashioned into a strong body armor.													
Centurion	**Imperial Body Armor**	20	91	6	0	-2	10	●	●	●	●			N/A
	Elite soldiers of the Imperial Army are awarded with Imperial Body Armor in honor of their duty to the Empire. It is the strongest armor that a centurion can equip.													
Channeler	**Mage's Robe**	18	70	6	0	0	16	●	●	●	●			Spell Range Up
	This magical robe, crafted by Channelers for Channelers, increases the range of spell skills.													
Dervish	**Royal Garb**	17	66	6	0	7	12	●	●	●	●			Crowd's Favor
	The high protectors of Queen Ibliis are gifted the Royal Garb in honor of their duty to Her Majesty. It is the strongest armor that a dervish can equip.													
Gwazi	**Unknown**	N/A	N/A	N/A	N/A	N/A	N/A					●		N/A
	N/A													
Legionnaire	**Soldier's Skirt**	12	15	5	0	8	N/A							N/A
	This medium-weight skirt offers fair protection and is used throughout the Imperial Armada. Since soldiers travel by foot, it is a light armor allowing for increased initiative.													
Legionnaire	**Segmented Gear**	20	79	6	0	-1	10	●	●	●	●			N/A
	For footsoldiers of the Imperial Army, there isn't a piece of armor better than the Segmented Imperial Gear--a modified version of the Lorica Segmentus.													
Ludo	**Shell of Darkness**	1	65	6	0	-3	18					●		N/A
	Ludo's armor													
Mongrel	**Bark Armor**	1	2	1	0	-1	4	●	●	●	●			N/A
	Made from sheets of bark strung together with leather, the Bark Armor offers weak protection.													
Mongrel	**Dried Bones**	4	14	2	0	-3	6			●				N/A
	This armor is made of bones tailored onto the outside of a standard leather backing. It is very fearsome looking armor.													
Mongrel	**Rabbit Pelt**	6	22	3	0	-5	0							N/A
	The Rabbit Pelt is a light fur coat worn mainly for protection from the elements, but has made its way into the gladiatorial games as a beginner's armor in Nordagh.													
Mongrel	**Bamboo Armor**	10	38	4	0	-8	10			●				N/A
	Found somewhere far to the east, this armor is fashioned by strapping multiple shoots of hard bamboo together with twine.													
Mongrel	**Human Skeleton**	14	54	5	0	-1	12			●				N/A
	Worn only by Mongrels, the Human Skeleton is a fearsome looking suit of armor. Made of human bones held together with leather, it strikes fear into the hearts of enemies.													
Mongrel	**Bear Skeleton**	18	70	6	0	-2	14			●				N/A
	Heavy bones from bears are tied together with bear hide to create this very strong and intimidating bone armor.													

CLASS	NAME	LEVEL	PWR	DEF	ACC	INI	AFF PWR	⊙	⊙	⊙	⊙	⊕	⊕	+ ABILITIES
Mongrel	Petrified Wood Plate	20	78	6	0	-3	16			●				N/A
Murmillo	Tidal Guard	20	79	6	0	1	16	●						N/A
Nephilli	Gown of Darkness	1	78	10	10	-1	20					●		N/A
Peltast	Imperial Breastplate	20	78	6	0	2	16				●			N/A
Samnite	Lamellar Shell	16	73	6	0	2	0	●	●	●				N/A
Samnite	Invulnero	20	91	6	0	-3	0							N/A
Samnite	Shell of Menat	20	91	6	0	-3	0							N/A
Secutor	Scarab Shell	18	70	6	5	3	8			●				N/A
Secutor	Platinum Guard	20	78	6	0	0	0							N/A
Secutor	Studded Mail Guard	20	78	6	0	0	0	●	●	●	●			N/A
Summoner	Robe of Rebirth	18	70	6	0	0	20	●	●	●	●			Auto Revive
Undead	Dark Gear	18	71	6	0	0	14					●		N/A
Undead Summoner	Interment Robes	13	50	5	5	4	20					●		Affinity Charge Up
Urlan	King's Armor	20	82	8	0	4	0							Affinity Charge Up
Valens	Munio's Armor	23	87	6	5	8	0							Damage Reduction
Valkyrie	Treanid	20	82	8	5	5	10					●		Damage Reduction
DarkLegion	Dark Mail	20	20	6	0	0	20					●		N/A
Galdr	Unknown	N/A	N/A	N/A	N/A	N/A	N/A	●	●	●	●			N/A
N/A														
Galverg	Unknown	1	91	10	0	-1	20					●		N/A
N/A														
Mutuus	Hate Mail	1	91	10	0	-1	20					●		N/A
Mutuus	Hero's Breastplate	1	60	8	2	-1	0							N/A

The Petrified Wood Plate is a very heavy, very strong breastplate only worn by the most robust warriors.

The Tidal Guard is a scaled guard with images of the ocean cast into arm and leg pieces. It covers almost a full arm and a full leg and carries with it a heavy water affinity charge.

Nephilia's Gown of Darkness ties her to the Dark God. While she wears it, every action she performs becomes known to the Dark God. Impossible to acquire!

Elite support troops of the Imperial Army are awarded with Imperial Breastplates in honor of their duty to the Empire. It is the strongest armor that a peltast can equip.

Made of hard leather plates strung together, a style mastered by the nomads of the Windward Steppes, allows for easier movement while offering high protection to the samnite.

The Invulnero is a shell designed solely for the samnite. Such an item is only awarded in the high tournaments for samnites who have faced many battles.

Inspired by the protective amulet passed down from generation to generation of the royal family. It keeps the Queen from harm, and so does the armor for the samnite.

This special secutor armor is fashioned from the husk of a fallen desert scarab. It is immensely strong for its weight.

This heavy guard is a favorite among secutors that can afford it, as it nearly steps them up from a light gladiator to a medium, as far as endurance is concerned.

This guard, made especially for the Secutor, is made of a robust metal and has studs on it to help deflect blows.

This robe, supposedly stripped from the tomb of an assassinated Pharaoh, has blessed all who have worn it throughout the ages with the power of rebirth if struck down.

This gear, stripped from the corpses of fallen Imperial soldiers, carries with it a strong affinity to the Darkness.

Casters who fell in battle in the days of old were dressed in this ceremonial garb. After being resurrected by the Dark God, their magical properties have become evil.

Although Urlan is only a prince when he first receives this armor, his talents for leadership and strength of character support the armor.

The armor worn by Valens' father grants Valens courage in battle. Usus gives this armor to Valens after Valens proves himself to the Affinity Titans.

Summoned by the Light affinity and made especially for Ursula, this legendary armor worn only once before, by Feighona the Queen of the Valkyrie, can deflect almost any blow.

Given by Mutuus to his troops. It is a fearsome breastplate with greaves and a gorget, atop which sits a fine black chainmail, making this suit shimmer with darkness.

Not actually crafted from any earthly material, the Hate Mail is the strongest armor worn by any of the Dark Legion.

This ornamental breastplate was given to Mutuus many years ago by the Emperor himself. It was awarded for Mutuus' gallantry in battle against the Visigoths.

SHIELDS

SHIELDS Shields can absorb their power worth of damage on a successful shield block. If they take more than that, they'll shatter, so you may want to bring a few spares, and set them to automatically re-equip in your Equipment screen.

CLASS	NAME	LEVEL	PWR	DEF	ACC	INI	AFF PWR	⊙	⊙	⊙	⊙	⊕	⊕	+ ABILITIES
Light	Parma	1	11	2	0	0	0							N/A
Light	Embossed Shield	2	20	3	-1	0	4	●	●	●	●			N/A
Light	Iron Buckler	2	20	3	-1	0	0							N/A
Light	Umbo	3	30	4	-1	0	4	●	●	●	●			N/A
Light	Cured Leather Shield	4	40	4	-1	0	4	●	●	●	●			N/A
Light	Wicker Shield	5	49	5	-2	0	4	●	●	●	●			N/A

The Parma is a small shield used in training. It is often the first shield that a gladiator uses until they can afford a stronger one.

This small leather shield has familial designs embossed in its center in the cyclical pattern so common throughout the Steppes. It's comparable to the Hardened Leather Shield.

The Buckler is the smallest shield you can buy. This Iron Buckler is strong for its size, but one has to be skilled to use it effectively.

The Umbo is a part of the larger scutum used by the Imperial Army. After scavenging the battleground, they are salvaged from damaged scutum and used as shields.

Predominantly crafted by nomads in the Windward Steppes, this is a basic lightweight cured leather shield.

The Wicker Shield is a predecessor to the Bamboo Shield and is only slightly less strong, and remains much lighter. It is an easy shield to use and is good for beginners.

Class	Name	Level	PWR	DEF	ACC	INI	AFF PWR							+ Abilities
Light	**Hardened Leather Shield**	6	59	6	-2	0	4	●	●	●	●			N/A
	The Hardened Leather Shield is made from the leather of a hunter's most prized kill. It is small and light and is easy to build.													
Light	**Bamboo Shield**	8	78	7	-2	0	6	●	●	●	●			N/A
	Just a bit stronger than the Wicker Shield, this round shield has a metal rim and a metal umbo in the middle.													
Light	**Wooden Shield**	9	88	7	-2	0	4	●	●	●	●			N/A
	The Wooden Shield is made of standard planks of wood doubled up, back to back, and has leather wrist straps on the back.													
Light	**Lacquered Shield**	10	98	8	-2	0	4	●	●	●	●			N/A
	A thick lacquer has been applied to this standard leather shield to afford additional protection.													
Light	**Studded Shield**	11	107	9	-3	0	6	●	●	●	●			Retaliation
	Made of wooden planks, doubled up and nailed together--the nails sticking out through the front of the shield. Damage is often returned to the attacker with this shield.													
Light	**Round Shield**	12	117	9	-3	0	4	●	●	●	●			N/A
	Rather than cast, this copper shield is hammered into a round shape and usually ends up smaller than other shields due to the weight of the metal.													
Light	**Bronze Shield**	13	127	10	-3	0	6	●	●	●	●			N/A
	The Bronze shield is a basic shield made from one solid piece of bronze hammered into a circle. It is a strong, albeit plain looking shield.													
Light	**Winged Shield**	13	127	10	-3	0	8	●	●	●	●			N/A
	The Bronze Winged Shield is a very robust shield with bladed wings on the top and the bottom.													
Light	**Bwaag Scaap**	14	136	10	-3	0	10				●			N/A
	The Bwaag Scaap is a small, round shield made of Iron with images of the sky over Nordagh etched into it.													
Light	**Coral Shield**	15	146	11	-3	0	14			●				N/A
	Made from the coral found at the delta of the Habaas river, just as it empties into the Aeonis Sea, this Shield is light, but very strong.													
Light	**Trainer's Scutum**	16	156	11	-3	0	0							N/A
	The Trainer's Scutum is a much smaller version of the standard Scutum and is used mainly in schools while training newly recruited gladiators.													
Light	**Boandey**	17	165	12	-4	0	12				●			N/A
	This traditional small, round shield has images of animals linked in a chain standing on a jewel centered in the middle meant to represent the earth.													
Light	**Eye of the Cyclops**	18	175	13	-4	0	16				●			Petrifying Block
	From the legendary Cyclops Island. It is said that whoever stares into the eye jewel mounted on this shield will become petrified if not pure of intention.													
Light	**Bladed Pendulum**	19	185	14	-5	0	6			●				N/A
	The Bladed Pendulum is a shield modeled after the swinging pendulum blades found in the ancient dungeon ruins of Khoru, deep in the Qaa Rah Desert.													
Light	**Dragon's Claw**	20	194	15	a-50	0	18	●						N/A
	Made from a section of a dragon's claw. Shaved thin enough to see through, this rock hard shield is imbued with the power of fire and is lighter than any metal.													
Medium	**Beast's Shield**	1	14	2	0	0	4	●	●	●	●			N/A
	The Beast's Shield is a wooden shield covered with the tanned hide and teeth of one or more animals.													
Medium	**Banded Shield**	3	35	4	-1	0	0							N/A
	This is a basic round wooden shield with iron reinforcing bands on the front and the back.													
Medium	**Hoplite**	6	69	6	-2	0	0							N/A
	A round wooden shield coated with a thick leather and painted with intimidating images of war and fear. There's a round metal umbo in the middle to add extra protection.													
Medium	**Spiked Round Shield**	8	91	7	-2	0	4	●	●	●	●			Slight Retaliation
	This round wooden shield has large metal spikes nailed through it which will occasionally damage an attacker in return.													
Medium	**Steel Guard Shield**	10	112	8	-2	0	0							N/A
	This is a cross between a guard and a shield. The longer sides guard the arm from the hand up to the elbow.													
Medium	**Nomad's Shield**	12	134	9	-3	0	0							N/A
	Crafted with blades on the top and bottom and spikes on the sides for extra protection, as there are many dangers while wandering the plains of the Windward Steppes.													
Medium	**Branded Shield**	14	156	10	-3	-0	0							N/A
	This heavy wooden shield is unique in that it has no concavity to it at all. It is a circular shield with images of war and nature branded onto its front.													
Medium	**Regius**	16	177	11	-3	0	0							N/A
	This shield has a unique design and is given as a trophy of one's courage in the arena. It has a cyprus crown etched into its façade, encircling the national symbol of Imperia.													
Medium	**Mirror Shield**	18	199	13	-4	0	8	●	●	●	●			Bungling Block
	The Mirror shield is a round shield with wedges of mirror mounted on the outside. If a blow is successfully blocked, the attacker's luck falls.													
Medium	**Poison Barbed Shield**	20	221	15	-5	0	10			●				Poisoning Block
	The Poison Barbed Shield has small barbs on its front that have been dipped in poison. If an attack is successfully blocked, there's a chance of poisoning the attacker.													
Heavy	**Komo**	1	18	2	0	-1	0							N/A
	The Komo is a traditional desert foot-soldier's shield. It is made of wicker and has small stones woven into it for added strength.													
Heavy	**Animal Hide Shield**	2	33	3	-1	0	0							N/A
	The Animal Hide Shield is made of a rough, heavy animal hide stretched over a simple shield frame, usually augmented with large metal studs or heavy rope.													
Heavy	**Skull Shield**	3	47	4	-1	0	4				●			N/A
	This shield is nothing more than the skull of a giant desert snake, with leather harnesses that wrap around the warrior's arm. It is extremely strong.													
Heavy	**Scutum**	4	62	4	-1	0	6	●	●	●	●			N/A
	The Scutum is a large rectangular wooden shield with elaborate designs painted onto its face. This shield is used very effectively in massive numbers by imperial troops.													
Heavy	**Heavy Bronze Shield**	6	91	6	-2	0	6	●	●	●	●			N/A
	The Heavy Bronze Shield is hammered from one solid piece of inch-thick bronze. It has etchings of the dieties on it, but otherwise, is a simple shield.													

CLASS	NAME	LEVEL	PWR	DEF	ACC	INI	AFF PWR	◐	◑	◒	◓	◆	⬆	+ ABILITIES
Heavy	Warlord's Shield	6	91	6	-2	0	0							N/A
	The Warlord's Shield has been forged from the broken weapons and armor collected on the battlefield after a large-scale battle.													
Heavy	Digladio	7	106	6	-2	0	8	●	●	●	●			Retaliation
	A round silver shield with a single long spike protruding out from the center of it. The defender can deal significant damage back to the attacker with this shield.													
Heavy	Night's Guardian	8	121	7	-2	0	6				●			N/A
	This is a large shield bearing the visage of an intimidating owl, the bottom point coming to a golden "beak" and the top peaking at two sharp, golden "ears."													
Heavy	Visigoth Shield	9	135	7	-2	0	12	●	●	●	●			N/A
	This large shield has the fierce face of a lion cast in bronze protruding from the front of it. It is a fearful looking shield with many HP.													
Heavy	Reinforced Targe	10	150	8	-2	0	0							N/A
	This is a rough targe shield reinforced with iron. It is bladed on the top and bottom of the shield, however these blades are more for show and offer little protection.													
Heavy	Diamond Shield	11	165	9	-3	0	0							Blind Counter
	The Diamond Shield is a polished solid gold shield studded with diamonds that shines like the sun, sometimes even blinding opponents.													
Heavy	Procerus	12	179	9	-3	0	4	●	●	●	●			N/A
	The Procerus is a tall tower shield made of wood with leather stretched over its surface. It's little more than a flat plank covered with soft leather.													
Heavy	Horned Shield	13	194	10	-3	0	4	●	●	●	●			Retaliation
	The Horned Shield is a light Tower shield that has horns from various plains animals mounted on it with the intention of harming the attacker while defending their blows.													
Heavy	Tower Shield	14	209	10	-3	0	0							N/A
	The Tower Shield is a large shield made of brass and steel that covers a great deal of the body. This is the favorite starting shield of Samnites.													
Heavy	Poison Quilt Shield	15	223	11	-3	0	10		●					Poisoning Block
	Has a quilted leather front, underneath which are pockets of poisonous spores. If a leather pocket is ripped open, these spores will poison the attacker.													
Heavy	Jeweled Tower	16	238	11	-3	0	0							Crowd's Favor
	This shield is more for show than combat. Very heavy, it's only used by those who are too good to necessitate a shield. The crowd loves it when someone wields this shield.													
Heavy	Pointed Tower	18	267	13	-4	0	0							N/A
	An ovoid tower shield that comes to a point both at the top and the bottom. It is an uncharacteristic shape for a tower shield, but its shape makes it easier to use.													
Heavy	Obsidian Tower	19	282	14	-5	0	16				●			N/A
	This tall shield made entirely of Obsidian is one of the heaviest shields there is. It is black as night, serving as even more of an imposition than the samnite behind it.													
Heavy	Tower of Pain	20	297	15	-5	0	18	●						Fire Retaliation
	The Tower of Pain is imbued with the power of Exuro. Made of a magical metal found only deep in the Expanse, it can cause fire damage to those you're guarding against.													
Centurion	Imperial Tower	18	267	13	-4	0	16	●	●	●	●			N/A
	The Imperial Tower is a combination of a traditionally gladiatorial shiled and a standard issue military scutum. Very suitable for a centurion.													
Centurion	Heavy Scutum	21	311	15	-5	0	0							N/A
	The Heavy Scutum differs from standard military issue scuti, which are traditionally made of wood. This heavy shield is made entirely of metal and offers very high defense.													
Gungnir	Barricade Shield	16	156	11	-3	0	14			●	●			N/A
	Made of bound branches sharpened at both ends, the Gungnir have been known to plant this shield use it as a light barricade from behind which they hurl their javelins.													
Gwazi	Desert Carapace	18	175	13	-4	0	0							N/A
	Following a tradition of old, Gwazi prefers to use the shell of a giant desert scarab beetle as his shield. The light weight of this shield keeps movement unhindered.													
Legionnaire	Soldier's Scutum	5	57	5	-2	0	10	●	●	●	●			N/A
	The Soldier's Scutum is an Imperial Army issue shield for heavy ground troops. These shields are lightweight, reliable shields adorned with Imperial iconography.													
Legionnaire	Angled Scutum	15	156	11	-3	0	16	●	●	●	●			N/A
	Used solely in the arena is based on shields used by the Imperial Army. The head and foot are bent outward so the legionnaire can hold it as close to their body as possible.													
Legionnaire	Clypeus	19	290	14	-5	0	0							N/A
	The Clypeus was once used for Imperial infantrymen doubling as scouts. It is a tall slender shield.													
Legionnaire	Ovoid Scutum	19	209	14	-5	0	0							N/A
	Due to its unique shape and wooden construction, this shield hinders movement only slightly. It is the perfect blend between a military type shield and a gladiatorial shield.													
Ludo	Demon Shield	1	253	12	-4	0	10					●		N/A
	N/A													
Murmillo	Iron Targe	4	77	4	-1	0	0							N/A
	This targe is a heavy metal shield with a bronze rim and a decorated enamel center. Although it is heavy, it has been weighted perfectly for skilled Murmillo to throw.													
Murmillo	Throwing Hoplite	7	106	6	-2	0	0							N/A
	This is a sub-standard sized hoplite shield balanced perfectly for throwing. It is covered in hardened leather.													
Murmillo	The Cat's Claw	9	135	7	-2	0	12	●	●	●	●			N/A
	The Cat's Claw has retractable "claws" around the rim of the shield that only come out once thrown. They retract before the gladiator catches the shield.													
Murmillo	Teres Moles	11	165	9	0	0	14				●			N/A
	The Teres Moles is a powerful round shield made of thick steel with a bronze enamel, then polished to complete smoothness for precise throwing.													
Murmillo	Razor Shield	13	194	10	-3	0	16	●	●	●	●			Bleeding
	The rim of this shield is razor sharp. When thrown, the Razor Shield is very devastating.													
Murmillo	Shisa Vika	15	223	11	-3	0	12	●						N/A
	This small round shield has a beautiful sun sculpted onto the front of it. When thrown, it raises up into the sky and comes down with the flaming power of the sun.													
Ogre	Charging Rhino	18	267	13	-4	0	0							N/A
	Originally designed to be used by the mighty samnite, until put in practice, when it was realized that nary a samnite could use such a shield. It is now a favorite of the ogre.													

CLASS	NAME	LEVEL	PWR	DEF	ACC	INI	AFF PWR							+ ABILITIES
Peltast	Elongated Guard	16	156	11	-3	0	16	●	●	●	●			N/A

This light wooden arm guard is larger than most arm guards and because of its size and shape is very versatile. The paintings on the face call up to the gods for their support.

| Samnite | Notched Tower | 17 | 253 | 12 | -4 | 0 | 10 | ● | ● | ● | ● | | | N/A |

The notches in this hard wooden tower shield allow for a better range of movement from one's joints, making this tower shield hinder movement less than others of the same type.

| Samnite | Batenkh's Bane | 18 | 267 | 13 | -4 | 0 | 0 | | | | | | | N/A |

Batenkh, a devil spirit said to wander the plains of the Windward Steppes has become a fearful icon among the nomads. His face adorns this heavy samnite shield.

| Samnite | Wing of Safat | 19 | 282 | 14 | -5 | 0 | 12 | | | | ● | | | N/A |

This tower shield is modeled after the mighty wings of the mythical bird Safat. It holds great meaning for all who reside in the Southern Expanse.

| Secutor | Fur Lined Shield | 15 | 146 | 11 | -3 | 0 | 16 | ● | ● | ● | ● | | | N/A |

Wielding this small, light shield allows for quicker movement while at the same time boosting one's affinity greatly.

| Secutor | Charioteer's Shield | 18 | 175 | 13 | -4 | 0 | 0 | | | | | | | N/A |

During the days of chariot racing, shields like this were used to completely cover one's upper body by bracing them against the wall of the chariot.

| Undead | Bwaag Scaap | 14 | 156 | 10 | -3 | 0 | 10 | | | | | ● | | N/A |

This small shield is a bastardized version of the beautiful Bwaag Scaap. Instead of images of a peaceful landscape it has images of death and hatred etched into its face.

| Valens | Munio's Shield | 21 | 233 | 16 | 0 | 0 | 0 | | | | | | | Power Increase / Affinity Charge Up |

The shield thought lost for generations lends its strength to Valens for the final battle against the Dark God.

| Valkyrie | Fendeil | 20 | 221 | 15 | 0 | 10 | 30 | | | | ● | | | Critical Defense |

Fendeil, the mythic protector of the Garden of Light has summoned a shield used by Valkyrie war goddesses for Ursula to use during her final battle against the Dark God.

| DarkLegion | Hoplite | 6 | 69 | 6 | -2 | 0 | 10 | | | | | ● | | N/A |

A standard Hoplite shield twisted and warped into a tool of the Dark God. This shield is distributed to the Dark God's troops in massive numbers.

| Mutuus | Devil's Shield | 1 | 357 | 10 | -1 | 0 | 20 | | | | ● | | | N/A |

The Devil's Shield is used by the Dark Centurions who protect the base of the Dark God from the scourge of Light.

HELMETS

Helmets have the smallest effect on your stats, but rarely come with any significant drawbacks. Certain attacks can destroy them, and while this happens rarely, you can set them to automatically re-equip if you have spares.

CLASS	NAME	LEVEL	PWR	DEF	ACC	INI	AFF PWR							+ ABILITIES
Amazon	Amazonian Headband	12	60	3	-4	0	18					●		N/A

The Amazonian Headband is the traditional headgear for the legendary amazon. Although it offers little physical protection, it's size allows for heightened accuracy.

| Arcane | Comptus | 5 | 25 | 1 | -2 | 0 | 4 | ● | ● | ● | ● | | | N/A |

The Comptus is a standard headdress for arcane classes that can be found almost anywhere in Imperia.

| Arcane | Contubernium | 6 | 30 | 2 | -3 | 0 | 6 | ● | | | | | | N/A |

Crafted by master smiths, the Contubernium weighs about the same as the Comptus, but offers much more protection.

| Arcane | Golden Headdress | 7 | 35 | 2 | -3 | 0 | 8 | | | | ● | | | N/A |

Since gold is a softer metal, this solid gold headdress will absorb much of the blow when physically attacked.

| Arcane | Infula | 8 | 40 | 2 | -3 | 0 | 0 | | | | | | | Disorientation |

This mirrored headdress can cause either blindness or confusion to melee attackers.

| Arcane | Miter | 14 | 70 | 3 | -4 | 0 | 0 | | | | | | | N/A |

The Miter is a stronger piece of headgear than the diadem or circlet, however it offers no affinity boost.

| Arcane | Sacred Miter | 15 | 75 | 3 | -4 | a01 | 18 | | ● | | | | | N/A |

The Sacred Miter is blessed such that the higher your water affinity, the more likely you are to avoid damage completely when attacked.

| Arcane | Holy Miter | 16 | 80 | 4 | -5 | 0 | 0 | | | | | | | Auto Revive |

The Holy Miter may only be average when it comes to protection from physical attacks, but it will sometimes revive the wearer once they've fallen in battle once per encounter.

| Arcane | Mythic Miter | 17 | 85 | 4 | -5 | 0 | 6 | | | | | ● | | Move Range Up |

The Mythic Miter makes the wearer light of foot, increasing one's movement range.

| Arcane | Crown of Air | 19 | 100 | 4 | -5 | 0 | 16 | | | | | ● | | Move Range Up |

Cast in silver and polished to complete smoothness, this crown embodies the spirit of Aeris and increases the wearer's movement range.

| Arcane | Crown of Earth | 19 | 100 | 4 | -5 | 0 | 16 | | | | ● | | | N/A |

Aged copper gives this crown a slight green tint. The heavy metal crown represents Solum and makes the wearer seem hard as rock, nearly impervious to physical attack.

| Arcane | Crown of Fire | 19 | 100 | 4 | -5 | 0 | 16 | ● | | | | | | N/A |

Made of sanded brass, this crown gets its power from Exuro. The wearer is protected from all manner of Flame attacks and lower level water attacks.

| Arcane | Crown of Water | 19 | 100 | 4 | -5 | 0 | 16 | | | ● | | | | N/A |

A polished iron crown under the influence of Maritimus, this crown protects the wearer from all water attacks and lower level fire attacks.

| Archer | Stained Fur Hat | 16 | 80 | 4 | -5 | 0 | 14 | ● | ● | ● | ● | | | N/A |

Made of a heavy fur and is worn throughout the Windward Steppes by archers. The color of the stain depends on which affinity the wearer is strongest with.

| Archer | Spiked Fur Hat | 17 | 85 | 4 | -5 | 0 | 16 | ● | ● | ● | ● | | | N/A |

A fearsome looking lightweight headpiece worn by archers throughout the Windward Steppes. Its color and affinity depends upon the affinity preference of the wearer.

| Barbarian | Spiked Helm | 19 | 95 | 4 | -5 | 0 | 16 | ● | ● | ● | ● | | | N/A |

Crafted by the most hardened Barbarian blacksmiths, the Amtower Brothers, the Spiked Helm is a fearsome piece of armor, unparalleled in quality.

CLASS	NAME	LEVEL	PWR	DEF	ACC	INI	AFF PWR	◉	◉	◉	◉	◉	◉	+ ABILITIES
Barbarian	Rhinoceros Spangenhelm	20	100	4	-5	0	0							N/A

A standard spangenhelm, reinforced with iron plates and the horn of a fallen rhinoceros attached to it. This is a very strong helmet for the Barbarian.

CLASS	NAME	LEVEL	PWR	DEF	ACC	INI	AFF PWR	◉	◉	◉	◉	◉	◉	+ ABILITIES
Centurion	Bladed Gallic	19	100	4	-5	0	0							N/A

This heavy gallic helmet has a more gladiatorial feel to it with its crest comprising of six sharp blades running along its length.

| Centurion | Closed Gallic | 19 | 100 | 4 | -5 | 0 | 18 | ● | ● | ● | ● | | | N/A |

After the Imperial Empire spread throughout the lands, this helmet was conceived. The ears are closed to offer protection and the crest shrunken to call less attention on the battlefield.

| Channeler | Skeletal Headdress | 20 | 100 | 4 | -5 | 0 | 0 | | | | | | | N/A |

Covers a fair amount of the head while at the same time adding very little weight to the channeler. The gold in the metal also helps to channel her psychic abilities.

| Cyclops | Cycloptic Corinthian | 18 | 90 | 4 | -5 | 0 | 12 | ● | ● | ● | ● | | | N/A |

This is one of the few helmets that a cyclops is ever seen wearing. As they are not very vain creatures, they opt for functionality first and foremost.

| Dervish | Silk Fez | 2 | 10 | 1 | -1 | 0 | 6 | ● | | | | | | N/A |

This fez has a shimmering blue silk band crowning it. Wearing it will increase one's affinity with Maritimus. This helmet is unbreakable.

| Dervish | Dancer's Fez | 3 | 15 | 1 | -2 | 0 | 6 | | ● | | | | | N/A |

This is a fez of moderate height with no tassel that is worn by the dancers of the Southern Expanse. This helmet is unbreakable.

| Dervish | Tasseled Fez | 4 | 20 | 1 | -2 | 0 | 4 | | | ● | | | | N/A |

This is a standard felt fez with a golden tassel attached at its apex. This helmet is unbreakable.

| Dervish | Tall Fez | 5 | 25 | 1 | -2 | 0 | 0 | | | | | ● | | N/A |

This fez stands tall above the Dervish's head. Such headgear shows off one's stature in the arts of the Whirling Dervish. This helmet is unbreakable.

| Dervish | Rigid Fez | 6 | 30 | 2 | -3 | 0 | 8 | ● | | | | | | N/A |

This is a rare fez made of a hardened leather. Being that it is quite robust, it is traditionally worn while traveling. This helmet is unbreakable.

| Dervish | Dervish Helmet | 7 | 35 | 2 | -3 | 0 | 4 | | | ● | | | | N/A |

This is a very short fez made of a thin metal. It is Nordagh's attempt at making a southern type helmet for their tournaments.

| Dervish | Veil | 8 | 40 | 2 | -3 | 0 | 6 | | ● | | | | | N/A |

The Veil is a small turban that drapes down the back and has a veil that falls from it, down over the face. This helmet is unbreakable.

| Dervish | Turban | 9 | 45 | 2 | -3 | 0 | 0 | | | | | | | N/A |

The Turban is simply a piece of cloth wrapped around the head many times. It offers decent protection for dervishes. This helmet is unbreakable.

| Dervish | Woven Turban | 10 | 50 | 2 | -3 | 0 | 8 | | | | ● | | | N/A |

A standard turban which instead of being wrapped around the head, is woven into itself and set upon the head. This keeps it from unravelling during battle. It is unbreakable.

| Dervish | Cote Fez | 11 | 55 | 3 | -4 | 0 | 12 | ● | | | | | | N/A |

Legends from the south link this fez to a dubious secret society, which is rumored to have formed in an attempt to tame and control the Cyclops for its own sinister purposes.It is unbreakable.

| Dervish | Desert Turban | 12 | 60 | 3 | -4 | 0 | 10 | | | ● | | | | N/A |

Sitting low on the head, the Desert Turban is worn when going deep into the desert and therefore covers the whole head, leaving only the eyes visible. It is unbreakable.

| Dervish | Leather Wrap | 13 | 65 | 3 | -4 | 0 | 0 | | | | | | | N/A |

This is a turban made of a thin leather. The Nordagh people have put their spin on a traditionally Southern helmet. It adds a lot of HP, but detracts from one's Initiative.

| Dervish | Royal Turban | 14 | 70 | 3 | -4 | 0 | 6 | | | | | ● | | N/A |

A turban which sports the patterns and colors of the royal family of Ibliis. It is inlaid with gold thread and dyed with rich colors, then wrapped many times around the head. It is unbreakable.

| Dervish | Cotton Sikke | 15 | 75 | 3 | -4 | 0 | 0 | | | | | | | N/A |

The Cotton Sikke is all cotton adn often looks dented and worn, beign that this sikke is made by Imperials who don't know how to make sikkes very well. It is unbreakable.

| Dervish | Wool Sikke | 16 | 80 | 4 | -5 | 0 | 4 | | | | ● | | | N/A |

The wool sikke is made entirely of wool. The middle stands only a little taller than the wrapped, turbany part, and although it is wool, it is very tightly woven and still rigid.

| Dervish | Veiled Sikke | 17 | 85 | 4 | -5 | 0 | 12 | | ● | | | | | N/A |

This is a mixture of two traditional dervish headpieces, the veil and the sikke. It hides the face of the dervish and protects the head at the same time.

| Dervish | Royal Sikke | 18 | 90 | 4 | -5 | 0 | 14 | ● | ● | ● | ● | | | N/A |

The Royal Sikke is the only Sikke that has a tassel. It is brightly decorated much like the Royal Turban, with gold threads and rich colors. This helmet is unbreakable.

| Dervish | Tekuja Sikke | 19 | 95 | 4 | -5 | 0 | 8 | ● | ● | ● | ● | | | N/A |

This Sikke has a jewel embedded in the front of it that enhances one's strongest affinity greatly. It is wrapped in such a way as to mimic the headwear of the Tekuja statues. It is unbreakable.

| Dervish | Sufi's Sikke | 20 | 100 | 4 | -5 | 0 | 16 | | | | | ● | | N/A |

This is the holiest of all Sikkes. It is wrapped perfectly and has no loose ends of fabric. Showing off its stature, it has a small pom-pom at its apex. It is unbreakable.

| Diadem | Rigid Circlet | 1 | 5 | 1 | -1 | 0 | 10 | ● | ● | ● | ● | | | N/A |

The Rigid Circlet is made of one hammered piece of steel that is worn as decoration more than it is for function.

| Diadem | Plated Circlet | 2 | 10 | 1 | -1 | 0 | 10 | ● | ● | ● | ● | | | N/A |

The Plated Circlet has a leather underside with steel plates mounted on the outside.

| Diadem | Jeweled Circlet | 3 | 15 | 1 | -2 | 0 | 4 | ● | ● | ● | ● | | | N/A |

Worn by the elite warriors of the Southern Expanse. Depending on which god your affinity is strongest with, its jewel is placed ornamentally in the center of the circlet.

| Dervish | Circlet of the Gods | 4 | 20 | 1 | -2 | 0 | 12 | ● | ● | ● | ● | | | N/A |

The Circlet of the Gods is a metal headpiece which raises your affinity greatly once equipped.

| Diadem | Diadem | 9 | 45 | 2 | -3 | 0 | 0 | | | | | | | N/A |

The Diadem is a basic tiara worn as a traditional headpiece more than it is for functionality.

| Diadem | Golden Diadem | 10 | 50 | 2 | -3 | 0 | 0 | | | | | | | N/A |

The Golden Diadem is physically stronger than the standard Diadem and is traditionally worn by those just beginning to explore their piety.

CLASS	NAME	LEVEL	PWR	DEF	ACC	INI	AFF PWR	Aff1	Aff2	Aff3	Aff4	Aff5	Aff6	+ ABILITIES
Diadem	Soul's Diadem	11	55	3	-4	0	4	•	•	•	•			N/A
Diadem	Jeweled Diadem	12	60	3	-4	0	10	•						N/A
Diadem	Ringed Diadem	13	65	3	-4	0	14		•					N/A
Eiji	Archer's Crown	18	90	4	-5	0	18				•			N/A
Gladiatorial	Iron Thracian	3	15	1	-2	0	0							N/A
Gladiatorial	Mosaic Thracian	4	20	1	-2	0	0							N/A
Gladiatorial	Rimmed Thracian	6	30	2	-3	0	0							N/A
Gladiatorial	Shumpula	8	40	2	-3	0	0							N/A
Gladiatorial	Nex	10	50	2	-3	0	0							N/A
Gladiatorial	Carnifico	11	55	3	-4	0	0							N/A
Gladiatorial	Casus	12	60	3	-4	0	0							N/A
Gladiatorial	Horned Thracian	13	65	3	-4	0	0							N/A
Gladiatorial	Pondus Fabula	15	75	3	-4	0	8	•						N/A
Gladiatorial	The Steel Skull	16	80	4	-5	0	0							N/A
Gladiatorial	Grinning Pondus	17	85	4	-5	0	8	•	•	•	•			N/A
Gladiatorial	Heavy Pondus	18	90	4	-5	0	6	•	•	•	•			N/A
Gladiatorial	Studded Pondus	19	95	4	-5	0	8	•	•	•	•			N/A
Gladiatorial	Crested Pondus	20	100	4	-5	0	4	•	•	•	•			N/A
Gungnir	Wolf Cowl	5	25	1	-2	0	14		•					N/A
Gungnir	Unknown	N/A	N/A	N/A	N/A	N/A	N/A		•					N/A
Gungnir	Bear Cowl	20	100	4	-5	0	14		•					N/A
Hat	Fur Band	1	5	1	-1	0	6	•	•	•	•			N/A
Hat	Warrior's Band	2	10	1	-1	0	8		•					N/A
Hat	Dark Band	3	15	1	-2	0	6		•					N/A
Hat	Death's Head Cap	4	20	1	-2	0	6	•	•	•	•			N/A
Hat	Fur Hat	5	25	1	-2	0	4	•	•	•	•			N/A
Hat	Horned Band	5	25	1	-2	0	4	•	•	•	•			N/A
Hat	Plated Band	5	25	1	-2	0	6	•	•	•	•			N/A
Hat	Leather Hat	6	30	2	-3	0	0							N/A
Hat	Wing Hat	6	30	2	-3	0	10	•	•	•	•			N/A

The Soul's Diadem accents whatever the wearer's strongest affinity tie is, and adds a bonus to that affinity.

The Jeweled Diadem shimmers like the sea with polished aquamarine inlaid.

Three thin pieces of unique precious metals joined by thin ornamental chain pay homage to the Earth when donned.

The Archer's Crown was designed as an alternative to a standard helmet. This "crown" allows the archer to aim and move without compromise while offering high defense.

A long time favorite of samnites and secutors, the Iron Thracian is a powerful headpiece which offers full head protection, leaving nothing exposed.

This helmet is made by melting down old helmets, weapons and armor and forming them together into this strong, yet somewhat motley looking headpiece.

The Bronze Rimmed Thracian is merely a standard Iron Thracian helmet reinforced with bronze edging.

Carrying with it the meaning of beheading, the Shumpula has the visage of a fallen gladiator's final scream cast in its face.

The Nex's meaning, slaughter, is displayed prominently in the form of a bladed crest running the length of this intimidating ferinus helmet.

The Carnifico is a heavy ferinus helmet, cast in metal, with hooks, horns and claws covering it. Looking upon it sends images of mutilation through one's mind.

The Casus, meaning violent death, speaks for itself, as it is one solid piece of metal crafted in the visage of a saber-toothed tiger.

This helmet has metal horns protruding from the top of the helmet. Although uncommon, some have been known to use this helmet to attack like a charging bull.

This is a legendary Pondus Helmet crafted in the likeness of fabled gladiatorial champion Armofortis' helmet.

One of the few Thracian helmets to have more than just eye holes, this one has nose holes and a mouth carved into it, representing a skull.

This helmet is crafted by only one blacksmith in the Windward Steppes. He gives his helmets frightening visages and his work houses the affinities of the gods.

A hybrid of the thracian and ferinus types. This pondus helmet is made of steel and has hinges and doors for ease of equipping quickly before battle.

Not only does this iron Pondus have a full face shield, but it's also covered in studs of Bronze that will glance blows off its surface, lessening damage greatly.

The Crested Pondus is molded from one solid piece of metal. The face plate doesn't open and the tall, thick crest protects from nearly all head attacks.

The Wolf Cowl is a wolf's hide with the skull still intact. Worn on the head of a gungnir, this decoration of one's hunt serves as a reliable helmet.

N/A

This bear hide serves as a very strong defense for the gungnir, yet allows them their connection with Solum, the god of earth.

The Fur Band is just a step above plain leather and offers some magical support.

Gifted to the best warrior in a given tribe, the Warrior's Band is an intimidating headpiece made of leather and spent arrowheads.

The Dark Band is made of cured leather soaked in the great bogs until it is nearly rigid. The dark tint it gets from the bog is fearsome to opponents.

This skull cap is made from cast iron and has icons of death engraved on its surface.

The Fur Hat is a light-weight hat that not only protects from the elements, but pads against medium attacks.

The Horned Band has horns of animals slain mounted on it. It is a fearsome looking headpiece.

The Plated Band has a thick leather underside with small plates of precious metals sewn onto the outside for added protection.

This hat fits the wearer tightly and offers minimal protection from attacks, but is better than nothing.

The Wing Hat is made from the wings of the giant bats that haunt the Wastes. Their leather is thin, but strong.

CLASS	NAME	LEVEL	PWR	DEF	ACC	INI	AFF PWR							+ ABILITIES
Hat	**Ring of Fangs**	7	35	2	-3	0	6			●				N/A
	This helmet has two rings of animal fangs adorning it. Not only do they create a fearsome look for this helmet, but they also help in deflecting blows from melee attackers.													
Hat	**Wood Armored Hat**	8	40	2	-3	0	10		●					N/A
	With thin pieces of wood stitched into this thick leather hat, it's light enough that it won't hinder movement and offers high protection.													
Hat	**Cured Leather Hat**	9	45	2	-3	0	4				●			N/A
	This leather hat is about the strongest hat there is for how much it weighs. Imbued with the air affinity, it allows for faster movement.													
Hat	**Silk Cap**	10	50	2	-3	0	6	●	●	●	●			N/A
	The Silk cap is an ornate cap from the Steppes worn more or less to show your tribe than for protection.													
Hat	**Patched Cap**	12	60	3	-4	0	0							N/A
	This cap is patched together from scraps of leather salvaged after a hunt. It has ear flaps that protect the ears from the brisk winds of the Windward Steppes.													
Hat	**Leather Cap**	13	65	3	-4	0	0							N/A
	This is a small thin cap made of scraps of leather, usually salvaged after a hunt.													
Hat	**Clawed Cap**	14	70	3	-4	0	4				●			N/A
	The Clawed Cap is a double layered leather cap with the talons of an Eagle adorning the rim.													
Hat	**Steel Cap**	15	75	3	-4	0								N/A
	The Steel Cap covers just the top of the wearer's head, offering great protection from physical attacks to the head.													
Helm	**Shielded Ridge Helmet**	3	15	1	-2	0	0							N/A
	The Shielded Ridge Helmet has large cheek flaps and a lower brow. For a crude helmet, it's quite reliable.													
Helm	**Confortari**	9	45	2	-3	0	4	●	●	●	●			N/A
	The Confortari is the peoples' answer to the Consenesco. Consenesco are reworked and reinforced by traders and the resulting Confortari is actually a decent starting helmet.													
Helm	**Consenesco**	11	55	3	-4	0	0							N/A
	The Consenesco is a ridge type helmet that has been manufactured by small factories in Caltha and due to the mass production, suffers from lower standards of quality.													
Helm	**Hooked Ridge Helmet**	11	55	3	-4	0	10	●	●	●	●			N/A
	This ridge helmet has a tall hook protruding from its summit. Often, the god of one's affinity will be the visage on the end of the hook.													
Helm	**Ridged Fortis**	11	55	3	-4	0	0							N/A
	The Ridged Fortis is forged by armor dealers as a cheap means of income. There's always someone who wants one and they're not difficult to make.													
Helm	**Iron Helm**	18	90	4	-5	0	4	●	●	●	●			N/A
	The Iron Helm has no eye cover, but instead, protects the nose with a noseguard extending down from the forehead. It is similar to the helmets worn by the Nordagh army.													
Helm	**Pointed Helm**	18	90	4	-5	0	10	●	●	●	●			N/A
	The Pointed Helm has no face covering whatsoever, but extends well above the top of the head to a point. It is made from riveted metal plates.													
Helm	**Bronze Horned Helm**	19	95	4	-5	0	0							N/A
	The Bronze Horned Helm is a heavy helmet cast in iron. From the sides of this helmet protrude two imposing looking bronze horns.													
Helm	**Heavy Helm**	19	95	4	-5	0	6	●	●	●	●			N/A
	This Gjermundbu Helm has both eye covering and a noseguard and comes to a point at the top of the crown. Helmets like this were worn by front line infantry in the King's Army.													
Helm	**Iron Horned Helm**	19	95	4	-5	0	0							N/A
	The Iron Horned Helm is a heavy helmet forged deep in the womb of Nordagh. It is one solid piece of metal with two iron horns sticking out from the sides.													
Helm	**Horned Spangenhelm**	20	100	4	-5	0	10	●	●	●	●			N/A
	The Horned Spangenhelm adds strength in defense to the standard Spangenhelm by attaching strong horns that can potentially catch weapons.													
Helm	**Spangenhelm**	20	100	4	-5	0	0							N/A
	The Spangenhelm is the basic metal helmet of the Barbarians. Made from riveted metal, it covers the top of the head and the eyes.													
Legionnaire	**Soldier's Helmet**	12	60	3	-4	0	0							N/A
	Issued to the slaves turned soldier under Imperial rule, these helmets are designed to be a touch above average in protection, but exemplary for initiative.													
Legionnaire	**Mask of Argos**	17	85	4	-5	0	16	●	●	●	●			N/A
	This corinthian helmet is unique in that it has a full face plate, although it is sculpted to look as though it still is an open faced helmet.													
Legionnaire	**Brimmed Corinthian**	19	100	4	-5	0	12		●					N/A
	This corinthian helmet is crossed perfectly with a gallic helmet, taking advantage of the positives of both helmet types.													
Military	**Glossy Attic**	2	10	1	-1	0	0							N/A
	Only the richest schools have attics made especially for their pupils. Of which, the Glossy Attic is one of the finest training helmets money can buy.													
Military	**Pedes Attic**	4	20	1	-2	0	4	●	●	●	●			N/A
	This Imperial issue helmet is generally used by the infantrymen in the Imperial army and is only used for troops considered expendable.													
Military	**Worn Attic**	4	20	1	-2	0	0							N/A
	The Worn Attic is one of many helmets left behind after a war, never to be used again. Gladiatorial schools pick them up and use them for training.													
Military	**Attic Durus**	5	25	1	-2	0	4			●				N/A
	This helmet is a custom-made piece of armor. Hardly standard with the dual metal casting process it goes through, this attic is superior to all others of its type.													
Military	**Brass Coolus**	6	30	2	-3	0	4				●			N/A
	Forged in brass, this thin headpiece is a light helmet that offers decent protection.													
Military	**Frons Coolus**	6	30	2	-3	0	6	●	●	●	●			N/A
	The Frons Coolus offers average protection and has a brow guard as well as a longer neck guard.													
Military	**Iron Coolus**	6	30	2	-3	0	6		●					N/A
	Although the Iron Coolus offers fair protection, the weight of the metal often makes this helmet more of a hindrance than a help.													

CLASS	NAME	LEVEL	PWR	DEF	ACC	INI	AFF PWR	🌀	🔵	🟢	🌙	✦	✛	+ ABILITIES
Military	**Crested Coolus**	7	35	2	-3	0	4				●			N/A
The Crested Coolus is typically worn by higher ranking soldiers and can be fitted with a crest.															
Military	**Hooked Coolus**	7	35	2	-3	0	8	●	●	●	●			N/A
A thick coolus helmet worn both for protection and for guidance by the gods. The likeness of the god of the particular affinity is cast into the hook on top of the helmet.															
Military	**Ornamental Italic**	8	40	2	-3	0	0							N/A
Initially made for display purposes, the Ornamental Italic Helmet is forged from a heavy combination of metals and is covered in images from past battles won.															
Military	**Bronze Italic**	10	50	2	-3	0	4	●	●	●	●			N/A
The Bronze Italic helmet offers decent protection for beginners or those who aren't in the front of the lines during battle.															
Military	**Crested Italic**	10	50	2	-3	0	0							N/A
This standard Italic helmet has attachments for a crest, but is more often used without one, being that the crest alone costs more than the helmet.															
Military	**Ornate Italic Helmet**	10	50	2	-3	0	0							N/A
The ornate designs on this helmet showcase your status as a warrior while at the same time adding a little more protection than the standard Bronze Italic Helmet.															
Military	**Praetorian Italic Helmet**	11	55	3	-4	0	10	●	●	●	●			N/A
The crested Praetorian Italic Helmet is the strongest of the italic helmets and is generally awarded only to the bravest of the Imperial infantry, hence the high cost.															
Military	**Attic Cuspis**	12	60	3	-4	0	6				●			N/A
This attic helmet is only a step above the Pedes Attic. It has a single metal spike at its summit.															
Military	**Corinthian Helmet**	16	80	4	-5	0	4	●						N/A
The Corinthian is the only helmet in this class with even a partial faceguard. Made from one solid piece of metal, it's custom built to fit the warrior who bought it.															
Military	**Crested Corinthian**	17	85	4	-5	0	4				●			N/A
The Crested Corinthian is one of the most expensive helmets there is. Made of heavy-cast bronze, and with a rigid crest mount, this is a very tough helmet.															
Military	**Regal Corinthian**	17	85	4	-5	0	8	●	●	●	●			N/A
The Dual Crested Corinthian helmet offers amazing protection and is equipped with two regal crests to intimidate opponents.															
Military	**Gallic Helmet**	17	85	4	-5	0	0							N/A
The Gallic Helmet is a stronger version of the Italic Helmet worn by Imperial light infantry. Gallic type helmets are only worn by Centurions.															
Military	**Ornate Gallic Helmet**	18	90	4	-5	-8	6	●	●	●	●			N/A
The Crested Ornate Gallic helmet is a heavy military helmet with a tall crest symbolizing one's faith in The Gods.															
Military	**Gallic Aquincum**	18	90	4	-5	-7	6	●	●	●	●			N/A
The Gallic Aquincum is a bronze gallic helmet with a tall spike on the top.															
Military	**Enforced Gallic**	19	95	4	-5	0	8	●	●	●	●			N/A
The Enforced Gallic looks hardly different from the Gallic Aquincum, but under the bronze, it's reinforced with an Iron skeleton.															
Military	**Metal Crested Gallic**	19	95	4	-5	0	12				●			N/A
The is a heavy gallic helmet with a tall metal crest running from left to right instead of the standard front to back. This helmet offers superior protection.															
Minotaur	**Scorched Skull Cap**	3	20	1	-2	0	14	●						N/A
This leather cap is made from the viscera of a dragon, and has been scorched to near rigidity.															
Minotaur	**Flowing Chainmail**	5	25	1	-2	0	10	●	●	●	●	●	●	N/A
This helmet is a small band that fits around the horns and head of a minotaur and allows the chainmail to drape down the minotaur's back, offering protection from behind.															
Minotaur	**Bladed Fin**	7	40	2	-3	0	10	●						N/A
This small minotaur helmet is a skull-cap type helmet with short metal blades extending from the top of it, symbolizing the fins of a fish.															
Minotaur	**Crested Beast Helm**	9	60	2	-3	0	0							N/A
This is a crested helm usually worn by the horses of the Imperial army, but it has been customized to fit the mighty minotaur. It has a tall crest and looks very gladiatorial.															
Minotaur	**Spiked Beast Helm**	12	80	3	-4	0	16			●				N/A
This minotaur helmet was designed with the idea of a charging bull in mind. It has a single iron spike extending out from the top of it.															
Minotaur	**Horn Guard Helmet**	15	100	3	-4	0	0							N/A
This helmet is the only Minotaur helmet that has metal pieces that extend out and cover the horns, protecting them from battle.															
Mongrel	**Shattered Thracian**	18	90	4	-5	0	0							N/A
It is rare for a mongrel to wear a helmet, but on occasion one will be seen sporting the remaining shell of their latest victim's. The Shattered Thracian is an example of such a helmet.															
Murmillo	**Mosaic Campana**	4	20	1	-2	0	6	●						N/A
Much like the Mosaic Thracian helmet, this campana is made from melting down all kinds of metal, giving this helmet a semi-quilted looking quality.															
Murmillo	**Copper Campana**	6	30	2	-3	0	0							N/A
One of the most basic Murmillo specific helmets you can buy, the Copper Campana is a simple, lightweight piece of headgear.															
Murmillo	**Polished Campana**	8	40	2	-3	0	0							N/A
The Polished Campana is uncharacteristically plain for a Murmillo helmet. It is polished to a bright sheen and is elegant in its simplicity.															
Murmillo	**Iron Campana**	10	50	2	-3	0	8			●				N/A
This dull looking heavy helmet made by the blacksmiths of Nordagh and therefore isn't much more than a protective piece of headwear without much show.															
Murmillo	**Maritus**	12	60	3	-4	0	12	●						N/A
This steel campana helmet has images reminiscent of the sea and its power engraved into its surface.															
Murmillo	**Jeweled Campana**	14	70	3	-4	0	10	●	●	●	●			N/A
The Jeweled Campana helmet has six affinity jewels set into its elegant surface.															
Murmillo	**Spiked Campana**	16	80	4	-5	0	8			●				N/A
This bell shaped helmet is the traditional headgear of the Murmillo. At its apex is a tall spike.															

CLASS	NAME	LEVEL	PWR	DEF	ACC	INI	AFF PWR							+ ABILITIES
Murmillo	Winged Campana	18	90	4	-5	0	8				●			N/A
	This bronze Murmillo helmet has tall metal wings sticking up towards the heavens.													
Murmillo	Crested Campana	20	100	4	-5	0	10	●						N/A
	This is a heavily decorated Murmillo helmet with a tall crest on top of it, showing off its grandiosity.													
Nephilli	Crown of Mortuus	N/A	N/A	N/A	N/A	N/A	N/A					●		N/A
	N/A													
Ogre	Open Pondus	17	85	4	-5	0	0							N/A
	While the Ogre can equip most Pondus helmets, the Open Pondus has been pounded out of shape by a blacksmith so it's more comfortable in combat.													
Peltast	Infantry Helm	18	90	4	-5	0	20				●			N/A
	This infantry helm is given to peltasts in the Imperial army. The wings and the strong affinity to air make the wearer light of foot.													
Plain	In Cognito	22	120	5	-6	0	0							N/A
	No one will be able to recognize you with this brilliant disguise. Fool your friends and confuse your enemies. And it retails for only 3 Dinars!													
Plain	The Laughmaster	22	0	5	-6	0	0							N/A
	Now you too can look and act just like Bongo Happyxander Flappy Smiley Chuckafeller Rocko Bestertesterlester Slippo Flippo of Poindexter, everyone's favorite clown!													
Plain	The Marksman	22	120	5	-6	0	0							N/A
	This favorite joke among archers is as old as the wind itself. When sparring in the school, many a samnite have been known to play possum with this headpiece.													
Samnite	Boar's Head	17	85	4	-5	0	12			●				N/A
	The Boar's Head pays homage to Solum, the boar god of earth. Made of metal and lamellar plates, this is a strong helmet.													
Samnite	Chainmail Thracian	17	85	4	-5	0	0							N/A
	The Chainmail Thracian helmet is an exotic looking helmet with a desert artistry atop an Imperial base. One of the strongest helmets that a samnite can equip.													
Samnite	Chainmail Corinthian	18	90	4	-5	0	6	●	●	●	●			N/A
	The Chainmail Corinthian is a standard corinthian, but instead of a noseguard, there's a chainmail covering that hangs down from the eyes to the chest.													
Samnite	Chainmail Pondus	18	90	4	-5	0	0							N/A
	The Chainmail Pondus uses a heavy pondus base, but allows for better movement due to its chainmail faceguard.													
Samnite	Plated Corinthian	18	90	4	-5	0	8	●	●	●	●			N/A
	The Plated Corinthian helmet is stronger than the Chainmail Corinthian helmet, as the face covering is one rigid piece of metal.													
Samnite	Shielded Corinthian	18	90	4	-5	0	10	●	●	●	●			N/A
	The Shielded Corinthian has a full faceguard with holes in it, similar to a pondus type helmet. It is only considered a corinthian because of its base shape.													
Samnite	Nomad's Pondus	19	100	4	-5	0	0							N/A
	Those of the Windward Steppes who have accepted the Imperial sport of arena combat have crafted amazing armor to be worn by Steppes nationals. This is one such item.													
Secutor	Finned Ferinus	17	85	4	-5	0	16	●						N/A
	A heavy helmet with a strong affinity for the fire god Exuro and has fins mimicking the serpent god's gills, which adds extra protection for the sides of the wearer's head.													
Secutor	Decorated Pondus	18	90	4	-5	0	12	●	●	●	●			N/A
	The Decorated Pondus is a strong pondus type helmet that has become almost standard among Imperial secutors, in spite of its cost.													
Summoner	Pharaoh's Miter	18	90	4	-5	0	14			●				N/A
	The Pharaoh's Miter is a legendary miter once worn by the rulers of ancient times. This miter was exhumed from ancient tombs and is imbued with the power of Solum.													
Undead	Nex	10	50	2	-3	0	10					●		N/A
	The Nex's meaning, slaughter, is displayed prominently in the form of a bladed crest running the length of this intimidating ferinus helmet.													
Undead	Shumpula	10	50	2	-3	0	12					●		N/A
	Carrying with it the meaning of beheading, the Shumpula has the visage of a fallen gladiator's final scream cast in its face.													
Undead	The Steel Skull	10	50	2	-3	0	10					●		N/A
	One of the few Thracian helmets to have more than just eye holes, this one has nose holes and a mouth carved into it, representing a skull.													
Undead Summoner	Crown of Darkness	20	100	4	-5	0	16					●		Fatal Retaliation
	This obsidian crown clamps itself to the wearer's head with sharp claws and embodies the strength of the Dark God. It can strike attackers down in retaliation against physical attack.													
Urlan	Barbarian's Pride	20	100	6	-5	0	0							Damage Reduction
	This unbreakable helmet is the most ornate helmet a barbarian can find. It is suiting that Urlan wears such a crown. It is an iron helm with fierce horns made of solid gold.													
Valens	Munio's Helmet	20	100	4	-5	0	0							Move to Attack Up
	This ancient warlord's helmet was the inspiration for Munio's legendary gladiatorial headgear. Donning this unbreakable helmet makes Valens feel impervious.													
Valkyrie	Iolair	1	100	6	-1	0	10					●		Magic Defenses
	Iolair, the ancient son of the union of Aeris and Victus is reawakened and takes the form of this valkyrie helmet to watch over and protect Ursula.													
Dark Legion	Carnifico	1	90	1	-1	0	10					●		N/A
	The Carnifico is a heavy ferinus helmet, cast in metal, with hooks, horns and claws covering it. Looking upon it sends images of mutilation through one's mind.													
Dark Legion	Casus	N/A	N/A	N/A	N/A	N/A	N/A					●		N/A
	N/A													
Dark Legion	Cruor	1	90	1	-1	0	10					●		N/A
	Streaks of tarnished bronze pouring from the solitary horn on top of this otherwise plain helmet make it one of the most intimidating helmets there is.													
Dark Ludo	Darl Cowl	1	90	4	-5	0	18					●		N/A
	The Dark Cowl is Ludo's standard corinthian helmet transformed by the power of the Dark God into a menacing looking cowl with a dark crest.													
Galdr	Mask of Mourning	1	20	1	-1	0	6			●				N/A
	This sad looking mask is meant to symbolize the pain and suffering that one goes through while in mourning for somone returned to the Earth.													

CLASS	NAME	LEVEL	PWR	DEF	ACC	INI	AFF PWR	💧	🌀	🌍	☀	✦	➤	+ ABILITIES
Galdr	**Death Mask**	7	35	2	-3	0	6					●		N/A
The skull of a giant vulture is what gives this mask its strong affinity with Death. Everything the Galdr sees while looking through this mask is dying and in decay.														
Galdr	**Mask of Fertility**	8	40	2	-3	0	8				●			N/A
This light mask carries with it a soft glow. It has beautiful images of angels and ancestors ascending into the heavens adorning it. It increases one's Life affinity greatly.														
Galdr	**Mask of the Boar**	9	50	2	-3	0	20			●				N/A
This mask heightens the Galdr's affinity with the earth greatly, allowing the Galdr to see through the very eyes of Solum himself.														
Galdr	**Mask of the Dragon**	10	50	2	-3	0	20	●						N/A
Although this mask is made from standard leather, it is formed into the burning visage of a savage dragon. Wearing it pays homage to Exuro.														
Galdr	**Mask of the Eagle**	10	50	2	-3	0	20				●			N/A
This ceramic mask adorned with feathers is made to look like the predatory face of the vicious eagle god, Aeris. Wearing it increases one's air affinity immensely.														
Galdr	**Mask of the Turtle**	10	50	2	-3	0	20		●					N/A
Made from the leather of a sea tortoise, this mask heightens the Galdr's connection with Maritimus, the God of Water.														
Mutuus	**Gallus Helmet**	1	60	1	-1	0	0							N/A
Mutuus' Gallus Helmet is a custom made helmet of his own design based on the legendary warriors of old.														
Mutuus	**Gallus Infectus**	1	100	1	-1	0	20					●		N/A
Mutuus' Gallus Infectus is the twisted version of his standard Gallus helmet from before he became a pawn of the Dark God. It has strengthened him beyond belief.														

ACCESSORIES

 ACCESSORIES — Most accessories have no effect on your primary stats. Instead, they boost one Affinity type by ten, or grant him or her an innate ability. Accessories can be won in combat, or purchased at Althaag's traveling accessory cart.

ITEM	NAME	EFFECT
Anklet	**Anklet of Oasis**	+ 10 Water Affinity
This anklet is said to contain the waters of a mythical oasis deep in the Qaa Rah Desert in its ornamental jewel. It will raise Water affinity.		
Anklet	**Anklet of Will**	Steadfast
This unique anklet protects the wearer against charm and confusion attacks. It is woven of seaweed found on the beaches of Trikata.		
Anklet	**Chain Anklet**	Damage Reduction
This heavy anklet is crafted by the robust blacksmiths of Nordagh. It will decrease the amount of damage received by the wearer in battle.		
Anklet	**Desert Viper**	Power Increase
Made from the shed skin of the most feared snake in all the known regions, this anklet will increase the wearer's PWR while in battle.		
Anklet	**Earthen Anklet**	+ 10 Earth Affinity
Crafted from pounded down raw ore, this anklet will increase the wearer's Earth affinity.		
Anklet	**Golden Anklet**	+ 10 Life Affinity
The Golden Anklet is a light piece of jewelry crafted by the Queen's royal jewelers. It will increase the Life affinity of the wearer.		
Anklet	**Ivory Anklet**	+ 10 Death Affinity
Braided Elephant hair and an ornamental tusk section make up the Ivory Anklet. It is a testament to the Death affinity.		
Anklet	**Jeweled Anklet**	Affinity Charge Up
Adorned with the six jewels of the gods, this anklet doubles the rate at which the wearer's affinity charges.		
Anklet	**Lace Anklet**	+ 10 Air Affinity
Made by the finest seamstresses of Imperia in the artisan city of Syrna, this lace anklet will increase the wearer's Air affinity.		
Anklet	**Mark of Rank**	Lucidity
Once a Dervish completes their training Akar An, they are awarded with the Mark of Rank which will guard them against stun attacks.		
Anklet	**Myth of the Sands**	Supreme Critical
This anklet is made from the vines of the carnivorous Snakeleaf plant deep in the desert. It increases critical hit damage.		
Anklet	**Queen's Anklet**	Crowd's Grace
Wearing the Queen's Anklet means that you have her favor and therefore, it is impossible for you to make enemies with the crowd, even if you make poor battle choices.		
Anklet	**Scarlet Anklet**	+ 10 Fire Affinity
The deep red color of this anklet is reminiscent of the glow off the volcano in Orus and will increase the wearer's Fire affinity.		

ITEM	NAME	EFFECT
Anklet	**Silken Anklet**	Move to Attack Up
This delicate accessory increases the wearer's Move to Attack range.		
Anklet	**Steel Anklet**	Defense +5
This is a thick anklet crafted from sub-weapon grade steel which is worn to increase defense.		
Anklet	**Tekuja Anklet**	Positive Reaction
Modeled after the jewelry adorning the mystical Tekuja statues, this anklet will boost the wearer's popularity.		
Armband	**Birch Armband**	+ 10 Earth Affinity
The soft bark of the birch tree contains the energy of the Earth and when worn, channels it into and through the human, increasing one's Earth affinity.		
Armband	**Bone Armband**	+ 10 Death Affinity
Made of bones strung together with sinew, the Bone Armband increases one's Death affinity when worn.		
Armband	**Brute's Armband**	Supreme Critical
This is a tight leather armband worn to accentuate one's muscle tone. Equipping it makes criticals achieved deal more damage than normal.		
Armband	**Chainmail Armband**	Damage Reduction
The strongest chainmail in all the known regions decreases the amount of damage received in battle when this armband is equipped.		
Armband	**Feathered Armband**	+ 10 Air Affinity
Feathers of an unknown bird said to have fallen from Aeris' great sky chariot embellish this armband. Wearing it increases one's Air affinity.		
Armband	**Fur Armband**	Power Increase
With trimmings of fur, this armband is very similar to the types of garb that Barbarians and other warriors from the North wear. It increases PWR while in battle.		
Armband	**Insignia Band**	Crowd's Grace
With insignias from all four regions, this item can be worn so any region's insignia is visible, making it impossible for a crowd's favor to diminish due to poor battle choices.		
Armband	**Leather Armband**	Critical Defense
The Leather Armband protects the wearer from critical hits, making them cause less damage than they normally would.		
Armband	**Plated Armband**	Defense + 5
The Plated Armband is nearly classified as armor, except for its small size. Wearing it increases one's DF.		
Armband	**Revenge Armband**	Supreme Counter
Equipping this armband will ensure counterattacks to all incoming melee attacks.		

ITEM	NAME	EFFECT
Armband	**Silken Armband**	Move to Attack Up

The flowing silk imported from the Windward Steppes is worn throughout all the regions to increase one's Move to Attack range.

Armband	**Snakeskin Armband**	+ 10 Fire Affinity

The rare skin of this nocturnal python shines with a fiery glow in faint light. Wearing this armband increases one's Fire affinity.

Armband	**Soldier's Armband**	Face Enemy

This armband is scavenged off of fallen soldiers by bandits after massive battles have been fought. Wearing it prevents flank attacks.

Armband	**Steel Armband**	+ 10 Water Affinity

This shimmering, polished armband has a very faint blue tint to it and is reminiscent of the sea. Equipping it increases one's Water affinity.

Armband	**Thief's Armband**	Bandit's Luck

The Thief's Armband is worn by master thieves. Equipping one of these increases the likelihood of receiving unique items after a battle.

Armband	**Woven Armband**	+ 10 Life Affinity

The peaceful patterns woven into this white armband pay homage to Victus, the God of Life. Equipping it increases one's Life affinity.

Belt	**Archer's Belt**	Power Increase

A standard and plain belt worn by archers all throughout the Steppes, this belt will increase the wearer's PWR while in battle.

Belt	**Assassin's Belt**	Ambush Range Up

The Assassin's Belt is awarded as an honor among the mercenary killers throughout the regions. It will increase the Cover range of the wearer.

Belt	**Belt of Willpower**	Steadfast

This belt protects the wearer against charm and confusion attacks. It is woven of seaweed found on the beaches of Trikata.

Belt	**Chain Belt**	Damage Reduction

This heavy belt is made of chain formerly used in the castles of Nordagh for their drawbridges. It decreases the amount of damage received in battle.

Belt	**Dark Belt**	+ 10 Death Affinity

The Dark Belt is made from the slain and tanned hides of horses and beasts of burden fallen in battles past. It increases the wearer's Death affinity.

Belt	**Fisherman's Belt**	+ 10 Water Affinity

Generally worn by mariners of Imperia, the Fisherman's Belt increases the wearer's Water affinity.

Belt	**Leather Belt**	Defense +5

The Leather Belt is a thick belt crafted from the toughest leather in the entire region of Nordagh. It increases the wearer's Defense.

Belt	**Magic Belt**	Spell Range Up

This belt has been magically charged and is a natural assistant to casting spells. Wearing it increases the range of spell skills.

Belt	**Master's Belt**	Range Up

This is a master archer's belt. It will allow an archer's range to increase once equipped.

Belt	**Nomad's Belt**	Crowd's Grace

Carrying with it the famed history of the nomadic order, this belt makes it impossible for the wearer to lose the crowd's favor through poor battle choices.

Belt	**Quarryman's Belt**	+ 10 Earth Affinity

This belt is worn by the quarrymen of the Expanse and is adorned with stones found in abundance in the mines. It increases the Earth affinity.

Belt	**Rider's Belt**	+ 10 Air Affinity

Crafted in honor of the wispy clouds of Aeris' realm, the Rider's Belt increases the wearer's Air affinity.

Belt	**Scarlet Belt**	+ 10 Fire Affinity

Paying homage to the fire god Exuro, this belt is crafted from a flaming red fabric, dyed to match the lava of Exuro's Eye, increasing the Fire affinity.

Belt	**Silk Belt**	Move to Attack Up

This normally ceremonial belt offers the wearer such ease of movement that it will increase their Move to Attack range.

ITEM	NAME	EFFECT
Belt	**Soul Belt**	Supreme Critical

The Soul Belt channels the energy of the wearer's soul and increases their critical hit damage output.

Belt	**Temple Belt**	+ 10 Life Affinity

The temple belt is given to high class Imperials when they are born. It signifies new life and will increase the wearer's Life affinity.

Bracelet	**Amazon's Bracelet**	Power Increase

The only thing more fierce than an Amazon's presence as a warrior, is her pride. Wearing this trophy will increase her PWR while in battle.

Bracelet	**Bone Bracelet**	+ 10 Death Affinity

The Bone Bracelet is a chain of thin vertebrae from small game animals. Wearing this bracelet will increase the Wearer's Death affinity.

Bracelet	**Bracelet of Force**	Supreme Critical

This is a heavy bracelet which allows the wearer to do more critical damage when equipped.

Bracelet	**Bronze Bracelet**	+ 10 Death Affinity

The Bronze Bracelet pays homage to Aeris and increases the wearer's Air affinity.

Bracelet	**Gold Bracelet**	Damage Reduction

Made from the purest gold quarried from the mines of the Qaa Rah Desert, this bracelet decreases damage received in battle.

Bracelet	**Jeweled Bracelet**	Affinity Charge Up

With the six jewels of the gods set in it, this bracelet doubles the rate at which the wearer's affinity charges.

Bracelet	**Leather Bracelet**	Defense +5

The Leather Bracelet acts as a type of padding for the wrist as well as a decoration. It increases the wearer's DF.

Bracelet	**Magical Bracelet**	Spell Range Up

This mythical bracelet comes from Saraa Izel and possesses the magical energy of the mysterious city. Wearing it increases the range of spell skills.

Bracelet	**Mythical Bracelet**	Crowd's Grace

Fashioned after the mighty Armofortis' bracelet worn in the first gladiatorial battle in Caltha. The crowd chooses to ignore poor sportsmanship when this item is equipped.

Bracelet	**Ornate Bracelet**	Positive Reaction

This bracelet is so beautifully crafted by the artisans of Syrna that it boosts one's Popularity in battle.

Bracelet	**Pretty Bracelet**	Hard to Get

This feminine charm is so beguiling that it will increase the chances of evading attacks from male opponents.

Bracelet	**Steel Bracelet**	+ 10 Water Affinity

Crafted to mimic the rolling waves of the Aeonis Sea, this bracelet increases the wearer's Water affinity.

Bracelet	**Steppes Bracelet**	Range Up

This bracelet gives the wearer the power of the mighty archers of the Steppes and increases the range of attack when using bows.

Bracelet	**Stone Bracelet**	+ 10 Earth Affinity

The Stone Bracelet is a heavy accessory which will increase the wearer's Earth affinity.

Bracelet	**Vermillion Bracelet**	+ 10 Fire Affinity

Straight from the Steppes, where the threat of volcanic eruption constantly looms on the horizon, the Vermillion Bracelet increases one's Fire affinity.

Bracelet	**Woven Bracelet**	+ 10 Life Affinity

Woven from the thick wool of Vargen's fame, this bracelet's bright white color honors Victus and increases one's Life affinity.

Bullring	**Bone Nosering**	+ 10 Death Affinity

The Bone Nosering, a favorite trinket of Mortuus', increases one's Death affinity when equipped.

Bullring	**Bronze Nosering**	+ 10 Air Affinity

Made of the metal of choice for the Air god Aeris, the Bronze Nosering increases one's Air affinity.

General Strategy · Character Classes · World Atlas · Bonus Material

ITEM	NAME	EFFECT
Bullring	**Bull Ring**	Power Increase
This is the standard Bull Ring used by farmers for pack and farm animals. Equipping it increases one's PWR while in battle..		
Bullring	**Glass Nosering**	+ 10 Light Affinity
The thick, and surprisingly robust Glass Nosering looks as fragile as life itself and increases one's affinity with Victus when equipped.		
Bullring	**Gold Nosering**	Positive Reaction
This beautiful yet simple gold nosering shines brightly on the sunlit battle-field. Wearing it boosts one's popularity gained in battle.		
Bullring	**Heavy Nosering**	Damage Reduction
This heavy adornment bolsters one's vitality when worn, dramatically decreasing the amount of damage received in battle.		
Bullring	**Jeweled Nosering**	Affinity Charge Up
The Jeweled Nosering is studded with jewels representative of all six affinities. This nosering makes one's affinity charge twice as fast.		
Bullring	**Linked Nosering**	Critical Defense
The Linked Nosering is a chain rather than a proper "ring." Wearing this item makes criticals received deal no more than a normal hit would.		
Bullring	**Polished Nosering**	Crowd's Grace
This nosering has a violet sheen to it and never tarnishes. This nosering makes it impossible for the Minotaur to lose the crowd's favor through poor battle choices.		
Bullring	**Soul Ring**	Supreme Critical
The Soul Ring is a comfortable nosering which, when equipped, will make criticals achieved deal more damage than they normally would.		
Bullring	**Steel Nosering**	+ 10 Water Affinity
The Steel Nosering is fashioned after the earring sometimes worn by the mighty Water god, Maritimus, and will increase one's affinity with him.		
Bullring	**Stone Nosering**	+ 10 Earth Affinity
The strong Stone Nosering pleases the Earth god Solum and will increase one's affinity with him when equipped.		
Bullring	**Studded Nosering**	Negate Stun
This nosering is made of steel with bronze studs pounded into it. Wearing it will guard against stun attacks.		
Bullring	**Thorned Nosering**	Steadfast
Equipped on bulls taken on long journeys to keep them alert, the Thorned Nosering guards against charm and confusion attacks.		
Bullring	**Titanium Nosering**	Defense +5
The strong Titanium Nosering is made of a material found only in the deep mines of The Southern Expanse. It raises one's Defense when equipped.		
Bullring	**Vermillion Nosering**	+ 10 Fire Affinity
The brilliant red enamel on this piece of jewelry is reminiscent of the flames of Exuro's glory. Wearing it increases one's Fire affinity.		
Charm	**Amber Gemstone**	Crowd's Grace
The Amber that comes from Nordagh is a matter of such pride for the citizens that one who carries the Amber Gemstone is unable to adversely affect the crowd.		
Charm	**Ankh**	+ 10 Light Affinity
The Ankh is an age-old symbol of life from deep within the Expanse. Carrying it will increase one's Light Affinity.		
Charm	**Aquamarine Shard**	+ 10 Water Affinity
This unrefined shard of Aquamarine crystal increases the Water affinity when carried.		
Charm	**Cat's Eye**	Move to Attack Up
This is a marble with a Cat's Eye shape in its center. Holding this increases one's Move to Attack range		
Charm	**Crystal Ball**	Magic Defenses
The Crystal Ball serves as a receiver for magic and therefore lessens the effect of magic attacks against anyone who possesses it.		
Charm	**Eye of the Gods**	Affinity Charge Up
It is said that everyone who looks into the Eye of the Gods sees something different. Holding this will make your affinity charge twice as fast.		

ITEM	NAME	EFFECT
Charm	**Heart Star**	Damage Reduction
The Heart Star is a symbol of physical vigor and strong life presence. When in possession of this vitality boosting charm, damge received in battle is lessened.		
Charm	**Knuckle Bones**	Positive Reaction
As a symbol of divine knowledge, carrying the Knuckle Bones boosts one's popularity gained in battle.		
Charm	**Lucky Charm**	Critical Defense
A traditional Imperial symbol of fortune, this charm lessens the effect of critical damage done against the person holding it.		
Charm	**Moon Charm**	Spell Range Up
This charm helps to channel the magic powers of those holding it, increasing the range of magic used in battle.		
Charm	**Ruby Earrings**	+ 10 Fire Affinity
The fiery red color of these precious earrings increase the wearer's Fire affinity.		
Charm	**Scarab Beetle**	Defense +5
Throughout the Expanse, the Scarab Beetle is a symbol of protection. Holding this charm increases DF.		
Charm	**Talisman**	Magic Attack Up
As an icon of one's magical faith, this charm will bring the wearer's Magic Strength up dramatically.		
Charm	**Talon of Safat**	+ 10 Air Affinity
This rare talon of the mystical bird, Safat, is found in the desert sands of the Southern Expanse. It is carried to increase one's Air affinity.		
Charm	**Voodoo Doll**	+ 10 Dark Affinity
Made to represent all enemies, the Voodoo Doll is a powerful device of those who worship Mortuus. Holding this item increases one's Dark Affinity.		
Charm	**Worm of Orion**	+ 10 Earth Affinity
Found deep in the forests of Nordagh, this worm's nocturnal luminescence makes it shine in the starlight. It is used to heighten the Earth affinity.		
Collar	**Battle Collar**	Supreme Critical
The Battle Collar is given to Imperial War Hounds and will make criticals deal more damage when achieved in battle.		
Collar	**Black Band**	+ 10 Dark Affinity
The Black Band, made from the foul sinew of animal carcasses found deep in the Qaa Rah Desert increases one's Dark Affinity when equipped.		
Collar	**Chain Collar**	Damage Reduction
This thick iron chain crafted by the famous blacksmiths of Nordagh reduces one's damage received in battle		
Collar	**Collar of Force**	Power Increase
Wearing the Collar of Force shows just how mighty a fighter you are. It increases one's PWR while in battle.		
Collar	**Collar of Spite**	Counter Attack
Wearing the Collar of Spite makes one bolder, more aggressive. It allows one to counterattack 50% of the time, after receiving physical damage.		
Collar	**Dragon's Choker**	+ 10 Fire Affinity
The Dragon's Choker is actually an ancient bracelet worn by the vain dragons of ages past. Wearing this as a collar increases one's Fire affinity.		
Collar	**Guard's Band**	Steadfast
The Guard's Band is a collar for watch dogs throughout the Imperial Empire. Wearing it guards against charm and confusion attacks in battle.		
Collar	**Halter of Light**	+ 10 Light Affinity
This sparkling collar of fine silver and lace made in the artisan district of Syrna increases one's Light Affinity when equipped.		
Collar	**Iron Choker**	Critical Defense
The Iron choker serves almost as a piece of armor. Equipping it causes incoming critical attacks to deal no more damage than standard heavy attacks would.		
Collar	**Leather Collar**	Defense +5
The Leather Collar is put on wet, so that it dries into a tight grip around the strong muscles of the beast's neck. It increases defense greatly.		

ITEM	NAME	EFFECT
Collar	**Mad Choker**	Berserk

This uncomfortable collar will drive nearly any animal to insanity if it is worn for too long. It places the wearer in a constant state of berserk.

ITEM	NAME	EFFECT
Collar	**Ornamental Collar**	Crowd's Grace

The Ornamental Collar is fashioned after those worn by the Royal family's pets in Khorhu. Wearing it keeps the crowd's favor from falling due to poor battle choices.

ITEM	NAME	EFFECT
Collar	**Silken Collar**	Move to Attack Up

The Silken Collar, a decorative collar worn by pets of the nomadic tribes throughout the Windward Steppes, will increase one's Move to Attack range.

ITEM	NAME	EFFECT
Collar	**Steel Collar**	+ 10 Water Affinity

Rough and heavy, the Steel Collar is indicative of the type of craftsmanship found throughout Nordagh. Wearing this collar increases the Water affinity.

ITEM	NAME	EFFECT
Collar	**Wind Collar**	+ 10 Air Affinity

The Wind Collar is adorned with feathers, giving the impression of a blowing wind when worn. This collar increases one's Air affinity.

ITEM	NAME	EFFECT
Collar	**Woven Collar**	+ 10 Earth Affinity

This collar is made from the thick fern stalks found covering the forest floor in Nordagh. Wearing this collar increases the Earth affinity.

ITEM	NAME	EFFECT
Eye	**Barbarian's Eye**	Power Increase

Barbarians are famed throughout all the known regions for their massive strength. Carrying this item will increase one's PWR while in battle.

ITEM	NAME	EFFECT
Eye	**Bear's Eye**	Critical Defense

The strength of the Bear lies not solely within its muscle, but also in its stern eyes. Criticals against you do no more than normal damage when carrying this item.

ITEM	NAME	EFFECT
Eye	**Berserker's Eye**	Defense + 5

The Berserker's Eye increases one's DF greatly, as the conditioning they endure to become warriors allows them to fight without armor.

ITEM	NAME	EFFECT
Eye	**Blindman's Eye**	Accuracy +99

Tapping into the sixth sense said to be common among the blind, equipping this trinket makes every physical attack performed 100% accurate.

ITEM	NAME	EFFECT
Eye	**Boar's Eye**	+ 10 Earth Affinity

Carrying the Boar's Eye brings you closer to the element of earth, increasing your affinity with Solum greatly.

ITEM	NAME	EFFECT
Eye	**Centurion's Eye**	Face Enemy

Carrying the watchful eye of this important and powerful Imperial soldier prevents side and back attacks.

ITEM	NAME	EFFECT
Eye	**Cyclops Eye**	Crowd's Grace

The Cyclops eye ensures that the crowd's reaction will not be adversely affected by poor combat choices. The crowd loves seeing the Cyclops wielding an eye of its own people.

ITEM	NAME	EFFECT
Eye	**Dervish's Eye**	Move to Attack Up

The Dervish's Eye holds the secret to all their rigorous training. Carrying this item increases one's Move to Attack range.

ITEM	NAME	EFFECT
Eye	**Eagle's Eye**	+ 10 Air Affinity

Carrying the Eagle's Eye brings you closer to the element of air, increasing your affinity with Aeris greatly.

ITEM	NAME	EFFECT
Eye	**Glass Eye**	Ever Sight

The Glass Eye, crafted of the finest glass and jewels can be equipped to act as a guard against attacks causing blind.

ITEM	NAME	EFFECT
Eye	**Jackal's Eye**	+ 10 Dark Affinity

Carrying the Jackal's Eye brings you closer to the element of death, increasing your affinity with Mortuus greatly.

ITEM	NAME	EFFECT
Eye	**Samnite's Eye**	Damage Reduction

Equip this item to absorb the vitality of the mighty Samnite, decreasing the amount of damage received during battle.

ITEM	NAME	EFFECT
Eye	**Serpent's Eye**	+ 10 Fire Affinity

Carrying the Serpent's Eye brings you closer to the element of fire, increasing your affinity with Exuro greatly.

ITEM	NAME	EFFECT
Eye	**Tiger's Eye**	Supreme Critical

Carrying the trophy of the most vicious predator of the Steppes makes criticals achieved deal more damage than they normally would.

ITEM	NAME	EFFECT
Eye	**Tortoise's Eye**	+ 10 Water Affinity

Carrying the Tortoise's Eye brings you closer to the element of water, increasing your affinity with Maritimus greatly.

ITEM	NAME	EFFECT
Eye	**Valkyrie's Eye**	+ 10 Light Affinity

Carrying the Valkyrie's Eye brings you closer to the element of life, increasing your affinity with Victus greatly.

ITEM	NAME	EFFECT
Jewel	**Amber**	Defense +5

Amber has for so long been regarded as a protector and giver of longevity that equipping this jewel increases one's Defense greatly.

ITEM	NAME	EFFECT
Jewel	**Amethyst**	Antidote

The Amethyst protects the wearer from poisons and sicknesses, nullifying all poison attacks.

ITEM	NAME	EFFECT
Jewel	**Aquamarine**	+ 10 Water Affinity

Aquamarine always has a place on long sea voyages, as it pleases Maritimus greatly. Equipping this jewel increases one's Water affinity.

ITEM	NAME	EFFECT
Jewel	**Bloodstone**	Face Enemy

Generally carried into battle by soldiers, the Bloodstone gives a warrior unrivaled strength in combat. Equipping it will prohibit flank attacks.

ITEM	NAME	EFFECT
Jewel	**Coral**	Damage Reduction

Coral is an organic jewel and is believed to help to increase one's vitality. Wearing this jewel decreases the amount of damage received in battle.

ITEM	NAME	EFFECT
Jewel	**Crystal**	+ 10 Air Affinity

Crystal, being little more than fashioned glass pays homage to the skies wherein dwells Aeris, the air god. Equipping it increases one's Air affinity.

ITEM	NAME	EFFECT
Jewel	**Diamond**	+ 10 Light Affinity

The only jewel in the known world to completely exemplify goodness, when equipped, the Diamond will increase one's Light Affinity.

ITEM	NAME	EFFECT
Jewel	**Emerald**	+ 10 Earth Affinity

The Emerald has had many meanings, but recently has been adopted by those worshiping Solum. Equipping it will increase one's Earth Affinity.

ITEM	NAME	EFFECT
Jewel	**Garnet**	Crowd's Grace

The Garnet is a rare gem very popular among the highest classes. Equipping a jewel of such high regard insures one's favor with the crowd.

ITEM	NAME	EFFECT
Jewel	**Jade**	Move to Attack Up

Equipping Jade enhances one's motivation, thereby increasing their Move to Attack range.

ITEM	NAME	EFFECT
Jewel	**Jet**	Initiative +10

This dark gem is a natural absorber of energy and when equipped, lends this energy to its master, nearly doubling their initiative.

ITEM	NAME	EFFECT
Jewel	**Moonstone**	Critical Defense

The Moonstone protects the wearer from great harm making criticals achieved against the wearer do no more than normal damage would.

ITEM	NAME	EFFECT
Jewel	**Onyx**	+ 10 Dark Affinity

For those weak of heart, Equipping Onyx is said to bring on nightmares and depression, but for those strong of heart, it increases one's Dark Affinity.

ITEM	NAME	EFFECT
Jewel	**Quartz**	Power Increase

The foggy, transparent quality of this stone makes it one of the stronger jewels in the known regions. Equipping it increases one's PWR while in battle.

ITEM	NAME	EFFECT
Jewel	**Ruby**	+ 10 Fire Affinity

It is said that rubies spring up from the shed blood of the mighty Fire god, Exuro. Equipping this jewel increases one's Fire affinity.

ITEM	NAME	EFFECT
Jewel	**Sapphire**	Affinity Charge Up

Historically considered an amplifier of all things mystic, equipping the Sapphire will enable your affinities to charge twice as fast as normal.

ITEM	NAME	EFFECT
Medal	**Badge of Aeris**	+ 10 Air Affinity

This medal proves one's allegiance with the god Aeris and will increase one's Air affinity.

ITEM	NAME	EFFECT
Medal	**Badge of Exuro**	+ 10 Fire Affinity

This medal proves one's allegiance with the god Exuro and will increase one's Fire affinity.

ITEM	NAME	EFFECT
Medal	**Badge of Maritimus**	+ 10 Water Affinity
This medal proves one's allegiance with the god Maritimus and will increase one's Water affinity.		
Medal	**Badge of Mortuus**	+ 10 Dark Affinity
This medal proves one's allegiance with the god Mortuus and will increase one's Dark Affinity.		
Medal	**Badge of Solum**	+ 10 Earth Affinity
This medal proves one's allegiance with the god Solum and will increase one's Earth affinity.		
Medal	**Emperor's Insignia**	Crowd's Grace
No matter how you perform in battle, if you've got the Emperor's Insignia equipped, you cannot lose the favor of the crowd by poor battle choices.		
Medal	**Impervious Heart**	Defense + 5
This medal increases the wearer's defense. It symbolizes the pride of Nordagh and has the same insignia as is on the gate of the border wall.		
Medal	**Iron Fist**	Critical Defense
The Iron Fist is a symbol of strength familiar throughout the known regions. When equipped, criticals received will do no more than normal damage would.		
Medal	**Iron Will**	Steadfast
With the Iron Will equipped, one finds themselves with all the strength of the Northern pride and it is impossible to be charmed or confused.		
Medal	**Medal of Bravery**	Face Enemy
Wearing the Medal of Bravery allows you to always face your opponent, whether they are attacking you from the side, from behind or in front of you.		
Medal	**Medal of Rank**	Supreme Motivation
When worn by a Centurion, The Medal of Rank gives the wearer the authority for their commands to be doubly effective when motivating team members.		
Medal	**Medal of Stature**	Damage Reduction
From the age old strength of the Expanse comes the Medal of Stature. After equipping this item, one's damage received in battle lessens greatly..		
Medal	**Medal of Valor**	Positive Reaction
The Medal of Valor is awarded to generals in the Imperial Army who have become inspirations. Equipping this medal will boost PP received in battle.		
Medal	**War Hero**	Supreme Critical
Soldiers known for fighting fiercely in the Imperial Army are awarded with the War Hero medal. When equipped, it increases critical damage.		
Medal	**Warrior's Medal**	Power Increase
The Warrior's Medal is what separates regular fighters from the true "Warriors." Wearing this medal increases your PWR while in battle.		
Necklace	**Aquamarine Pendant**	+ 10 Water Affinity
One of the favorite stones of the Imperial high class, the Aquamarine has always been associated with the Sea and will increase one's Water affinity.		
Necklace	**Assassin's Necklace**	Ambush Range Up
The Assassin's Necklace increases the Ambush range of any Peltast or Gungnir who wears it.		
Necklace	**Bone Pendant**	+ 10 Dark Affinity
As the harsh environment of the desert has always been linked with death, this necklace embraces that fact and increases one's Dark Affinity.		
Necklace	**Chain Necklace**	Damage Reduction
Nordagh is known for their heavy and crude mastery of raw metal ore and this necklace is no exception. Its robust craftsmanship lessens damage received in battle.		
Necklace	**Clay Pendant**	+ 10 Earth Affinity
Made to resemble the tusk of the mighty boar-god Solum, this necklace increases one's Earth affinity when equipped.		
Necklace	**Dancer's Necklace**	Move to Attack Up
This decorative necklace is worn by the performers in the royal palace of Ibliis. Equipping it increases one's Move to Attack range.		
Necklace	**Gold Necklace**	+ 10 Light Affinity
This precious and fine necklace is characteristic of the craftsmanship in jewelry of the Expanse. It's simple beauty increases one's Light Affinity.		

ITEM	NAME	EFFECT
Necklace	**Heirloom Pendant**	Crowd's Grace
The Heirloom Pendant is a trinket reminiscent of the glorious history of Imperia. Wearing it keeps the crowd from reacting negatively to one's poor battle choices.		
Necklace	**Iron Pendant**	Critical Defense
The Iron Pendant not only acts as a symbol of one's strength as an aggressor, but also as a defender. Equipping it reduces critical damage received.		
Necklace	**Lace Necklace**	+ 10 Air Affinity
The world-famous artisans of Syrna have long been influenced by Aeris and it is seen in much of their art. This necklace will increase one's Air affinity.		
Necklace	**Leather Choker**	Defense +5
The Leather Choker is made of a thick leather doubly cured and is worn to protect the neck. It increases the wearer's Defense.		
Necklace	**Necklace of Vigilance**	Face Enemy
Worn by the guards of the nomadic pitches, the Necklace of Vigilance is believed to heighten the senses and will prevent any side or back attacks.		
Necklace	**Olympic Necklace**	Range Up
Equipping the Olympic Necklace increases the distance one can throw a javelin.		
Necklace	**Pendant of the Valkyrie**	Supreme Critical
Wearing Pendants of the Valkyrie honors the sacrifice the Valkyries made during the Great War. This item will increase one's critical attack strength.		
Necklace	**Ranger's Necklace**	Move to Attack Up
Worn to distinguish among rank in the Imperial army, the Ranger's Necklace will increase one's movement range when equipped.		
Necklace	**Ruby Pendant**	+ 10 Fire Affinity
Made from the most precious stone found in the Steppes, the flashing glimmer of this necklace will increase one's affinity with Fire when equipped.		
Necklace	**Tooth Necklace**	Power Increase
Worn as a trophy to show off one's strength, the Tooth Necklace is generally made from a vicious animal's fang. It will increase one's PWR while in battle.		
Poem	**A Jingle for Me**	Crowd's Grace
Like the players on the stage / I play to the crowd / I act perhaps less than my age / So cheer for me out loud!		
Poem	**Death's March**	+ 10 Dark Affinity
Death will come to every one / Death brings us together / Mortuus, with your great dark power / Surround me altogether		
Poem	**Doggerel of Defense**	Defense +5
Like the thickest hardest leather / Like the strongest Nordagh chain / Any assault I will weather / As if it were as light as rain		
Poem	**Elegy of Perception**	Steadfast
In the darkness I can see / By nothing I am bound / For clarity of sight and mind / With me are always found		
Poem	**From the Cup**	Damage Reduction
Within this cup, vitality / New vigor and new energy / Drink the contents with much glee / And fight on much more happily		
Poem	**Lion's Pride**	Face Enemy
Like a Lion in his pride / No one hits him from the side / If you try you'll be denied / 'Cause I'm a warrior bona fide		
Poem	**Ode to Aeris**	+ 10 Air Affinity
Aeris, the mighty god of sky / Rain your wrath not down on I / Gaze upon me with your eye / Instead to grant me power		
Poem	**Plea for Strength**	Power Increase
Mighty gods on high, I plead / Lend me strength unrivaled / Every ounce you have I need / Lest I be defiled		
Poem	**Plead to Maritimus**	+ 10 Water Affinity
Water cleanses, feeds the soul / Maritimus see me / Feed me, cleanse me whole / And through your graces free me		
Poem	**Rise of the Mediocre**	+5 Accuracy
Knocked and battered to the ground / Throughout the lands I'm hated / Someday, though, I swear you'll see / I'm underestimated		

ITEM	NAME	EFFECT
Poem	**Showman's Rhyme**	Positive Reaction
	I've got moves unlike no other / Gather all your family 'round / Your mother, father, sister, brother / Can watch me beat the enemies down	
Poem	**Solum Rises**	+ 10 Earth Affinity
	From the mighty mother earth / Solum rises strong / Lift me up upon your back / And carry me along	
Poem	**Strength of the Fire**	+ 10 Fire Affinity
	Fire rising through the night / Cast your light upon me / Shroud me fully and I'll fight / With your great strength beside me	
Poem	**The Pledge to Light**	+ 10 Light Affinity
	God of Light and God of Life / A good man lives in me / In times of trouble and of strife / I'll always turn to thee	
Poem	**Traveler's Verse**	Move Range Up
	Wandering and wondering / I travel 'cross this land / With want for nothing other / Than a flask of mead in hand	
Poem	**What it Takes**	Supreme Critical
	Watch yourself when fighting me / I may be small by all accounts / But I play cheap and take my pride / In hitting where it counts	
Quest	**Desert-Yeti Head**	N/A
	The severed head of the Desert-Yeti should clear Aziza's name in the eyes of the citizens of Saraa Izel. Bring it back to her and she might have a reward waiting.	
Quest	**Mysterious Tablet**	N/A
	The surface of the Mysterious Tablet has been marred beyond legibility.	
Quest	**Signet of the Valkyrie**	N/A
	This charm was given to Ursula by Sigi, A Galdr. she said that when the time comes, Ursula will know what its purpose is. This item can not be equipped.	
Quest	**Stolen Items**	N/A
	This looks like the items from The Loyalist that Agamede was talking about. If they return the her, she might see fit to offering the school a reward.	
Quest	**The Promise Stone**	N/A
	This is the charm give to Valens be a strange man imprisoned inside the Mysterious Tablet. He said that when the time comes, Valens will know what its purpose is.	
Ring	**Band of the Emperor**	Crowd's Grace
	Wearing a ring with the Emperor's royal standard etched into its face, like the Band of the Emperor, makes it impossible to lose the crowd's favor by performing poorly in battle.	
Ring	**Gladiatorial Legend**	Supreme Critical
	Rings like this used to be awarded to powerful gladiators and will often end up on the black market. Equipping it will increase critical damage dealt.	
Ring	**Golden Ring**	HP Up
	The heavy Golden Ring covers almost one finger entirely and bends in parts. Equipping it decreases damage received in battle.	
Ring	**Jeweled Ring**	Affinity Charge Up
	Studded with all six of the affinity stones, this precious ring is unparalleled in beauty. Equipping it will make one's affinity charge twice as fast.	
Ring	**Ring of Aeris**	+ 10 Air Affinity
	The Ring of Aeris, fashioned after the ring worn by the mighty god known for his vanity as well as his infinite power, will increase one's Air affinity.	
Ring	**Ring of Exuro**	+ 10 Fire Affinity
	This ring is covered with a rich red enamel and is reminiscent of the ring worn by the mighty Exuro himself. Equipping it will increase the Fire affinity.	
Ring	**Ring of Honor**	Positive Reaction
	As Imperials honor glory through war, the Ring of Honor will boost any Popularity gained in battle.	
Ring	**Ring of Maritimus**	+ 10 Water Affinity
	This coral ring is rumored to have been created by Maritimus himself. Wearing it increases one's Water affinity.	
Ring	**Ring of Might**	Power Increase
	Wearing the crudely crafted and raw looking Ring of Might will increase one's PWR while in battle.	

ITEM	NAME	EFFECT
Ring	**Ring of Mortuus**	+ 10 Dark Affinity
	The Ring of Mortuus, fashioned after the ring worn by the mighty god known for his cruel and unrelenting character, will increase one's Dark Affinity.	
Ring	**Ring of Purity**	Antidote
	This crystalline ring is made from a healing gem and will guard the wearer against becoming poisoned.	
Ring	**Ring of Refuge**	Move to Attack Up
	Wearing the Ring of Refuge will increase one's Move to Attack range.	
Ring	**Ring of Solum**	+ 10 Earth Affinity
	The Ring of Solum is fashioned after the ring worn on the tusk of the mighty Boar god of the Earth. Equipping it will increase one's Earth affinity.	
Ring	**Ring of the Brave**	Face Enemy
	This ornate ring is a trophy of sorts, awarded to the bravest warriors of the nomadic tribes. Equipping it will prevent side and back attacks.	
Ring	**Ring of Victus**	+ 10 Light Affinity
	Made of white gold, the Ring of Victus is cast in the likeness of the ring worn by the peaceful god of Life. Equipping it increases one's Light Affinity.	
Ring	**Titanium Ring**	Defense +5
	Made of the rare Titanium found in the deepest areas of the mines of the Qaa Rah Desert, this ring is of such a robust nature that it will increase Defense.	
Runestone	**Algiz**	Critical Defense
	The runestone for protection, Algiz, is made of black tourmaline and makes criticals deal no more than normal damage against whoever equips it.	
Runestone	**Ansuz**	Affinity Charge Up
	The runestone Ansuz symbolizes the gods and is made of lapis lazuli. Equipping this runestone will make one's affinity charge twice as fast.	
Runestone	**Berkana**	+ 10 Earth Affinity
	Berkana, the rune of the great Mother Earth, is carved into earthy jet. It will increase one's affinity with Solum when equipped.	
Runestone	**Eihwaz**	+ 10 Dark Affinity
	Eihwaz is the rune of death. It is made of smoky quartz and carries with it an unsettling presence. Equipping it increases one's Dark Affinity.	
Runestone	**Eow**	Move to Attack Up
	This runestone represents the power of one's inner self. Made of turquoise, when equipped it increases one's move to attack range.	
Runestone	**Fehu**	+ 10 Light Affinity
	Fehu is the rune of fertility and life-force. It is made of amber and will increase one's Light Affinity when equipped.	
Runestone	**Gebo**	Positive Reaction
	The emerald runestone Gebo represents giving and boosts the possessor's Popularity in battle.	
Runestone	**Hagalaz**	+ 10 Air Affinity
	Hagalaz, or "hailstone" represents the torments of the weather from high in the heavens above. It is made of crystal and increases one's Air affinity.	
Runestone	**Ingwaz**	Damage Reduction
	Ingwaz, the rune of rebirth and life anew, is appropriately found carved into sacred ivory from felled war elephants. Holding this runestone decreases damage received in battle.	
Runestone	**Kenaz**	+ 10 Fire Affinity
	Kenaz, in the old Nordish tongue meant "fire." This stone is made of flint and will increase one's Fire affinity when equipped.	
Runestone	**Lauguz**	Ever Sight
	The rune of revelations, Lauguz is made of malachite and will guard against blinding attacks when equipped.	
Runestone	**Mannaz**	+ 10 Water Affinity
	Wise like Maritimus, the Tortoise god of Water, this rune's essence is that of intelligence. It is carved into amethyst and will increase one's Water affinity.	
Runestone	**Sowilo**	Defense +5
	Representing wholeness, Sowilo increases the possessor's Defense. It is generally found carved into the handsome sunstone.	

ITEM	NAME	EFFECT
Runestone	**Tiewaz**	Face Enemy

Symbolizing justice, this hematite runestone protects the one in possession of it from side and back attacks.

ITEM	NAME	EFFECT
Runestone	**Uruz**	Power Increase

At the basest understanding of Uruz, lies true Strength. This rune is carved into the rare tiger eye jewel and increases PWR when equipped.

| Runestone | **Wunjo** | Crowd's Grace |

Wunjo represents joy and the fulfillment of wishes and is carved into rose quartz. Holding this item makes it impossible for the crowd's favor to wane due to poor battle choices.

| Scalp | **Boar's Scalp** | + 10 Air Affinity |

The Boar's Scalp pleases the Air god, Aeris, and therefore raises one's Air affinity.

| Scalp | **Corpse's Scalp** | + 10 Light Affinity |

The Corpse's Scalp pleases the Life god, Victus, and therefore raises one's Light Affinity.

| Scalp | **Dervish's Scalp** | Defense + 5 |

Having a Dervish's Scalp will increase one's agility, making it more likely to evade attacks.

| Scalp | **Eagle's Scalp** | + 10 Earth Affinity |

The Eagle's Scalp pleases the Earth god, Solum, and therefore raises one's Earth affinity.

| Scalp | **Galdr's Scalp** | Regenerate |

Treasured by Ogres and Mongrels for its revitalizing effects, the Galdr Scalp is very hard to come by. It will slowly regenerate HP when equipped.

| Scalp | **Giant's Scalp** | Power Increase |

It is said that the strength of the giants who wandered the world long ago lives on in their remains. This scalp increases one's PWR while in battle.

| Scalp | **Minotaur's Scalp** | Supreme Critical |

Carrying the heavy scalp of the mighty Minotaur makes criticals achieved against the carrier deal less damage than they normally would.

| Scalp | **Mongrel's Scalp** | Crowd's Grace |

Mongrels are hated by most of the civilized world. As such, their scalps are a favorite of the public's, insuring no negative reactions from the crowd for poor battle choices.

| Scalp | **Mummy's Scalp** | Auto Revive |

Recovered by grave robbers and sold to the rougher classes in the world, the Mummy's Scalp will revive a warrior with 1/2 HP when they're downed.

| Scalp | **Ogre's Scalp** | Crowd's Grace |

Ogres are hated by most of the civilized world. As such, their scalps are a favorite of the public's, insuring no negative reactions from the crowd for poor battle choices.

| Scalp | **Phoenix Scalp** | + 10 Water Affinity |

The Phoenix' Scalp pleases the Water god, Maritimus, and therefore raises one's Water affinity.

| Scalp | **Samnite's Scalp** | Damage Reduction |

Taking a scalp from the mighty Samnite will also steal their vitality. Equipping this scalp decreases the amount of damage received in battle.

| Scalp | **Satyr's Scalp** | Steadfast |

Carrying the scalp of the wily Satyr will guard against charm and confusion attacks.

| Scalp | **Soldier's Scalp** | Face Enemy |

Much like the innate ability of the military classes, the person who has this scalp equipped will always turn to face the enemy when under attack.

| Scalp | **Tortoise's Scalp** | + 10 Fire Affinity |

The Tortoise's Scalp pleases the Fire god, Exuro, and therefore raises one's Fire affinity.

| Scalp | **Valkyrie's Scalp** | + 10 Dark Affinity |

The Valkyrie's Scalp pleases the Death god, Mortuus, and therefore raises one's Dark Affinity.

| Scalp | **Warrior's Scalp** | Defense +5 |

Scalping a true warrior is no easy task but once accomplished, the one who equips this scalp will gain a greatly increased DF.

ITEM	NAME	EFFECT
Tooth	**Bear Tooth**	Supreme Critical

Pulling from the legendary strength of the Bear. This tooth makes criticals achieved deal more damage.

| Tooth | **Boar Tooth** | + 10 Earth Affinity |

The Boar Tooth, sometimes referred to as an Earth Tusk, shows one's devotion to the mighty Earth god Solum and increases one's Earth affinity.

| Tooth | **Buffalo Tooth** | Defense +5 |

This large trophy from the robust plains buffalo increases one's Defense through the spirit of the animal it was taken from.

| Tooth | **Cat Tooth** | Crowd's Grace |

The deification of the cat throughout the known regions keeps the crowd from reacting negatively when someone possesses this accessory.

| Tooth | **Crocodile Tooth** | Critical Defense |

This strong tooth protects the carrier from critical damage, reducing any critical hits to merely normal ones.

| Tooth | **Eagle Beak** | + 10 Air Affinity |

Possession of the Eagle Beak increases one's affinity with the mighty Eagle-God, Aeris.

| Tooth | **Horse Tooth** | Power Increase |

Carrying this beast-of-burden's tooth greatly increases one's PWR while in battle, as the Horse is a strong pack animal used throughout all the regions.

| Tooth | **Hyena Tooth** | Berserk |

The tooth of this wild animal causes a constant state of berserk when someone possesses it.

| Tooth | **Jackal Tooth** | + 10 Dark Affinity |

Recovered from burial sites deep within the Expanse, the Jackal tooth increases one's affinity with Death.

| Tooth | **Lion Tooth** | Face Enemy |

The tooth of the Lion gives the possessor the great pride of the noble beast. Flank attacks against the one carrying this tooth become impossible.

| Tooth | **Owl Beak** | Steadfast |

Carrying the Owl Beak will guard against charm and confusion attacks in battle.

| Tooth | **Ox Tooth** | Damage Reduction |

With an energy combining the perfect aspects of the horse with those of the buffalo, this tooth, through the spirit of the Ox, decreases the amount of damage received in battle.

| Tooth | **Pegasus Tooth** | + 10 Light Affinity |

Rarely found on the battlefield is a fallen Pegasus, but if one manages to find one and keeps their tooth as a trophy, one's Light Affinity will rise greatly.

| Tooth | **Serpent Tooth** | + 10 Fire Affinity |

The Serpent, a creature forever bound to fire among all folklores of the known world will increase one's Fire affinity when in possession of its fang.

| Tooth | **Turtle Beak** | + 10 Water Affinity |

Sensing your strength in devotion to his affinity, Maritimus, the great Tortoise god will increase your Water affinity powers when carrying this item.

| Tooth | **Wolf Tooth** | Hidden Power |

When in possession of this trophy of the Wolf's great fighting strength, one's ST will increase with each hit received.

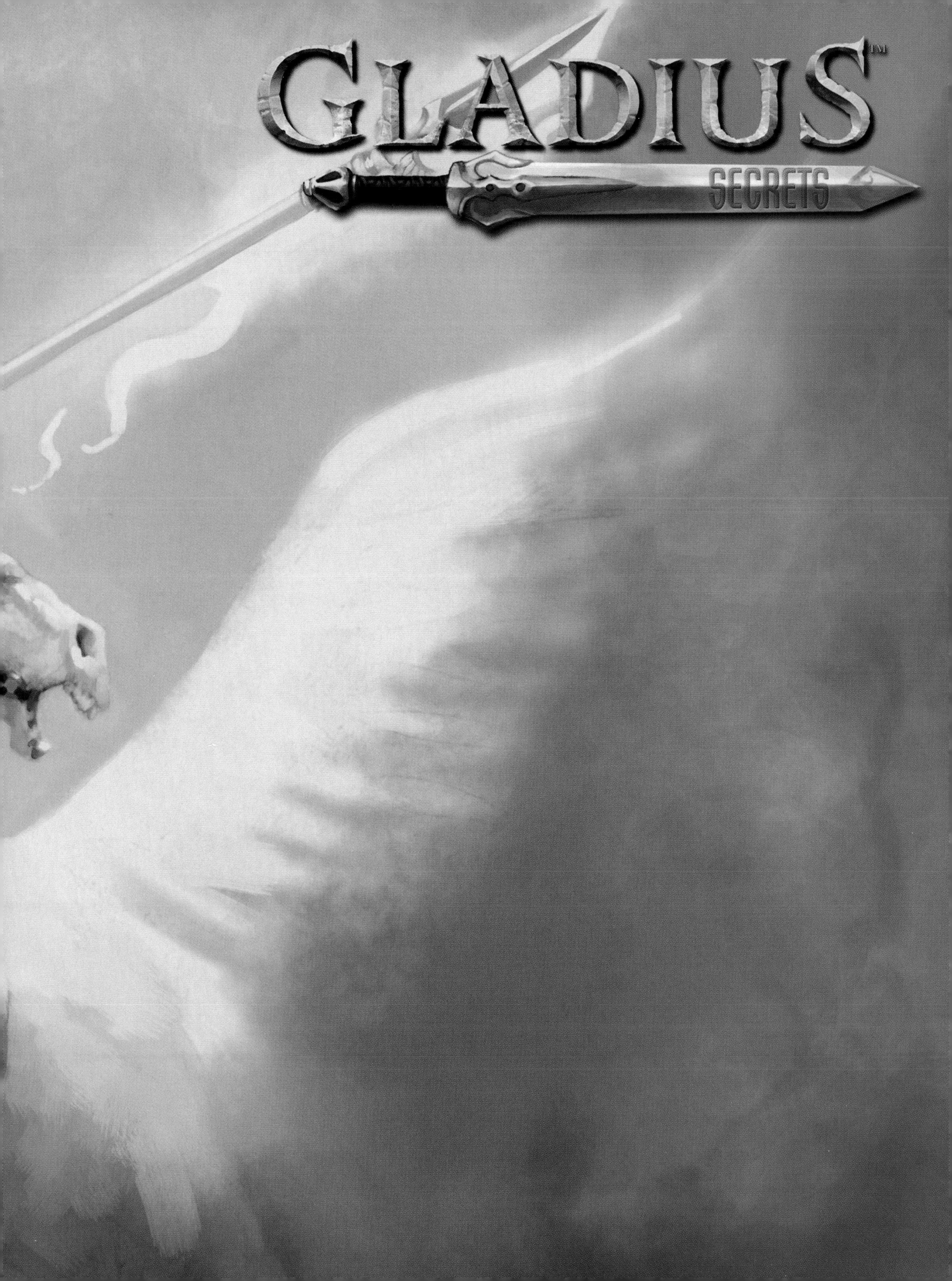
GLADIUS™
SECRETS

SECRETS

THE HELLS GATE QUEST

Gladius has one final hidden league for those who have been diligently completing the game's various Shopkeeper Quests.
To open Hell's Gate, you must do the following things:

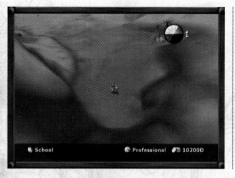  

- Earn the Signet of the Valkyrie from the first Mördare's Den shopkeeper quest.
- Earn the Promise Stone from the Mysterious Tablet shopkeeper quest in Saraa Izel,
  by reading the Mysterious Tablet Aziza gives you.
- Defeat Sarenenutet in the final Saraa Izel shopkeeper quest.
- Raise at least six characters to level 18 or higher.

When you've completed all of the prerequisites, glowing lights will lead you to the southern tip of the Southern Expanse, where Usus will locate a hidden portal. When you enter, you'll be automatically enrolled in the Fulfill Your Promise league, a five round wilderness battle that is perhaps the toughest challenge in the game. You will do battle with four Summoners in each of the first four rounds, and take on a reborn Sarenenutet in the final battle.

Surviving characters will each learn the Hell's Fury skill, which Sarenenutet demonstrates in the first round of the battle. This area damage skill is by far the strongest attack in the game, and the game will be a breeze after you earn it. You'll also earn a few strange pieces of equipment: In Cognito, The Marksman, The Laughmaster, and No. 1 Fan.

RARE RECRUITS

Most of the 29 character classes in Gladius can easily be recruited from the game's various recruitment offices. But a few require a bit of legwork first. Here's how to recruit members of the game's hardest-to-find classes:

I MINOTAUR

To recruit a Minotaur, you must enroll in the Historian's League in the Imperial city of Cro Beska. After you earn the Mongrel Butcher badge, talk to the proprietor of the shop (Scotia's) and she'll set up for the league for 7 days later. Return on that day, make sure you have an open slot in your school, and save the game. If you can beat the league, one of your opponents will randomly offer to join you, so you have a 50/50 shot of getting a Minotaur. If you get a Satyr instead, just reset and try again.

II SCARABS & SCORPIONS

To recruit members of the game's final two beast classes, you need to conquer the Insect Ze league in Qaa Rah. After your victory, you'll begin to randomly see Scarabs and Scorpions in the Qaa Rah recruiting office.

III SUMMONER

After you win the tournament in Qaa Rah, Gwazi will lead you to the hidden city of Saraa Izel. After your battle there, head towards Akar An to trigger an event scene, then enter the city of Akar An and recruit the game's only Summoner in the Palace Ibliis recruiting office.

V UNDEAD LEGIONNAIRE

After completing the first shopkeeper quest in Mördare, and attempting the Dead of Night league, return to the Dragonslayer and ask the shopkeeper how he's doing. He'll tell you of a nearby hill where the unalive prowl at night, and ask you to do something about it. Visit that hill after dark, and defeat the skeleton-generating tombstones to earn the Talisman of Unlife. Bring that to the gravestones elsewhere in the game (there is one in each continent), and an Undead Legionnaire will arise and join your school.

IV UNDEAD SUMMONER

Recruiting an Undead Summoner is much easier. Visit Nordagh's Mördare's Den at night, complete the Dead of Night series league, and you'll get a message about a visitor in the recruiting office. Head down there and recruit Taithleach the Undead Summoner for free.

VI YETI

There are two Yetis that will fight for you, but only one will join your school permanently. To recruit him, clear the Trial of the Elders league in Vargen, and then visit Vargen's recruiting office.

GLADIUS™

ART GALLERY

CHANNELER
(CONCEPT)

DERVISH
(CONCEPT)

SECUTOR
(CONCEPT)

CHANNELER
(FINAL)

DERVISH
(FINAL)

SECUTOR
(FINAL)

GREATER CAT
(CONCEPT)

GREATER WOLF
(CONCEPT)

DERVISH
(CONCEPT)

CAVALRY
(CONCEPT)

SAMNITE
(CONCEPT)

CAVALRY
(CONCEPT)

DARK EARTH
BEAST

DARK AIR
BEAST

DARK WATER
BEAST

FIRE
BEAST

DARK FIRE
BEAST

AIR
TITAN